DANCING IN THE SHADOWS OF THE MOON

Dancing in the Shadows of the Moon

Machaelle Small Wright

PERELANDRA

CENTER FOR NATURE RESEARCH
JEFFERSONTON, VIRGINIA

For information, write Perelandra, Ltd.
This book is manufactured in the United States of America.
Designed by Machaelle Wright and James F. Brisson.
Cover design and artwork by James F. Brisson, Williamsville, VT 05362.
Copyediting and indexing by Elizabeth McHale, Bennington, VT 05201.
Diagram designs by Machaelle Wright.
Diagram preparation for publication by Sandra Hirth.
Split Molecular Process chart by Albert Schatz, Ph.D.
Production assistance by Clarence N. Wright.
Formatting, typesetting and computer wizardry
by Machaelle Wright.

This book was formatted, laid out and produced
using the Xerox Ventura Publisher software along with
the Hewlett Packard Laser Jet 4 printer.

Printed on recycled paper.

Published by Perelandra, Ltd.,
P.O. Box 3603, Warrenton, VA 22186

Library of Congress Card Catalog Number: 94-74999
Wright, Machaelle Small
Dancing in the Shadows of the Moon

ISBN 0-927978-20-2

2 4 6 8 9 7 5 3

To David,
Tex, Butch, Mickey,
Max, Seamus, Lorpuris
and Hyperithon.
Thank you.

Contents

DANCING IN THE SHADOWS OF THE MOON

The Setup

THE CHOCOLATE SUGGESTION

This is important. Have a large box of the best chocolates you can find at your fingertips when you are reading this book. This may not make any sense to you now, but about halfway through the book you will be grateful for this suggestion.

THE KEY WORD
Expansion

This is also important. There will be times while you are reading when you will look to the heavens and ask the question, "What is this book about and why am I reading it?" That's when you'll need to turn to this page and read the word "Expansion." Then pop a couple of those chocolates in your mouth, and continue reading.

READER INSTRUCTIONS

Pace yourself well. While reading this book, pay close attention to your physical and emotional reactions. If you *begin* to feel uncomfortable, put the book down and let what you have read settle in. This may take fifteen minutes, a couple of hours, a couple of days or several weeks. When you feel comfortable again, continue reading.

For those of you who use flower essences, I suggest that you test yourself for essences after each reading session. This will assist you in integrating the material. And for those of you who use MAP (the Co-Creative White Brotherhood Medical Assistance Program), tell your team that you are reading this book and have frequent MAP sessions. If you do not know what MAP or flower essences are, have patience. They are explained in this book.

SETTING THE TONE

Imagine you are in the middle of Manhattan, and you are suddenly
faced with this somewhat defiant-looking bag lady. She's clutching
several junk-filled shopping bags. She's wearing an old, stained raincoat that you know is going to smell if you get too close, and she has
several scarves loosely draped around her shoulders. She has one of
those umbrella hats plunked on her head—the umbrella open, of
course. She's wearing a high-top sneaker on one foot and a running
shoe on the other. Only the running shoe has the added benefit of a
shoelace. And she has on stockings. You know this because she likes
to wear them rolled down to her ankles. She puts down her bags and
starts scratching herself. You react a little. She notices your reaction
and explains that she scratches so much because her neurons are on
fire. At hearing her razor-edged voice, you react again. She tells you
she got her raspy voice because she has to yell all the time since
nobody ever listens to her. Her name is Trudy, and she starts talking:

TRUDY:

I know what you're thinkin'; you're thinkin' I'm crazy.
You think I give a hoot? You people
look at my shopping bags,
call me crazy 'cause I save this junk. What should we call the
ones who
buy it?
It's my belief we all, at one time or another,
secretly ask ourselves the question,
"Am *I* crazy?"
In my case, the answer came back: A resounding
YES!

You're thinkin': How does a person know if they're crazy
or not? Well, sometimes you don't know. Sometimes you
can go through life suspecting you *are*
but never really knowing for sure. Sometimes you know for sure

'cause you got so many people tellin' you you're crazy
that it's your word against everyone else's.
Another sign is when you see life so clear sometimes
you black out.
This is your typical visionary variety
who has flashes of insight
but can't get anyone to listen to 'em
'cause their insights make 'em sound so *crazy!*

In my case,
the symptoms are subtle
but unmistakable to the trained eye. For instance,
here I am,
standing at the corner of "Walk, Don't Walk,"
waiting for these aliens from outer space to show up.
I call that crazy, don't you? If I were sane,
I should be waiting for the light like everybody else.

They're late
as usual.

You'd think,
as much as they know about time travel,
they could be on time *once* in a while.

I could kick myself.
I told 'em I'd meet 'em on the corner of "Walk, Don't Walk"
'round lunchtime.
Do they even know what "lunch" means?
I doubt it.

And "'round." Why did I say "'round"? Why wasn't I more
specific? This is so typical of what I do.

Now they're probably stuck somewhere in time, wondering
what I meant by
"'round lunchtime." And when they get here, they'll be
dying to know what "lunchtime" means. And when they
find out it means going to Howard Johnson's for fried
clams, I wonder, will they be just a bit let down?

I dread having to explain
tartar sauce.

This problem of time just points out
how far apart we really are.
See, our ideas about time and space are different
from theirs. When we think of time, we tend to think of
clock radios, coffee breaks, afternoon naps, leisure time,
halftime activities, parole time, doing time, Minute Rice, instant
tea, mid-life crises, that time of the month, cocktail hour.
And if I should suddenly
mention *space*—aha! I bet most of you thought of your
closets. But when they think of time and space, they *really* think of
Time and Space.

They asked me once my thoughts on infinity and I told 'em
with all I had to think about, infinity was not on my list
of things to think about. It could be time on an ego trip,
for all I know. After all, when you're pressed for time,
infinity may as well
not be there.
They said, to them, infinity is
time-released time.

Frankly, infinity doesn't affect
me personally one way or the other.

You think too long about infinity, you could go
stark raving mad.
But I don't ever want to sound negative about going crazy.
I don't want to overromanticize it either, but frankly,
goin' crazy was the *best* thing ever happened to me.
I don't say it's for everybody;
some people couldn't cope.

But for me it came at a time when nothing else seemed to be
working. I got the kind of madness Socrates talked about,
"A divine release of the soul from the yoke of
custom and convention." I refuse to be intimidated by

reality anymore.
After all, what is reality anyway? Nothin' but a
collective hunch. My space chums think reality was once a
primitive method of
crowd control that got out of hand.
In my view, it's absurdity dressed up
in a three-piece business suit.

I made some studies, and
reality is the leading cause of stress amongst those in
touch with it. I can take it in small doses, but as a lifestyle
I found it too confining.
It was just too needful;
it expected me to be there for it *all* the time, and with all
I have to do—
I had to let something go.

Now, since I put reality on a back burner, my days are
jam-packed and fun-filled. Like some days, I go hang out
around Seventh Avenue; I love to do this old joke:
I wait for some music-loving tourist from one of the hotels
on Central Park to go up and ask someone,
"How do I get to Carnegie Hall?"
Then I run up and yell,
"Practice!"
The expression on people's faces is priceless. I never
could've done stuff like that when I was in my *right* mind.
I'd be worried people would think I was *crazy*.
When I think of the fun I missed,
I try not to be bitter.

See, the human mind is kind of like . . .

a piñata. When it breaks open,
there's a lot of surprises inside. Once you get the piñata
perspective, you see that losing your mind
can be a peak experience.*

* From *The Search for Signs of Intelligent Life in the Universe* by Jane Wagner.
Reprinted with permission.

Chapter 1

Explaining
Tartar Sauce

The Concepts and Terms

In 1982 I experienced the expansion that I describe in this book. Prior to that event, I did not have the benefit of any information or understanding of the following concepts and terms. As I moved through the long process of integrating the expansion, I gained this knowledge. I feel that by becoming familiar with the terms *before* you read the story, you will be able to more fully absorb, understand and learn from my expansion experience as you read about it.

EXPANSION

A person undergoes expansion when an experience or event affects the electrical, central nervous and sensory systems *in new ways*.

Everything in our immediate environment affects us physically. We experience stimulus first in our electrical system, a complex electrical gridwork that is located within and surrounding the body. Once the electrical system responds to the new stimulus, the new impulses are immediately shifted to the central nervous and sensory systems for identification, sorting and integration. All of this happens within a split second.

There are two main areas of difficulty in an expansion experience. The first is physical. Because an expansion experience affects these three systems in new ways, if the systems are unable to immediately adjust to the new input, they may become over-energized, overloaded and, as a result, nonfunctional as far as the new experience is concerned. As a consequence of this physical breakdown, the person feels confused and is unable to discern what he is actually experiencing. What a person intellectually perceives is a direct result of the function of and interaction between the electrical system, central nervous system and sensory system. Sometimes an experience is so far beyond a person's present ability to sort, identify and integrate within these three systems that he is not even conscious of being influenced by it at all. It is as if the experience never happened.

The second area of difficulty is intellectual. During expansion, our intellectual understanding of what we are experiencing is challenged because it is new to us. If we try to force understanding, we shove the experience through the framework of what we already know. An expansion renders that framework obsolete as far as this experience is concerned. If we persist in pushing the experience through the old framework, we end up confused and we (via these three systems) misinterpret the experience.

We can actually distort an expansion by forcing it through our old intellectual framework. In essence, we experience what we *think* we are experiencing. I have met a number of people who have described some pretty frightening "sixth-sense" events to me. While I listen to them, I can see that their ordeals were actually benign in nature, but because it was new to them, they quickly shoved it through their already-existing intellectual framework. Invariably, these were people who had read a lot about other people's frightening tales or black magic. So they pushed their benign experience into a frightening framework and literally forced themselves to have a frightening experience that they could describe, even understand. In the process of finding intellectual satisfaction, they managed to scare the bejeezus out of themselves.

The way I've been taught to deal with the intellect during expansion is to simply *suspend* the intellect: I just focus on the experience, let it integrate—and observe. This enables the organic formation of a new logic or intellectual framework. As a result, we gain a completely different understanding. Before expansion, we don't have the ability to understand because the new pieces aren't yet in place. The experience itself builds the new logical framework.

By approaching expansion in this manner, I allow the intellect to work for me and not against me.

THE OZZIE AND HARRIET SCHOOL OF EXPANSION vs THE SCUZZBALL SCHOOL OF EXPANSION

If we believed the stuff that is written about expansion experiences, "enlightenment" or eureka moments, we'd swear that all we need to do to achieve such heights is to desire, apply ourselves a little, maybe have a life-threatening accident or two to knock some sense into us and, voilà—we come into enlightenment. Oh yes, it also helps to be special in the first place. Our lives magically change, and we now live in enlightenment. Our hair never gets mussed, our fingernails never break, the crease in our pants (if we have one) never flattens, and we never lose that saintly smile of the enlightened one. This is what I call the Ozzie and Harriet School of Expansion. Nothing ever goes wrong.

This book is about the Scuzzball School of Expansion, the one I belong to. We get down and dirty. We also have a strong yearning to demythologize and deglamorize expansion. After all, it's not a gift from God. We are all evolving, and sometimes this means we have the opportunity to expand in major ways. If we take the step, we feel like we just got blown to smithereens. There's nothing subtle about this kind of expansion.

Expansion, by definition, implies that we are now faced with an experience that was heretofore unknown to us. If we are already personally familiar with the experience, it's not expansion—it's just an experience. Now, the people from the Ozzie and Harriet School want us to believe that we function well when faced with the unknown. Well, balderdash. I happen to find the situation very challenging (as they say), and I suspect this is true for most of us.

MUNDANE-FANTASTIC LIFE

"Mundane" refers to our everyday life. It's getting up in the morning, drinking coffee, going to work, doing the laundry, picking up the kids, reading the newspaper and watching your favorite TV program. The mundane is the glue that holds our life together.

"Fantastic" refers to those experiences that are beyond the mundane. They are the magical part of life. They are those moments or events that fall out of the scope of our logic—they are unexplainable. This includes expansion.

Often, people keep a separation between the mundane and the fantastic in their lives. They don't see a relationship between the two. They see the mundane as boring, tedious and a necessary evil—sometimes even a trap. They see the fantastic as the "perfect" life, as something to aim for, if they could just release themselves from their mundane trap.

But there is a strong relationship between mundane and fantastic. The mundane part stabilizes our life, provides life's tools and training, and creates the platform from which the fantastic springs. The fantastic—those magical moments and events that propel us beyond our logic—then wraps around and becomes integrated in the mundane, resulting in an enfolding and expansion of the breadth and depth of the mundane. The fantastic gives new meaning to the mundane. The more we allow this interrelationship to occur, the more the mundane and fantastic come together and the more they feel indistinguishable. They each become an extension of the other. When the mundane and the fantastic fully interweave, we have what I call the "mundane-fantastic life."

The story I present in this book is an example of the interweaving of the mundane and the fantastic events into one cohesive mundane-fantastic life.

Mundane   Fantastic   Allowing the mundane   The integrated
                               and fantastic to inter-   mundane-fantastic
                               relate and integrate   life

FORM: Defined by Nature

We consider reality to be in the form state when there is order, organization and life vitality combined with a state of consciousness.

We do not consider form to be only that which can be perceived by the five senses. In fact, we see form from this perspective to be most limited, both in its life reality and in its ability to function. We see form from the perspective of the five senses to be useful only for the most basic and fundamental level of identification. From this perspective, there is very little relationship to the full understanding and knowledge of how a unit or form system functions.

All energy contains order, organization and life vitality; therefore, all energy is form. If one were to use the term "form" to identify that which can be perceived by the basic five senses and the word "energy" to refer to that aspect of an animal, human, plant or object's reality that cannot be readily perceived by the basic senses, then one would be accurate in the use of these two words. However, if one were to use the word "form" to refer to that which can be perceived by the basic five senses and assume that form to be a complete unit of reality unto itself, and use the word "energy" to refer to a level beyond form, one would then be using these two words inaccurately. From our perspective, form and energy create one unit of reality and are differentiated from one another solely by the individual's ability to perceive them with his or her sensory system. In short, the differentiation between form and energy within any given object, plant, animal or human lies with the observer.

On the planet Earth, the personality, character, emotional make-up, intellectual capacity, strong points and gifts of a human are all form. They are that which gives order, organization and life vitality to consciousness.

Order and organization are the physical structures that create a framework for form. In short, they define the walls. But we have included the dynamic of life vitality when we refer to form because one of the elements of form is action, and it is life vitality that initiates and creates action.

NATURE: Defined by Nature

In the larger universe and beyond, on its many levels and dimensions, there are a number of groups of consciousnesses that, although equal in importance, are quite different in expression and function. Together, they make up the full expression of the larger, total life picture. No one piece, no one expression, can be missing or the larger life picture on all its levels and dimensions will cease to exist. One such consciousness has been universally termed "nature." Because of what we are saying about the larger picture not existing without all of its parts, you may assume that nature as both a reality and a consciousness exists on all dimensions and all levels. It cannot be excluded.

Each group of consciousnesses has what can be termed an area of expertise. As we said, all groups are equal in importance but express and function differently from one another. These different expressions and functions are vital to the overall balance of reality. A truly symbiotic relationship exists among the groups and is based on balance—universal balance. The human soul-oriented dynamic is **evolution** *in scope and function. Nature is a massive, intelligent consciousness group that expresses and functions within the many areas of* **involution***, that is, moving soul-oriented consciousness into any dimension or level of form.*

Nature **is** *the conscious reality that supplies order, organization and life vitality for this shift. Nature is the consciousness that is, for your working understanding, intimately linked with form. Nature is the consciousness that comprises all form on all levels and dimensions. It is form's order, organization and life vitality. Nature is first and foremost a consciousness of equal importance with all other consciousnesses in the largest scheme of reality. It expresses and functions uniquely in that it comprises all form on all levels and dimensions and is responsible for and creates all of form's order, organization and life vitality.*

REALITY: Defined by Nature

From our perspective, reality refers to all levels and dimensions of life experience within form and beyond form. Reality does not depend on an individual's perception of it in order to exist. We call an individual's perception of reality his "perceived reality." Any life system that was created in form—which occurred at the moment of the Big Bang*—has inherent in it all dimensions and levels that exist both within form and beyond. How a person relates to an individual, object or event depends on his present ability to enfold and envelop its many levels. The scope within which one exists, the reality of one's existence, is truly beyond form, beyond description. If one understands that the evolutionary force that moves all life systems forward is endless—beyond time—then one must also consider that it is the continuous discovery of these vast levels inherent in all life systems that creates that evolutionary momentum. Since that dynamic is beyond time, it is endless.

RING-PASS-NOT

I did not coin this term. It's something I picked up in my travels. I have since made the term mine, and the following is what I mean when I say "ring-pass-not."

All reality is available to every one of us. Now, I know there are some people who would like us to believe that some reality is available to most of us and more reality is available to a chosen few. But the fact is, reality is not withheld from any of us.

However, we have chosen to function in form. This means that reality has to become integrated in order to become operational in our form life. Integrating reality is called evolution. It is a gradual process and it is a learning process. At any given time we have a range of reality that we are capable of integrating and using. Beyond that range is the rest of reality. No one is withholding this larger

---

* The Big Bang: The gigantic explosion in which the universe, as we know it, began. According to scientists, it occurred between 12 and 20 billion years ago. The Big Bang brought about two major dynamics: individuation and the fusion of soul to form.

reality from us. It's just that we have not figured out how to physically incorporate it and successfully activate it in our life. Consequently, we have no use for it—yet.

The ring-pass-not refers to the "dividing line" or "mystical membrane" between the part of reality we can work with (our perceived reality) and the rest of infinite reality. It's like we have a ring around us. Inside the ring is a "safety zone" and outside the ring is something larger than we can presently handle. Therefore, the ring becomes a "border" beyond which we should not venture—if we're smart.

But I've said that reality is not withheld from us. At some point, we have to be able to access what is beyond the ring-pass-not. When we are capable of integrating and working with a larger picture, our ring-pass-not is triggered and we have what I call a "ring-pass-not expansion." When this occurs, the ring expands, we suddenly see a larger picture, and *everything* we had previously experienced, known or understood gets thrown into the air and must be reexamined in light of the new information.

This kind of expansion does not happen every day. If we're lucky, it happens once in a lifetime. If we're unlucky, it happens twice! I'm one of those unlucky ones. My first ring-pass-not expansion occurred in 1976 when I opened to the world of nature intelligences. An expansion such as this forces us to redefine and upgrade every aspect of our life. It can be exhausting, bewildering and even scary. However, it never creates a situation that is beyond our coping ability. This expansion is triggered by the soul, and it occurs only when we are ready to take on a larger picture.

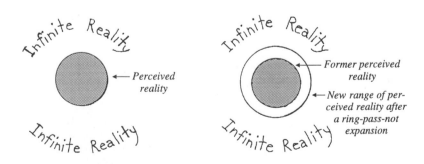

A ring-pass-not expansion is not a subtle event. You won't miss it when it happens. (You also don't have any clear warning that it is about to happen.) It is something that occurs inside you even though it may be triggered by an external event. You will feel as if the entire rug has been pulled out from under you and your life. It comes without clear warning, so you will feel both surprised and, often, confused. One day you are peacefully driving the kids to school, and you feel life has never been better. The next day you are driving those same kids to that same school, and you cannot for the life of you figure out what it's all about and what you are doing. You start doing things like questioning the purpose and meaning of stop signs. You chalk it up to having a *really* bad day that will go away after a good night's rest. But you wake up the next morning, and everything is still floating around in the air. The real meaning of stop signs still alludes you. After a few days of this, you realize that the feeling of uncertainty and everything being airborne is not going to resolve itself.

I have said that ring-pass-not expansions are exhausting. They require that you diligently identify *every* element of your life and life's knowledge, and expand it to include the larger picture. This does not happen automatically. Only the expansion itself, which is triggered by the soul, happens automatically. Once it occurs, we are left with the job of making the larger reality useful. This can take many years. For the first two years, you will feel like you are holding on to your sanity for dear life. (Because a ring-pass-not expansion suddenly includes reality that is beyond your present range of logic, questioning your sanity is something that will come up fairly often!) As you address each area of your life, you will apply what you now know from the larger picture to it and experience a mini-expansion as that area "upgrades" to incorporate the new information. I call this an "in-house expansion," meaning that it is not an all-encompassing ring-pass-not expansion but an identification and upgrading of one area among many in your life that was affected as a result of the larger expansion. In-house expansions can feel so dramatic at times that you could

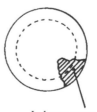

In-house expansion

mistake them for the larger ring-pass-not expansion. But, unlike the larger expansion, in-house expansions focus on one specific area at a time. Once you upgrade it, you will feel comfort and stability in that area again.

You may feel by now that if you should ever have a ring-pass-not expansion you might as well quit everything and go hide out in Tahiti for a few years while you work on getting your life back in order. But don't forget that I have said it does not happen until you are ready. And despite all the "symptoms" and feelings I have described, you are still capable of functioning. Your mundane life becomes especially important during these times. You will still be quite capable of driving the kids to school and functioning at work. It's just all the questions and changes that arise as a result of doing these mundane things will threaten to drive you mad.

In *Dancing in the Shadows of the Moon*, I describe what I faced as a result of my 1982 expansion, its effects on me, what I learned that might be helpful to you, and the tools we created as a result of this expansion that might also be helpful.

HOW WE PHYSICALLY SUPPORT EXPANSION
A Perelandra Coning Session

An expanded experience does not by definition mean it is nonphysical or beyond five-senses form. It simply implies that the experience is beyond that which the person has experienced prior to that time— thus, the sense of expansion. We have said to Machaelle that the band of form is quite complex, and this is true. It includes all that a person can potentially experience while participating within any given level of form such as Earth. . . .

The laws of form are much broader than what is encompassed when one thinks of the five-sense sensory system. In fact, an expanded experience is simply learning or allowing the sensory system, as most individuals know it, to operate in a fuller capacity. The problem is that individuals tend to see the five-senses system as the one and only sensory system, and anything beyond or outside this basic functioning as being something entirely different. In fact, they are both functions of the same system.

When a child is born, its sensory system is quite sensitive and expanded. It is, after all, just moving from a state prior to birth in which the sensory system naturally functions in a broader state. If left on its own, the child would continue to develop its sensory system from the point of this broader perspective. And what one might call "expanded experiences" would be the norm. Societal preconceptions are what encourage the child to limit the sensory scope, and the development of the sensory system throughout childhood then takes place from this more limited perspective. Along with this, the limited definition of the sensory system and its scope of discernment becomes the rule of thumb by which to judge experience.

Now, if the sensory system is naturally capable of operating in a much broader scope than most individuals can at present imagine, it follows that the physical body must respond to and support that operation. The sensory system itself is a part of that overall body response and support system. Everything works as a team, ideally. Consequently, one cannot have what is known as an expansion experience without the sensory system and the physical body system as a whole responding to and attempting to support it. So, one may see entering a meditative state as an expanded experience, but, in fact, it is a broader use of the sensory system and draws appropriate response and support from within the physical body itself. Just as one cannot move a finger or toe without the entire body's muscular and skeletal systems responding, one cannot shift from one state of mind to another without a similar physical response and shift.

There is a saying many on the Earth level use: "If you don't use it, you lose it." Normally, this refers to muscle and body tone. When a child limits the scope of operation within the sensory system, the complementary scope of physical response and support is no longer needed or utilized. In those areas, a person stiffens and atrophies. Then, later on, when the individual is an adult and consciously chooses to reactivate the sensory system in a broader way, the physical body no longer "knows" how to respond and support that expansion. The person will experience nothing, no matter how much willpower he musters, or the experience will be partially perceived and most likely distorted, as well.

Let's address the body system itself and what happens when the sensory system responds to an experience. Any experience initially strikes the human body through the electrical system. This occurs whether the experience is easily perceived or not. The initial receptor of experience is not the brain or the senses but the electrical system. The impact immediately, almost simultaneously, shifts and translates into the nervous system and routes itself throughout the nervous system appropriately as it begins its identification and experience process. This includes activating the sensory system in an appropriate manner. (All this occurs within a split second.) The point to remember is that the initial level of impact is electrical, followed by an impact on the nervous system. If the experience is within the individual's perceived notion of "acceptable," the person probably knows how to perceive the experience on all levels operating within the physical body.

Two things can occur if the individual does not know what to do with the experience. Either the physical body does not know how to respond and support the experience and is in need of assistance, or the experience itself is so beyond the person's operating scope of reality that it takes on an intensification that literally overwhelms the body and requires of it a level of operation well beyond its present range of capability.

In the latter case, the person must have a good foundation for such a stretch, or else he risks damaging himself physically. You would not want a person who is not capable of walking a half-mile to suddenly be forced to run three miles. But you could expect someone who easily runs three miles to be able to tackle a seven-mile run without sustaining damage. It's a challenge, but it is not beyond the scope of possibility—and most likely not dangerous, but it could result in soreness and discomfort until the body learns to better support the longer run. . . .

Let me sum up the relationship of the cranials, spine and sacrum in the expanded experience. The experience is received electrically and shifted to the central nervous system for sorting and identification. At this point, the physical body systems move to support what is being identified. If the body cannot adequately shift, the electrical system will overload or break, and the corresponding vertebrae, sacrum or cranials will most likely react by misaligning. Hence, you have the sensation of trying to catch six balls all at once while only being able to catch four.

A special note about the cranials: An expanded experience carries with it an intensity that registers through the electrical system, moves into the nervous system and continues its impact into the cerebrospinal fluid (CSF). The brain is impacted by both the nervous system activity and the CSF pulse response to the impact. The cranial plates must respond accordingly to accommodate this two-pronged impact. The range of plate movement will be affected. If the cranials have lost their knowledge of how to move within this new range or if they are three-milers stretching for the seven-mile run, they run the risk of jamming or misaligning. This is when you have head pain associated with expanded experience. Cranial adjustments may be necessary over a period of time in order to allow the plates to properly adjust to and move in a more expanded range.

Just as the leg muscles need to adjust to the seven-mile run, the cranials need time to adjust to expansion. Because of the close working proximity with the electrical and nervous systems, the cranials must be considered one of the primary areas for assistance during times of expansion. In a relatively short period of time, the cranials, as well as the rest of the physical body system, will learn how to operate within the expanded range of experience with ease, accuracy and efficiency.

PERTINENT ANATOMY IDENTIFICATION

The Cranials

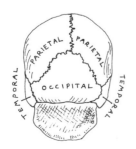
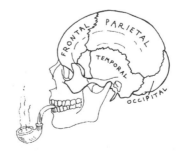

The Cervical, Thoracic and Lumbar Vertebrae, and the Sacrum

The Psoas Muscles and the Pelvis

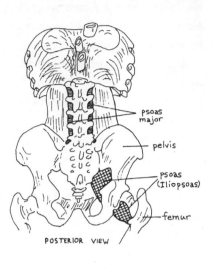

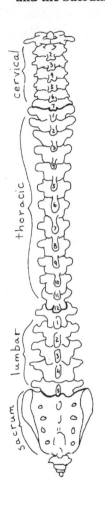

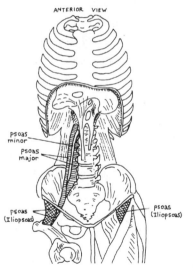

BASIC SENSORY SYSTEM

PERCEPTION: Defined by Nature

We define basic sensory system perception as being that which the vast majority of individuals on Earth experience. The acts of seeing, hearing, touching, tasting and smelling fall within what we acknowl-

edge as a basic, fundamental range of sensory development that is dominant on the Earth level. What is referred to as an "expansion experience" is, in fact, an act or experience that is perceived by an individual because of an expansion of the range in which his sensory system operates. Expansion experiences are not perceived outside or beyond an individual's electrical system, central nervous system and sensory system. These three systems are interrelated, and an accurate perception of an expansion experience requires that the three systems operate in concert. Therefore, it is quite possible for something to occur in an individual's life that registers in the person's electrical system and central nervous system but then short-circuits, is altered or is blocked simply because the person's present sensory system does not have the ability to process, due to its present range of operation, what has registered in the other two systems.

People say that "these kinds of strange things never happen to me." This is inaccurate. "Strange" things, experiences and moments beyond the present state of their sensory systems are continuously happening around them and to them. They are simply not at the point where their sensory systems are capable of clear, useful processing. They waste time by directing their will and focus to "make things happen." That is useless since things are happening all the time around them. Instead they should relax and continue through an organic developmental process that is already in effect and that will gradually allow them to accurately perceive what is happening around them. In some cases, events or experiences are vaguely perceived or processed in outrageous, useless ways because their sensory system is expanding but still not operating in a range where events can be usefully processed.

LIFE LOOPS

This is a term I coined. It may sound like a breakfast cereal, but it's really a term I use to describe a specific dynamic in life.

You are going along in life, and you experience an event or moment that in itself feels complete once it's over. At the time it may

Life Loops

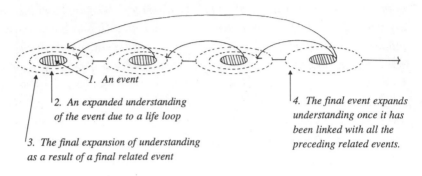

1. An event

2. An expanded understanding
of the event due to a life loop

3. The final expansion of understanding
as a result of a final related event

4. The final event expands
understanding once it has
been linked with all the
preceding related events.

not strike you as being important. The event itself may not even make much sense to you. It is just something you experienced—and now it is complete and you go on with the next thing in your life. Then you get further down life's road—it may be a week, a month, ten years, fifty years, even lifetimes—and you experience something else. Suddenly you remember the original event, and you realize that this latest happening is actually related to the earlier event. In fact, it is so related that you realize it is a continuation of the earlier event. This is a "life loop." The most recent event loops back and connects with the original event right at the point where the original event stopped. As a result, the original event combines with the latest event, and you move forward with a new understanding about both events. At the time, you were convinced that the original event was complete. It felt self-contained—like it had a period at the end of it. But in actuality, the original event doesn't make sense until you connect the later event to it. The original event actually had a comma, not a period, after it.

Life loops can encompass several events that stretch out over much of your life. Each one loops back to the previous event and adds more information. At some point the last piece falls into place, and the whole series of events has meaning and clarity. *Now* you sense the period. There are no more commas.

Life loops are not karmic patterns. They are simply related experiences that in themselves have little meaning, but when put together, create one larger, significant experience. When you complete a life loop, you are likely to say, "Oh, *that's* what it's all about!"

We all experience a lot of life loops. They can be particularly maddening to people who insist on knowing the meaning of everything that is happening to them at the moment it is happening. Actually, it is a waste of time trying to figure out what a life-loop event is all about—until *after* all the loops are in place. In short, the experience isn't really over until all the life loops are in place. Then the events clarify themselves with no effort on our part. With a life loop in progress, the most efficient thing you can do is shrug your shoulders, mutter "I don't know what the hell is going on" and tuck the event in your back pocket. Trust that at some point, after another loop or two, it will clarify itself.

Life loops are particularly prevalent just before and after ring-pass-not experiences. As I tell you the story of my expansion, I point out several life loops by ending the sentence with [comma]. This way you will get a clearer idea of what they are and how they operate.

SPIRITUAL THREAD

This is another term I coined. The spiritual thread is woven within the fabric of our mundane life. It is comprised of the experiences that serve to teach and train us for moving forward in evolution. In short, it prepares us for the next stage. It is also an integral part of the mundane foundation from which expansion springs.

The interesting thing about the spiritual thread is that it does not feel spiritual at all. It is not only woven into the mundane fabric, it is also part of the mundane that creates that life fabric. It feels ordinary to us, and as we move along it feels like the thread is meandering all over the place. In reality, the spiritual thread cuts straight through the life fabric and gives us all that is needed for the next stage.

Feels like:

Its actual path:

One other thing about the spiritual thread: It is nearly impossible to identify our spiritual thread as we move along its path. It is only in hindsight that we can look back and see the clear and undeniable events that make up the thread. Sometimes the events can be difficult, sometimes joyful; sometimes they are so subtle that we nearly miss them. But once we move into the new stage, how they prepared us is unmistakable.

BAND OF FORM

At some point in my early twenties, I heard or read that Earth was the only form planet that existed, and souls on Earth were the only souls operating in form. Since I saw no evidence to the contrary, and since I really didn't care anyway, I didn't bother to question this piece of information—for years. Even after I began to work with nature in 1976, I still didn't challenge it. Although nature was teaching me a lot about form and the underlying dynamics of form, I assumed that what I was learning applied to my Earth reality only.

In order to understand my ring-pass-not expansion, I had to learn something new about this form business. I learned that form as I

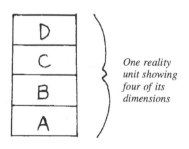

One reality unit showing four of its dimensions

experience it on Earth is not the only form experience there is. In fact, there is a complex, broad "band of form" made up of many different dimensions—some of which we on Earth are capable of seeing and some of which we can't see—or experience—in any of our usual ways.

I eventually learned that no matter how "unique" the dimension, it operates with the same universal laws of form as every other dimension within the band of form. Only the way those laws are demonstrated are different.

I learned that there are many realities. Within each reality there is a corresponding large, complex band of form. We presently experience the one reality that includes our Earth. Perhaps a better way of saying this is that there exists one large, complex band of form that moves through and is reflected in all the different realities.

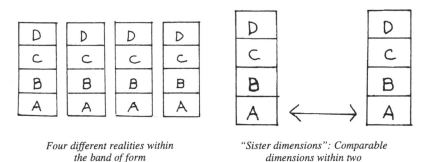

Four different realities within   "Sister dimensions": Comparable
the band of form   dimensions within two
                                                 different realities

Within any single reality there are dimensions that are comparable
in every way to specific dimensions in all other realities. In short,
each reality has a dimension or "sister dimension" that corresponds
in every way to what we are experiencing on Earth. This does not
mean that each reality's "Earth" dimension is the mirror image of
everything that exists on our planet. Rather, it means that our sister
dimensions have a planet *similar* to ours. People live on these
planets in dwellings similar to the ones we use. The planet has trees,
mountains, deserts, rivers and oceans. There are animals and plants
that we would recognize. There are also some we wouldn't. The
people wear clothes, work in jobs and travel by means similar to
ours. And their social structures are comparable.

A ring-pass-not expansion may occur if you begin to *consciously*
perceive and experience another dimension within your "base"
reality. That is, another dimension within the reality in which you
currently reside and operate. In fact, this is a common ring-pass-not
expansion. Although rare from the Earth perspective, you may also
undergo expansion if you begin to consciously perceive and experience another dimension from a reality other than your base
reality. In either case, the level that you live on remains your "home
base." It functions as your foundation. You aren't released from it.
The new level that you begin to consciously perceive and experience
is an expansion of your perceived reality as lived out on your home

base, and what you learn from the experience becomes integrated into your home-base life. As you might imagine, this adds a whole new meaning to "life on Earth as you know it!"

HORIZONTAL COMPATIBILITY PRINCIPLE

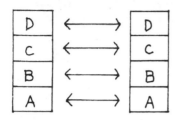

Horizontally compatible dimensions between two different realities

Horizontal Compatibility is a universal principle that occurs between "sister dimensions" where the laws of form are demonstrated in similar ways. For example, we on planet Earth live out and experience life that is horizontally compatible with every level in all other realities that live and experience life in comparable ways.

The Horizontal Healing Principle that is often referred to in the Perelandra material is part of the Horizontal Compatibility Principle. In short, the easiest, most efficient and effective means of healing are horizontally compatible with the object, being or person in need of healing. *Like healing like.* The most effective means for healing those of us living on Earth are found on this planet or created as a result of combining several ingredients native to the planet.

To take this a step further, because of the Horizontal Compatibility Principle, what constitutes quality health practice on Earth can have a similar positive health impact for those living on a "sister dimension" in another reality and vice versa.

SOUL RAYS/LIFETIMES
A Perelandra Coning Session

When souls took on individuation as a result of the Big Bang, they became involved in a vast array of experiences that were also created during the same Big Bang. As a result, individuated souls*

---

* The Big Bang: The gigantic explosion in which the universe, as we know it, began. According to scientists, it occurred between 12 and 20 billion years ago. The Big Bang contained two major dynamics: individuation and the fusion of soul to form. (I have repeated this footnote for your reference.)

had to have the tools for experiencing. *Not to have these tools would have rendered the soul incapable of experience. In essence, souls that are incapable of experience are also **beyond** experience, and are in the same state they were in prior to becoming individuated by the Big Bang.*

*The tools souls use to experience come from nature and are fully contained in one "package"—the human body. Nature supplies the **order, organization** and **life vitality** that create the human body. All the various elements and systems that make up the human body are the tools needed by souls for functioning in form.*

*All experiences after the Big Bang have been and are **in form**. The Big Bang was a soul/nature phenomenon that added order, organization and life vitality to the One, and from this came individuation. Consequently, in order for the soul to function in a post–Big Bang dynamic, it needed to fuse with a form that could expand and modify in ways that would allow the soul to operate appropriately on any level or experience.*

*When most people consider the human body, they conclude that the form of that body is the form that is needed for operating on Earth, and that this form is unique to Earth and Earth-related locations. They reason further that once beyond this level, the human body is no longer needed and, therefore, does not exist. These conclusions are wrong. The basic "design" of the human body was created by nature at the moment of the Big Bang. Once the One Soul individuated, it was imperative that the individual souls immediately fuse with appropriate form. The elements and systems present in the human body on Earth are the same as the basic elements and systems that made up the original form that received the individuated soul at the Big Bang. The form system as you see it today **is** the appropriate system through which the human soul can best operate, experience and express. It forms a structure and foundation through which the soul operates—no matter what level, state or dimension the soul chooses to participate in. It is not unique to the Earth level.*

*This is not to say that on every level and dimension the human body is present **exactly** as you experience it on the Earth level.*

Remember, every level and dimension was created at the time of the Big Bang. Therefore, because everything created at the Big Bang is form, every level, whether it is seen or not, is also in form. But the many levels and dimensions within the band of form are quite extensive, complex and comprehensive. The body through which the soul operates must be fully compatible with the prevailing life dynamics of the level upon which the soul is presently choosing to participate. This is natural law and falls within the scope of the Horizontal Compatibility Principle. So, although the human body is capable of being present on any level and dimension, the **state** *of that body at any given time will correspond with the prevailing life dynamics of the actual level it is on. For example, from Earth's perspective, the human body is visible to the naked eye. On another level, that same body may be invisible. But the body is fully present and operating on each level whether it is visible or not.*

In short, the relationship between the soul and its physical body **has been present since the Big Bang.** *Soul and body have worked in partnership through every soul experience, no matter the level on which it has occurred. It is important to understand that the relationship of soul to body has been present since the moment that soul originated in its individual expression and has not been solely a relationship unique to Earth.*

No matter what level or dimension a body is functioning on, it still has all the components that make up the physical body that is familiar to the person on Earth. It has a basic form with all its parts. Although the basic form may modify itself to accommodate the prevailing dynamics of a specific level or dimension, its parts all function in surprisingly similar patterns despite the level. A sensory system on the Earth level functions in much the same manner as the sensory system on any other level. Only the **range** *of function may differ.*

Individuated souls operate beyond time and space. Although time and space are form structures, they do not meet the criteria in the definition of form. Form is any reality that has order, organization, life vitality and consciousness. Time and space are but two kinds of order and organization. There can be form reality without time and

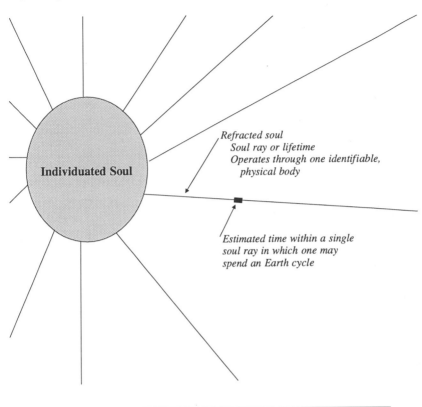

Refracted soul
Soul ray or lifetime
Operates through one identifiable,
physical body

Individuated Soul

Estimated time within a single
soul ray in which one may
spend an Earth cycle

space. Individuated souls are in a form reality that does not include time and space.

*Because of this, all that is experienced by the individuated soul, no matter what level or dimension, occurs **simultaneously**. That is, all that is experienced by the individuated soul is beyond time and space. It has no linear or spatial dynamics to it. However, many of the levels and dimensions within which a soul may have an experience include time and space as part of their dynamics. In order to participate within these levels and dimensions, the individuated soul must modify itself to accommodate time and space. To do this, the soul creates what have been commonly called "lifetimes." At Perelandra, these are called "soul rays." The individuated soul **refracts** itself into a smaller unit that includes all of the qualities necessary for experiencing within a specific range of time and* *space. Each individuated soul has countless such refractions that are functioning in concert with it at all times.*

Each lifetime or soul ray has a body through which the refracted soul operates and experiences. The soul-ray bodies are linked to and harmonious with the individuated soul's body. The common notion on the Earth level is that a lifetime begins at conception or birth and ends at death. The soul-ray lifetime is much more extensive than this. Its birth/death cycle on Earth is but a small part of the overall range of experience that occurs within a soul-ray lifetime. It may include many different experiences on many dimensions and levels— Earth being just one of its levels. [See diagram on page 29.] *What distinguishes one soul ray from another is its human body. Each soul ray has one consistent human body that is uniquely developed for allowing the refracted soul of that ray to operate and have experiences on its many different levels and dimensions.*

The soul-ray body is capable of functioning well beyond what is required in a birth/death cycle on Earth. It operates in an overall range that envelopes all activities that make up the full soul-ray experience. What is important to understand for anyone on the Earth level is that this massive array of functioning within a soul ray is occurring in a complex, highly synchronized manner every day. The fact that a person on the Earth level is not aware of this expanded activity has to do with the unique development and expansion of consciousness that is part of the Earth experience. The Earth experience includes a highly structured sense of time, space and consciousness. These properties do not make the Earth experience lesser in importance than experiences on other dimensions. They are simply elements of reality that the refracted soul, in partnership with its body, must learn to operate with. So, from the perspective of the Earth experience, one may not be consciously aware of any other activity being experienced except for the present Earth activity. As one moves through the Earth experience and one's understanding of time, space and consciousness expands, the Earth body develops and is able to process that greater understanding. There will come a time when an individual operating on the Earth level will be consciously aware of the full scope of his refracted soul activity.

We have said that a single soul ray contains a single body. Yet the refracted soul of that ray may have many experiences on many different levels and dimensions. In order to understand how one body functions simultaneously on many different levels and dimensions, one must understand that the body has a far more expansive reality than what you know from the Earth perspective. We have said that the Earth experience includes a highly structured sense of time, space and consciousness. While operating within the Earth level, the body functions with a comparably high structure of time, space and consciousness. However, this is but one small range of function for that body. It is also capable of operating in any structure that comprises any of the other levels and dimensions that are part of that soul-ray experience. So, for example, the sensory system as viewed from the Earth perspective can be defined scientifically as to its properties, characteristics and range of operation. But this is just the sensory system as viewed from the Earth perspective. From a different perspective in the soul ray's experience, the same sensory system includes different properties, characteristics and range of operation. It can also include some of the same elements that are part of the sensory system from the Earth perspective. Properties, characteristics and range of operation can overlap.

Perhaps an easier way to understand this is to see the sensory system as a vast, expanded unit capable of functioning on many different levels. Within each separate level, the sensory system operates with only those properties and characteristics needed for functioning within the range appropriate to that level.

From the Earth perspective, the key to knowing one's soul-ray activity is **consciousness.** *As the refracted soul and body learn to work with and through the highly structured elements of time, space and consciousness from the Earth perspective, they (the soul and body) will be capable of expanding their awareness and equally capable of processing the results of that awareness. They will operate with a greater and more conscious expanded sense of the self.*

Expanding one's consciousness to incorporate new levels of operation has an impact on the body. One does not simply expand consciousness. The body must **shift** *to incorporate this new con-*

*sciousness, and it must then learn to **function** in light of the new consciousness. To consciously understand that one's sensory system is capable of functioning in a more expanded manner than is defined by one level of experience literally allows that sensory system to expand. At that point, it can begin to operate in its more expanded manner. It feels as if the one sensory system as defined from one level is uniting with the sensory systems that are defined by other levels to form a larger, more complex unit. Because they may have different properties, characteristics and range of operation, they feel like completely different sensory systems. In fact, it is the different levels of functioning of one sensory system that are being united within one consciousness.*

VERIFICATION

When something fantastic happens to us, we get catapulted out of our framework of logic. Many times, the fantastic event includes

verification. It is as if a "hand" reaches out of the fantastic event and touches our mundane life in a small but special way that will catch our attention and serve to say, "You are not crazy. This is really happening." For example, one morning something fantastic happens to you that has

Verification: A fantastic event touches our mundane life in a small but special way.

really challenged your sense of logic. You wonder if it is actually happening or if somehow you are conjuring the whole thing up in your mind. That afternoon, as usual, you walk to the mailbox at the end of your driveway. You take the same route you take every day. But this afternoon you notice a wildflower in full bloom growing where you *know* no flower was growing the day before. And this is a plant that you have never before noticed growing wild in your area. There is absolutely no question in your mind that this flower is new on the scene—and it is gorgeous. And at the same time, you know that this flower is saying to you that the fantastic event that occurred that morning really did happen. This is verification.

One of the characteristics of verification is that it is extremely personal in nature. It is designed to communicate only with those involved with the fantastic event. Consequently, when you try to describe verification to others, they tend to look at you as if you're obsessing or have truly lost your mind. In the example above, *you* are the only person who knows for certain no flower was growing in that spot the day before because you are the only one who routinely goes for the mail. Verification alters *your* mundane and no one else's.

What generally happens when we try to share verification with others is that everyone will come up with theories that will satisfy them and reposition *your* verification back into *their* framework of logic. In short, they try to shoot it down. My suggestion to you is to share verification carefully and only with those who already support the "illogic" in your life. Having people pick apart your verification can be painful—and unnecessary.

THE PC PAT ON THE BACK

This is a concept I use to honor a friend of mine named Peter Caddy (hence the "PC"). Peter, who just recently died, was one of the co-founders of the Findhorn Community in Scotland. We met when I visited that community for three months in 1978, and we have been friends ever since. From all outward appearances, Peter always looked like the proper English gentleman. He generally wore a sport coat and turtleneck—or tie. And he abhorred the American custom of drinking coffee out of a mug. He liked a cup and saucer. Once, when he was visiting Perelandra, we put the half-gallon milk carton on the table as a creamer for coffee. He didn't say a word, but I could tell he thought this was very crass.

But Peter had another side, and this is where the pat on the back comes in. Early on in life, he had a spiritual teacher who had a lot of drill-sergeant qualities about her. She taught him to act immediately on intuition and guidance: Never stop to question it. Just do it. Peter listened—and learned—well. As a result, he went through one crazy, totally insane adventure after another—all because of his intuition or someone else's guidance. When he was on the move—and he traveled a lot—it was as if the whole world would reposition itself to accommodate whatever he needed to do. His adventures were nuts, and his stories were magical.

As I have moved through the years since meeting Peter, I've been challenged to do some pretty outrageous things myself—as this book will attest to. Whenever I have hesitated moving forward into absurdity, I have thought of Peter. And I'd say to myself, "Peter wouldn't even blink an eye at this." Then I'd go ahead, knowing that I'm not the only person who'd be crazy enough to do this thing. In this way, he's given me terrific support. And that's his "pat on the back."

I suspect—and hope—that by the time you finish this book, you'll look at my life and use it as your "MSW Pat on the Back" when you need a little encouragement to keep moving.

PISCEAN ERA

The Piscean era is that period of time, roughly 2000 years long, out of which the planet Earth and the universe are presently passing, and during which specific universal laws were grounded on the planet. In a broad and loose sense, one may say that the Piscean era explored, developed and worked with the dynamic of the parent/child, higher/lower and masculine-energy–dominate relationship, and expressed this dynamic in both action and structure throughout all levels of form.

AQUARIAN ERA

The Aquarian era is the term used to describe the coming phase of evolution facing not only those on planet Earth, but all souls and all life forms within the universe as well. Although it is termed "Aquarian" because of its loose connection to the astronomical alignment of Aquarius, it is more importantly a term that connotes an emphasized pattern and rhythm in life behavior. The Age of Aquarius will see the coming to the fore of the concepts of balance, teamwork and partnership played out on all levels of life.

THE INFORMATION POLICY

I began operating with what I call "The Information Policy" after my 1982 ring-pass-not expansion. To put it simply, those involved in the expansion suggested, and I agreed, that they would give me information about what I was experiencing only when I specifically asked for it. This meant I had to ask a direct question, and then I'd be given only the information that was needed to answer that specific question. We did this so that I would not be overwhelmed by the mammoth task of identifying and integrating everything that was involved in the expansion. It was—and still is—critical that I move through the post-expansion process at my own rate and in my own timing. (This happens to be true with anyone moving through post-expansion.) The only way we could assure that my timing was being fully adhered to was to address only what I could question.

Actually, it was more complex than this. The issue centered around the information I was ready to integrate. This didn't just hinge on my asking a direct question. We all can override our ability to integrate information by asking questions for purely intellectual curiosity. We are taught to do this in school. I had to also *need* the information.

I had to learn the difference between an intellectual question and an integration question. When we ask a question just for the sake of asking the question, and have no intention of doing anything with the answer, this is an intellectual question. It springs from our curiosity about something. An integration question is one in which the answer is received in right timing, and we are able to integrate the information we receive from the answer into our life. It can change the way we think, how we perceive the reality around us, how we act, and how we move through our daily schedule. It is a question whose answer moves through a complete experiential grounding process. It is information we need.

There is no general, hard-and-fast formula for discerning an intellectual question from an integration question. What is intellectual for one person is integration for another. But here is what I did to learn to distinguish between the two for myself:

1. I stopped asking questions that did not apply to whatever I was experiencing at that moment. That automatically cut out a lot of questions.

2. When I mistakenly asked an intellectual question, I paid attention to how the answer affected me. I noticed that when I couldn't integrate the answer, it would bounce off me as a rubber ball off a brick wall. I could physically hear the words, but my body felt "hard," and the word energy was bouncing off it. As a result, I had difficulty comprehending the answer or retaining it. I wasn't ready to absorb it. Whenever I felt an answer bounce, I would disregard my question and the answer. If I could discern the bounce fast enough, I would stop the person who was answering, tell him I wasn't ready to ask that question, and apologize.

3. After a while, I could anticipate the effect an answer would have on me by thinking out a question I had doubts about ahead of time and feeling whether the energy would be absorbed or bounce off. Even if I didn't know the answer, I could still feel an "answer energy." Once I felt the impact, I could decide whether or not to even open my mouth.

Don't forget: I went through this exercise because the expansion I took was so large that, had I not learned to discern intellectual questions from integration ones, I would have quickly become overloaded with information. This would have made it extremely difficult to function in the post-expansion stages. I still adhere to the Information Policy. I found that my life became so much more efficient when I didn't weigh it down with useless information that I extended the policy into my mundane life, as well.

FREE WILL, OPTION, SYNCHRONICITY, ACCIDENTS

Our lives operate on free will. When a human soul individuates, it takes on free will. Without it, we could not experience individuation. When an individuated soul activates a soul ray, we take on the task of developing *conscious* free will. Conscious free will is the dynamic that allows us complete freedom of choice in all that we do and how we develop within a soul-ray lifetime. In order to fully participate in the larger universal picture, we must learn to function responsibly, intelligently and ethically in ways that are consistent with the universal dynamics of that larger picture—and we must choose to do this consciously and freely.

Within each soul-ray experience, we intentionally choose (from our individuated soul level) to focus on specific areas of experience and learning. This is the extent of our "preplanning" prior to birth. As a result, we are born with a sense of direction and purpose.

After birth we take on the challenge of how best to accomplish our direction and purpose. Some people like to think that we come into a lifetime not only with direction and purpose, but also with the exact game plan we need to execute to fulfill that direction and purpose. If you think about this for a minute, you'll see that this preset game-plan idea eliminates conscious free will. Our participation in the larger universal picture is so important that we simply cannot sidestep our growth and development in the area of conscious free will. It seems like everyone in the universe and all the intelligences in nature know this—except us. Some of us work awfully hard to sidestep our responsibility in this matter. We must learn to consciously weigh situations and issues, and to say "yes" and "no" and "maybe." In this way, we learn to deliberately choose options that are consistent with universal dynamics and law and to consciously participate in the larger picture. Full participation implies knowledgeable and free participation. The only way we can learn this is through conscious growth and development around free will.

At any given point along the way, we are faced with many options for accomplishing direction and purpose. Some options are harmonious with our direction and purpose—and the universal larger picture. Some are not. We have to learn to discern and choose. We choose one option over the others for various reasons. It is the one that we find most attractive or exciting. It is the one that seems easiest. Perhaps it is the option that seems most efficient. Maybe it is the one we have the strongest gut reaction to. Or perhaps it's the option that seems the most difficult out of all the others, and, for whatever reason, we feel it is the important one for us to take. As we choose each option along the way, we begin to weave a unique pattern based on who we are and our ability to use free will to make choices. And over time we learn the formula for choosing that works best for us.

Three issues tend to come up whenever I have talked about this. The first is synchronicity. Usually people use synchronicity to describe an event where one's need or desire is suddenly and unexpectedly met by the perfect opportunity. There is a sense that "someone has heard them" and magically met their need.

In actuality, this kind of synchronicity is an illusion. They have simply chosen the option out of all the different ones available to them that allowed for their need to be met in this manner. They could have chosen another option that was equally available to them that would have also met their need, but in a different and less "magical" manner.

At any given point along the way, we are surrounded with a number of options for meeting need and desire. Most of them are positive in nature and can meet need and desire well. If we choose one of these, we experience our lives moving easily and well—even magically. This causes some to think that they "received" the one and only option for fulfilling need and desire. In fact, they chose one of several options. And had they chosen one of the difficult options or one of the options that was not consistent with their direction and purpose, their tough experiences might have been labeled "bad luck."

Both concepts—synchronicity and bad luck—distance us from our personal responsibility in life and complicate our growth and development in the area of conscious free will.

The second issue that is raised has to do with victimization and/or terrible outside circumstances that seem to eliminate any possibility of choice. When a person is suffering from victimization, he has already relinquished free will to another person or social structure. For whatever reason, he has chosen to step back from his life's responsibilities. When we look at these situations, we tend to focus on the difficult (and real) circumstances they now find themselves in as a result of victimization and say that this person's situation is caused by these circumstances. In order to understand free will, we have to look at the choices (or lack of choices) the person made prior to the situation. What decisions led the person into the situation in the first place? The situation is the *result* of these decisions. And now they are faced with far more difficult decisions to make in order to extricate themselves from the situation—and reestablish control over their free will. If the circumstance itself was the sole reason a person experiences victimization, then all we would have to do is remove any person from their circumstance to eliminate their problem of victimization. Addressing these kinds of issues have shown us that the real answers come from within, and without those internal answers—without personal growth and change—the person will simply move into another victimization situation.

There is no doubt that some of these situations are horrible—child or spouse abuse, institutional abuse, prison, genocide, mass starvation, the Holocaust.... Obviously, children are the most vulnerable to difficult and dangerous outside circumstances. They have the least-developed conscious free will and the fewest options. But children do have a strong survival instinct that pushes many of them to take control as best they can and reach out to options. Don't misunderstand me. I'm not suggesting that it is okay for children to face survival situations. I feel deeply that it is not fair and it is wrong. What I am saying is that, when addressing difficult or dangerous outside circumstances, the survival instinct gives children options and opportunity that is relative to their age and ability. Children can survive, and many do.

Adults are another matter. They have had the opportunity to develop free will and the ability to identify, consider and choose options. Some adults make decisions and choose options that enable them to avoid the difficult situation altogether. Others make choices that seem to "flirt" with fate. Still others position themselves in such a way that the situation becomes inevitable. But the fact that people who are faced with these horrible situations manage to have very different experiences (some disastrous, some breathtakingly heroic) illustrates that there are many different options available to each of them prior to the situation and during it. These situations may *limit* free will and choice, but they do not *eliminate* them.

The last issue generally raised centers around accidents. Many feel that there are no accidents in life. All events and opportunities are in right timing or predestined. Although this concept can be comforting at times—especially when dealing with what we call "someone's untimely death"—it eliminates free will. You simply cannot have over five billion people running around the planet exercising free will and not have accidents occur.

One last thing about free will: You will see in this book that I did not *consciously* know that a major expansion was before me or what impact it would have on my life. This is not at all unusual about expansion. On the surface, it appears that I moved into the expansion blindly and had no opportunity to exercise my free will. But as you read along, you'll see that at every critical juncture along the way, I had to consciously decide if I chose to go on. I didn't know what I was heading into, but I had to say "let's go" before the expansion continued. Had I decided to go no further (which would have been based on my gut instinct), I would not have continued beyond that point. I would have put the whole expansion experience on the back burner until I *felt* ready. Remember, ring-pass-not expansion is triggered by the soul and *only occurs when we are able to enfold it into our perceived reality.* However, this is all unconscious. Once we start to *consciously* move into the expansion we may feel unprepared, but we can still call a halt. Expansion overrides intellect—but not free will. *And the growth and development of free will is so critical to our evolution that, during our soul-ray lifetime, we do not relinquish free will to our own soul.*

FACTOR-X

Sometimes, something comes into our lives suddenly that we were not expecting, and we have no plans for dealing with it. This is factor-x. It can be part of whatever we are dealing with that we simply didn't know existed until it popped up. Or it can be the result of an accident. Something has happened that was not only unexpected but was also never meant to be part of whatever we are trying to address. Wherever it originates, we have to deal with it.

No matter how well we plan, how hard we try to figure things out ahead of time, a factor-x will show up. In fact, we're damn lucky if only one factor-x hits us! They like to travel in packs.

The keys to dealing with a factor-x are flexibility and creativity.

CONINGS

A coning is a balanced vortex of conscious energy. The simplest way to explain a coning is to say that it is a conference call between levels. With a coning, we are working with more than one intelligence simultaneously.

The reason a coning is needed for multilevel processes is because of the greater stability, clarity and balance it offers. With multilevel processes, we are working with many different facets and levels of intelligences at one time. Consequently, it is better to work with an organized team of all those involved in the area we are focusing on.

A coning, by nature, has a high degree of protection built into it. Because of the larger scope of multilevel work, it is important to define exactly who and what are involved in that work. All others are excluded by the mere fact that they have not been activated in the coning. In essence, a coning creates not only the team but also the "room" in which the team is meeting. It is important, when activating a coning, to discern between those team members who are a part of the work to be done and those others who are not involved. The coning is created and activated by us—the human team member. Only those with whom we seek connection will be included. Members will not "slide" in and out of a coning on their own. This adds to the exceptional degree of protection contained within the coning.

Any combination of team members can be activated for the purpose of simultaneous input. But this does not constitute a coning. A true coning has balance built into it. By this I mean a balance between nature and the human soul. In order for us to experience anything fully, we must perceive it in a balanced state; that is, it must have an equal reflection of the soul dynamics (evolution), combined with an equal reflection of the form or nature dynamics (involution). A coning contains both dynamics.

CONSCIOUSNESS: Defined by Nature

The concept of consciousness has been vastly misunderstood. To put it simply, consciousness is the working state of the soul. In human expression, as one sees it demonstrated on the planet Earth, the personality, character, emotional makeup, intellectual capacity, strong points and gifts of a human are all form. They are that which give order, organization and life vitality to consciousness.

We say "working state of the soul" because there are levels of soul existence that are different than the working state and can best be described as a simple and complete state of being.

Humans tend to think of the soul as being something that exists far away from them because they are in form. This is an illusion. The core of any life is the soul. It cannot exist apart from itself. Like the heart in the human body, it is an essential part of the life unit. A human in form is, by definition, a soul fused with nature. Personality and character are a part of the nature/form package that allows the soul to function and to express itself in form. Personality and character are not the soul; they are the order and organization of that soul.

Consciousness physically fuses into the body system first through the electrical system and then through the central nervous system and the brain. This is another aspect of nature supplying order, organization and life vitality. Consciousness itself cannot be measured or monitored as a reality. But what can be measured and monitored is the order, organization and life vitality of consciousness. Consciousness is the working state of the soul and is not form. It is nature, not consciousness, that supplies form.

We wish to add a thought here so that there will be no confusion about the relationship between nature and the soul. Nature does not, with its own power, superimpose its interpretation of form onto a soul. We have said that nature and soul are intimately and symbiotically related. This implies a give and take. No one consciousness group operates in isolation of the whole or of all other parts of the whole. When a soul chooses to move within the vast band of form, it communicates its intent and purpose to nature. It is from this that nature derives the specifics that will be needed for the soul to function in form. It is a perfect marriage of purpose with the order, or-

ganization and life vitality that is needed for the fulfillment of that purpose. Nature, therefore, does not define purpose and impose it on a soul. It orders, organizes and gives life vitality to purpose for expression in form.

SOUL: Defined by Nature

It is most difficult to define soul since—at its point of central essence—the soul is beyond form. Consequently, it is beyond words. However, it is not beyond any specific life form. As we have said, an individual is not separate or distant from his or her soul. Souls, as individuated life forces, were created and fused with form at the moment of the Big Bang. Beyond form, souls are also beyond the notion of creation. So we refer to the moment of the Big Bang regarding the soul, since this gives you a description of soul that will be most meaningful to you.

The Big Bang was the nature-designed order, organization and life force used to differentiate soul into sparks of individuated light energy. The power of the Big Bang was created by intent. And that intent originated from the massive collective soul reality beyond form.

It is reasonable to look at the Big Bang as the soul's gateway to the immense band of form. To perceive the soul and how it functions exclusively from the perspective of human form on Earth is akin to seeing that planet from the perspective of one grain of sand. The soul's options of function and expression in form are endless. What we see occurring more frequently now on Earth is the shift from the individual soul unknowingly functioning in an array of options, all chosen only because they are compatible with the immediate purpose of the soul, to the individual beginning to function with discrimination and intent in more expanded ways. Using the words in their more limited, parochial definitions, we can say that we see the beginning of a shift from soul function in which an individuated personality remains unaware of many of its options to soul function in which the personality begins to take on conscious awareness of all its options.

INTENT: Defined by Nature

Intent refers to the conscious dynamic within all life that links life vitality (action) with soul purpose and direction. When an individual uses free will to manipulate what he or she willfully desires instead of what is within the scope of higher soul purpose, then intent is combined with the manipulative power of free will and this combination is linked with life vitality. Life vitality adds action to order and organization. It both initiates and creates action. To maintain harmonious movement with soul purpose and direction, life vitality must be linked with the soul dynamic. This linkage occurs on two levels. One is unconscious, allowing for a natural patterning and rhythm of action through form that is consistent with soul purpose. As the body/soul fusion moves through its own evolutionary process as a functioning unit, it takes on a greater level of consciousness and an expanded level of awareness and knowing. As a result, the unconscious link between soul dynamic and life vitality takes on a new level of operation, thus shifting it into a state of consciousness. The shift is a gradual, step-by-step evolutionary process in itself. ***Intent is therefore defined as conscious awareness of soul purpose, what is required within the scope of form to achieve soul purpose, and how the two function as a unit.*** *Consequently, when one wishes to express soul purpose, one need only consciously fuse this purpose with appropriate form and action. This act is what is referred to when one speaks of intent.*

Intent as a dynamic is an evolutionary process in itself and, as we have said, does not suddenly envelop one's entire life fully and completely. Intent is only gradually incorporated into one's everyday life. Therefore, one does not suddenly and immediately function within the full scope of the dynamic in those areas of life where intent is present. Intent as a dynamic is as broad a learning arena as life itself. And in the beginning, intent can often be confused with or intermingled with free will. However, as it is developed, it becomes the cutting edge of the body/soul unit and how it operates. Intent is the key to unlimited life within the scope of form.

INTUITION: Defined by Nature

Intuition, as it is popularly defined, relates to a sixth sense of operation. This is false. This is not a sixth sense. When individuals experience a phenomenon that they consider to be beyond their five senses, they tend to attribute this experience to another category, the sixth sense, and call it intuition. The fact is that the phenomenon is processed through their five senses in an expanded manner.

Intuition, in fact, is related to and linked with intent. It is the bridge between an individual's conscious body/soul fusion—that state in which he knows and understands the body/soul fusion and how it functions—and the individual's unconscious body/soul fusion. **Intuition bridges the unconscious and the conscious.** *This enables what is known on the level of the unconscious body/soul fusion to be incorporated with and become a part of the conscious body/soul fusion. Intuition is the communication bridge between the two that makes it possible for the conscious body/soul unit to benefit from those aspects of the unconscious body/soul unit. This benefit results when the conscious unit opens to and moves through the lessons surrounding intent. Where intent is functioning fully, these two levels, the unconscious and the conscious, are no longer separate but have become one—the expanded conscious level. Consequently, there is then no need for the bridge known as intuition.*

However, lest you think otherwise, intent is not considered greater than intuition; rather, they are two excellent tools utilized equally by the highest developed souls functioning within form. We say this to caution those who read this not to think intent is "greater" than intuition and to be aimed for at the exclusion of intuition. Evolution as seen from the highest perspective is endless. Therefore, discovery of all there is to know about both intuition and intent is endless. For all practical purposes, an individual can safely consider that there will never be a time in which the development of intuition will be unnecessary. As we have said, the highest souls who function to the fullest within the scope of form do so with an equal development and expansion of both intent and intuition.

GROUNDING: Defined by Nature

Quite simply, the word "grounded" is used to acknowledge full body/soul fusion or full matter/soul fusion. The word "grounding" refers to what must be accomplished or activated in order to both ensure and stabilize body or matter/soul fusion. To be grounded refers to the state of being a fused body (matter)–soul unit. To achieve this fusion and to function fully as a fused unit is the primary goal one accepts when choosing to experience life within form. Functioning as a grounded body (matter)–soul unit is a goal on all levels and dimensions of form, whether the form can or cannot be perceived by the five senses.

Nature plays two key roles in grounding: First, it is through and with nature that the grounding occurs. Nature, which organizes, orders and adds life vitality to create form, is what creates and maintains grounding. Second, the levels of nature know what is required to fuse the soul dynamic within form. Nature provides the best examples of body (matter)–soul fusion. Humans have recognized the form or matter existence of nature on the planet, but have only recently begun to understand that within all form there are fully functioning soul dynamics. On the other hand, humans acknowledge or concentrate on their personal soul dynamics but have little understanding as to how they, in order to be functional within form, must allow the soul to fuse with and operate through their form body. Humans do not see the examples or learn the lessons of the master teachers of body (matter)–soul fusion that surround them in all the kingdoms of nature. Humans also deny the fusion within themselves. The relative extent of this denial interferes proportionately with the quality and stabilization of the fusion.

BALANCE: Defined by Nature

Balance is relative and measured, shall we say, by an individual's ability to faithfully demonstrate the various elements that make up his larger reality through the specific frameworks of form in which one has chosen to develop. When what one is demonstrating is faith-

ful in intent and clarity with these elements and the larger reality, he experiences balance. And those interacting with this individual will experience his balance. One experiences imbalance when there is distortion between what he demonstrates through the form frame- work and the intent and clarity of the elements that make up the larger reality as well as the larger reality itself.

If you seriously consider what we are saying here, you will see that balance as a phenomenon is not an elusive state that only an exalted few can achieve. Balance is, in fact, inherent in all reality, in all life systems. Balance is defined by the many elements within any individual's reality. And it is the dominant state of being within any reality and any form system. It is also the state of being that links individual life systems to one another and to the larger whole. When someone says that he is a child of the universe, what he is acknowl- edging is the relationship and link of his higher state of balance to the universe's state of balance. Whether he feels linked to or distant from this relationship depends on the closeness or distance he creates within himself with respect to his larger personal state of balance—that dynamic that is part of his overall reality.

THE WHITE BROTHERHOOD

Much has been written about the White Brotherhood, but I think a lot of it is garbage. Some people have felt or said that they were the sole "channellers" of the White Brotherhood, and this simply isn't true. The Brotherhood is a huge organization that is constantly con- nected to us in general and to many of us individually. It's just that usually they are only able to work with us on an intuitive level, and our link with them is unconscious on our part.

The White Brotherhood is a large group of highly evolved souls dedicated to assisting the evolutionary process of moving universal reality, principles, laws and patterns through all planes and levels of form. They hold the major patterning and rhythms now being util- ized for the shift we are all going through from the Piscean to the Aquarian era. When we link with them, they support and assist us by assuring that any work we do maintains its forward evolutionary motion and its connection to the new Aquarian dynamics.

They exist beyond time and history. I first heard about them during my stay at the Findhorn community in Scotland in 1977. St. Germaine, who had a close relationship with several Findhorn members, was referred to often and described as being a master teacher from the White Brotherhood. I was also told that the Order of Melchizedek was a part of the Brotherhood, and it is from this group that all of the major religious leaders come who have been a part of our history. I ignored the Brotherhood and its existence for years, assuming that they knew how to do their job, whatever that was, very well without me and that my focus was primarily on nature, not on human-oriented evolution. After all, this is the age of specialization.

My understanding of how the Brotherhood functions is, I'm sure, somewhat simplistic. I see them operating in a *co-creative* role with us on this planet. As a result of this role, they design and infuse purpose and direction into the various frameworks of social order through which we on Earth move in order to learn, experience and evolve. In essence, they create the schools through which we move. We call these schools religions, governmental structures, educational movements, philosophy, science...all those massive social frameworks with which we associate and within which we function.

Let me say something about the name "White Brotherhood." Several people have written to me questioning—and sometimes complaining about—that name. They want to make sure this isn't some white supremacist/sexist organization. Trust me, the White Brotherhood is neither. It includes males, females and souls beyond both persuasions, and some of them can outdo us any day when it comes to color.

The name "White Brotherhood" has been used for this group for centuries. We did not coin the name here at Perelandra. It was coined by those folks on the Earth level who first began to consciously work with this group. It is not a name the group chose for itself. It is a name *we* chose for it. The words "white brotherhood" maintained the intent and integrity of the group, so it has always been acceptable to them. "White" is used to signify *all* the rays of the light spectrum. "Brotherhood" is used to signify not only the family of all *people* but also the family of all *life*.

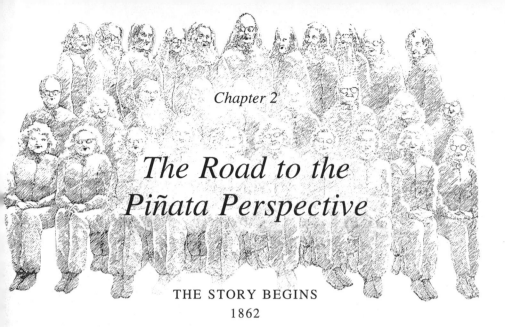

Chapter 2

The Road to the
Piñata Perspective

THE STORY BEGINS
1862

Somewhere near Jamestown, Virginia.

A schizophrenic plantation owner had many slaves who constantly tended to his land and enlarged its productivity. The opportunity in that lifetime for him to understand the law of karma was to see it outside of himself in the form of slavery. Simultaneously, he was being exposed to talk of revolution and the formation of a new order, a new country, giving equal vote and equal taxation to all. In that life, the three extremes—the high and mighty soul, the personality repressed unjustly and unfairly by the rule of the country, and the exposure to serfdom and slavery outside of self—*rent* the personality in two. At age forty, he had a complete nervous breakdown, manifesting that one must split in order to understand the reality that is Oneness. [comma]

THE STORY CONTINUES
1969

Washington, D.C.

In 1969, I was twenty-three years old. I had survived a childhood of abuse and abandonment.* Today the experts would say that I was a

---

* I describe my childhood and early life in the book *Behaving As If the God In All Life Mattered.*

"throwaway child." I had been on my own since age twelve. But back in the late 50s and early 60s, when I was a girl faced with the somewhat formidable task of surviving on my own, this term had not yet been coined. I had also survived two years in a Catholic boarding school for girls. I'm not sure which was tougher. By 1969, I had successfully come through the survival years and was now building my own life.

I had been working at the National Gallery of Art for two years. I managed to land this job after my return in 1967 from a year traveling in Europe. Hiring me had been a major gamble on the Gallery's part—not only did I not have a master's degree in fine arts or art history (a Gallery requirement in those days), I had not even attended college. I convinced the head of the publications department that spending a year looking at the real paintings of the masters had more value than studying reproductions in an art history book. I further wowed her with stories about my three-month job with the Florence marble restoration team that had taken on cleaning all the marble art that had been damaged in the devastating 1967 Florence flood. When I told her about working on some of Michelangelo's pieces, she was convinced I would be an asset to the Gallery and overlooked all those college requirements.

I wanted to work at the National Gallery of Art after my return to the States because I wanted to continue the "softer" lifestyle I had discovered (and appreciated) in Europe. I didn't want to return to the fast-paced life I left behind when I departed on a freighter for England. I had worked in the classified advertising department at *The Washington Post* for three and a half years. Although it was an exciting job, and although I had been invited to rejoin *The Post* after I returned, I came back to the States knowing I needed to change my life. I might have functioned quite well under the daily pressures of a major newspaper, but it was no longer a lifestyle that made me comfortable. In Europe, I realized it was too hard-edged for me, and I was afraid I would not like the person I might become if I spent year after year in that environment.

Just before I went to Europe, a friend hauled me to the National Gallery of Art for a two-hour crash course in art history. I had no interest in this kind of thing, but he was sure I'd be a better person for it. And it was "good preparation" for my Europe trip. After being dragged from room to room, I can honestly say that I left with a headache, nausea and an even stronger disinterest in art.

I wasn't sure what I was going to do in Europe. I only knew that it was important for me to go. I didn't even have an itinerary. In fact, I left the States not knowing where the freighter was going to dock. It all depended on the weather. If we had good weather— which was doubtful for a January crossing—we would dock at Southampton. If we had questionable or bad weather, we would dock at Liverpool. Two days before we arrived, I found out I would be disembarking at Liverpool.

And so, I arrived with no plans. I spent only a few days in Liverpool, then I headed to London. I was nearly paralyzed by the shock of realizing I was in a foreign country and I didn't know one other person. I quickly became homesick for the States—actually I think I was just yearning for *anything* that was familiar. There I was— twenty-one, in England, and without a clue as to why I was there. But I couldn't turn back. I had worked too hard to earn the money for the trip; I had quit my job, given up my apartment, stored my stuff and farmed out my cat. So I took a deep breath and slowly, *slowly* began to pull myself together. Sort of. I had a copy of *Europe on $5 a Day*, which listed inexpensive places to stay, inexpensive places to eat and equally inexpensive things to do. Museum-hopping is very inexpensive. It was also about the only thing listed that I felt comfortable doing. I wasn't interested in the night life in bars and pubs. I had lived with an alcoholic mother before being thrown out on the streets, so I really was not drawn to people who sat around getting half looped and acting silly. Besides, I didn't drink or smoke. I did not have enough money for fancy restaurants, and I was not that interested in food anyway. That left museums, art galleries and your basic historical points of interest.

I wish I could say that I walked into my first museum in London and fell madly in love with what I saw. It's not that I hated what I saw. I just didn't understand what the big deal was. Oh sure, some of the objects were interesting and some of the paintings were actually quite pretty. I continued visiting museums because I wanted to figure out what was the point of it all. After about my fourth country and approximately the thirtieth museum, I began to gain an appreciation and respect. (Years later, when I was working at the Gallery, a boy about nine years old came up to me and asked, "What's the big deal with all this stuff? All they had to do was follow the numbers." I said, "Oh no. *These* are the fellows who figured out what numbers to use." Well, this kid left with a whole new respect for what he was seeing.) By the time I got to Florence and joined the marble restoration team, I was actually beginning to feel a little knowledgeable about art.

Now, if you're beginning to think that culture was influencing me by the time I arrived in Florence, and that this is the reason I joined the marble restoration team, don't. I arrived in March 1967. The Arno River overflowed in November 1966—just after everyone in the city had received their first delivery of heating oil for the winter. The flood waters burst all the storage tanks. The water alone, which reached a height of twenty feet in some streets, did a great deal of damage. But that thick heating oil did a great deal more damage, particularly to the artwork. Large numbers of international teams of art restoration experts rushed into Florence to take over the massive cleanup job. The English worked on the restoration of paintings. The Americans sent in teams to deal with the cleanup of old books. But no one came to work on the marble because there were no experts in this field of restoration. A small, ragged group of English and Americans banded together on their own and took on the challenge. Washing mud off the marble was the easy part. The oil was the main problem.

Marble is porous and, although it has a smooth surface or patina, it acts very much like skin. When the oil hit the surface, it was absorbed through the pores, into the marble, leaving a dark, brown stain on the surface. This small group of people, armed with a few implements (dental tools, de-ionized water and toothpaste), set to work, but no amount of scrubbing affected the oil problem. Eventually, a scientist from England brought in a chemical solvent to draw the oil out without damaging the patina or breaking down the marble. A thin layer of solvent mixed with talcum powder was hand-packed on the marble. The solvent drew out the oil, which then absorbed in the talc. The talc dried, was brushed off, and the whole process was repeated. This procedure was done over and over until the surface of the marble was once again white.

The whole city of Florence is a museum. There is marble art everywhere: statues, plaques, tombs, fountains, cathedral walls. And this group of about fifteen people was trying to hand-pack everything before the oil left a permanent stain on the marble. This is the situation I walked into. I appreciated their efforts; they were in need of help; and I volunteered because I became fascinated with the technical challenge of how to get oil out of marble. I did not have a deep love for marble art—at least not before I began cleaning it. It was just the thing to do.

We worked long hours six days a week. The Italian government paid us $100 a month. For me that wasn't bad. It paid for all my living expenses while I stayed in Florence. A few more people joined the group. We were making progress and began to feel we could get this job done. We ignored the fact that the solvent left chemical burns on our hands. (We couldn't protect ourselves with rubber gloves because the solvent ate through the gloves too.) We packed the hell out of that city. Then, around mid-June, the intense summer heat rolled in. All the marble we had cleaned began to show new brown stains on the surface. The heat was drawing out the remaining oil from the very center of the marble that had not been drawn out with the solvent. All of Florence had to be repacked. That's when I looked at my hands that were becoming more raw by the day, and handed over my tools to a new volunteer.

I left Florence at the end of June and continued my travels. With each month, I became more comfortable with tackling new countries, new customs, new languages. My self-confidence steadily rose. I became a seasoned and intelligent traveler. I became less an American and more a European. Traveling alone gave me a lot of time by myself, and I became quiet and more at peace. I was healing from my tumultuous childhood.

I returned to the States with a very different feeling about myself and how I wanted to live. That's when I made the decision not to rejoin *The Post* and, instead, look for a completely different kind of job. The National Gallery of Art was not advertising for help when I showed up. I decided that I wanted to continue with what I had learned in Europe about art, and so I simply presented myself at their personnel office. I walked out with a job in the publications department.

I then decided I wanted to live in an area of town that had a neighborhood feeling rather than renting another apartment in a high-rise. Not far from the National Gallery of Art is an area called Capitol Hill. I found an English basement apartment in a house owned by a couple with two small children. It was perfect. I was now living only thirteen blocks from work, so I bought a gold Robin Hood bicycle, which became my main mode of transportation.

Now, that bicycle became quite the source of adventure for me. I rode it for several years, and in all those years I rarely passed another cyclist. It took a few more years before cycling came into vogue in Washington, D.C. I was determined not to get run over by a car and wore bright clothing so folks would see me. I had great rain gear; I bought a piece of oil cloth (white with black polka dots), a shiny black, broad-brimmed hat that tied under my chin, and shiny black plastic boots. I looked like a whacky witch from the west as I rode through town with my oilcloth poncho flapping in the breeze. It drew a lot of attention—which was the point. No one ran over me.

I, on the other hand, ran over—or into—someone. Each day I cut through the grounds of the U.S. Capitol Building on the way to and from work. All the Capitol guards knew me, and I'd wave as I rode by. One summer evening, there was an amazingly beautiful sunset going on just behind the rotunda. I was pedaling slowly, watching the sunset along with just about everyone else—except Robert Kennedy. He was coming down the east steps of the Capitol Building with his head down—I assume he was thinking. As he stepped off the curb, I ran right into him. Actually, my front wheel lodged between his legs. (He had been mid-stride when we collided.) Our heads were about a foot apart. He didn't say anything, but he sure had tears of pain in his eyes. I didn't know what to do, so I said, "Tough day, huh." He said something like, "It's an appropriate end to the day." Thank god the guards knew me and didn't come flying over to wrestle me to the ground. Senator Kennedy and I "disconnected." I asked if he was okay, hoping he wouldn't go into any kind of detail. He said, in a strained voice, that he'd be fine. I apologized (a lot), then said, "Bye," and pedaled on.

I didn't always attack people with this bike. (Although there were many times when I wanted to turn it into a Sherman tank so that I could rumble down the street taking off every car door that swung open in my face.) Once Golda Meir crossed the street right in front of me—apparently she hadn't heard how dangerous I was. I dutifully stopped and said "Hi" to her. (What else do you do when someone of her stature is looking right at you? You can't just stare. Well, I guess I proved you could run into them, but just saying "hi" seems a lot easier.) She graciously said "Hello," and continued on. I went on my way, thinking she really looked like a short grandmother and not like the prime minister of Israel.

One time I rode my bicycle through the hallways of the National Gallery of Art, but I felt I had good reason. The Gallery was closed, and I was getting ready to go home. I was allowed to park my bike in the Gallery garage. When I arrived in the garage one evening, I realized I had left my wool gloves in the publications room, which was a good block away from the garage. It was the dead of winter and downright cold outside, and I was tired. So I hopped on the bike and pedaled down the hallway to publications. Unfortunately, John Walker, the dignified director of the National Gallery at the time, picked that very moment to come down the hallway. You know how it is when someone sees something they can't believe, so they refuse to believe they're seeing it? That's how John Walker looked. I have the feeling that the last thing he expected to see was someone riding a bicycle through the hallowed halls of the Gallery. He was walking with two other equally dignified-looking men, and it was clear they didn't know what to say. I decided to take advantage of the confusion, so I pedaled right passed them, said "Good night," and kept right on going to publications as if it were the most natural thing in the world. After I passed, I heard Mr. Walker saying to the others, "Did you just see that?" I assume he never got it straight in his head because I didn't see any memos about prohibiting bike-riding in the Gallery.

I was probably an asset to the Gallery, as the head of publications predicted I might be, but I was also a challenge to them. I was just

too different for them. I had never considered myself a "free spirit"
because back then this was synonymous with "hippie." I certainly
was not a hippie—at heart or lifestyle. I wanted a "normal" life. I
wanted a real "home"—a place where I belonged. I had already had
enough freedom, challenge and adventure, thank you. But I *thought*
differently—and I especially thought differently than most people
who worked at the Gallery. They took themselves very seriously,
and they got upset about the smallest things. An accidental food
stain on a silk tie could wreck a man's day there. They didn't like to
think about practical things. They were the "gentrified folks" who
were meticulously dressed, and I always looked like I just rolled in
on a bicycle. Sure, I wore dresses, but they were ones that I had
sewn and not bought from Bloomingdale's. And I didn't have a
single piece of gold (real gold) jewelry to sport around.

Actually, what I had to offer the Gallery was common sense. We
really thought differently. When I began working in publications, no
one knew which reproductions were in stock, which ones were out
of stock, or which were on order from the printer. People would ask
for maybe twenty reproductions, and at least half of them would be
out of stock—and we never knew when they'd be available again.
Some prints had been out of stock for years. After a while, I offered
to do an inventory for these people. This involved crawling around
storage areas, identifying stacks of stuff and counting. You wouldn't
believe the junk I found. Trudy would have been ecstatic. I set up
the first, organized inventory/restocking/reprinting process for all
publications at the Gallery. They were impressed.

The people that I understood were the tourists. They drove me
nuts, but I understood where they were coming from. They didn't
get what the big deal was either. But the National Gallery of Art was
on the list of things to see in Washington, so in they trooped. A lot
of people came through the doors in the summertime just for the air
conditioning and the chance to walk around on the cool marble
floors in bare feet. Many people never bothered looking at the real
paintings—they'd just come into the publications room and look at
the postcards and 11-x-14-inch reproductions of the paintings. It
saved time.

Lots of people bought those reproductions, and this is when it got interesting. When I worked at the Gallery, the publications area was not self-service, as it is today. Now you just walk around and pick up the postcards, 11-x-14 prints or poster-size reproductions you want, and then go pay for them. You don't have to identify the pictures to the clerk. Back when I worked there, only the postcards were self-service. Everything else was displayed with stock numbers. You brought your list of stock numbers to a staff person, and we got your stack of "artwork." Consequently, I'm one of the generation of publications staff who knows most of the Gallery paintings not by artist and name, but by stock number. Renoir's *Girl with a Watering Can* was forever known by us as "good ole 1870."

You could tell that people really didn't get the overall concept of what the Gallery was about based on what they said to us in publications. A fair number of people thought that this was where John Kennedy was buried. (He had lain in state in the Capitol Building under the rotunda, and since the Gallery had a big rotunda, visitors got confused.) Another person came to the Gallery for a special show and asked afterwards what the building was normally used for once "this show left." One woman asked for an 11-x-14 print of Picasso's *The Tragedy*. This is a rather somber picture of a man, woman and child from his blue period. Hence, the entire picture is in shades of blue. I pulled the print out, but the woman looked at it a few seconds and said, "Oh, do you have this in green? It'll go better with my bathroom if it's in green." Another fellow, who had clearly been sent to the Gallery on a mission by his wife, asked if we had any pictures by "Genre." (This is like asking if there are any poems by "Anonymous.")

By far, the biggest seller was the 11-x-14 reproduction of Salvador Dali's *Last Supper*, which sold for a quarter. The traditional depiction of the Last Supper often features the torso of God with outstretched arms just above Jesus and the disciples. Dali did not include the head of God. In his depiction of the Last Supper, the painting stops at His neck. A number of people, when seeing the inexpensive reproductions of the painting, would ask if we had a more expensive copy that included God's head. I guess they figured the cheap reproductions didn't necessarily include the entire painting. One fellow argued that Dali could not have possibly painted that picture because there were no bent watches anywhere in it. (Ahhh...you're not getting this one. Let me help. Dali painted a bunch of pictures that included watches with bent faces. They looked as if they were liquid rather than solid.) Another time, a woman proudly presented herself at the desk and asked for a copy of Dolly Madison's "Last Dinner."

I may not have had a master's degree in art history like other staffpersons, but, compared to many of the people who visited the Gallery, I was an expert. But I can't say I ever got comfortable at the Gallery. It just wasn't my world.

During the two-and-a half-year period that I worked at the Gallery, I began to make changes in how I practiced my religion. In 1964, I had converted to Catholicism, despite my high school experiences in a Catholic boarding school. I had been born into a nonpracticing Jewish family. So I converted from no religious experience to Catholicism. It gave me a moral and ethical framework in which to live my life, and I was grateful for this because I didn't have parents or family to supply the structure. I took my religion quite seriously. I examined every aspect in Catholicism that directly affected me. I had to know why I was to do or say something—I couldn't just do it. Sometimes this led me to take stands that drove the priests I knew a little nuts. Before I went to Europe, my parish was St. Matthew's, in the diocese of Washington, D.C. It was then headed by the conservative Archbishop O'Boyle, who later became a cardinal. Since I was a convert and had not grown up around the deification of priests by parishioners, I had a fairly secular attitude toward priests in general and Archbishop O'Boyle in particular. In the evenings I worked at the rectory with a group called "Apostolic Action." This meant that I was around the place a lot and saw the priests and archbishop fairly frequently. To me they were people and capable of making mistakes. Consequently, I didn't hesitate to challenge them if I had questions about something they said or did.

One Sunday morning at Mass, I noticed that many of the women were wearing expensive, somewhat showy hats and mantillas. This was during the time when women were required to cover their heads. In my convert's zeal, I had done some research and discovered that the cover-your-head rule developed during the early church when women's hair was a great source of pride. Consequently, it was an act of humility to cover their heads during Mass. Based on this, I had accepted the cover-your-head rule. But looking at the women around me at St. Matthew's, I felt that things had reversed themselves. What women chose to cover their heads with had now *become* the source of pride. So I reversed the rule. The next Sunday, I showed up with nothing on my head but hair. Well, you would have thought from some of the reactions around me that I had just dragged road-kill up and laid it on the altar. Archbishop O'Boyle was saying the Mass. I went up to the communion rail at the appropriate time and knelt, waiting to be "served" communion. The archbishop got to me, took one look at my bare head and walked right by me to the next person. I looked at him and thought something defiant like, "I'm not going to let you get between me and my religion. How dare you." So I continued kneeling at the altar railing—and I knelt, and I knelt. . . .

He finished giving everyone else communion and was back up at the altar "cleaning up"—I was still kneeling. Nothing like this had ever occurred at St. Matthew's, and especially not to the archbishop. Of course, in a few years the church would go through a testy period of change, upheaval and lots of protest, but that was two or three years down the road. You just didn't protest anything back in 1964. When the archbishop finally turned around, I was still kneeling at the railing. I stared at him, and he stared right back at me. I was clearly taking him on. By this time, the congregation was pretending I didn't exist and went right on with the rest of the Mass.

After Mass, as is the tradition, Archbishop O'Boyle stood by the main door, greeting the departing parishioners. At that time, the custom included the archbishop taking the parishioner's hand, the parishioner doing a little genuflection, and then kissing the archbishop's ring. When I came to him, I refused to let him take my hand and I refused to kiss his ring. In fact, from that moment on, I never kissed another ring. He was flustered, and I was angry. I just said, "Have a good afternoon" and walked out.

The next Sunday, I saw a handful of women in the congregation who had nothing on their heads. It didn't take long before half the women attended Mass bareheaded. I had not intended to create a movement. I just did what *I* had to do in order to align my actions with my intent. For the others, I think it was a change that was ready to happen. Oh yes—Archbishop O'Boyle started serving me communion again and continued speaking to me whenever he saw me at the rectory as if nothing had happened.

I didn't just challenge archbishops. I took on priests, too. For example, I was serious about the sacrament of confession. I went every week and, after trying out several of the priests at St. Matthew's, I asked the one I liked best to be my confessor. This meant that I always went to him for confession. Although they're not supposed to know who is confessing, a priest recognizes the voices of those who come to him regularly. He always knew who I was, and going to him regularly gave me a sense of continuity upon which to build my confessional experiences. I didn't have a lot of sins to unload since I was honestly trying to live my religious convictions. So I used confession to fine-tune my religious thinking as much as possible. They were more like quick, moral counseling sessions—with a sin or two thrown in from time to time for good measure. My confessor believed in developing the sacrament of confession to its fullest. We got along very well. One of the things he did was listen to what was actually being said, and after giving his thoughts on the subject, he would give a penance that was related to what I had said. This may sound reasonable, but it was actually very unusual. Unlike other priests, he didn't just hand out a bunch of Hail Marys and Our Fathers for penance. Often, he would tell me to kneel at the altar for ten or fifteen minutes and think about what we had talked about. And that was it. I learned a lot and grew in my understanding of Catholicism quite a bit with him.

Some weeks my confessor's schedule changed, and I'd have to go to another priest if I wanted to maintain the weekly rhythm. (I can't for the life of me remember why I chose this specific weekly rhythm, but I did and I was reluctant to change it even if my confessor wasn't there.) I knew all the other priests because I worked with them at the rectory. Also, I had "auditioned" them for the confessor position—and rejected all but one. So, on the days my confessor was out, I'd try one of the other ones anyway. This is when problems cropped up.

One priest was intently reading his Daily Office—a bunch of prayers priests are required to read each day—when I went into his confessional. It's not unusual for them to read these prayers while they're waiting for people to have their confessions heard. Some days they could sit in their little booths and read *War and Peace* between confessions. But normally, when someone comes into their confessional, they stop reading and turn off the light. Then the priest proceeds with the business at hand. This priest wouldn't stop reading, nor would he turn out the light. He just huffed a little when I knelt down, and continued reading. When he realized I wasn't saying anything, he told me to speak, then continued reading. I still waited for him to pay attention to the confession. After all, this was a sacrament, not a sharing of brownie recipes. When I realized he wasn't going to stop, I said, "I'll be in a pew right outside. When you're ready to hear my confession, you just step out and let me know." Then I got up and sat in the pew outside his door. At first he didn't make any noise, but I was sure I had gotten his attention. So I waited. It didn't take long for him to emerge from the booth—no more than five minutes, I'm sure. He said, "All right. You can come back," and quickly ducked back into the booth. We got through the confession without further incident. I never went back to him.

The next pinch hitter I tried out was attentive during confession, but he gave me one of those throwaway penances: twenty-five Hail Marys and eighteen Our Fathers, or something like that. It had nothing to do with what had been said by him or me. When he gave me the penance, I said, "No." He said, "What do you mean 'no'?" I said, "That's not acceptable. It has nothing to do with the confession." He was quiet for a minute, then said, "What penance would you like?" I replied, "How about telling me to think about . . . ," and then I came up with some esoteric topic that somehow wove together the issues of that confession. He thought about it and said, "Well, that sounds good. Go ahead and do that." I left happy, but I didn't go back to him either. I figured if I had to come in with the sins, organize my thinking and go through the process of confessing them, the least the priest can do is come up with a reasonable penance. I didn't see why I had to do *all* the work.

Now, I wouldn't want you to think I was tedious about religion in general or confession in particular. I had my share of "mirthful moments." For example, I liked to go to St. Matthew's just before confessions were to begin. There could be as many as five or six priests working at one time. St. Matthew's is an international parish, and the priests would post language signs outside their booths so that everyone would know which foreign languages were understood and spoken by which priests. I'd wait until the priests were settled in their booths and quietly switch all the language signs. The French-speaking priest would be listening to Spanish confessions. The German-speaking priest would be hearing Italian confessions, and so on. (I learned during my European trip that confession was valid even if the priest didn't understand the language of the person confessing, so I knew I wasn't nullifying anyone's confession with this stunt.) After they'd get a few confessions they couldn't understand, they'd all come out of their booths and meet in the middle of the Cathedral to exchange language signs. They never figured out who was doing that.

I also coordinated one of the world's greatest short-sheeting events. As I've said, I knew each one of these fellows, and we were all prone to playing pranks now and then. I picked an evening when all five were in the rectory. I got a friend and we began making phone calls. I called the first priest and talked him into short-sheeting the bed of one of the other priests. (It didn't take much convincing on my part.) I promised I would keep the other priest busy on the phone while he (the first priest) was short-sheeting his (the second priest's) bed. Then while I had the second priest on the phone, I talked him into short-sheeting the bed of the third priest, with the promise that I'd have someone call and keep the third priest busy while the deed was being done. My friend then called the third priest and talked him into short-sheeting the fourth priest's bed, and so on. The long and short of it (so to speak) is that all five priests short-sheeted each others' beds all on the same night while each was present in the rectory and presumably protecting his quarters.

So, this is the kind of Catholic I was prior to going to Europe—

diligent but cheeky. I maintained this attitude toward religion throughout my trip. I not only visited many churches and cathedrals, I made it a point to attend Mass in as many as possible so that I could experience the building in its "working state." I visited the Vatican several times, attended Mass in the different chapels, and attended Easter Mass with the pope in St. Peter's Square. I even found the bar in the Vatican. Yes, there's a regular bar right in the Cathedral. It's supposed to be open to the public, at least that's what one priest told me. I found out, however, that hardly anyone knows about it except priests, and they don't like it when a young woman walks in alone and orders an espresso. (I won't tell you where the bar is. Next time you're at the Vatican, just poke around a little. Go on in and order something. Tell the boys Machaelle sent you.)

After returning to the States in 1967, I began to gravitate more and more toward the liberal end of the church spectrum. I can't explain why this occurred. It just automatically happened. I found the new parish church on Capitol Hill too traditional—and therefore unacceptable. I wasn't sure what I was looking for, but I felt clear about what I no longer wanted. A friend of mine heard about a "neat" Mass going on at George Washington University. So I rode my bike across town to the George Washington University Newman Center and found the Mass for me.

This was an interesting Mass in many ways. First of all, Newman Centers operate on university campuses for the benefit of the students. This Newman Center had a Mass that was so unique and alive that it drew people to it from all over the Washington metropolitan area. Families drove in from the suburbs to attend this Mass. At the same time, there weren't many university students in the congregation. We could never figure out how to appeal to the students. It was a folk Mass, which was a format that was just coming into vogue at that time. Most of the music was original, and the musicians were either professional or semi-professional. No one in the congregation winced when these people played. In fact, they could rip off a jazzy version of the "Our Father," featuring an outstanding trombonist that was so good the congregation would applaud. The "church" was the university amphitheater, and the seating was almost in the round. This fostered a completely different relationship between the congregation, the altar and the priest. The priest was personable and a little nuts—which helped him communicate the Mass in direct ways to the congregation. He had a great sense of humor and a well-honed ability to laugh at the absurd. And he allowed the liturgy to include the congregation in significant ways. For example, people from the congregation assisted him during Mass and helped hand out communion. Unlike the traditional church, they placed the bread/host into the hands of the person rather than place it directly on their tongue. This was an important symbolic gesture because it allowed us to take responsibility for giving ourselves communion, rather than depending on a priest to "feed" it to us. It was also a gesture that reconnected me in an indirect way to the archbishop. The archdiocese considered this Mass to be close to heretical. Each Sunday, a priest from the archdiocese was assigned to attend our Mass and observe. We assumed he was waiting for us to "cross the line." He'd even take notes. We all knew who he was and would say "hello" to him each Sunday, even try to get him to join in. He didn't smile much.

The Mass I remember most was the one that marked the twenty-fifth anniversary of the bombing of Hiroshima. During that summer, each Mass focused on a specific issue in the areas of peace and nonviolence. Four of the Masses were devoted to ecology, and one of those Masses centered around world population and birth control. At the time this was scandalous. The priest from the archdiocese nearly went mad from taking so many notes that day. But our priest and the congregation maintained a good balance by talking through an issue without promoting it, which was tricky. The final Mass of the summer series was the one centered around the bombing at Hiroshima. It was a multimedia event, and its focal point was a short, original "play" that we had obtained from the Japanese Embassy.

The play was read by three people who were interspersed throughout the congregation, each taking a "voice" or role. One person represented straight history and simply gave us the facts of the event. The second person represented the voice of social consciousness at the time of the bombing. The third voice expressed the current social consciousness regarding war and bombing. This was at the height of the Vietnam War, so there were a lot of opinions on the subject. The three "voices" interwove and created a tapestry about history, war and nonviolence. Somehow, word got out that the Japanese Embassy was offering this play to anyone who wished to use it for the anniversary of Hiroshima. It was considered by many to be fair, moving and politically noncontroversial, but the GWU Newman Center was the only group that accepted their offer. When we did, an aide who had worked with Robert Kennedy heard about it, called and requested to be one of the "voices."

While the lines were being read, slides were projected onto a huge screen behind the altar that made the whole experience audio *and* visual. The play ended with the bombing, and the final slide was an abstract picture of colored lights. The musicians quietly played an instrumental piece for several minutes. Then the Mass continued. When it was over, it was the first (and only) time I saw no one move. The priest ended the Mass, and everyone sat there for a good fifteen minutes—silently. Then gradually they left, without saying a word.

By 1969, my life had settled into a comfortable, efficient, creative routine that I enjoyed very much. In fact, it was one of the most satisfying times of my life, and I still look back on it with great fondness.

One event occurred that year that later proved to be significant, even though it seemed irrelevant at the time. I attended a portion of the state funeral for Dwight D. Eisenhower. I hadn't intended to go. As a matter of a fact, I couldn't have cared less about the event. This was a man who was president when I was a child. I began to wake up politically with the Kennedys, like a lot of impressionable youth around the country. Eisenhower was the old golfer who we wanted to go away and fade quietly into the background. Let the new blood take over and get all those world problems straightened out. The only real memory I had of him was when I was seven. He was delivering his first State of the Union Address on television. I remember sitting right in front of the TV, watching this guy yammer away while constantly taking his glasses off and putting them back on. I had figured out he was nervous, and I thought this was fascinating—for about five minutes. Then I announced, "This man is boring," and went off to find something more interesting to do.

In March 1969, I was only vaguely aware he had died. I didn't even know the coffin had been brought to the Capitol Building to lie in state. What made me aware of all this was a small controversy that centered around street parking. Whenever anything remotely important went on at the Capitol, police would post signs all over our area of Capitol Hill announcing that on a certain day, during certain hours, residents were not allowed to park their cars along those streets. (It's like all the residents were supposed to drive their cars into their living rooms for those hours.) Although I only had a bicycle to contend with—which was actually already parked in my living room—I joined in the neighborhood complaining whenever we saw those signs posted around. When the signs went up early in the week to announce that, once again, we'd have to vaporize the cars for the next Saturday afternoon, I was grumbling and griping along with everyone else. It didn't help when I found out it was because of Eisenhower's funeral. How insignificant can the reason get?

That Saturday morning, I ignored the car shuffle and headed out to the local grocery store. I got back to the apartment, put away my groceries and was settling down for a cup of coffee when I heard the twenty-one gun salute start. Living just seven blocks from the Capitol, I was pretty used to hearing ceremonial gunfire. We used to say that if it's slow and steady gunfire, it's a salute. If it's rapid and erratic, it's a gunfight—so duck. This was slow and steady, so I continued drinking my coffee.

After the first round, something strange happened. The sound of the second and third rounds intensified. It was as if the "honor shooters" were moving closer to the apartment. By the fourth round, it sounded like I was sitting in a tin can, and they were standing right next to it, firing directly at it. It intensified so much that I had to cover my ears. But this didn't help. The sound just kept getting louder. All of a sudden, I decided I had to get out of that apartment before my head burst. (I really thought my head was going to blow apart.) I grabbed my bicycle, went outside and, without thinking, hopped on and started pedaling towards the Capitol Building. I arrived at the east entrance just as the twenty-one gun salute was ending. There was a huge crowd standing on both sides of the entrance behind ropes. There were so many people that it looked like an inauguration. It certainly didn't look like the funeral of some old, forgotten past president.

Because I had the bike, I couldn't fit into the crowds too easily, so the police quickly placed me on the sidewalk just in front of the crowd. That's when dignitaries began coming out of the Capitol and lining up on either side of the door just at the top of the steps. I remember recognizing Charles de Gaulle and Omar Bradley, who was in a wheelchair. I looked at this group of old men, and for some reason, I thought that this was a very special moment. These were the Allied leaders of World War II, and this was probably the last time they'd be together like this. Soon they would all be dead. I tried to take in as much of this scene as I possibly could.

I remember what I thought at that moment so clearly because I completely startled myself. The only thing I knew about World War II was that it had happened. I have no idea why I understood the significance of these men standing at the top of the steps. I only know that the moment completely filled me.

The coffin was carried slowly down the steps between the dignitaries. Everyone in the crowd was quiet and attentive—none of the jostling around to see what was going on and who was doing it that I was used to seeing in Washington. I was deeply impressed that those dignitaries and this crowd seemed to care about the death of Eisenhower.

It didn't take long to get the coffin into the hearse, and the family and dignitaries into the limousines. Still, no one in the crowd moved. The cars slowly filed out the east entrance, which was right in front of me. The hearse passed, then suddenly the cars stopped. Charles de Gaulle was in the limousine directly in front of me. The window was down, and while the cars were stopped, we stared at one another. I was no more than five feet from him. He had a serious expression on his face. At first I thought he disapproved of my being there with my bike, and considered it undignified of me. But then I realized that, although he had looked right at me, he was now actually looking through me, and his expression was one of deep sadness—even despair. This puzzled me, because I couldn't figure out why he would feel this way over the death of an old man whose death was inevitable. De Gaulle was a soldier, and surely he had a better grip on death than this. (The insolence of youth!) I don't know how long we stared at one another. It seemed like forever. Oddly, neither one of us broke away from our staring. I thought I felt his pain and I wanted to reach out and touch his arm, but I knew I'd be shot on the spot if I tried that. Finally, the procession started up again. When the final cars left, the crowd broke up— and I headed back to my apartment to have another cup of coffee and to continue with my day. [comma]

1970–1971

Life for me was still comfortable. I had returned from my second trip to Europe—this time, just for six weeks. Because of the oppressive Washington summer heat and humidity, I had added a Lambretta 200cc motorscooter to my "garage," which gave me a lot more mobility. And I was attending some classes at George Washington University. Actually, life was beginning to feel too comfortable. This little nagging thought kept popping up in the back of my mind that had something to do with needing to make a change. It didn't make sense because things were going so well.

Two opportunities fell into my lap. First, I was asked if I wanted to help start what would be called the Community for Creative Non-Violence (CCNV). It was the brainchild of a lawyer I had not met before and a newly ordained Paulist priest who I knew from the GWU Newman Center. They wanted to develop a Christian center for the study and education of nonviolence, and they wanted to bring together a small group of people to live out these principles together under one roof. We would offer classes and sponsor lectures at CCNV and give talks about the concepts of nonviolence at any area school that would have us. And since this was at the height of the protests against the war in Vietnam, we would serve the country and the world by *responsibly* joining in the protests. ("Responsibly" became defined as anything from peaceful marching to dumping gravel at the entrances of the Pentagon in an attempt to close down the "war machine." The definition depended on who you were talking to at the time. I was pro-march and anti-gravel.)

I had developed strong beliefs in nonviolence as a principle and as a tactic for social change. I accepted the offer to be part of this community because I felt it would give me a unique chance to further develop in this area and actually live the principles with a group of like-minded people. The offer felt both socially responsible and personally challenging. I had lived by myself since I was twelve, except for one six-month period and my stint in Catholic boarding school. CCNV felt like just what I needed to stir my life up and kick it out of that complacency zone I felt I was in.

The second opportunity was given to me by a minister from one of the local churches in the GWU area. He was interested in having his church become more connected with the local community, so he offered space for a craft shop. The church was just three blocks from the house where we were going to begin CCNV. I loved crafts, and I especially liked the idea of creating a place where local craftsmen could display their work. Plus, I was intrigued with the notion of applying nonviolent principles to the world of retail. So I accepted this challenge.

It wasn't easy leaving my nice little apartment on Capitol Hill. I had grown fond of the family who lived upstairs, and this was the closest I had experienced to living in a family—and now I was deliberately leaving it. But while I packed I could tell it was time to move on, even though it was painful and scary. I tried to keep my focus on the adventure of it all just so I could get through the difficult transition period of closing down the old and walking into the new.

Walking into CCNV was an adventure. And it sure did stir up my life. I don't think I could have placed myself in a more difficult environment. First of all, I quickly found out that I'm not someone who enjoys community life. I like quiet. This was a big old house, right on Washington Circle just across from the GW University Hospital Emergency Room. And I was used to a great deal of order in my life. I liked things neat—a trait not shared by my five housemates. I needed time to myself and spent a fair amount of it in my room reading, writing or softly plucking away on my guitar. My housemates declared me antisocial. I loved animals and liked spending time with my cat. My housemates assured me that they looked forward to having my cat as part of the community. That was before we all moved in together. Actually, they hated cats. She didn't make things any easier. She could be a real charmer, except when she was in heat. For some reason, she shifted from a once-every-six-months heat rhythm to a once-every-six-weeks rhythm when we moved into the house. I didn't have the money to have her spayed, so we all endured—I with as much understanding as I could muster under the circumstances, and my housemates with a mixture of hostility and general crankiness toward me and the cat.

We all tried to hold things together by focusing on the central purpose of the community. However, we didn't agree on what that was. One fellow wanted to focus on world hunger, several others on the Vietnam War, and I wanted to focus on the concept of ecology as environmental nonviolence.

Every once in a while we'd have a speaker in to lecture about nonviolence. Sometimes they were thought-provoking, and sometimes they were smelly little boors whose definition of nonviolence meant "You can't stop me from doing what I want to do." These were the guys who always showed up late because they felt being "forced" to keep a schedule was an act of violence. They were also the ones who made sure they used the greatest possible variety and amount of foul language in their lecture. (You guessed it: Expecting them to speak in a socially inoffensive manner was also an act of violence.)

The Vietnam War took precedence over world hunger and ecology. The fellow interested in world hunger just quietly put together a project with an outside group and ignored his housemates. I kept trying to interest the others in ecology, but the war kept getting shouted over top of it. We didn't do anything unique about the war. Mostly we joined in on the big marches held in Washington during this time. There was the May Day Demonstration that was aimed at closing down all of Washington. Tens of thousands marched on the city and tried to block off all its street and bridge accesses. We chose not to participate in this demonstration because it was gearing up to deliberately promote violence—and we were a nonviolent community. So we tried to encourage cool heads by serving coffee and donuts to anyone stuck in traffic at Washington Circle. The cops totally lost their cool—they didn't get enough coffee and donuts—and began tossing tear gas all over the place. They arrested anyone who moved. All my housemates got arrested, along with about 23,000 other people (if I remember correctly). The multitudes were bused to a local stadium and processed there. Unfortunately, the majority of those arrested were "civilians" who had been trying to get to their offices.

My biggest distinction back then was that I was the member of CCNV who did *not* get arrested. I'd march and carry big placards just like everyone else, but when the cops announced, "If you don't leave, we'll arrest you," I was the one who immediately got up and left. This alone disqualifies me from the war protesters' rank-and-file in-good-standing list.

Speaking of lists: Richard Nixon was president during this time, and he had a real phobia about antiwar demonstrators. We didn't have to wait until Watergate to find out about his campaign to harass the "peaceniks." We knew firsthand. We were on Nixon's hit list primarily because of our name, "Community for Creative Non-Violence." His people took exception to the words "community" and "nonviolence." I think they were okay about "creative," but I'm not 100 percent sure about this. Anyway, we had to be checked out. The first thing they did was have our phone tapped. We knew it was tapped because they did such a lousy job with it. At times we couldn't hear the phone conversation due to all the static and cracking on the line. Periodically, we'd call the FBI and ask them to clean up the tap on our phone so we could hear our conversations—and, within a day or so, the phone would be fine. We took turns reading the Constitution over the phone, just to give them something to listen to. Sometimes we read articles from *The Washington Post*. We thought this would drive them a little nuts since the Nixon Administration seemed to feel that *The Post* was run by a bunch of pinko, commie, liberal conspirators.

The next thing they did was send someone out with a tripod and a *big* camera to photograph everyone who walked in and out of the house. We knew this was happening because the guy was just across the street in Washington Circle with all this paraphernalia pointed right at us. When someone would come or leave, he'd jump into action. He was there for about a week. We took pity on the poor sap and took him coffee and donuts—we were big on coffee and donuts. Honest to god, the man tried to pretend he wasn't taking pictures of us. We had pictures of him taking pictures of us. On the last day, he came to our door and rang the bell. When we opened the door, he didn't say anything. He just quickly took a bunch of pictures of the house interior from the front door, and then he left. I think my cat even made the FBI gallery.

We weren't the only ones I knew that got picked on. They also decided that the priest at the GWU Newman Center was suspect. They actually sent a guy out there who posed as a plumber (Was this a precursor of Watergate?) and who said he was there to fix the water heater. The only problem was there was nothing wrong with the water heater. And the guy's plumbing outfit looked new. Everyone who was at the Newman Center at the time (the priest included) just let the guy do his thing. After he left, they inspected the water heater, followed his fingerprints to a bugging device clamped on the back of the heater. They didn't remove the device. They just made it a point to have silly, weird conversations any time they were within range. They'd also sing into it from time to time. Part of the job description at Newman included entertaining the guys on the other end of the bugging device.

Aside from trying to stop the war, I was trying to start a shop. It wasn't hard to find craftspeople interested in my exhibiting their stuff. I told a couple people I knew that I'd accept quality crafts on consignment, run the shop and sell the goods—all for twenty-five percent. Craftspeople stampeded to my door. They told me that normally they had to give the retailer forty percent of anything sold. I didn't have to pay rent to the church, I wasn't looking for a big salary and I had no other employees. At twenty-five percent, I was a bargain they couldn't resist.

You'd think that running this shop would have been easy for me. But it wasn't. I was used to the security of a regular paycheck. I put in time and effort, and somebody would give me a paycheck. Now I put in time and effort, and there was no guarantee I'd get any money. Also, for the first time I was responsible for other people's livelihood. Even though the craftspeople got their money on time and I got some salary, this new responsibility felt like a terrific burden. I was constantly on edge for fear of failing others. The craftspeople and the minister could not have been kinder to me, but the bottom line was that I was working alone and all the responsibilities were mine. Whether something succeeded or failed rested on my shoulders, and I quickly saw that success was going to require efforts from me in areas I didn't naturally do well in. I felt like I was being slowly crushed in a vise.

During the winter months, the shop was in a large, sunny second-floor room above the entrance area to the church. I enjoyed setting up the displays and meeting the craftspeople. I advertised by posting announcements all around the GWU campus. That stirred up a little interest, but sales didn't really get going until after the weather warmed up, and I got the idea of setting up shop on the lawn in front of the church entrance. I figured if I kept this up throughout the warm months, I'd have a good customer base that would be willing to climb the stairs to the shop inside during the winter months. So, each day I was "open," I'd haul my blankets and boxes out to the lawn, set up, chat, sell, chat some more, pack up the boxes and haul everything back inside—just to do it all over again the next day. I have to admit that this routine started wearing on me physically rather quickly. But it sure did improve sales. Not enough to make us rich, but it helped us buy food. This was just enough encouragement to keep me plugging along, despite my fears and trepidations.

One of the seminarians who was working at the Newman Center visited the shop right after I opened in January to see if I'd be willing to sell some of his photography. His name was Clarence Wright, and his photography was wonderful—which surprised me. I had met this guy at a meeting back in the fall, and I thought he was a jerk. He had "accosted" a friend and me in the parking lot just after we had arrived for a meeting. We got out of the car, and he came bounding across the parking lot, hand outstretched, anxious to greet us. He shook hands with us in that enthusiastic way that makes you feel like someone's pumping you for oil. He said *most* sincerely, "Hi! I'm Clarence Wright! I'm the new seminarian at Newman, and I'm pleased to meet you!" (More heavy-duty arm pumping.) Then he bounded off to greet some other new arrivals. My friend and I looked at one another and said simultaneously, "What was that?" We steered clear of him during the meeting, and I made sure I gave him a wide berth throughout the rest of the fall and into the winter.

Now here he was in my shop showing me some terrific black-and-white photographs. I agreed to display them, but I was still keeping my distance and carefully watching this guy for any rising signs of severe jerkiness. I was poised to jump out of the way and save myself at the first indication. Actually, he was quite nice and left without incident. The next several times he visited to bring pictures, I enjoyed the visits. One day he noticed no one else was in the shop, so he asked if I wanted to close up for the day and have a cup of coffee with him. By now, I felt pretty confident that he wasn't suddenly going to snap back into that goofy state, so I closed the shop and off we went.

By this time in my life, I had learned that priests and seminarians dated. I had met priests and their mistresses, and I had seen seminarians with their dates at parties. I was kind of intrigued with what they were doing with that vow of celibacy, but I really didn't think about it too much. I entered the world of dating clergy with Clarence.

Sometimes he would take me to St. Paul's College for dinner with the other seminarians—many of whom also had dates. Everyone was quite gracious to me. It was as if the most natural thing in the world was to go to a seminary on Saturday night for a dinner date. They had a crew of nuns who had dedicated themselves to serving priests and seminarians. They were from Mexico and spoke little English. They did all the laundry—which included ironing the priests' underwear, so I'm told—and all the cooking. And they really put out a spread. By this time, I was beginning to question that vow of poverty, too. We'd have a wonderful meal, then "retire" to a large pub-like room that was complete with a bar and kegs—not bottles—of beer on tap. To get to the "pub," we passed the TV room that was outfitted with row after row of La-Z-Boy rockers, a very large TV and a bar with liquor in the economical half-gallon size bottles.

I enjoyed most of the priests and seminarians I met at St. Paul's. Some of them were . . . well, different. Once when I visited, I noticed a bunch of watercolor drawings on the wall down one of the hallways. It looked like they had invited a kindergarten class in, given them poster paper, brushes and paints, pointed to the hall and said, "Go to it, kids." I asked Clarence what it was. He said, "Oh, that's a final exam for the sacraments class. The priest told us to go out in the hallway and draw 'sin.' "

In the philosophy of science class one semester, the priest began by reading out of a book, "Twinkle, twinkle, little star." Then he closed the book and said, "Let's analyze that." They spent the entire semester discussing what this line actually meant. What do we mean by "twinkle?" What is a star? How do we know this thing is a star? Why do we say "little," and is this an accurate description? I met this priest at several of the Saturday dinners. He was a shy man, but fascinating. From everything I had heard about him from the seminarians who had been taught by him, he was a true genius. He even had some genius eccentricities. He once reviewed a fellow's paper by writing at the top, "This is interesting." Then he spent two pages defining what he meant by the word "interesting." He also *always* wore a black coat—indoors. In the summer, too. I'd be having dinner at his table, and he would be sitting at the table with a coat on. His only deference to the sweltering, humid Washington summers was to shift from a black wool coat to a black raincoat.

In June, Clarence left Washington for the summer to work in a pastoral counseling program in Atlanta. We had grown quite close by this time and parting wasn't easy. We quickly racked up some hefty phone bills, so we decided it would be more cost efficient if I flew down to Atlanta for a two-week visit beginning July 1. I arranged for one of my housemates to take over the shop while I was gone (I gave her my twenty-five-percent cut for her efforts), got another housemate to take care of my cat, and I went to Atlanta. During that two weeks, Clarence and I decided we didn't want to part. And that was that. I stayed in Atlanta an additional six weeks while he finished the pastoral counseling program. The two housemates agreed to continue running the shop and taking care of my cat. We lived in student housing at Emory University, and I got a temporary job working for one of the professors there. Clarence and I had long talks about what he was going to do about this seminary business, and he decided that he would leave the seminary in the fall when we returned to Washington.

Clarence's group in the pastoral counseling program was run by a feisty, tobacco-chewing counselor who could hit a spittoon from just about any distance. He and I got along very well. We respected and appreciated one another's blunt honesty. This character trait gave him the reputation among the students for running the toughest program. It wasn't a Catholic program. They had ministerial students from just about every denomination, many of whom were married. They were quite supportive of Clarence's and my relationship. To them, we were a new, but well-established couple. I was grateful for the support and comforted by the camaraderie I experienced from everyone connected with this program. After my six months with CCNV, I found the attitudes of these people to be both refreshing and healing.

The blunt and quick-challenging group leader wasn't the only thing that made the program tough. These guys were working with alcoholics and drug addicts, counseling them in groups and one-on-one. And the seminarians and ministerial students were participating in their own group counseling and one-on-one sessions with the therapists running the program. It was very intense; nothing was allowed to slip by. The patients themselves were encouraged to give the most direct, and sometimes brutal, feedback to the students. During our last week there, one of the ministerial students tried to commit suicide.

Just before leaving, every student was given an evaluation from their group leader. I felt that one of the things needed in this program was the recognition that spouses (and partners like myself) also experienced a great deal of intensity and challenge as the students moved through the program. The therapists treated the program as if it was self-contained and didn't impact anyone other than the students. I felt that for the sake of the mental and emotional well-being of the spouses and the future of their marriages, some kind of support needed to be offered while their husbands/partners got their guts ripped out of them. Basically, we women, as well as the therapists, did a lot of work to hold these guys together, and I felt that it would have helped if we had some direction and assistance from the program itself. So, when Clarence met his leader for his evaluation, I sent along a typed report—my evaluation of the program. In it, I outlined my suggestions and the reasons I felt the change was needed. I saw the leader one last time at the farewell party. This was just after the ministerial student had attempted suicide. The director had a twinkle in his eye when he saw me. I knew that it had been quite cheeky of me to give him my evaluation of the program, but apparently he appreciated it. He said he'd give my suggestions some serious consideration. Then he switched the subject, and we got into a discussion about what he does at a party when he's chewing tobacco and there are no spittoons around. (It wasn't hypothetical, since he was chewing and I didn't notice any spittoons anywhere.) He got another twinkle in his eye—he knew he was about to gross me out—and said, "I swallow it."

When Clarence and I arrived back in Washington, we stepped right into the proverbial hornets nest. We returned to our respective former "homes" until we could find an apartment. I arrived back at CCNV to a less than enthusiastic welcome. In fact, it had the distinct air of hostility about it. When I had phoned to talk over my plans about staying in Atlanta, my housemates sounded happy for me and supportive. When I returned, I found this was not really the case.

First of all, they rented out my room while I was away—even though I continued paying rent. My clothes had been rearranged to accommodate the sub-leaser, and the furniture had been shifted around to reflect that person's taste. Several of my ceramic things had been smashed, and the broken pieces had been pushed (or swept?) behind the dresser. I had not known that my housemates were planning to turn my room into a money-making venture, so I was quite surprised when I walked in.

I did receive one enthusiastic, even grateful, welcome—my cat. They fed her, but that's about all they did. They hadn't even washed her food dish in the two months I was away. Her litter box had been changed, but when the bag of litter was empty, no one bought another bag. So they just made her use an empty tray—and complained rather royally to me when I got back about the odor. Aside from minimal feeding and litter box detail, they ignored her. It had never occurred to me that people—especially *these* people—would treat any domestic animal so badly. I felt terrible that I hadn't seen this coming and made other arrangements, and I was furious that these people had not been honest and asked me to do something else with the cat. When I returned, she clearly saw me as her rescue and stuck close to me every minute I was in that house. I quickly began viewing her as my rescue as well.

My shop was another disaster. The woman who agreed to keep it open had apparently decided she no longer wanted to do this, and so she closed it. She said nothing to me about it, or to the minister or craftspeople. When I questioned her about her decision, she just said she hadn't felt like continuing the work. Her decision would be a little comprehensible if she had been holding down another job at the time, but this wasn't the case. On top of it all, the sales records from which I paid the craftspeople had been completely screwed up. A quick inventory showed me that she had not bothered recording what was sold—or she gave an awful lot of stuff away. In either case, the craftspeople still had to be paid. The little money I had saved from my job in Atlanta went toward squaring those accounts.

I started cleaning up the mess by first seeing the minister, basically to apologize for any inconvenience this might have caused him. That's when I found out that my housemate had also not bothered to pass a message along to him about my remaining in Atlanta until the end of August. (This was *my* mistake. I should have called him directly when I changed my plans.) So, when I talked with him after my return, he didn't have a high opinion of me. I apologized as best I could, which I'm sure was a pretty weak excuse for an apology. By now the pressures of my return were really getting to me, and I don't think I was functioning too well. Despite everything, he said I could continue the shop if I wished, but I could tell that his enthusiasm and support had waned quite a bit.

I decided to reopen the shop. In part I wanted to change this man's opinion of me, but also I wanted to move the merchandise that had been packed away in boxes for two months so that the craftspeople would get money back instead of unsold crafts. When I set up shop on the front lawn again, it quickly became evident that the base of customers I had developed prior to Atlanta was no longer there. I'd have to start over.

The relationship Clarence and I had was not settling well with lots of people. Prior to our going to Atlanta, the people who knew we were dating had accepted it as if it was the most normal thing in the world. Only once did an issue arise. The priest at CCNV, who was a Paulist and had been one of Clarence's roommates prior to his moving to the CCNV house, spent three hours trying to convince me that the relationship I had with Clarence was a figment of my imagination. Those were the precise words he used: a figment of my imagination. (My figment and I have just celebrated the twenty-third anniversary of our partnership.) After our return from Atlanta, many of the people we knew had difficulty accepting that we were now a couple. It seemed to me as if it was okay with them for us to be together as long as they thought it wasn't serious. Once we crossed that line they reacted—usually with hostility. For me, the sad part was how Clarence was being treated by his "brothers" from St. Paul's. Men he had known for seven years were now barely speaking to him. I watched several times as he would walk into a room, greet a fellow Paulist he hadn't seen during the summer, and that lovely "brother" would just look at him coldly, turn around and walk away. It was a sad time for Clarence.

Although Clarence faced his share of people's open hostility, I was the one they had declared open season on. Instead of confronting Clarence with their concerns about his decision to leave the order, they unloaded their anger and hostility on me about that decision. I had suddenly become the person who was responsible for "snatching him away." I wish I could say that Clarence and I represented a unique situation that had caught these men off guard, and shortly thereafter they came to their senses. But this simply isn't the case. That fall, there were several Paulist priests and seminarians who were in exactly the same situation as Clarence. We women quickly formed an informal "support group" just to get through this time. In each of the cases, the women were being treated as the sole cause of it all. Remember, these were the women who had been graciously wined and dined at St. Paul's College just a few months earlier. Now we had all suddenly become sex-starved, emotionally troubled "girls." The men in the relationships seemed as surprised by the turn of events as the women, but there didn't seem to be anything they could do to stop the anger from being directed toward the women.

Clarence and I moved into our new apartment within the first two weeks after our return.* My cat was thrilled. Just after we moved in, Clarence received a letter from the head of the Paulist order. He didn't live in Washington at the College. He lived at an estate in Scarsdale, New York. Clarence had written him before leaving Atlanta about his decision not to be ordained a priest that fall but to live with me instead.

The response was startling. He spent the first half of the letter discussing Clarence's decision to leave the order. He constantly referred to me throughout the letter as "the problem," even though Clarence had referred to me by name in his own letter. He never even referred to me as a human being—I was just "the problem." He spent the second half of the letter suggesting, in strong language, that the Paulists had given Clarence a lot over the years, and now that he was leaving, he owed them. He completely ignored anything Clarence had given the Paulists over the same period. Clarence was now leaving, and he should pay the order some money. To his credit, he was willing to wait for payment until Clarence and "his problem" got on their feet. And he wasn't discussing amount. He was leaving that up to Clarence's conscience.

Clarence fired back a letter explaining how he had already fulfilled any agreement made when he entered the order—implied or otherwise. Ordination had not been a guarantee or a promise. He listed everything he had given back to the order in return for what

---

* CCNV managed to survive quite well without me. About a year after I left, as the war was winding down, they turned their focus to establishing a soup kitchen. This became successful, and the community membership grew. They then expanded that focus to include shelters for the homeless. During this time, a man named Mitch Snyder joined the community and became the driving force for developing CCNV into a strong, politically active force for the homeless. CCNV still exists today as one of the nation's largest operations and strongest advocates for the homeless.

he had received. He also let the head of the order know that I wasn't his (Clarence's) "problem."

I took offense at the letter, as you might imagine, and I fired off my own response. My first lines were something like, "My name is Machaelle, not 'Problem,' and I am a human being. I expect that, from this point on, whenever you address me, you will address me by my name." Then I went on from there. I told him about what I and the other women who were in my position that fall had experienced from the order once the men announced they were leaving. I suggested that not facing their own issues around fellow "brothers" choosing to leave the order was "the problem." I also said that directing their hostilities and anger around this toward the women, instead of facing the real issues, was cowardly. I went on to suggest that perhaps every time a "brother" left the order, it challenged the others who were choosing not to leave. Perhaps all the questions, fears and other emotions the others had about staying in the order were surfacing—and that was what was behind the crap they were dumping on the women. (Was I a charmer, or what?)

He never responded to either of our letters. After much consideration, and after a deep search within the inner recesses of our consciousnesses, we chose not to give them any money.

Our new apartment was located on Capitol Hill. I was back in friendly territory. For a while, I continued running the shop. But now this meant that I had to travel across town. The customer base never improved much, and I couldn't figure out what to do to expand it. On top of this, I lost any desire I had to keep the shop open. I was beginning a new life, and it was located on the other side of town. Even so, I was sad to close it down because I knew I had never made a success out of it. It had been a small, but messy failure.

A degree in philosophy doesn't really get you far in the job market, but Clarence was able to get work teaching in a home-schooling program in a neighboring county in Maryland. It paid $500 a month, before taxes. He had a lot of commuting, so we got a second motor vehicle. We had a chance to buy a used 125cc Vespa motorscooter for $150. It stretched our budget, but we figured it was an investment for our future.

As soon as I closed the shop, I began looking through the employment ads. I spotted this ad about selling human hair wigs. Actually, the most intriguing part was the money it said could be earned—something like $500 a week. I dialed the number, and the man I spoke with said, after about five minutes of chatting, that he thought I might do well in this line of work. He suggested I come in for an interview. I jumped on my motorscooter, and off I went. The interview was exciting, very upbeat, and they seemed to like me a lot. I didn't know at the time that good salespeople are overly positive and super-enthusiastic when they're on, so I just thought these people were falling all over themselves for me. I was flattered, and, by the time I left, I was convinced I could sell wigs.

I attended sales classes, motivation meetings and went out with the veterans to observe and learn. I memorized my pitch and practiced it over and over. I picked up pointers and tricks of the trade. I even called my father, who was now calling me from time to time. He had been a highly successful traveling salesman for over thirty years, earning about $90,000 annually by the late 1950s. Now he owned the company and had his own "stable" of salesmen. I thought that learning that his daughter had entered the world of sales might make him pleased, or proud, or something. So I asked him for pointers. He gave me one: "If you don't think you're gonna close the sale, don't bother walking through the goddamn door." (Words to live by.)

Soon I was going on my own appointments. I'd go to the door carrying helmet and briefcase. The helmet was an icebreaker and a great selling point. We had to wear a sample of the product on all calls. The wigs ranged in price from $125 to $275, depending on the length. Most of the other women (ninety-nine percent of the sales force were women) wore shorter wigs in fancy hairstyles. I had a long-hair wig that perfectly matched my own long hair. I kept my hair down, plunked the wig on like a hat and combed my hair with the wig into two thick pigtails. If you're on a scooter, you can't get fancy about these things. Besides, it helped keep my head warm during the cold months. Customers never associated wigs with the casual look, and they wouldn't believe I had one on even when I told them. Just this alone would half sell them on our wigs.

I became a very good wig salesman. I guess I was a "method" salesman. I needed to understand why a person should buy the product before I could sell it. Well, I quickly discovered my reasons for selling wigs. All of our appointments were made with young women who already had an interest in wigs, and most of them already had wigs—in fact, several. Usually their wigs were synthetic, and looked it. We were taught to have them get out any wigs they had before we started our pitch so that they could see what their wigs looked like next to ours. Our wigs were made with human hair—Indonesian, not the coarser Oriental hair. I decided that if these women were prone to buying wigs anyway, they should buy quality instead of those Dynel clown-curl jobs. Also, our wigs could be styled, so the woman only had to have one wig for every length of hair she wanted. This was cost-effective, so I was saving women from wasting their hard-earned money.

I was filled with conviction and I sold a lot of wigs, but I never reached $500 a week in commissions. I don't know what we had to sell to get that kind of commission. Weeks passed between the signing of a contract and the receiving of the wig, and we weren't paid until the wigs were in the customer's hand—or on their head, as the case may be. But I was out there every evening—all appointments were in the evenings—working my heart out to sell these wigs. The weather turned cold, and I think my bosses took pity on me. I was the only one without a car, and I had been driving all over D.C. and the Virginia suburbs for my appointments. My bosses needed an office manager to coordinate the sales force and their appointments, and asked if I'd like the job. I didn't even hesitate. To be honest, I didn't like sales at all. I found it to be very stressful. I was grateful to get a regular paycheck and a warm office.

My selling wigs further diminished our circle of friends. These were the nonviolent people who basically felt that I had sold out to the sleazy business world. I might as well have been working for McDonnell Douglas, as far as they were concerned. We ended up with four friends: the lawyer who co-founded CCNV and his wife, a

Paulist priest and a seminarian. They were a small but very supportive group, and with this base we built our new life together.

Now when Clarence and I think about these early days on Capitol Hill, we get a little misty-eyed and wistful. This is the period when we experienced *free time*, and had to be creative about what we wanted to do with it. We actually sat around on weekends reading the paper and discussing what museum, shop or event we might like to go to in the afternoon.

We lived in an apartment on the third floor of an old row house on 4th Street, S.E. The rooms were long and narrow—the place resembled a bowling alley. It had a living room, kitchen, bathroom and a walk-in closet. The closet was big enough to be converted into a small bedroom. When we did this, however, we lost the only closet we had in the place. So Clarence built a new closet for our clothes out on the hallway landing. We painted each room a different color, and the place took on a nice cheery feeling.

The kitchen had a window that led out to the fire escape. My cat spent many hours out on her new "porch." Every once in a while she'd go down the steps to visit the fellow in the apartment below us. I still refer to her as "my cat" during this time because she didn't warm up to Clarence too quickly. To be honest, she kept looking at him as if he were the dumbest thing she had ever seen. She wouldn't let him near her. She'd just fix a stare on him with this strange you're-too-dumb-to-even-exist expression on her face. There was nothing Clarence could do to change her attitude. He tried petting her, talking to her, even feeding her. Nothing impressed her. Since I had had a similar initial reaction to Clarence, I felt certain she'd come out of it. After all, I did. So I counseled patience to them both. After a few months of this, I noticed that she would sit on the front window sill every day about the time he was due to come home. She'd watch him park the scooter, come into the building—she'd even listen to him coming up the stairs. As soon as he got in the door, she'd ignore him. Gradually, she began meeting him at the door. Then one night she jumped on his lap, curled up and went to sleep. At that moment, she became *our* cat.

We had our share of bumps as we went through the normal pangs of two people learning to live together without doing irreparable harm to each other. And Clarence almost froze himself to death riding the scooter out to the suburbs to teach during the winter months. We had our first argument during this time. Actually, it's the only flat-out argument we've ever had. It had to do with vampires. I insisted that since the word "vampire" existed, somewhere on some level, vampires had to actually exist. I concluded that the word could not exist without its corresponding reality. Clarence took the reasonable road and just declared that vampires did not exist, with or without the word. We argued these points until 4 A.M. One would think we would give it up after some sleep, but I continued referring back to the argument for four years. Finally, after seeing the "light," he says, he conceded the point. But aside from these little challenges, it was a pleasant time. I felt like I was really beginning to build a strong home life—finally.

Both of us were broadening our spiritual thinking at this time. I kept wondering about life after death. This was one area that the church didn't talk about too much, except to say that there was life after death. I wondered about that. If there was life after death, what did one do in the afterlife? How did one live? What were the practical aspects of this? You know—did they go to the bathroom? It seemed to me that if there was life after death there had to be practical considerations like this. The church made it sound like you die, you get judged, you go to heaven (eventually, depending on how severely you were judged), and you function in some angelic fashion. I felt that human beings demonstrated too much individuality for this kind of broad-brush approach. There had to be something more if all this individuality were going to be accommodated.

The Paulist priest and seminarian who had remained friends with us came over for dinner several times a month. We would talk about our latest thoughts on things spiritual, and then vigorously discuss their merits long into the night. Each of us had a strong intellect, and we would take stands on a subject until one of the others would convince us our stand needed to be modified or changed.

I held my own with these fellows. This wasn't the first time I had experienced intense discussions with men of keen mind. The family whose house I lived in on Capitol Hill used to invite me up to dinner when there were several priests from Catholic University present. They were all good friends; they were more traditional in thinking; and the men were all members of Mensa. They thought I was young and cute, and typically radical in my thinking. But I didn't let their opinions or reputations scare me, and I wouldn't let them back me away from a point I felt was correct. I learned to hold my own.

Clarence and the seminarian tended to hold out for reason. The priest and I were the wild thinkers in the group. Actually, the priest was just wild, and this influenced all aspects of his life, including thinking. He had been a Paulist priest for several years when I met him. He spoke fluent French—a talent he never flaunted in front of me—and received his doctorate in sacramental theology from a university in Paris. While there, he ministered to the prostitutes in Montmartre. He did most of his work and held Masses during the days because the prostitutes (his congregation) were busy at night. Prior to going to Paris, he had been straight-laced and conservative in thought and action. Everyone said he loosened up a lot after his return. Not long after he arrived back, he was in the priests' common room with a bunch of his fellow Paulists. Someone had given him a glass of wine. He took a sip, made a guttural gagging sound, spit the wine out and bellowed something like, "This is the worst wine I've ever had!" He punctuated his point by throwing the glass across the room. This was when the others started getting the idea that Paris had relaxed him some. When I met him, he was a lean man with long, straggly brown hair, a bushy beard and intense eyes that made him look like a genuine madman. He taught sacraments at the college—he was the one who told the students to go out in the hall and draw sin. I remember hearing that the day he talked about the Biblical notion of anointing with oil, he demonstrated the point by pouring cooking oil all over his head.

He had developed interesting table manners, too. At one of the infamous Saturday night dinners at St. Paul's College, a new seminarian asked him to pass the mashed potatoes. He grabbed a glob of potatoes with his hands and passed this to the seminarian. Then there was the time when we had one of our foursome dinners at a local restaurant, and after coffee, he got up and asked everyone else sitting in the restaurant for their attention. Once he got it, he proceeded to let them know that this was one of the most pleasant evenings he had ever spent, and he wished to thank them for helping to make it so. Then he sat down. I must admit that he was pretty well looped that night. And no one else in the restaurant seemed to know what to do with his declarations or gratitude.

He didn't mind creating that kind of situation one bit. He and two other Paulists drove from Washington to Colorado once. Throughout the entire trip, he wore flowered bibbed overalls, a flowered engineer's cap, and sat in the back of the car knitting a scarf. By the time they got into West Virginia, people would look at this "lunatic" and not want to pump gas for them. The further west they got, the worse it got—and the more outrageous he got. In one coffee shop, he ordered a bowl of soup, then proceeded to "pass out," falling face down into the soup. The other two just calmly told some story about escorting him back to the institution, explaining that he was really harmless.

In our spiritual discussions, this fellow and I took the outrageous positions and drove the other two nuts. The problem was that our "outrageous positions" weren't nuts at all—just new, or different. We didn't let tradition or convention stop us from thinking something. This left the other two in the unenviable position of having to defend God and country from absurdity that had a point.

About this time, both Clarence and I felt we needed to find a different Mass to attend. The GWU Newman Mass was still exciting, but we felt something was missing. Or perhaps our needs had changed. Our whacky friend invited us to attend the Mass at St. Paul's College. It was open to the public, it had a good-size congregation—and he was the one who said the Mass. I was curious to see what this guy would do to (or for) a Mass, so we went.

Well. I discovered that our friend was the best liturgist I have ever experienced. For one thing, he had memorized all the "fixed" parts of the Mass. The only things he read were the parts from the Old and New Testaments that were assigned for each liturgy. Having all the other parts memorized gave him tremendous flexibility in how he projected the Mass and how he related his role as the celebrant to the congregation. And not only had he memorized the Mass, he had also put some thought into what he was saying. So, as he delivered it, he did so with conviction and feeling. Consequently, many of us in the congregation were *hearing* it for the first time. Not being tied down to the printed page, as most priests are during Mass, allowed our friend to look at the congregation and make eye contact. He was actually a sensitive man (despite evidence to the contrary), and he could pick up on the prevailing mood of a congregation in the first couple of minutes of the Mass. Then he'd adjust his presentation to enhance or support or challenge the congregation—whatever was needed to convey the day's "theme." If it was a rainy day, and everyone was feeling quiet and contemplative, he would present the liturgy in a quiet format that encouraged thought. I would say that his Mass gave me a more direct and intimate fusion between the liturgy and myself, and this is what was missing for me at the Newman Mass.

1972

In January the whacky priest called us to say that a psychic was going to visit St. Paul's College that Saturday. He thought it might be interesting. Did we want to attend? We said yes, more out of curiosity than anything, since neither one of us had ever met a psychic.

Her name was Peggy Townsend. Even though she was invited to the College by one of the priests, I wouldn't say she was welcomed with open arms. There were about thirty-five priests and seminarians in a conference room, seated three deep around a long table. Clarence and I were seated at one end of the table facing her. One of the first things that struck me was that many of the men arrived in "formal" attire. I had rarely seen these guys wearing their black suits and clerical collars except at functions where they were officially at work. The rest of the time they wore normal, casual street clothes. Now they arrived, dressed to kill (pun intended).

I had no idea what to expect from Peggy. I knew virtually nothing about psychics—only that they did strange things, and I wasn't sure what the strange things were. I assumed she would be a thin woman dressed in white flowing robes, and that she'd float more than walk into the room. Well, she was thin alright, but she wore a wool pants suit and walked like a normal person.

She spoke for just a few minutes. I can't remember what she said during this time. Then she invited questions, and that's when many of the priests jumped into action. Besides showing up dressed in their clerical clothes, they also came armed with their Bibles. They spoke to her in respectful tones, but that was just veneer. Right away they attempted to blast holes in her work as a psychic by using scripture. Unfortunately for them, they picked on the wrong person. She happened to be equally versed in the Bible and quoted passages back to them that supported the role of the psychic within Christianity. This went on for a good hour—perhaps longer. Throughout this time, I sat quietly across the table from her, watching. She didn't take these men on with a sense of combat. Instead, she did two things. First, she quietly matched their challenges, Biblical point by Biblical point. She dodged nothing. And secondly, she opened some door in herself, letting out such a wave of love that it took the combative fire out of everyone in the room. This was a formidable thing to see—and feel.

Once the clergy backed down from the Bible battle, she was able to move on to different discussions. By this time, I was anxious to move on too, so I asked her to talk about life after death—of course. I asked her some specific questions that were based on what I had been thinking. Much to my surprise, she verified everything I had been saying in the foursome discussions. I don't remember all the different questions I asked, or her answers, for that matter, but I do know that she and I began conversing as if no one else was in the room. I remember that I asked her about ghosts. I wanted to understand where this phenomenon fit into the life-after-death scheme. She talked about some work she had just done at Gettysburg, Pennsylvania. Some people living in a house there had asked her for help. Several of them had experienced "seeing" children screaming and trying frantically to escape fire in a couple of rooms in the house. This experience was occurring more and more frequently, so they contacted Peggy for help. She did some research on the house and found that at that location, during the Battle of Gettysburg, there had been an orphanage. At the time of the battle, the orphanage burned to the ground, killing all the children inside. When Peggy entered a specific room in the house, she immediately saw the screaming children running around. She began to talk to them, calming them down. She told them they were now dead, and it was okay to move on. In fact, they needed to move on. Then, one by one, the children filed past her. I can't remember if Peggy just said something to each child or if she placed her hands on them. But after this private moment, which seemed to leave them at peace, the child lifted up and "floated" through the ceiling. After the last child had released, the "fire" in the room disappeared. Peggy and the others from the house who had observed the whole thing then walked out into the yard. She spread her hands over a large patch of daylilies, and they bloomed—even though it was night. One of the observers had been the priest who then invited her to speak at St. Paul's.

She went on to explain to me that ghosts are often people who are confused about what state they are in, and frightened at the possibility that it might be death. She said that normally when a person dies, they are met by someone who helps them through the transition. However, when there is mass death that is surrounded by great confusion such as a battle, slip-ups can occur. These children had fallen through the cracks, as it were, and had never been helped through the transition. So they kept reliving the moment of death, and this is what was being played out in the house that was now on the spot where the orphanage had once stood.

After the session at St. Paul's ended, I said to her, "I think I need to see you privately." She replied quietly, "I know," and we set a time for the next morning.

I spent the rest of the day quietly in the apartment. My experience with Peggy Townsend had both exhilarated and disoriented me. For one thing, she verified all the "crazy" things I had been saying about the afterlife. Although I was now excited about knowing I had been "on track," I couldn't help but wonder where in the world I had gotten all these ideas in the first place and what I was getting myself into now. All I knew for sure was that I needed to see Peggy Townsend. I needed to find out what was happening to me. And I desperately wanted to grab any bit of information she had on the afterlife.

That night, the temperature outside dropped below zero. The next morning, we could only get one of our motor scooters started—the smaller one that carried one person. I had wanted Clarence to be with me when I met with Peggy, but because of the weather I arrived back at St. Paul's College for the appointment alone. (I had arrived late because of the scooter problems, and she met me at the door saying, before I could even apologize, "I know. You couldn't get your cycle started." Technically, she was wrong. It was a motor scooter, not a cycle. But I wasn't going to fault her on that one. What does a nice suburban-looking lady in her fifties know about the differences between scooters and cycles? No matter. I was impressed.)

We went into a small room. I sat in a chair directly opposite her. I was quite nervous. She asked me to uncross my legs and arms so that the energy could flow through me, and then she explained that she had spent most of the previous night meditating on what she was to say to me. She had felt that there was much to tell me. But every time she considered areas to talk to me about, a steel curtain would drop before her. However, I was not to worry. She was going to try again with me there and see what came up.

She sat quietly with her eyes closed for about a minute, then she began to speak. Little things at first. Clarence had gotten heartburn from the garlic I had put in the spaghetti sauce the previous week and wasn't telling me for fear of hurting my feelings. Other little things about our apartment . . .

She sat quietly again. All the while, I said nothing. She said that the steel curtain had come down once more.* So she decided to use another tactic. She asked that it be revealed to her what was to be said to me at that moment. Then she was quiet. I was going crazy. I didn't know what she was doing. All I knew was that I had to keep my legs uncrossed and my mouth shut.

Finally, she spoke. She explained that I had the potential to

* I reconnected with Peggy in the late 1980s, and we had a chance to reminisce about this first meeting. Up until then, I had assumed that *I* had caused the steel curtain to drop. When I told her this, she laughed and said, "No! Think of where we were at the time. I could barely function in that atmosphere at St. Paul's. The College and those priests kept dropping the curtain on us!"

develop psychically in any area—it was all open to me. But I had to understand a few things first. There would come a time in my psychic growth when my relationship with Clarence could no longer come first in my life. At that time, I should decide carefully if I wanted to continue my development. I could decide at any time to go no further. Also, there were two conditions existing presently in me that were creating blocks and preventing Peggy from being fully open to me. First was my frantic desire to know, to obtain knowledge about this new world of the unseen. It was essential for me to learn to relax, to trust that everything would simply flow to me if only I would relax. Second, there was information, a piece of the puzzle, that was not yet a part of my consciousness, but that would shortly come to me. Without this piece, I could not absorb the things she could tell me. But again, I was to relax. Once the piece was in place, much of what Peggy wanted to say would simply fall into place inside me on its own.

The last thing: I was cautioned not to force any of my new awareness onto Clarence. Regarding these matters, he was more conservative, and I needed to respect his own sense of timing.

The session ended. It had lasted only twenty minutes. As I got up to leave, she hugged me. She wished me her love and support. I could tell she wasn't just handing me shallow, social politeness— she meant it. I walked out of the room, knowing I was about to embark on a brand new adventure.

I wish I could say that I followed the advice I got from her, that it was all a snap, that from the moment I left her, I was relaxed, open and calm, waiting patiently for the cosmos to smack me in the face. But anyone who has ever had this experience of getting information from a psychic would know I was lying. It's one thing to hear this information. It's quite something else to act on what's being said. And the last word I wanted to hear from anyone about all of this was "relax."

I told Clarence everything that happened with Peggy. She had been right about his heartburn. We agreed that if he ever felt I was ramming something down his throat, he'd tell me to back off. He stated that except for that one time about the vampires, he had always found our discussions about such matters enjoyable, interesting, even thought-provoking.

I didn't understand how my development in the psychic world, which I had been introduced to all of twenty-four hours ago, could ever force my relationship with Clarence to become secondary. Quite frankly, the thought of it scared me. Neither one of us wanted to touch this bit of information. We both ended up pushing it onto the back burner, fairly confident that when it became an issue, we'd understand and somehow know what to do. [comma]

Not long after seeing Peggy, the mysterious missing puzzle piece dropped into place. Clarence supplied it by discussing a book he was reading about reincarnation.

Reincarnation. That was *the* piece. As soon as he started talking about it, I saw a huge, old, arched wooden door slowly open inside of me. Suddenly, a wave of information washed through me. What I had been saying about the afterlife now took on a totally different dimension. A multitude of missing bits of information slipped into the mysterious gaps I had recognized that existed in what I had been saying. I now saw life—both afterlife and Earth life—from the perspective of many reflections of the soul rather than of just one reflection. I saw longevity, interconnectedness and interrelationship.

Over the months, the partnership between Clarence and me strengthened and stabilized. In late winter, we decided we'd like to have a Mass with our friends to celebrate what we were creating.

Clarence wanted to get married. I, on the other hand, had strong feelings about the subject—none of which pointed favorably toward marriage. I had read several papers on vows by Ivan Illich (renegade Jesuit), which fit neatly into my own thinking. Basically, I believed that vows are truly sacred, and should not be taken in the beginning of a relationship when there is only *hope* of living them out. One cannot vow today what he will do tomorrow. Instead, vows should be *earned*. A person demonstrates in his life the intent of the vow, and then earns the right to make it after a certain period of time. The vow becomes an honor one receives the right to make, rather than something one hopes to live out. I also felt that taking a marriage vow implied that I didn't have the integrity to maintain a long-term,

loving relationship with someone on my own. It said that I had to
have external structure and expectations imposed on me, or my intent wasn't valid or real. The bottom line is that I didn't like the
position I felt a marriage vow would have placed me in. It implied
that, on my own, I was missing something that only a marriage vow
could give.

Clarence listened to me, and even understood what I was saying.
In the end, he still wanted to get married, but my feelings about
marriage vows were more intense than his assumptions that we
should get married. He was willing to put his desires on hold for a
while with the assumption that some day I'd change my mind about
all of this and we'd be married.

In the meantime, we'd have a Mass that celebrated our *partnership*. We'd invite family, our few old friends, new friends... After
the Mass, we'd eat and play. The lawyer and his wife offered us the
use of their home for the gathering.

Everything moved along wonderfully until we asked our whacky
priest friend to say the Mass. He told us he would not say it unless it
was registered as a marriage. I was stunned. At first, this was not an
issue for Clarence, and he was willing to have it registered. But, as
you might imagine, I had a problem. We wanted a Mass to celebrate
a partnership, not a marriage, and I was furious that our priest friend
was refusing us this right. What we were requesting was not against
Canon Law. He never gave us a good reason for his stand.

Clarence and I talked it over. We decided that if we allowed the
celebration to be turned into a church-recognized wedding, we
would be saying that the decisions we had made in good faith up to
that time were secondary to the church. At this point in our religious
development, we were not willing to say this. We would also be
saying that the partnership we created in good conscience in August
1971 was no longer valid in *our* eyes and that we now wanted the
church to create a valid one for us. So, together, we told our friend
that we would not register the Mass as a marriage, and that we
would find someone else to say it.

We asked a Jesuit we knew from Georgetown University. He had
no problem with what we were requesting. In fact, he had as many
reasons for wanting to say our Mass as I had for not wanting to take

vows or make this Mass into a marriage celebration. He understood the concept of partnership, and felt that a Mass is a fine way to acknowledge partnership.

In early June, we celebrated that partnership with seventy-five friends. To honor what we had created, I took Clarence's last name. Our seminarian friend gave the homily, and our whacky priest friend attended. (Go figure.)

The controversy surrounding our Mass moved me into a new level of relationship with the Catholic church. When I first joined, I looked *within* its structure for what I called the essence of truth. Then when I focused on the concepts of nonviolence, my attention broadened to include world issues and social conditions. That's when I saw that the essence of truth was *outside* the church walls. Now, by standing up to the church and saying "no" to a registered marriage, I saw that the essence of truth lay *within myself*. It wasn't in the church, it wasn't floating around me, it was *inside* me. This resulted in my questioning the church even more than I had previously. Was the church an amplification and extension of my inner feelings about life, or was it unrelated to those feelings?

I continued working at the wig company while Clarence finished out the home-teaching year.

I don't know how or why I thought of the next adventure for us, but somehow I came up with the idea of visiting Canada. We were saving money at this point, and we figured we could afford to take eight weeks off to travel across Canada. Once we got out west, we'd loop down and drive across the United States back to Washington. The trip seemed important then, but I can't remember why. Clarence knew that he wanted to change jobs again in the fall, so if we left July 15 after his teaching was over for the year, we'd be back by September 15, just in time for him to look for another job. We put a downpayment on a new Ford Econoline van, fixed up the interior for traveling and loaded up our two cats (Gretel the old-timer and a new cat, Fred). We drove from Prince Edward Island in the east, all the way across the continent to Calgary. The cats became seasoned travelers after about three days of caterwauling. Fred liked to sit on the motor mount between us and watch the traffic go by. Gretel spent her travel time curled up on the shelving in the back. About halfway through the trip, Fred saved our lives. We left the sweltering heat of Washington not knowing how early it got cold in Canada. After a couple of freezing nights, we came up with the "brilliant" idea of heating the van at night with hot charcoal in a cast-iron dutch oven. Of course we weren't so stupid that we kept the windows shut. No sir. Clarence had been a boy scout, and we both knew to leave the windows open for ventilation. The only windows that could be opened were the front ones, which we rolled down about halfway. We were both reading in the bed in the back, and I had just put down my book and turned over to go to sleep. All of a sudden, we heard Fred let out a little chirp (he didn't meow, he chirped), and then we heard a thud. For some reason, call it mother's instinct, I knew right away that the cat had passed out and why. I told Clarence to get Fred out of the van quickly. We opened the sliding door, put his limp body on the ground, and I began massaging his lung area. He was out cold. After about a minute, he came to and got up. He seemed pleased to see us. It was then we realized how close we were to going off to sleep and never waking up.

The rest of the trip went uneventfully, except for the three-day search for Gretel in Choteau, Montana. Half the town was out on horseback looking for her. Actually, she and Clarence had had an argument over whether or not she really needed to go outside to pee late one night. She insisted. He got up, angry about the interruption of his sleep, and accidently squeezed her kidneys when he grabbed her to let her out. That's when she scratched his hand. He yelled, threw her out of the van, then slammed the door shut. When she tried to get back in, she couldn't. (We found little claw marks on the door where she had tried to get back in.) The next day, she was nowhere in sight. We began to comb the area, and that's when people joined in the search on horseback. She came back on her own after three days. The person most grateful to see her was Clarence. He had been trying to figure out how he was going to hitchhike back to D.C. after I left him in the middle of Montana. He was a lot more attentive to Gretel throughout the rest of the trip.

We arrived back on Capitol Hill with family intact. We settled into the apartment and began job hunting. Clarence switched from teaching to the more lucrative field of electrical wiring. He got this job based on his years of experience at St. Paul's as the in-house electrician. Finally, his six and a half years at St. Paul's were paying off. The new job paid enough for us both to live on, so I took some time to figure out what I wanted to do.

1973

In January, Clarence changed jobs again. Xerox opened a new facility in Springfield, Virginia, and, once again, he fell back on his electrical/technical skills to land a job refurbishing copiers. Xerox offered a terrific salary, paid vacation time, sick leave, family health insurance and profit sharing. Finally, we had some security. We were on our way to becoming a "regular" family.

I was pursuing a career in writing and the arts. I spent my time writing children's stories that centered around different themes of nonviolence and social consciousness. When I got tired of writing, I'd do these abstract crayon drawings that I called "waxed acrylic art." If we needed a quick infusion of money, I'd go to the local farmers' market, set up a booth outside and sell my stories and artwork. I was always a little surprised at how many people bought my stuff. I figured at $2, the price must have been right.

Springfield is located near the Beltway, ten miles outside of Washington. Every day Clarence drove out of the city to work, and back into the city to live. I began to think—Why not live ten miles outside the Beltway in the country and drive into the suburbs to work? It was the same commuting distance, and I had a strong desire to live someplace in a woods where I could begin to put into practice the things I knew about an ecologically responsible lifestyle. I had heard that there were "farmettes" with ten or twenty acres of land available just outside the Beltway—for $35 a month rent. (Obviously, I would believe anything.) Clarence thought this was worth looking into. (He'd believe anything, too.) By this time, the woman who owned the wig company had branched out into real estate, so we gave her a call.

On a bitter cold, drizzly day in late January, we set out with our real estate friend to find those farmettes. Well, first of all, the area ten miles out from the Beltway was nothing but middle- to upper-middle-class suburban sub-developments. If we wanted to live in a brick house with pillars and garage, next to similar brick houses with their pillars and garages, and if we had an extra $75,000 laying around to pay for the privilege, we were in luck. There wasn't a farmette in sight. The real estate friend told us that she never heard of "farmettes." She suggested that we buy property and have a small modular home built on it instead of trying to rent something. This was the more economical way for us to go. She had brought along several suitable property listings further out that we could look at.

The properties we looked at that afternoon were depressing. The weather didn't help matters. But we soon found out that if a listing said "wooded," it actually meant "the lot with the tree on it." As it was getting darker, our friend suggested we look at one more piece of land. It was a ten-acre, wooded lot with two streams. We weren't far from it, so we said okay. After such a disappointing day, I wasn't expecting much. Maybe, with a little luck, we'd get to see the lot that had two trees on it.

We kept driving further and further out into the country toward the Blue Ridge Mountains. Finally we turned onto a gravel road. About a half mile down this road, we stopped. All the way down the road on the right had been a woods. On the left were fenced fields with cattle. We got out of the car, I looked into the woods for about thirty seconds, and said, "This is it."

Clarence nearly passed out.

The first hurdle was the fifty-five mile drive to Xerox. On our way back to the city, we timed the trip—one hour and ten minutes. By the time we got back to our little apartment, Clarence had convinced himself that since he didn't mind driving anyway, he would be able to tolerate this commute.

The second hurdle was money. Clarence had just started working for Xerox, and banks weren't too impressed with my waxed-acrylic and story-selling business. Our real estate friend said that if we could somehow buy the land outright, we could use this as collateral for a loan for a modular home. She could fix us up with the right modular home people. Clarence's family didn't have money to lend, but I knew someone in my family who did. My father. We drove up to New York City, where he was living with his third wife, and just asked him flat out if he would loan us $11,000 to buy this piece of land. This is the man who had not supported me since I was twelve, so I had nothing to lose. He listened to our pitch, called his accountant to find out the most advantageous way (for tax purposes) to transfer the money, and we walked out with $11,000 cash. To us, this money represented our lives and the future. To him, it was pocket change.

By March, we had purchased the land and now needed to find a bank for a $27,000 house loan. We were too young (both twenty-eight), Clarence had not worked at Xerox long enough, and I could tell loan officers thought our hair should have been shorter. I could see we weren't going to get anywhere with these fellows unless we did something different. So I said to this one overly self-important guy: "Listen. Do me a favor and call my father. Perhaps he can put your mind at ease about giving us this loan." I'm not sure what I expected my father to do, but I figured this was the only shot we had at getting the loan. The bank guy humored me and called New York. He explained to my father that we were in his bank and what we wanted. Then he listened for about five minutes. I don't know what my father said to him. Personally, I think he threatened to buy the "goddamn bank" if this guy didn't snap to his senses and give us the loan. I know he wasn't asked to co-sign. But after the phone call, the bank fellow began processing our paperwork, and in less than a month we had the loan. (Did I tell you that my father had buddies in the Mafia with whom he played golf? No kidding.)

In June, we packed our belongings, grabbed our two cats and moved to the country to our new three-bedroom, two-bath, wood-paneled modular home nestled on ten acres of a ninety-acre woods.

For the first five months, we lived without electricity. The person at the electric company in charge of getting the right of ways signed simply sat on the paperwork for four and a half months. We called every day to find out the status of the right of way signatures, and every day he told us not to worry, the lines would be up shortly. We finally figured out that this guy was the kind who gave truth to the Peter Principle. He was incapable of getting sheets of paper signed.

So, Clarence took over the task, and in two weeks we had all the right of ways signed, sealed and delivered, as they say—and in another two weeks, we had electricity hooked up to the house.

I remember that day well. The linesman had come up to tell me that I'd have electricity in a few minutes. Perhaps I'd like to turn on a lamp so that I'd know when "juice was runnin'." I dutifully turned on a lamp in the living room, then stared at it so I wouldn't miss the momentous occasion. When the juice was runnin', nearly every light in the house lit up, and the refrigerator started humming. I laughed. I don't know whatever made either one of us think I might miss something this obvious!

Living those first five months without electricity meant no lights, no toilets, no refrigeration, no water and no stove. We improvised. We converted the refrigerator into an icebox by stuffing ten pounds of ice into the freezer every day. Clarence hauled ten gallons of water daily from Xerox, which covered our cooking, bathing and cleaning needs. For the toilet facility, we bought two cinder blocks, a toilet seat and a shovel. We'd go into the woods, dig a hole, put the cinder blocks on either side of the hole and set the toilet seat on top of the blocks. We thought about building an outhouse, but the inept electric company guy kept saying the lines would "be up shortly." It took us a while to realize that, his ineptness included forked-tongue talking.

These five months were actually helpful—but I'd never tell that to Mr. Inept. By the time the lines finally reached our house, we had made two major adjustments in our thinking. First, we were no longer concerned about the possibility of living out in the middle of nowhere and losing our electricity. We had become "country-sufficient." Second, we no longer had rosy, idealistic urges to embrace the pioneer, back-to-the-land lifestyle that was so prevalent at that time among those who sought the environmentally correct life. We had hauled enough water, dug enough latrine holes and lit enough kerosene lamps. For us, a simple lifestyle now included appropriate technology. A little bit of electricity seemed appropriate.

The move to the woods kicked me into a whole new life. First of all, I had to deal with the solitude. It took months before I was able to walk through the woods and *know* I wouldn't pass another human being, that I was truly alone. Rush hour now consisted of two cars coming down the gravel road at 5:30 in the evening. Maybe a tractor would go by in the afternoon. On real busy days, a horse or cow that had gotten out from a neighboring field might wander down the road. The city noises that I had grown so used to were now being replaced with country sounds.

Clarence was working the second shift at Xerox. This meant that he left the house at 2:30 in the afternoon and didn't arrive back home until 2 A.M.—or 4 A.M., if he had to work overtime. Consequently, I spent large blocks of time alone. During the daylight hours, I worked in the woods clearing out the brush and repairing the damage that resulted from the house construction. In the evenings, I read spy novels by kerosene light, or studied something of interest. For example, I decided I wanted to eat vegetarian, so I immersed myself in nutrition literature.

I first noticed something different about the woods when I was alone in the house at night. It sometimes felt spooky. I'd feel uncomfortable about walking in front of a window or by the sliding doors. The "energy" seemed to intensify during the full moon. I wasn't afraid that someone was going to get me. It was more a response to being surrounded by an air of intensity that I couldn't explain. It was just there.

In 1968, I read a book by C.S. Lewis, *Perelandra*, from his science fiction trilogy. It was about a planet that existed in perfection. In the book, the planet was named "Perelandra," and, according to some scholars, this was Lewis's name for the planet Venus. Perelandra is visited by two Earth men. One man embodied the dynamics of good and the other evil. The one could see the perfection in the planet and moved about in harmony with it. The other was blind to the perfection and moved in destruction, choosing to use the planet as he wished.

I felt that our woods, although badly damaged from being logged poorly by the farmer who owned it prior to us, contained within it perfection. And that once the debris had been cleared away and the damage healed, that perfection would surface and shine again. I felt that Clarence and I had a choice. We could either live in the woods in harmony or in destruction. Our goal was to live in harmony, but we didn't always know what that meant. We sometimes struggled in our efforts to create balance and harmony—the *perfection*—and avoid destruction. I realized that what we were experiencing was similar to the struggles that Lewis had set up in his book. Because I believed so deeply that the woods still embodied perfection, and because of the nature and heart intent of our struggles, we named our land "Perelandra."

1974

My quest for the "normal," environmentally friendly family life moved along just fine until that spring morning in 1974 when I heard those "voices."

I had been slowly slogging my way through the mists of the morning—that space between sleep and full wakefulness—when I suddenly heard a bunch of voices. Well, this delivered me out of the mist. In about two seconds, I was wide awake, bolted upright with eyes open, looking for a crowd of people in the bedroom. Clarence had gotten up earlier, and no one was there but me. The sounds continued. It was like a group of maybe twenty-five or thirty people standing around, all talking at the same time, and pretty loudly. You know how it is when you walk into a large gathering and everyone is yapping away, making it impossible to distinguish what anyone is saying? That's what this sounded like. I would have sworn to anyone that a group had gathered in our bedroom. The only problem was, I didn't see anyone.

I wasn't happy about this. In fact, I was scared. I immediately assumed I was having a nervous breakdown. Now, the idea of a breakdown wasn't new to me. I had frequently thought that the intense pressures of my difficult childhood might cause me to have a breakdown at some point. I had actually prepared myself for this mentally. I would accept the breakdown without guilt, work to pull myself back together and then move on, probably with a new life. But I always assumed it would come at a time when I was under a lot of pressure. I was now the happiest and most content I had ever been. I had survived the hard times, and I was safely nestled in a wonderful life. Why in the world would I have a breakdown now? I decided not to say anything to Clarence about the voices, hoping that I'd never hear them again.

The next morning, the same thing happened—same voices, all talking at once. I realized that they were not talking to one another. They were all talking to me. But I couldn't understand a word they were saying. The overall tone of their voices wasn't threatening, nor did it sound like they were trying to warn me about something.

Still I said nothing to Clarence. I needed some time to figure out how I was going to tell him that I needed to be hospitalized. Except for thinking about the voices and my new mental health needs, I went about my day as usual. I didn't feel like someone who was in the middle of having a nervous breakdown. In fact, I didn't feel like I was in trouble in any way.

The third morning. More voices. Sounded like the same group.

Obviously, I was deteriorating rapidly, and I needed to talk to Clarence right away.

Clarence listened to me and didn't say a word. Then, without batting an eye or missing the proverbial beat, he began talking about—and even quoting from—some letter written by St. Paul to the early Christians. He told me that the early Christians, at one point, heard voices and questioned Paul about whether or not he felt they were going insane. St. Paul wrote a letter assuring them that the voices they heard were of the Spirit and they were not to be afraid.

Clarence was saying all of this as if it were the most normal thing in the world to have your partner tell you over morning coffee she's hearing voices and needs to be institutionalized. I've since talked with him about his reaction that day. He said that at first he was "a little concerned." We hadn't been together that long, and already I had to be institutionalized. Then he says that he had a feeling that something else was going on here. I didn't look or act in trouble. I had already demonstrated to him that I was a "pretty intuitive" person, and he had developed a trust in this. That's when he began thinking about this letter from St. Paul to the early Christians. (The irony of this is that I am not a fan of St. Paul—not after some of his remarks about the role of women.)

It was clear to me that my declaration of insanity was being rejected, and I was going to have to deal with the voices from another perspective. Again, Clarence came to the rescue. He suggested that I meditate.

I didn't know anything about meditation. I hadn't read anything on the subject and I knew no one who meditated. Peggy Townsend had suggested that I learn to meditate in our session two years back. But I didn't know what she was talking about then either, so I shoved it aside. Now Clarence was suggesting the same thing. He felt that if I meditated, I could find out what the voices were.

That afternoon, I went into the bedroom to meditate—whatever that meant. As soon as I shut the door, I heard a voice. It was clear, but gentle. It told me to lie on the floor. I figured I had nothing to lose, so I stretched out on the floor. Then the voice told me to relax my muscles. I tried to relax. Then I was told to relax my mind the way I did when I was a child and had wanted to fantasize.

At last, something I understood. While I lived with my parents, I protected myself from abuse by isolating myself from them as much as possible. I used to sit for long periods of time in my room, and let my mind get quiet. I'd experience wonderful "fantasies" during this quiet time. I'd see strange places and people. I even experienced sounds and smells. These times became part of my survival.

This day at Perelandra, I shut my eyes and did what I had done a thousand times as a child. My body felt the familiar sensation of lifting and, at a particular point, it felt as if it had fallen over a ledge into space. The voice said: "*This* is meditation."

I was then instructed to recall one of my childhood fantasies. With little effort, I remembered an island I used to "go to" and, in a flash, I was once again experiencing that island. I felt like I was floating above it. I could see it, feel the sunshine, hear the waves break along the shoreline—even smell the water. The voice explained that this was a form of meditation called "astral traveling." All those childhood fantasies had actually been astral traveling experiences.

When I pulled myself out of the island and returned to my original sense of floating in space, the voice explained to me that it was important that I spend a portion of each day in meditation, that meditation wasn't just floating in space or astral traveling. It was a discipline that allowed us to experience a broader spectrum of life, and that life had many facets that were open to me, if I wished to experience them and learn from them. All I had to do was say that I wanted to learn, ask for the help and commit myself to getting into the same relaxed state daily. When I thought about the voices I had heard in the bedroom, I was told that I had not been responding to the more subtle hints I was receiving about meditation and was given something a bit more obvious to deal with.

The voice stopped. I waited for it to say something else, but there was just silence. I didn't need time to think about whether or not I would pursue meditation, so I said I wanted to continue and asked for help. There was no reply, and I wasn't sure if I was heard. I just brought myself "back to the bedroom"—something else I had learned to do in my childhood—and got on with the rest of my day.

The second day, I got into that relaxed state, slipped over the ledge into space—and nothing happened. No voices, no action, no visits to great places. I just hung out for awhile, then came back to the bedroom.

The third day, I slipped over the ledge, only this time the space felt very different. It was as if I had gone to a higher ledge before slipping over. Right away, I saw before me forms, like a group of people so out of focus that I could only make out that they were people, and not trees or cows. They had a "wispy" density to them, and I felt I could walk right through them—if I wanted to. I was standing on the outside and looking in at them through a window. Suddenly, I realized that I had *come home*. The realization was so powerful that I literally felt physically struck by it. I didn't know where this place was but I knew, without a doubt, that this was my real home and that I had left this home to come to Earth. A strong wave of homesickness washed over me, and I had a deep yearning to stay in this place. Then I realized that even though I didn't consciously know why I had chosen to come to Earth, I had made a sound decision. I felt a respect, from myself and the others, for having made that decision.

All the people were facing me and recognizing my presence. When they saw that I had focused my eyes on them, they sent me what I can only describe as a collective wave of love that I found to be quite overpowering. I knew that if I didn't do something with this wave, my body would explode from the intensity. So I focused on gathering the wave in my body, reversed its direction, added my love to it and sent it back to the people. They surprised me by sending the same wave back to me. So, I sent it back to them. It was like we were playing ping pong with a tidal wave of love.

The wave exchange went on for some time, and I began to sob— not just cry, but sob—from the magnitude of the experience. Then suddenly, without warning, I was standing in the Garden of Gethsemane, looking at Christ. He was by Himself, and apparently I wasn't visible to Him. I don't know how long He had been there, but it seemed to me like it had been a while. He was on his knees, and He, too, was sobbing. That's when I realized that He was having the exact experience that I was having. He had gone home. He was feeling the wave of love, and He now knew that He had made the right decision to leave this home and come to Earth. It was then that I realized that this was the experience that gave Him the strength to go through the crucifixion the next day.

Again without warning, I was standing in front of the people. Only, this time, I wasn't on the outside looking in through a window. Now I was facing them directly. The wave of love was still being exchanged between us. At the same time, I was aware that a thunderstorm was going on at Perelandra. The lightning and thunder felt right over the house. It was so noisy that I was certain Clarence, who was in the living room, could not hear me sobbing. In fact, I could barely hear myself. The experience with the wave intensified to the point that I didn't think I could take it any longer. My heart was pounding now, and I felt that if I didn't come out of the experience, my heart would explode from the pressure. I gathered myself and pulled out of the experience, moving through "levels of space" to where I could easily return to the bedroom. I "arrived" with the thunderstorm wildly unleashing over the house. [comma]

I couldn't stop crying. Eventually, I got up and went into the living room, hoping Clarence would hold me—which he did. I couldn't speak for the longest time. But, while Clarence held me, I remembered that the Bible says that Christ was saddened when He returned to His disciples and found them asleep in the Garden of Gethsemane—something about their not supporting Him in His hour of need. I realized that had I walked into the living room and found

Clarence asleep and unresponsive, I, too, would have felt deep sadness.

I was not able to talk to Clarence about the experience until many weeks later. He said to me that when I came into the living room, he thought I had experienced something that had to do with my death, and this was why I was so upset. Luckily, he didn't try to press for information. He just held me until I stopped crying.

I remember going for a walk down our gravel road the next day and feeling that something *big* had happened to me that had changed my life, and no one else knew about it. My whole perspective about my life had changed, and I now had a profound sense of peace. Life was going on as usual around me. I thought that this must be what it's like for someone to suddenly loose someone they love, and then have to go on dealing with life's normal routine. You know something major has happened and that your life is forever changed, but the postman doesn't know this. He still delivers the mail as usual, casually greeting you.

I don't want you to think that I am for one second comparing my life with Christ's. For the record, I am not. We had similar experiences, and we had similar responses. That's all. Since this time, a number of people have told me about their experiences of "visiting home." And they shared that they were overwhelmed by it also.

I returned to the bedroom the day after the "home" experience, but I was scared. Although it was joyful, profound, moving, amazing and awfully interesting, I was frightened by its intensity. I felt I had come close to physically exploding, and I had no idea how to ensure my safety. I didn't think anyone had put me in danger. I just didn't know if I was physically capable of handling these kinds of experiences. With this in mind, I slipped over the ledge and, once again, asked for help.

Immediately, I saw an arched, stone bridge over a wide, deep stream. I walked onto the bridge, leaned my elbows on the side and watched the water flow by. The current was swift. I bet I spent a good ten to fifteen minutes looking at the water rush by. After awhile, I felt a presence next to me. I looked to my left and there was a young man, about thirty-six, who had a shaved head and was dressed in robes like a Buddhist monk. He didn't say anything, he didn't even look at me. We were no more than eight inches apart, but I felt safe next to him. He had leaned his elbows on the bridge and was watching the water also.

He didn't waste time chatting. But he had a soft, gentle demeanor that put me at ease so much, it seemed like we were the best of friends. I completely trusted him. Without talking to or looking at me, he began transmitting information. It was as if he flowed his thoughts directly into my head. He started by giving me an understanding about meditation. He said that meditation is a tool that allows us to experience many levels of life that are different from the one we choose to live on as our home base, that it is not to be used as an escape from life on our chosen level. Rather, it is a tool for enhancing and expanding our understanding of and participation in life as a whole. He further explained that like any tool, meditation required learning and discipline to be used well. Then he started giving me some basics. I knew that this was the person who was going to help me, the person who was going to be my teacher.

I met this man on the bridge every day for the next two years. He always stood next to me on my left. He never spoke out loud, and he never looked me directly in the eye. We always started out by leaning our elbows on the bridge and watching the water flow by. I never asked him why he didn't speak out loud because his communication with me was so flawless and efficient that it didn't occur to me to question it. I, on the other hand, spoke out loud to him. We laughed together—he even thought my jokes were funny. Actually, he looked me in the eye once, and this was during our last meeting. It felt like a loving goodbye.

He was a kind but no-nonsense teacher. And he was extremely proficient at getting his point across. He just "filed" information into my head, and I'd get it. There wasn't a lot of confusion or questioning on my part.

In the beginning, we spent months on the concept of word energy and what it meant to *really* clear the mind. Every day he had me identify what was going on in my head, then assign one word to each thought that accurately described it. Then I had to "pull" each word out of my head, one at a time. I had to visually "see" the letters of the word as I pulled them out with my hand. Next, I'd wrap the word in brown paper and carefully tie string around the package. Once completed, I'd throw the package into the stream and watch it as it floated under the bridge. Then I'd pull the next word out and do the whole thing over again. I continued doing this each day until I had all the words I had assigned to thoughts out of my head, packaged and floating downstream. The next day I'd come back, identify my thoughts again, and start wrapping.

As I said, this went on for months. Each day I became more adept at identifying what was going on in my head. I'd clear out one layer and realize a whole new layer of activity surfaced as a result. Then I'd have to clear that layer out. I got to the point that I was clearing out the expectation of having to clear my mind. It felt like mirrors within mirrors within mirrors. When we finished, finally, I had a much better understanding of clearing the mind. I also had the tool for doing it.

Several times, while we were working, I "crashed" out of the meditation because of some outside disturbance like the phone ringing or one of our dogs barking. I found the experience physically painful. My heart felt like it had dropped out of my body, and my head felt like it had received an internal whip lash. So he gave me lessons on how to protect myself when these intrusions occur. The *split second* something happened, he had me respond by "seeing" a huge air pillow under my body—the body that I could see at the bridge, not my body lying on the floor at Perelandra. This way my focus never shifted away from the bridge. The pillow supported me so that, as I felt the urge to "drop," I would feel this pillow "catching" me. I'd end up "falling" only a few inches, so to speak, rather than completely out of the meditation. I was still on the bridge, and all I had to do was collect myself a little bit. Then we'd continue with the lesson. It took me weeks before I could get the pillow under me in time, but once I got it down, it worked perfectly.

The most exciting, interesting and fun sessions were the astral traveling lessons. I learned that while with the monk I could ask to be of service to others by giving assistance to people in distress. I needed to request this; it wasn't decided for me. I quickly grew to love this form of service and requested it often for quite a few months.

Once, after asking for a "service day," I immediately found my-self on a train in the former Yugoslavia. I was always a little bit disoriented when I first "arrived" in these situations, but I found that all I had to do was stand and observe for about thirty seconds and my confusion would clear up. I'd know where I was and what I was to do. Of course, no one could ever see me. (At least no one ever looked like they could see me.) On this occasion, there was an East-ern Orthodox priest on the train. I was to feed into his mind my "coming home" experience. I found him sitting at the opposite end of the car from where I had "arrived." As soon as I found him, I recreated my experience in my mind and completely moved it into his mind. After the many months of pulling words out of my head to send down the river, this was a snap. As soon as I finished with the experience, I left the train and returned to the bridge. The monk told me that the priest had been in despair over his life, that the train was going to crash and that he would most likely die. Had he died in that state, his soul would have had great difficulty crossing over into the afterlife. When I placed my "going home" experience into his mind, *he* experienced it and was able to release himself from despair as a result.

The next day at Perelandra, I was leafing through the newspaper and saw a tiny filler article on one of the back pages about a train crash in Yugoslavia that had occurred the day before. Over a hundred people were killed.

Another time, I ended up in Liberia watching a large parade. It was government-sanctioned, and members from various tribes were participating. All of a sudden, machine-gun fire opened up and I watched six of the marchers in front of me get killed. One of the marchers seemed to be looking directly into my eyes as he was hit. His eyes showed a deep sense of horror and shock. Finally, his body slammed against the ground from the impact of the gunfire.

Then I watched the entire scene play out before my eyes again— from the start to the man's body slamming against the ground. When it was over, it played again. And again. And again.

I realized that the men who had been killed had not released themselves from the massacre and were in a kind of limbo, reliving the horror over and over and over. They were actually recreating the scene that I was watching. I remembered Peggy's work with the orphans and began calmly telling the men that they had died. They had been massacred. They needed to let go and move on. They would be fine, once they moved on. The horror would end once they let go. The person who had the most difficulty understanding what I was saying was the fellow whose eyes I had looked into during the shooting. His intensity about the massacre was somehow preventing the others from releasing. I then realized he had been a respected tribal leader. No one was going to let go unless he let go first. So I concentrated on him. I just kept repeating all the information that I had with as calm a voice as possible. I don't know how long it took, but eventually the massacre stopped repeating, and the leader lifted right out of the scene with the other five following.

Each time I requested to be of service was different, and I learned something new about the wondrous, unseen complex activity that goes on around us all the time.

Then, one day I decided to stop. I had not experienced anything that left me jaded or disappointed. All the experiences were amazing. The monk never said anything to me about stopping. He never even hinted that this was something I might consider. It's just that one day I had a deep, gut feeling that this was not my true work and that I needed to move on. For me to continue would be, in effect, avoiding my real work—whatever that was. That day, I said to the monk that it was time for me to learn something different, to move on. I haven't done any astral travel work since. Nor have I ever regretted my decision.

The more I worked with the monk, learning about new aspects of life, the more distant I felt from the Catholic church. The church was not being replaced by the monk. I didn't have a "religious" feeling about him. But the church in general was not supportive of what I was experiencing, and what I was experiencing was more vital and real than anything the church had given me or could give me. Having found that the essence of truth was within myself meant that I no longer needed the clergy or church to act as middleman.

In early June, I read in the newspaper that a civil rights bill that would have guaranteed homosexuals the right to housing and jobs had been defeated in New York City, and that the Catholic church was the primary force behind its defeat. For me, this was the last straw. I could not be a member of a church that actively campaigned against these basic rights for anyone. I was embarrassed to be a member of this church.

On June 12, I wrote to Pope Paul VI.

> Your Holiness:
>
> This is to formally notify you that, as of this date, I am resigning from the Catholic church.
>
> Ten years ago, I joined the Catholic church with great joy, anticipation and hope that I personally was on the best road to discovering the true essence of Christianity. Since then, I have seen a church that adamantly and vocally opposes killing through abortion while remaining silent about killing through war. . . . I have seen a church that forces those few young men out of the priesthood simply because they choose to speak out against war or live in ghettos in order to help the poor while, at the same time, supports and maintains the majority of its silent priests who have taken a vow of poverty, yet live in what we in America would call an upper-middle-class lifestyle. I have seen a church that claims to be Christian yet refuses to recognize full participation in its ranks of fifty percent of the world's population—women. I have seen a church that allows the Archdiocese of New York to lobby *against* a human rights bill in New York City. Thanks to their diligent and successful efforts, that bill, which would have provided housing and job security, was voted down purely because the Archdiocese took a stand against the humans involved: homosexuals.
>
> Because of these incidents and many others that I have seen and experienced, my conscience does not allow me to support or remain a member of the Catholic church. I have found that Christianity and the Catholic church are not necessarily one and the same. . . . Therefore, I can no longer remain a Catholic, and hereby tender you my resignation.

Of course, we all know that the Catholic church, the pope and the archbishop for the Arlington Diocese (to whom I sent a photocopy) could not have cared less about my little letter, but it was important for me to write it and formally cut my ties. I didn't care what anyone in the church was going to do with this letter. In fact, I assumed they would just throw it away. However, as far as I was concerned, their inability to appreciate what this letter was all about or to take it seriously was their problem. What was important were my actions. I had entered the church—via baptism—with a clear act of intent, and I needed to leave with an act of equally clear intent.

As soon as I placed my signature on the letter, I flipped over the ledge into a meditative state that I did not come out of for a full twenty-four hours. At first, I saw myself in space, floating, with my oxygen cord connected to a spacecraft. Then the cord was cut, and I was free-floating in the universe. That was how I remained for twenty-four hours. While floating, I dealt with two strong emotions. One was freedom. I now was free to move about in any direction. It was as if the whole universe was suddenly mine. The second was responsibility. I was struck with the heavy realization that from this point on, my movement, my direction, my very life, depended on no one but me. There was no structure or institution to fall back on. I now was truly operating on my own steam. Both the responsibility and the freedom felt awesome.

By the way, the pope never answered my letter.

1975

I continued working with the monk on the bridge. Not long after I stopped astral travel work, I began to have a new experience: the Void. Each day, I'd show up at the bridge, all bright-eyed and bushy-tailed, and the monk would give me instructions that would move me into levels well beyond anything I had experienced up to that time. When I got to a certain level, I would tip over the ledge into the Void. I'd hang out for a while, then I'd come back through the levels and return to the bridge. We did this for about six months.

There's not a lot I can say about the Void. It's nothing—it's a void. That's the point. I had no sense of self or of anything else, for that matter. I had no consciousness, and I had no awareness of being in a void until after I was out of it and could reflect back on the experience. It wasn't like a black hole in my life—a black hole would have had some substance to it. A lot of books are written

about the Void, mostly from Zen masters who claim this is the ultimate meditative state and the goal toward which all should aim. I
gotta tell you, in comparison to astral traveling work (or just about
anything else in life), the Void is pretty boring. I guess you could
say it's a state of being, but I couldn't find any way to fit this state
of being into my life. It was something that I experienced for six
months that didn't seem to have any useful purpose, and the monk
wasn't giving out any hints. [comma]

I admit that this was quite a letdown after the excitement of the
astral traveling work. I also have to admit that I never thought about
quitting. In fact, I don't recall complaining—at least not to the
monk. I'm sure I was grumbling to myself, however. I knew I had to
keep moving forward. To quit would have felt like I was moving
backwards. If I just stayed with this, I'd eventually come out the
other end, and I was curious about where this was leading.

1976

Despite my daily lessons with some monk on a bridge that only I
could see, life was pretty normal at Perelandra. (Actually, the lessons ended around September of 1976. That's when he finally
looked directly at me, and I knew the lessons were over.) Clarence
was still working at Xerox, we had expanded our family to include
two dogs, and I was into my third year of vegetable gardening. One
of the first things I wanted to do when we moved to the country was
put in a vegetable garden. I didn't have this great, loving hankering
to garden. That wasn't why I wanted to do this. I just felt that if a
person was going to live in the country, they were *supposed* to have
a garden. And it was the ecological thing to do, as well.

Having absolutely no experience with gardening, I had to rely on
what the "experts" in books had to say on the subject. I dutifully
followed instructions, including using insecticide that first year.
Then I learned to can and got busy canning vegetables and jams for
the winter. I canned huge vats of soup—sixteen quarts per vat.

The second year of the garden, I happened to read the fine print
on the insecticide bag and immediately felt that this stuff may have
ensured our supply of vegetables, but I wasn't sure how healthy

those vegetables were for us to eat. So I turned to organic gardening. By 1976, I was deeply immersed in the world of soil conditioning, mulching and interplanting. Frankly, it was easier using the insecticide, but it wasn't as interesting.

During this time, there was a couple we were friends with who we visited fairly frequently. He had been a priest, and she had been a nun—now they were married. Both had doctorates in philosophy, and he taught philosophy at a nearby college. I particularly liked visiting them because I enjoyed getting into arguments with the husband about any variety of esoteric points. He enjoyed the arguments, too. He was a tall man with a full beard and a deep voice. He said his students used to treat him as if he were Moses and would never challenge him on anything. So he liked the fact that I didn't care about his size, voice pitch or facial hair.

One afternoon in November, we got into a discussion that lasted ten hours—nonstop. I started by announcing that a human being could be a hermit living on a mountain, tending a garden and still learn all there is to know about life and living. Our friend's position was that human beings were meant to be social and family-oriented. There were some crucial aspects of life that could only be learned through social interaction with other humans—particularly within the family structure. After ten hours, neither one of us had budged from our respective positions. It was a standoff, and we were both exhausted. [comma]

The interesting thing to me about that argument is that I didn't plan to have it in the first place, and I said things in defense of my position that I had never before thought about. When I heard myself say them, I knew they were true—at least, in terms of *my* truth. I talked about a garden being a key to the universe, and that it was an access to spiritual truth and universal law. By the time I left my friends' house, I *knew* these things were true.

In December, I became fascinated with the concept of regressive self-hypnosis and had a terrific urge to learn to do this. I had to find out about all those past lives of mine. Since the monk on the bridge hadn't covered this in our lessons, I decided I was just going to march right out, buy some books on the subject and teach myself.

One Saturday afternoon, Clarence and I went into D.C. to the *Yes!*

Bookstore where I found seven books on my newest interest. While we were browsing, Clarence handed me two books and said, "Here, I think you'll be interested in these." I looked at them. They were on something called "Findhorn" (pronounced: fend' horn): *The Magic of Findhorn* and *The Findhorn Garden*. I asked why I would find them interesting, and he said, "They're about gardening." I thought, "Oh joy. More books on organic gardening. How boring," and then stuck the books in with my other ones, figuring "what the hell, they're paperback. They're cheap. I'll buy the things and that way I won't hurt his feelings. Maybe I'll get bored this winter and have time to read them." [comma]

Immediately after returning to Perelandra that day, I sat down with my new books. I was excited about this regressive hypnosis business. No matter which one of the books I picked up on the subject, my attention would automatically shift to the Findhorn books. So I began reading *The Findhorn Garden*—and I didn't put it down until I had finished it.

I couldn't believe what I was reading. Everything that I had said in that ten-hour argument was laid out on the pages before my eyes. I fell right into the world of nature intelligences, and nothing could have made me more ecstatic. I was being told that the vague energies I had felt around me at Perelandra actually had names: devas and nature spirits. They weren't my imagination. That spooky feeling I had felt at night from the woods was a life force that was now identified and could consciously be worked with. I saw that my goal of achieving ecological balance at Perelandra rested on my willingness to work with these life forces, these nature intelligences.

1977

By reading about the example of the garden that was growing in sand at Findhorn, Scotland, and how the people who started that garden worked with nature intelligences, I received the encouragement I needed to open up to a new world. One evening in early January, I walked into the woods and announced in a loud, clear voice, "I want to do at Perelandra what they did at Findhorn. I want to work with the devas, and I want to work with nature spirits. I invite all of you to make yourselves known to me. I am ready to learn from you."

With this declaration, I triggered my first ring-pass-not expansion. I left the woods, returned to the house, put myself into a quiet state and waited. By doing this, I sealed my declaration by physically acting on it—by opening myself to whatever was to happen next.

The response was immediate. In fact, I had the same experience that Dorothy Maclean had at Findhorn when she first connected with devas. I had a "crowd of voices" coming at me, all talking at the same time. I could tell from what they were saying that they had been waiting for this for some time. I remembered that in the Findhorn book, when Dorothy described this experience, she said she simply asked the devas to speak to her one at a time. Having nothing to lose, I tried the same thing. Much to my amazement, they responded instantaneously. And from that point on, I received the nature intelligences one voice at a time.

I spent every day in nature's classroom from January through October of 1977, where I was taught reality from nature's perspective. I describe this first garden in detail in Chapter 2 of *Behaving As If the God In All Life Mattered*, so I won't repeat it here. But I'd like to give you an overall sense of my first ring-pass-not experience and what it taught me.

Each morning I would open to nature and ask what I was to do that day. I let nature decide the curriculum. I made the assumption that I knew nothing—and I must say that, looking back after eighteen years with nature, my initial assumption could not have been more accurate. From this garden, I received my early lessons about the universal laws of nature and how they apply to the nature that we experience on our planet. I also started learning about partnership, teamwork, leadership and peer relationships. And as much as I learned about universal laws, nature and these other things, I learned about myself—my power, equality, balance, health, heart and soul.

A pattern for my daily lessons was quickly established. Nature would give me something specific to do. I would then do it, observe the results, then sometimes receive more instructions about what to do next. Again I'd do what I was told and observe the results. Often,

I got the understanding of what nature was trying to teach me simply through the conclusions I could draw from doing and observing.
The act itself became the explanation. At other times, I would act,
observe and still be blank regarding what I was seeing. That's when
nature would sometimes "step in" and give me the additional insight
I needed for understanding.

And then there were those times when I would act, observe, stare
blankly and *not* receive any insight. I would close the day not understanding anything I did. That's when I'd scratch my head a lot. I'd
come back the next day, open to nature and start the whole process
over again. I may end up with a string of days where I had absolutely no understanding about what I was doing or observing. But I'd
keep plugging along. Eventually, I'd observe something I had just
done and that would be the piece I needed to pull that day and all
the previous blank days together into one large, comprehensible
package. I'd finally get it.

Nature taught me that life is a learning process that doesn't necessarily include comprehension at given points along the way, and that
one must proceed in this process in faith and with patience. I experienced from nature a complete reversal of just about everything I
thought I knew, including many things I took for granted. Years
later, when I reflected back on this time, I realized that nature was
carefully dismantling my previous sense of logic and replacing it
with a completely different and more expanded logic. And nature
was doing this by giving me the actual experiences rather than "lectures" about such experiences. For example, one day nature told me
to hold a yellow squash in my hands. I was told to just watch it
sitting in my hands. I'd say I had been looking at it for about five
minutes when, right before my eyes, the yellow squash turned into a
green cucumber that was slightly larger in size than the squash had
been. The switch took less than fifteen seconds. And it was gradual,
so I knew that someone had not sneaked up on me and switched the
squash with a cucumber while I blinked. I saw the squash actually
change into a cucumber. Now, somewhere along the line I had been
taught that if you pick up a squash and hold it in your hands, chances were it would remain a squash. It was one of those assumptions I
had grown to trust. Here nature was showing me that this wasn't

necessarily the case. Form could change. And nature could change the form of anything it wanted—at any time.

I have to tell you—holding a squash that turns into a cucumber right before your eyes is a dumbfounding experience. Particularly if you haven't been forewarned. I just stared at the thing for a good half hour, trying to get my wits about me. My way of dealing with these things is to basically say, "Hold on. Nobody move. Let me get this." Then I just stare and touch and sniff until I am completely convinced that what I am presently seeing, feeling and smelling is what I think it is. I don't want you to think I moved through these kinds of experiences without batting an eye. While looking at this cucumber, I even accused nature of not playing by the rules. Of course, that was the point. Whose rules were we talking about here? Just as I was getting used to that cucumber, they changed it back to the yellow squash. (I never ate that squash. I just wasn't sure if the thing that ended up on my plate would be the thing I cooked. I mean, what if I started out—in good faith—steaming this squash, and ended up with a plate of steamed watermelon, for god's sake. Actually, I was a little nervous about everything I harvested from that garden!)

My summer was filled with these kinds of experiences. Each one, as I've said, taught me something different about gardening, form, reality and life. I talked to Clarence about what was happening in the early part of the season—the late winter, early spring months. Once again, he didn't show any evidence that he thought I was mentally disturbed. But as the lessons intensified, I became more quiet and I stopped sharing with him. I just needed to keep it to myself. He continued to support me by not questioning what I was doing and not getting in my way. (I'm still more comfortable not talking about this stuff while it's happening. It feels like I'm dispersing myself and the work, so Clarence reads about what I've been doing in my books!)

In early summer, without any warning, nature moved my lessons onto a new level. I went to the garden as I usually did, asked what they wanted me to do and then followed the new instructions. I had no idea that I was stepping into a carefully planned series of lessons on manifestation. Because each step was based on all the previous ones, I did not feel like nature was asking me to do something alien, nor was it seriously challenging my sanity. Everything I had experienced up to that point led to the lessons for the first stage of manifestation, and each step after that led to the second and third stages of manifestation. So, while I was experiencing these lessons that summer, I didn't feel I was doing anything outrageous or unbelievable, even though I had never heard about direct manifestation prior to that time. Also, nature did not use the word "manifestation" when instructing me on what to do. Our entire focus was on action and experience, not labeling or intellectual understanding. So within the context of that summer, and within the reality that nature had placed me in, manifestation made sense. In short, I was not shocked.

The first stage focused on *clearly* identifying a need. I was told to recognize something that was required in the garden—for example, hay to mulch our garden. Our usual supply from local farmers had been wiped out because of severe drought conditions. First, I had to recognize the need. Then nature told me to define precisely what we required—the kinds of hay that were acceptable, the condition of the hay, the amount, the timing for actually having it on hand.... Things like this. Once I defined everything, I was told to "present" the whole package of what I needed to nature, then let it go. Don't think about it again, and especially don't worry about it. I was to *assume* the need would be met. Within a couple of days, we received a phone call from a neighbor telling us about a farmer who had a huge pile of wet hay he wanted to get rid of. All we had to do was come get it. That hay supply lasted exactly the period of time I had requested.

The second stage of manifestation focused on the actual "inner mechanism" of how energy became form on our planet from the perspective of the nature spirits* within nature intelligence. I was again told to identify and define something that was required in the garden. I chose manure. I was then told to connect with the nature spirits of this specific kind of manure and to follow their direction. I did as instructed and experienced how the nature spirits interacted

* Nature spirits are regional implementors of creation's blueprints into form and action.

with a devically created energy reality in order to bring it into the band of form in which our planet operates. Nature slowed the process down considerably so that I could feel it through my sensory system. What normally takes less than a split second took us about two hours. I experienced the manure's movement through several different energy levels, then I sensed that it was beginning to take on the form I was familiar with. When I felt it had completed its process, I opened my eyes. There before me was a pile of perfectly rotted manure. I stared and poked at it for a long time, eventually convincing myself that indeed it was a pile of manure. I asked nature if they wanted me to place it on the garden where I needed it, and they said yes. So I did.

I spent several weeks working with nature in this manner. Each day, I identified and defined a need, and then, with the nature spirits, I experienced the object's movement through a series of levels that culminated in full form. It took tremendous focus on my part just to stay with the entire process. If I released or lost my focus for a split second, the object would not materialize, and we would have to start over.

The third stage focused on manifestation in its entirety. This meant that I had to begin the experience of the inner mechanism from the perspective of the devic level. For this, I was told to identify and define something else for the garden. Once completed, I was then told to "go into the Void." Now, that was a bit of a surprise. Finally, my earlier experiences around the Void and the monk on the bridge were going to be put to use! From the Void, I *felt* the instant of creation when the soul individuates and is devically fused to form. I experienced the process of all the various pieces of individuation being drawn together into a single comprehensive "package." This occurred right "outside" the Void. Then I moved with the package as it shifted through what seemed like levels where its pieces became more and more defined. At a certain point, the package was complete and was released to the nature spirit level for us to move it through the now-familiar process of taking on full form. [comma]

I spent several more weeks working on this third stage of manifestation. The whole process, from the Void to five-senses form, took between three and four hours. It was actually easier for me to maintain focus when I started out in the Void. I felt as if I were naturally more in sync with the movement from the beginning.

Experiencing the inner mechanism of creation like this changed how I looked at everything around me. You know how it is when you are present at the moment of birth—be it a human baby, kittens, puppies, a calf, a foal—and you feel you are sharing in the experience with the mother, and then you feel a deep heart bonding with the newborn? Those of you who have participated in birth know that there's a world of difference between hearing about it and being present. Through manifestation I was present for creation and birth—and I bonded with all life. My relationship to all reality around me changed. It took on an intimacy that has never diminished. And how I saw myself in relationship to reality also changed. I *experienced* the intimate kinship I have with everything. I do not have a me/it division when I look at life, the planet and the universe. Instead, I feel a deeply bonded "us."

By mid-August, the manifestation lessons stopped, and we moved the garden through its final weeks. I continued doing what I was instructed to do, and nature continued teaching me about life. Although I felt quiet and even vulnerable, I was able to keep up with every facet of my daily routine. I still washed clothes, cooked vats of soup and spaghetti sauce, canned said soup and sauce, cleaned house, did grounds-maintenance work beyond the garden and cared for our animals. I talked with Clarence, but not about anything that was going on in the garden. None of this felt like a strain, and actually the daily chores helped me feel anchored throughout the summer.

Sometime in May, Clarence and I had attended a talk given by Peter and Eileen Caddy, the co-founders of the Findhorn Community in Scotland. It was their books about their work in the garden with nature spirits and devas that had triggered my own garden work. At the gathering, they talked about a three-month educational and work program that was held at the Community each winter. I decided that it would be good for me to go to Findhorn and be part of this program. I figured that this was where I could talk about my garden with people who understood what I was saying because of their own similar work with nature. I wanted to discuss the nuts and bolts of this partnership with nature—from the human perspective.

I didn't know how I was going to get to Findhorn. I just knew I was going. The program cost $900, which we didn't have. And I'd need travel and living expenses on top of this. In mid-July, right in the middle of my manifestation lessons, my father called and said he wanted to send us to Las Vegas for a week-long vacation. This is the first (and last) time he made such a gesture. He explained that he was a "high roller." To emphasize the point, he told us he had once dropped $76,000 in one evening at the craps table. To ensure his presence at their gambling tables, the MGM Grand Hotel always paid for all his travel expenses to the hotel and living expenses during his stay. He would work it out with them to pay for us as his guests. All we'd have to do is take enough money for tips. Plane fare, room and meals at any restaurant in the hotel would be courtesy of the MGM Grand. Also, we could attend any show in Vegas for free. All we had to do was present ourselves to the pit boss at the hotel and tell him Isadore (my father) sent us—and give him a list of the shows we wanted to see for each day.

Well, Clarence and I thought this was too weird of an opportunity to pass up. I could go on and on about the craziness of this trip. I thought I had gone to another planet, quite frankly. There was the suite with the cheap Mae West decor including mirrors over the monster-size round bed. The bed was raised on a platform that was surrounded by a white and gold-gilt wrought-iron railing. We wondered if this was a safety feature for guests who got too rambunctious on that bed and needed to be fenced in. Clarence had "allotted" $20 for gambling—he's such a conservative, safe gambler that it took him four days to lose the entire $20. We saw some terrific shows. In fact, that was the thing that kept us there. Everything else bored us. We couldn't go for walks outside because the temperature was over 110 degrees each day. All we could do was eat (at the MGM Grand), visit the casinos in other hotels just to see what they were like (basically the same), and go to a show each night. About five days into this thing, we both admitted that we wanted to go home. Besides, we were running out of tip money. So we cut the "vacation" short and went back to Perelandra. Somehow, in the shuffle of the plane tickets created by our early departure, we ended up with over $900 in our hands. We called Isadore about the snafu, and he told us to forget it, he'd square it with the hotel, if necessary. That's how I got the money to go to Findhorn.

I put the garden to bed just before leaving for Scotland. I've never really been able to fully describe that experience. This garden had truly been my entryway into a whole new life—and it had functioned as my teacher, as well. I knew I would continue my work with nature, and that this was not the end of our relationship, by any means. But closing down *this* garden was like saying goodbye to an extraordinary teacher and leaving the best classroom experience I had ever had. I just didn't want it to end. It took a week to complete, and throughout the entire time I felt a deep peace and calm that permeated the garden and me. Within days after the garden was closed down I left for Findhorn.

1978

My four months at Findhorn (I had to take an additional two-week introductory program since I had not visited the community before, and Clarence came over for two weeks after my longer program, making it a four-month stay) served to remind me that I was not cut out for community life. I noticed a lot of the goofiness I had experienced at CCNV—only now it was among 150 people instead of six, and it was couched in new age lingo. I couldn't find one person who worked with nature the way I had back in Virginia. The three-month program that year was poorly organized and staffed by well-meaning people who had been "guided" to run it, even though they had no prior experience leading an intense, international group of thirty-five adults. The two main leaders (focalizers) of the group argued the first week and spent the rest of the program not talking to one another. Terrible mistakes were made, and the atmosphere was full of angst. It was difficult for us to try to suggest changes to the program because, at that time, any suggestions or feedback were seen as negativity—and "dwelling on negativity" was "forbidden." They liked addressing problems by hugging them away. They were very big on loooong hugs. We had a professional group leader in our program who was willing to help straighten out our mess, but his efforts were rebuffed by the leaders of our program and of the community. So most of us who had traveled to Findhorn for these three months basically managed to stagger through and survive the program.

Like any experience, even this one wasn't completely awful or useless. I made friends who I still maintain a connection with. I accomplished a few things while I was there as well. For one thing, I made flowered signs for the thirty-six bathroom doors at Cluny Hill College. I was part of the Cluny housekeeping group, and it was murder trying to describe to one another which bathroom needed what. So someone got the brilliant idea of naming each bathroom after a flower or herb. (I was part of the bathroom-naming group, too.) Then I made the signs with a drawing of the honored plant and its name, and posted it on the door.

As a result of my being in the Cluny housekeeping group, I developed (with nature) the Energy Cleansing Process. After each Saturday cleaning blitz, we housekeepers would meet in the Cluny sanctuary, and I would lead them through the Energy Cleansing Process. This was the final thing we would do to/for the building before the new week's guests arrived.

I also created Clyde Hornblower, the inept but good-hearted angel who became famous in the annual Findhorn angel/mortal game held at Christmastime. Clyde had botched so many past games that he was now on probation and would have to prove himself worthy if he was to continue with the game in future years.

The idea of this game is that everyone who wants to play throws his/her name into a bowl two weeks before Christmas. Then each person draws a name. You are now the angel to the person whose name you drew (your mortal). The angel is supposed to do nice things for his/her mortal for the next two weeks without the mortal discovering the identity of his/her angel. It makes for a lot of clandestine activity for two weeks. My mortal's husband (family members and friends could participate in the "web of deception") told me that she had a good sense of humor and that her hot water bottle was kept in the bathroom next to their room at Cluny. Then he smiled conspiratorially. I figured my mortal was into practical jokes, so I invented Clyde Hornblower.

Each day, Clyde came up with some whacky scheme that he was *sure* would please his mortal—except that he always somehow failed to pull it off. One day he gave her a packet of cookies, but when his mortal unwrapped them, she found them crushed to dust because Clyde had missed his landing approach as he flew in to Cluny and had fallen on his butt, thus inadvertently crushing the cookies that had been in his back pocket. He changed the sheets on her bed for her, but couldn't find clean sheets—so he used a bunch of towels. In his enthusiasm, he bought her flowers three weeks before the game even started, so they were a smidge dead when he left them for her. He crowned her "Queen for the Day" and made a lovely, elaborate breakfast for her that he left on a tray in the dining room with a fine toilet paper trail from her napkin ring to the tray so she wouldn't miss it. Unfortunately, he made the breakfast about six hours before she arrived. It was a bit cold and curdled.

You get the gist of this. Clyde tried the whole two weeks. Each day he left her a note with a story about his adventures around the latest attempt. Clyde's notes came to be a daily feature in the Cluny dining room. A large group would gather around my mortal's table while she read Clyde's latest installment. Everyone knew who Clyde was, except my mortal. They were all telling me when she would be out of her room or busy at a meeting or away in town for the afternoon so that Clyde could strike. One day at the daily reading, my mortal announced that Clyde had to be a *male* community member because no one but a member could play the game that well, and only a man could have this kind of sense of humor. She also decided that Clyde was really her best friend, because no one else but this friend could know her that well.

On Christmas day, all the angels were to give a small gift to their mortals and, in the accompanying card, reveal their identity. Clyde had become so endearing to all of us that I didn't want to "kill him off" by admitting that I was her angel. So I wrote her a note saying that for two weeks I had been "possessed" by this strange angel, and, I had been told, this entity was now before some angel review board. They would determine if he would be allowed to play the game again. He knew he "goofed" on a few things, but he hoped she had liked some of his efforts. He asked me to give her this last gift: a very nice, *undamaged* book on herbs.

When she read the card aloud, the expression on her face was priceless. She was *convinced* that her good friend was Clyde. She could not believe I, a female and not a member, could be this angel. Her face dropped. We all could tell she was scrambling mentally to put together this new reality—and she was having difficulty. Everyone was laughing. She and I ended up having lunch together that day, and we decided that old Clyde was not to "die." In fact, he "visited" her one last time (just before I left) to let her know that he had passed the board's review and that he would be allowed to play the game next year. In celebration, he left another gift in the dining room. She arrived to find a sandwich. The two pieces of bread were spread with a half-inch thick slab of butter with whole peanuts smashed down into it—Clyde's version of a peanut butter sandwich.

One other significant thing happened while I was at Findhorn. The schedule for our program included one week devoted to nature and gardening. It was to be led by members of the gardening group. Just before that week, one of our leaders asked me if I'd like to talk to the group about my gardening experiences. During group discussions over the previous weeks, they had caught on that I had finished an unusual year in my garden. I said, "Sure." It was a casual offer and an equally casual acceptance. She suggested that I write an outline of the things I wanted to talk about and said she'd be happy to go over the outline with me, if I wished. She said I should plan to speak for about an hour.

For the first time, I sat down and wrote an outline of the things that had happened to me in the garden that summer. When I saw the whole thing on paper, I was overwhelmed by the extent of the experiences—and I cried.

I met with the focalizer to go over what I was going to say. Actually, we sat in a broom closet while I went through the outline. She was a smoker, and smoking was prohibited everywhere in Cluny but the bar—and, apparently, broom closets. We wanted more privacy than the bar could give us. As I talked through my gardening year, she smoked with more intensity. She kept saying something like, "I don't believe this." Finally, after over two hours, we stumbled out of the closet, surrounded by a thick cloud of smoke. She told me I'd probably need three hours to say everything, and that I could have the morning of the first day of nature week to talk about the Perelandra garden.

I was quite nervous that morning, but I launched into the adventure of my garden. I wasn't able to finish in the three hours, so my group-mates *insisted* that I continue the next morning. (We had group discussions in the mornings only. During the afternoons, we worked.) The next morning I arrived to find several of the gardeners sitting in our group. They had heard about what I was saying and decided they wanted to hear for themselves. They had never experienced anything like the things I was talking about. I still didn't finish the second morning. In fact, I had just gotten through manifestation. (I omitted the Vegas trip.) So, they gave me the next morning, too. More gardeners joined. In all, it took me nine hours to describe what had happened in the Perelandra garden. When I got to the last part about putting the garden to bed, I couldn't go on. It had been just a few weeks prior that I had experienced that special time with nature. I had to leave the room and be alone. I kept wondering over and over what in the world I was doing at Findhorn.

I arrived home from Findhorn in mid-March physically and emotionally drained. Once I spoke publicly about the Perelandra garden, I became a "nature intelligence expert" in the community and was much in demand as a guest speaker in just about every group meeting imaginable. I felt the responsible thing to do was to accept all invitations and to share my experiences and lessons as openly and honestly as possible. After all, I had been given this tremendous gift from nature. I *owed* it to nature to give something back by sharing what nature had given me.

In actuality, I needed a business manager—some cigar-chewing guy from Brooklyn named Sol who would take me under his wing and say things like, "Listen, doll. Ya can't keep goin' through life respondin' to everybody else's beck and call. You'll end up killin' yourself."

By the time I got back to Perelandra, I felt I had turned myself inside out. I literally could not look at the garden. Instead, I stayed inside the house for several weeks and worried that perhaps I had spoken too much. Even though it made no sense to me, I wondered if nature preferred I had kept my mouth shut. I even questioned if my actions had violated some trust, and as a result my connection with nature would end.

Of course, I didn't bother asking nature about any of this. That would have been too reasonable and too easy. Instead, I stewed about it. Ironically, at the same time I was going through all of this hand-wringing, I felt the most loving, healing support from nature. It was as if the intelligences had created a platform right under my feet that stayed with me no matter where I walked. Wherever I moved, nature was with me—and I could feel it. And their support was completely free. There were no strings attached—no desires, wishes, hopes or urges for me to talk with them. They were just there for me.

My energy gradually returned after several weeks. With it came my confidence, and I began the new year's garden—with nature.

This garden was completely different from the first. As usual, nature told me what to plant and where. But once everything was planted, they told me not to do anything else for the garden for the rest of the season, except harvest. Also, each day I was to walk down all the rows and observe. They didn't say what to observe, just to do it. I thought they were crazy, quite frankly.

To guarantee that I not fiddle with the garden, they told me to prepare and erect the Native American tipi that we had just purchased. It was an eighteen-foot-in-diameter, canvas, Sioux tipi in kit form—meaning that I had to sew the pieces together, and cut and prepare about sixteen or seventeen poles. You haven't lived until you've sewn fifty-six-foot zigzag seams through three layers of heavy-duty canvas. I sat with my sewing machine on the kitchen floor and opened the kitchen door so that, as I sewed the seams, the canvas would slide across the linoleum floor and out the door.

Straight pine trees make the best tipi poles. We didn't have the right pine, so we had to use young oak trees. They needed to be four to six inches in diameter at the base and about twenty-five feet long. Once cut, they needed to cure for a couple of weeks, then the bark had to be removed. I didn't have a draw knife—a knife that is especially made for such jobs that has a handle on both ends of the blade—so I used a regular large butcher knife. Because I used oak, I needed to sand the poles to give them the proper smooth surface. When rain hits a good tipi pole, it forms rivulets on the underside that stream down to the base of the pole. That's the ingenious way the Native Americans kept water from pouring in. But the whole system requires a smooth pole. So, for the sake of the system, I sanded and sanded and sanded. By the time I finished, I was convinced that the circumference of a tipi pole was eternity.

The entire job took me ten weeks. In September, Clarence and I raised the tipi together. I had read that the Native Americans of old could erect their tipis in twenty minutes. It took us days. I set up the interior in the traditional manner, complete with fire pit. It was such a magical, beautiful, quiet, peaceful place that I slept in it every night throughout the fall and winter.

Each day during the summer weeks, I'd take a break from the Great Tipi Project and stroll along the rows in the garden. To be honest, the garden looked like hell. Weeds were growing everywhere. Some plants were overrun with insects. And some plants could not have looked happier. I had no idea what was going on. When I asked for a hint from nature, they'd say, "You'll see." Throughout the summer, we had a number of visitors from Findhorn who stopped by to see the "famous" Perelandra garden. They'd look at this mess and say things like, "Gee. I know a fellow who is a really fine gardener. Maybe you'd like to talk to him. I'll give you his number." Instead of taking my cue from nature and replying that this is what nature wanted me to do this year, and trust that it would eventually make sense to me, I told them what I *thought* was going on. Of course, I was completely off base.

Unlike the previous year, I was pretty happy to put this garden to bed. As winter approached, I still didn't know what it was all about. But I was at peace in my tipi, diligently learning how to make a smokeless fire in my pit.

1979

As winter moved into spring, the tipi shifted from a Native American experience to a Perelandra nature sanctuary. I changed the interior layout to reflect this by bringing in specific objects from the woods according to what nature was telling me.

I also began to have unusual experiences in the tipi. One morning, Clarence was calling—actually yelling—to me from outside the front door flap. I heard him and asked what he wanted, and why he was yelling. He said he had been calling me for a good twenty minutes or so, and I wasn't responding. (I guess he thought I was dead and didn't want to see for himself.) I had not heard him calling at all, and I realized that I had been "off someplace," but I had no idea where that was. The whole incident scared me a little.

Then there was the night I was lying in the tipi watching the stars through the smoke hole. All of a sudden, I was consumed by fear. It was fear that wasn't attached to anything specific, so there wasn't any logic to it. The fear intensified, and I spent the entire night wide awake, huddled in my sleeping bag. I was shivering from fright and sweating at the same time. The odd thing is, I knew I was okay, and that this was something I just had to get through. In the morning, I was drenched in cold sweat. I went on about my day as usual.

The garden was back to having order. Nature was giving me all kinds of different input about what needed to be planted where and how to tend to everything throughout the season. Just after the garden was planted, it dawned on me what the previous year had been all about. It was a fact-finding year. Nature had me plant the garden, then back away so that it (nature) and I could observe what happens to that garden's balance when left on its own within a specific environment. While nature was doing an environmental impact study, I was watching the results of the study playing out in the garden. So now, as I moved into the new garden, I understood why nature was making so many changes and what was behind the changes.

In the spring, I intuitively sensed that I needed to dedicate myself to taking the next step with nature. I didn't know what the next step was, but I knew I was not supposed to ask. I was simply supposed to decide if I wanted to go on, then announce my decision. I thought it over a bit. I didn't see any reason to back away from this adventure. So, one afternoon in the tipi, I announced that I wanted to go on to the next step. It was as simple as that.

In midsummer, I was told to move the garden from its present location beside the house to an open-field area four hundred feet away. It was to be done by the next gardening season. Well. Moving a garden is a chore. I didn't know how I was going to break the news to Clarence (I'd need his help), so I didn't say anything for several weeks. Then one day, as Clarence and I were returning from a walk, he looked right at the "proposed" new site and said, "You know, that's a much better location for the garden." Sensing an advantageous moment, I told him about the move. He said that in the fall we could get one of the local farmers to come plow the field for the new garden.

That winter, I received instructions from nature for constructing a sanctuary on the tipi site that was loosely modeled after the tipi design. It was to have eight sides, six feet high. Using this as a base, we were to build an eight-sided fiberglass roof that came together in the center at a point. The point was to be capped in copper, with copper wires running from the cap down the corners of the fiberglass roof and to the ground. The structure was to have a wooden floor that covered the fire-pit area, but the pit was to remain unchanged in the ground. On the floor directly over the fire-pit area, I was to place square slate pieces in the shape of a celtic cross. Nature then gave me a detailed list of what was to go on each slate slab. The new sanctuary was to be completed by and activated on the following summer solstice. I winced when I gave Clarence this information. He winced too. But we started making plans for the construction of this new sanctuary. (Are we troopers, or what?)

1980

"The next step" moved me from a private, family-oriented gardener seeking to work in partnership with nature within that garden to a co-creative nature researcher using a garden as her laboratory. Much of my efforts in 1980 were centered around getting the new garden in place and settled. It was three times larger than the old one and consisted of eighteen concentric circles—the last of which was one hundred feet in diameter. Clarence built a small shed/office for me, and I worked every weekday from the time he left Perelandra in late morning until sundown—sometimes longer.

On weekends, Clarence and I worked on the new sanctuary. It was positioned right on the spot where the tipi had been. It was a difficult structure to build because of its unusual shape. Slowly, and with a great deal of work and effort, we got the thing up in time for the summer solstice. It just so happened that Peter Caddy was in town that week. By this time we were friends, so I asked him if he would like to "officiate" at the activation of our sanctuary. He not only eagerly accepted but showed up with a couple of friends to help witness the moment. As we walked into the sanctuary, Peter stopped at the door, turned and said to me, "*This* is where the Pan/Christ* energies will come together." I had no idea what he was talking about.

That summer, my father died. Over the past ten years, we had struck an uneasy truce. Among other things, we agreed that he would never understand my life (I hadn't told him *anything* about my nature work; he was basing his decision on the fact that I had long hair, was unmarried, lived with Clarence in the woods and didn't even have a garbage disposal, for god's sake), and I certainly would never understand his life. I did not make it to his funeral. Instead, I was in New York City following his instructions about what to do with a safe deposit box that was supposed to be loaded with money. However, there was a broken combination lock on the office safe that held the key to the safe deposit box. I ended up spending all afternoon dealing with this situation. Meanwhile, Clarence was in Connecticut attending the funeral along with a handful of assorted, and sometimes hysterical, family members and several gentlemen from the Mafia—Isadore's golfing buddies. (By the way, there was nothing in the safe deposit box but a large stack

---

* "Pan/Christ" is the ancient metaphysical term used to describe what I now call "the involution/evolution dynamic." Involution or Pan is the dynamic of grounding and coming into form. "Evolution" or "christ" are used to describe the dynamic of moving forward. In this instance, "christ" does not refer to the historical figure named Jesus Christ.

of empty, used envelopes, paper clips and rubber bands. He had lost all the money gambling.)

I inherited some money from Isadore. Not a fortune, mind you, but enough for Perelandra and us to be a bit more financially stable. Clarence and I were grateful. We celebrated by getting a used lawn tractor. We were in heaven.

In the fall, a woman who I had met at Findhorn visited. She told me about this space soul she was hooked up to and about some of the adventures she had had as a result. The adventures sounded pretty goofy to me, but the space soul sounded kind of neat. She asked me if I'd like to get hooked up. I said, "Sure." She said she'd have to ask if it was okay with the space soul, and, if so, she'd assist him as he inserted a gold disk in my forehead. Right in front of me, she connected with this guy and asked him if he'd like to be connected with me. Apparently, he said, "Yes," because in less than five minutes, I was in the sanctuary with this woman getting a gold disk implanted in my forehead. I actually felt an object enter my head. The woman then drew a pattern on a piece of paper and told me that I could connect with this fellow any time by visualizing the pattern. The pattern activated the disk. The space soul's name was Hyper-ithon (pronounced: hi-pear'-eh-thon).

For about five days, I couldn't stop thinking about that pattern. You know how someone says to you not to think about a specific word, and all you can do from that point on is think about that word? That's how it was with me and that damn pattern. And every time I pictured it, this space soul would suddenly be saying hello to me. I'd apologize for the disturbance—again—and he'd laugh. Then we'd disconnect. I never said anything beyond an apology to him. I just couldn't think of anything to talk over with him. Eventually, I stopped accidentally "dialing his phone number," and I basically forgot about him—for two years. [comma]

1981

This was a relatively calm year. Clarence continued working the second shift at Xerox, and there were no major construction projects facing us. Basically, life had settled into a nice rhythm for both of us.

I concentrated on the garden and my work with nature, and we began developing many of the processes that I eventually wrote about in the *Perelandra Garden Workbook*. Nature showed me how to set up a coning—an interlevel energy vortex that contains balance between the involution and evolution dynamics—and I began to have all my nature sessions while in conings. I also began fine-tuning the translation process of long tracts of interlevel information. My days were long, but peaceful.

Early in the spring, a friend of mine visited, and as I showed her the garden, she stopped, looked at me, and said, "You ought to write a book about this. I think you ought to call it *Behaving As If the God In All Life Mattered*." As soon as she said that, I knew exactly what was to go in that book. It was as if all the information entered my head, and I was suddenly walking around with a book inside me.

I have to say, however, that I didn't take this moment too gracefully. The last thing I wanted to do was write a book. For one thing, I felt people were reading too much about all this kind of stuff and not doing enough with the information. I certainly did not want to add to the prevailing couch-potato syndrome. Plus, the idea of writing a book seemed like a pretty laborious task that no sane person would take on. (I was still under the impression that I was sane at this time.)

Despite my misgivings, I began to write *Behaving* in midsummer, and finished the first draft by that October.

Clarence was working with a fellow at Xerox whose mother worked at Harper and Row Publishers—the publishers of the Findhorn books. She was willing to have me send her my manuscript and see to it that someone actually looked at it. I took this as a good omen.

About three months later, I received the manuscript back with a note from the mother saying that the editors felt my book was not saying anything new and that I couldn't write a book that was in a story format in the first half and an essay format in the second half. Along with my returned manuscript and this critique, the mother sent a gift—a copy of a book titled *How to Happily Self-Publish*.

She didn't say I *should* self-publish. In fact, I couldn't figure out if she was saying that the book was good and I should get it published no matter what, or the book was so bad that the only way I could get it published was to do it myself. For some reason that has long since been lost in the recesses of my mind, I decided that she was telling me to go for it and self-publish the book. I sat on the manuscript for about a year while I read up on self-publishing and pondered my next move.

1982

I moved into this year with two instructions from nature: (1) Set up an office in the house; (2) Take an R&R. The ease with which I would face the near future depended on my doing these two things during the first six to nine months of this year. My focus in the spring was to remain on planting the garden. I was not to think beyond this.

Setting up my office and taking an R&R actually went well together. I was one of those kids who loved getting new supplies at the beginning of each school year. You know—buying just the right notebook and pens, and setting up the notebook *perfectly*. Then, going to school that first day with everything nice and clean and organized. What a hopeful time it was for me. I had a ball setting up an office in one of our spare bedrooms. The adult got to go back to school—big time!

My only problem was that I had no idea why I was creating an office or what work I was going to put in it. I kept notes about the garden work and sessions I had with nature, which I stored in my closet and in the garden shed. It was just a couple of boxes—so it seemed. When I found out that I had enough papers to fill a two-drawer filing cabinet, I was surprised. In fact, once I pulled everything out of the hidden-away corners, I had a pretty full office.

Around March, emotional issues concerning my relationship with Clarence began to surface. Not only was I not talking to him about what I was doing with nature, he was also not "asking." In the earlier years, while he didn't verbalize any questions, I still felt a deep heart support from him. I sensed that we could sit down together

any time and get into a lively conversation about what was going
on. The fact that we weren't doing this didn't mean that he wasn't
right there with me. But now I wasn't feeling this. It seemed to me
that over the previous year or so, he had backed away and had
begun moving in a different direction that was separate and distinct
from mine, one that didn't require my presence.

At the same time, I was feeling the need for more emotional support. As my work with nature intensified, my need for emotional
support also intensified. The only problem was that Clarence was no
longer there. As a result, I felt alone and lonely.

We had a handful of friends who knew I was doing this work with
nature, but none of them ever wanted to hear about it even in the
most casual context. In fact, I felt that they preferred I never mention it for fear that some of it might rub off and make them "crazy,"
too. We'd all go out to dinner together, and everyone would talk
about what new and exciting things were happening to them—until
it came to my turn. Then everyone would shut up or quickly change
the subject.

It was a terribly painful time for me. I tried to reach out to nature
for the kind of emotional support that I needed, but that never fully
solved the problem. I seriously considered ending my ten-year
partnership with Clarence, but I kept sensing that, even with this, we
still belonged together. I just didn't know why. I even thought about
filling the emotional void by having a clandestine affair or two, but
this seemed too complicated and like too much work. Besides, I
didn't want to divert my attention away from the nature research.

I cried a lot—for weeks, it seemed. I said nothing to Clarence
about what I was thinking because it seemed to me that this was *my*
issue, not his. Finally, I made a decision. I would stay with Clarence
and continue my work with nature alone. I accepted that I would
live out my life without personal, loving support, and that this was
okay. It's what I had to do for this lifetime, but it didn't mean that I
wouldn't experience it in some future lifetime.

I am not giving you a bunch of details about this because it was
such a personal time for me. However, I'll tell you that by the time I
made my decision—which took about six weeks—I was completely
drained, emotionally and physically. I was also completely in the

dark about my personal life. I didn't know where this partnership with Clarence was leading—I only knew that it was right for me to keep it together. If he wished to end it, he'd have to come to that conclusion on his own. Although he was focused on his own personal direction, he was giving me no indication that he wanted to end the relationship.

My partnership was now no longer first in my life. [comma]

Turning my attention back to the garden for spring preparations and planting was a healing experience for me. The more I focused on the garden, the more my life made sense. And gradually I strengthened both emotionally and physically.

In late April, I attended a Feldenkrais* "Awareness through Movement" Workshop given by one of the top Israeli teachers. I didn't really feel like going, but this man's reputation was so special and his presence in our area was so unusual, that I couldn't pass up the opportunity. I was lucky enough to get a private lesson with him, as well. On the day of my appointment, I drove with several friends who also had appointments to the house where he was staying. My session was incredible—worth all the effort, time and money it took for me to have the experience.

But something else happened that was equally extraordinary—if not more so. The Feldenkrais teacher gave his private lessons in the home of friends with whom he was staying during his Washington visit. Those of us who came for lessons waited on a balcony. At one point, I was alone on the balcony, reading a book and enjoying the beautiful early spring day, when the woman whose house we were in joined me. I didn't know her, but before we could even engage in small talk, she sat next to me, held both of my hands in hers, looked me right in the eye, and said calmly, "I am a camp survivor." I was so taken off guard that I had no idea what she was talking about at first. Then, from the look in her eyes, I realized she meant she was a

* The Feldenkrais Method was developed by physicist, judo master, athlete, mechanical engineer and educator Moshe Feldenkrais, D.Sc. It is an educational method for improving the function of the body and the state of mind. It is a unique approach to feeling better, moving better and performing better. Gentle lessons explore and improve the quality of habitual daily actions and bring about new movement skills and coordination. Results are better dynamic posture, greater ease of movement, new movement possibilities, increased flexibility and the awakening of inner vitality.

survivor of the concentration camps. She continued speaking in a calm, soft manner: "They don't know what to do with us. They don't know what to do with us." Each time, she emphasized the words. Then she said softly, "Our experience has moved us beyond therapy they have to offer, and none of the doctors know how to help us. They can't even hear what we tell them." She smiled at me in such a way that made me feel completely connected to her, squeezed my hands, then left to go back into the house.

I sat quietly, thinking about what she had said. First of all, I wondered how she knew I was Jewish. I didn't think a survivor would say these things to a non-Jew. Then I thought about what she had *really* said to me. She was telling me that there were some experiences a human can have that are beyond the ability of anyone else in society to comprehend or assist with. That it is possible for us to experience something so outside the realm of the prevailing reality that the experience itself effectively removes us from that society.

As wonderful as the experience was, I don't know how much I actually learned in the Feldenkrais lesson, but the echo of the woman's words stayed with me a long time. [comma]

One morning in early May, Clarence and I were having lunch at a local diner with an acquaintance. We started talking about Paris. This fellow reminisced about a trip he had taken to Paris years before, and that got me thinking about how much I missed Paris— just like the songs say. I mentioned this to the two men, and they both said right away, "Well, why don't you go back?" I hemmed and hawed a bit, and they urged me to take a trip back to Paris by myself. I started laughing at the absurdity of resisting a trip to Paris. Finally I said, "Alright. I'll do it!" I decided I would go in the fall for ten days—alone. [comma]

In late June, I scanned the *TV Guide* for something semi-decent to watch. I had spent a long day in the garden, and I wanted to be entertained—even mildly—while I ate dinner. My attention was immediately drawn to a movie miniseries based on Dwight Eisenhower's war years. It was a three-parter and a repeat. The first time it aired, I could not have been less interested. Now, despite the fact that I didn't think a movie on Eisenhower's war years could be entertaining in any way, I felt *compelled* to watch.

I had an odd reaction to this movie. I kept shouting at the screen things like, "That isn't what happened! You've botched the story!" The movie infuriated me. Yet, each night, I diligently watched—and each night I ranted and raved. Now, I have to say that I was beginning to question my sanity again. I had never reacted so viscerally and vocally to a TV program before. Plus, I was getting into a flap about an historical period I knew nothing about. How in the world did I know they were using full creative license with this story? [comma]

For you to understand the full absurdity of my response to the movie, I need to confess the somewhat amazing relationship I have with history. I was an Honor Society student in high school, which took a lot of work to achieve since I suffered from dyslexia. But grasping history—memorizing all those dates, names and places, and figuring out the significance of events—overwhelmed me. In my high school world history class, the teacher gave us a test at the beginning of the year to discover how much we already knew about the subject. I scored 23 on the test—the lowest mark. At the end of the year, he gave us the same test to see how much we had learned. I scored 67. Despite the fact that I had failed the test again, he gave me a B for the year and announced to all that I was the person who had learned the most because I had improved my score more than anyone. When I was taking classes at George Washington University, I took the required World History 1 course during the fall semester. My final grade was C. I worked very hard for that C. The next semester I made a mistake and signed up for World History 1 again, thinking I was signing up for World History 2. I sat through the entire semester, took notes, took all the exams, and didn't recognize that I was hearing the same information a second time. Not one thing sounded familiar. Again, I got a C. I didn't know I had made this mistake until I cleaned out some old boxes after moving to Perelandra and found my school records and class notes.

So, here I am, telling this TV screen that it is misrepresenting events from World War II. At the end of the third evening, I noticed in the credits that the movie was based on a book. I copied down the title and author, and gave the note to Clarence when he got home that evening. I asked him to pick up the book at the library on his way to work the next day. I was determined to rectify the misconceptions of the movie and prove my gut instincts to be correct by reading this book. [comma]

Clarence handed me the book the next evening, and I stayed up all night reading. When I finished, I couldn't say I was now an expert on World War II, but I did have another odd reaction. When I closed the book and put it down, I saw an old, arched wooden door inside my chest—just like the door I had seen open when I learned about reincarnation. Only this time, the door didn't open slowly. Instead, it *blasted* open, as if someone with a great deal of power had kicked it. The sensation startled me, and I felt a physical ripping sensation as the door bolted open. It was not pleasant, by any means. Instantly, I began to think about Eisenhower. It was as if I suddenly knew him. Not only that, I felt as if I knew him in a warm, familial, personal context. The whole experience scared me, and I backed away fast, choosing to focus on my day instead.

I couldn't get Eisenhower out of my mind, no matter how hard I tried. Instead of rolling with the thoughts and discovering what was going on, I resisted them. I didn't know what all of this was leading to, but I sure didn't like it one bit. I didn't have much respect for people who claimed they were connected with famous dead people and then used this connection to further their own status. To me, it was a cheap trick to gain fame and fortune off someone else's accomplishments, and no one could prove or disprove the claims. This was exactly the kind of situation I wanted to avoid at any cost—and now here it was, sitting in my lap.

The constant flow of thoughts combined with my efforts to resist them were so shattering and set up a tension that was so great in me that I began to cry every time I was alone—and I didn't stop for three weeks. Finally, I realized that this wasn't a situation that was going to dissipate on its own, nor was it something I was going to be able to cry through. In fact, if I was going to stop crying and get on with the rest of my life, I was going to need help.

That's when I remembered Hyperithon. I had not talked to him in two years, so he couldn't accuse me of pestering him. Maybe he could give me some insight on what was going on. I felt a little shy about "dialing his number" after all this time, but he "answered" with that same cheerful "Hi!" I had grown accustomed to two years ago. I reintroduced myself, just in case he had forgotten me. He assured me he knew who I was, and then, to my surprise, he said he could help me with this Eisenhower situation. He'd be glad to answer any questions I might have.

I first asked him if I had lost my mind. He stated flat out that I had not. So, there I was, asking some invisible space soul if I was sane—and I actually felt comforted by his answer!

I asked him if what I was perceiving about Eisenhower was accurate. I then gave him a brief description of my perceptions. He listened and said it was accurate. This meant I had some past connection with this dead, famous fellow, and that did *not* comfort me.

Hyperithon asked if I'd like him to give me an overview of what was happening to me. I said "yes."

He confirmed that I had been linked with Eisenhower as an aide and assistant in several lifetimes, the last being World War II. I did not have special military knowledge, nor did I have any extensive military training. Our connection was not that of military peers. Instead, it was more personal. I was a minor aide and, eventually, a friend who functioned as part of his military support staff in these different lifetimes. I didn't give him the benefit of expertise. Instead, I was someone who could listen, and someone who he could trust and with whom he could relax.

Hyperithon ended by saying: *Your relationship in World War II with the soul you know as Eisenhower was one of clarity, closeness and strength. As you have touched into his life through the movie and book, it is most natural that these things be remembered by you. Dynamics between people—more accurately, between souls—are not lost or forgotten. But it is only his high accomplishments as the military leader that attract you, because that is the part of his soul journey you have experienced. His presidency and his relationship with his family are all experiences outside your relationship. Therefore, they sound none of your chords.*

This was all I could absorb for the moment, and I wanted to know nothing more. At least it was enough to stop me from all that crying. However, it wasn't enough to stop the flow of Eisenhower thoughts. And I still felt discomfort about all of this.

Five days later, on July 28, I asked Hyperithon for more information.

*I understand the difficulty you are having with what you are presently learning. It is never easy to significantly expand one's working knowledge about life. Some of the emotions you feel are your reactions to moving within life on a much more expansive level. You are not consciously used to balancing and absorbing so many aspects of life at one time. But you must realize that you are quite capable of doing this. You have been trained. You have evolved into this. Again, the discomfort you feel has to do with seeing these various aspects of life **consciously** come together into one whole. The sense of inner stretch you feel comes from **consciously** dealing with the interrelationship of the past, present and future in an experiential, grounded manner. In essence, you are experiencing the grounding of a higher, more complete, spiritual concept, and finding out that the more conventional, seemingly more "grounded" way of looking at relationships (i.e., in a linear manner within the context of one's present lifetime) is no longer appropriate....*

Finally, he suggested that I relax as much as possible and allow my thoughts to surface and commingle at their own pace. If I let this happen, I would release a lot of the stress I was presently feeling.

I decided not to try to figure anything out. I would follow Hyperithon's suggestions to relax and let things surface on their own. I would not try to make anything come up nor would I try to understand anything. I figured that eventually things would come together, and I'd know what was going on—just like in the garden. Or, things would not come together, and I'd fall apart and start crying again. If the latter happened, I'd call Hyperithon for help. In the meantime, I would try to get on with my life as best I could for a person who was now constantly inundated with thoughts about Dwight Eisenhower.

Almost at the same time all of this was going on, I began to get a strange urge to have my hair cut. Not only that, I wanted to get a permanent to make it curly. I had not been to a hairdresser in over twenty years, and I had worn my hair long and straight for about fifteen years. It wasn't that I had an emotional attachment to long, straight hair. My grandmother (on my mother's side) was Native American, and about the only trait I inherited from her was hair that refused to curl. So, I never bothered fighting this—until now. I looked at hair styles in magazines, on TV and on passing heads. I found a picture of a style I liked, so I cut it out and, on a sweltering August afternoon, I presented it and myself at a local hair salon. [comma] When I walked out, I looked like a completely different person. Clarence didn't even recognize me!

On September 16, I wrote a letter to a friend of mine from the old Findhorn days.

> ...I am now on the last leg of what looks to be a four-year cycle. I knew I was coming out of something and going on to something different when I was "told" in January to go on a sabbatical this year and basically rest at Perelandra until the fall. I was to pay attention to the quality of my rest because the next stage depended on it. So, like a good kid, I hid out at Perelandra doing my nature spirit and deva thing. To complete the process, I'm leaving Monday (September 20) to spend ten days alone in Paris—an entirely different environment, and one that I love—where I can't expect to function as a nature researcher. I feel that these ten days will be the icing on my "sabbatical cake." Then I will return to Perelandra and move into the new. . . .

On September 17, I awoke in the night with such an intense pain in the left side of my chest that I couldn't move or call out to Clarence for help. All I could do was lie as still as possible and focus on trying to breathe. I assumed I was having a heart attack. The pain was beyond anything I had ever felt. However, I noticed that it was localized in one specific part of my body—the left side of my chest—and was not affecting or moving into any other part. I didn't have pain shooting down my left arm or into the right side of my chest. Based on these observations, I decided I was not having a heart attack, and only needed to ride this thing out—whatever it was. I estimate that I was in pain for about twenty or thirty minutes.

Then the pain quickly subsided, and I drifted back to sleep. The next morning I told Clarence that I thought I had had a heart attack in the night. He looked at me, then said, "I don't think so. You're still alive." And that was the end of that. [comma]

I left for Paris on September 20. It was the most wonderful personal ten days I had experienced in a long time. I stayed at the little hotel I had stayed in during my previous two trips. It was still run by the same family. I found a wonderful tiny restaurant just about three blocks away where I went for dinner every night. After about my third evening, the staff "assigned" me my own table that was complete with an ashtray for propping up the books I read during dinner. I did nothing cultural or significant during these ten days. In fact, I window shopped. Now, I *never* window shop. But during this trip, it was all I wanted to do. I would go into these extravagantly expensive shops and look around, pretending I had money. I walked all over Paris, visited cafes, watched traffic roll by on busy streets. One afternoon I sat in a cafe near the Arc de Triomphe and watched tourists and traffic avoid one another. I made it a point to have a pastry and espresso every day. Another afternoon, as I was stuffing my face with the day's pastry delight, I said to myself, "I'm *really* having a good time!" Not once did I think about Perelandra or Eisenhower.

I had one piece of business to take care of, however. The fall equinox fell on September 23, at around 10:30 A.M. This is nature's "new year," and each year, at the precise moment of the equinox, I call in the new cycle for Perelandra and for me. On the morning of the 23rd, I set out to find *the* spot in a Paris park where it felt appropriate for me to be during the equinox. After a bit of walking around, I ended up at a park right off the Avenue des Champs Elysées. It just so happened that there was a dahlia show going on in this park. Consequently, every garden was filled with blooming dahlias. It was an amazing sight. Dahlia colors are so vibrant and clear, and this park was literally pulsating with color. I found one garden I especially liked and stood in front of it waiting for the equinox time. I happened to look down at my feet several times. I wasn't looking at anything in particular—it was just something to do to pass the time. At the moment of the equinox, I looked at the large dahlia display in front of me and quietly called for the next cycle for both Perelandra and me. That was all I said. I never try to define what that next cycle will be; I let the future take care of itself. I felt the equinox energy pass through me. I stood quietly for several minutes longer, then looked down at my feet again. Right between them was a chestnut that I knew had not been there a few minutes ago. I figured it was nature's verification that the equinox "took," so I picked up the nut and put it in my jacket pocket. [comma] Then I headed to find just the right pastry to celebrate the New Year with.

Chapter 3

A Divine Release of the Soul from the Yoke of Custom and Convention

—Socrates

I returned to Perelandra resolved to settle the Eisenhower thing so that I could get on with my life.

I figured Hyperithon was my best bet for getting some answers. Plus, in our earlier sessions, he sounded like he knew something about what was going on. On October 12, I called him. Right up front, I asked if the experience I had been going through the past two and a half months around the Eisenhower situation was one of "growth and correctness," or was it one that "negated growth and balance" for either me or the Eisenhower soul. In short, I wanted the cards put on the table. Using my own words, he verified that my experience was one of growth and correctness. Then he went on to say that the opportunity before me was mutually beneficial to both me and Eisenhower, and that Eisenhower was creating a professional family in which he (Eisenhower) hoped I would participate.

Hyperithon continued by explaining how social mores and expectations that have nothing to do with a person or soul can interfere with development. When we take on patterns that are established and passed down by souls whose development is different from our own—mores and pressures that have nothing to do with us—it is not only inappropriate, but it can render our souls impotent. The energy one absorbs through incompatible social mores and expectations surrounds the individual with a debilitating fog. The key to functioning as a fully potent human being lies in the individual's ability to shed inappropriate energies and to return to his own sense of balance. In order for me to move with the opportunity that lay before me, I would have to cast off all such discordant patterns.

He said that Eisenhower and I were "soul friends" and that we had a strong bond that formed over several lifetimes. It was this bond that drew me to his funeral, for I was one of the souls there supporting his transition. We had worked a number of lifetimes as a team and could reconnect, if I so desired, in areas concerning work and "pure soul development." My knowledge of various disciplines allowed me to transcend levels easily and well. This enabled me to experience and grow by utilizing more options available to those on and around Earth. I had not gone into this experience blindly, even though it presently felt that way to me. Our reconnection, which occurred at the funeral, had been unconscious until the television movie activated it again and moved it into consciousness.

At this point, Hyperithon suggested that I "speak" with Eisenhower directly, since he had been present with Hyperithon during the entire session. That startled me. Luckily, I did not have time to think about it, or I might have refused the invitation. Instead, I agreed. Eisenhower began speaking immediately by addressing the difficulty I was having with this whole situation. In fact, he commiserated with me, saying that if he were in my shoes, he would have dismissed everything as being too nuts to seriously consider.

While Eisenhower spoke, I "saw" myself standing in a room. I couldn't see him, but I could sure feel his presence in the room. The realization of who I was talking to so disconcerted me that I immediately asked to speak to Hyperithon again. I had my hand on the door knob and was about to bolt, when I turned and said, "Wait. Do I call you 'Eisenhower'?" That got us into a short discussion about names. He explained that he now chose to use the name David, which was the name he had been given at birth. David Dwight Eisenhower. Since his father's name was also David, to avoid confusion everyone in the family called him Dwight. Now he preferred David. By the time we finished this discussion, the ice had been broken, and I was no longer frightened of this man. He was no longer Dwight Eisenhower, former Allied Commander, former U.S.

president and present dead guy. He was now David, the friendly fellow who just happened to be dead.

We ended our conversation, and I refocused my attention back on Hyperithon. That's when I brought up for the first time my fears that I might be fantasizing this whole thing, and that I might be confusing fantasy with reality. I once again talked about my fear of losing my mind. I said, "This is crazy. You *must* know this." He said no, he didn't know this. In fact, for him the opposite was true. This was not crazy, it was an opportunity and it was very real. Then he reminded me that they were looking at this opportunity from a broader perspective than I was. More pieces would come to me to assist with the shift and pattern re-alignment. This would allow me to function in a far more expanded and powerful manner. He assured me that I would be able to deal with more power, that I would do so with balance and care, and that this re-alignment would give me a new dimension of operating.

I asked Hyperithon what advice he could offer to help me more fully understand and participate in what was happening. He said my favorite word in the English language—relax. (Frankly, I think the most *un*relaxing word is "relax.") He also said that I needed to trust. Although what was happening to me was not the "average" occurrence that I observed (*there's* an understatement), it was, nonetheless, reality. And it was an enormous opportunity to explore life on a level far beyond what I could presently imagine. I also had the opportunity to free myself from limitations that were totally unnecessary to me now. The more I understood about human potential, the more I would be willing to let go of karma and function as a spiritualized soul in form.

I asked him one last question: "Does this experience with David disrupt or remove me in any way from the spiritual purpose and path I came into this lifetime to experience?" He told me no, that this was part of that spiritual path and purpose.

I could think of no other way to word another question about correct purpose and reality, so I closed the session feeling fairly satisfied that by continuing to pursue this opportunity, I was doing the right thing.

The next day I was ready for more information, and so I had another session with Hyperithon. He immediately began addressing my drive to "do well" in my life and spoke about it as a dynamic I needed to understand more fully.

When an individual has a *balanced* drive to do well, he uses it to help propel himself along in his journey during those times when he finds it difficult to move. Also, it helps keep him alert and reflective about his own evolution. When this dynamic is *unbalanced*, it can be used as a catalyst to do risky, splashy, even extraordinary things in order to be recognized by others. The motivation for movement shifts from inside the individual to someone or something outside him. For example, he may link his desire to do well with his fear of not being accepted. This will cause him to shift his actions to do well in a way that will ensure that people around him acknowledge his efforts in a positive and accepting way. He has stepped over the line and shifted his motivation to strive for quality to doing something for the purpose of bringing outside recognition to himself. In order to maintain balance, a person must be very clear of his motivation to do well. As a person remains on course, striving to be the best he can be, he will automatically draw to him quality, pure, sincere, encouraging, nurturing recognition.

Hyperithon then went on to talk about my spiritual development over the past two and a half years:

Spiritual potential lies in one's horizontal and vertical actions. It is not just how much you affect others around you (horizontal), it is also how well you connect with and operate in multilevel communication and connection (vertical). Your spiritual potential relates to both "directions." Over the past two and a half years, you have trained and disciplined yourself to connect with and to receive clear, usable information from various levels available to the soul. You have developed your writing, your ability to translate interlevel material, kinesiology and the conings. Now you have both the skills and opportunity to move in a new way. The fact that you are taking this information in presently is the sign that "all systems are go." You have grounded yourself and established the necessary tools needed for this job. Perelandra, the sanctuary, your close communion with nature that serves to support and clarify your physical systems, your new partnership relationship with Clarence, your sources of finance. . . . You cannot possibly look around and not see the evidence of readiness—of achievement.

You are experiencing being on the threshold of change. It is quite difficult to relax during these times because the "threshold of change" means that one is still living out the old patterns but has vision into and is moving toward the new patterns. This makes him anxious to leave the old in order to fulfill his vision of the new. The resulting anxiety takes him out of step with the present and lessens the quality of the intermediate steps one needs to move through in order to enter the vision of the new. Again, relax. . . .

With this session, I started to feel more confident about moving forward. I now knew how to watch out for a potential problem and how to maintain balance so that I would not get snared into the problem in the first place. Hyperithon had given me an overview of what I had done to prepare for this change, and now I felt less like I was hanging in space by my toes. And he also gave me more insight about the difficulties I was experiencing in just dealing with the information I was presently facing.

When I opened another session with Hyperithon the next day, I asked him to address my confusion about overlapping lifetimes. Hyperithon had told me that the person I was in my lifetime with David during World War II did not die until the 1970s. I, Machaelle, was born in 1945. That meant that for about twenty-five years we were both alive and living in the same country. Hyperithon said:

See yourself as the sun. A bright, vibrant, pulsating light sphere that continuously sends out individual rays to gather experiences. Each set of experiences travels from the ray to the sphere, where it becomes part of the total reality of the sphere, part of its memory bank. All the rays going out are equal in their connection with the sphere. No ray is more distant than the next. They are all equi- distant, all "equi-close."

Understanding this phenomenon by allowing yourself to accept the two rays that function within the same time span and under- standing that both rays are but individual reflections of your soul will free you further from the limitations of time and space. This, in turn, will enable your many rays to function with more agility.

By time and space limitations, we don't mean the escape from physicalness. Rather, it is a different reflection of physicalness. Our preconceptions of time and space are directly reflected in the physical reality around us. The broader truth of time and space does not demand that different lifetimes on Earth occur linearly. Once a person releases such notions, nothing is left to stop him from having lunch with another reflection or ray of his own soul—two simultaneous experiences, one might say.

He then added: *As you relate to David, you need not strive in any way to take on or affect any characteristics or mannerisms that you have discovered belong uniquely to your ray in the World War II life. To David, you are all the reflections the two of you have shared in other lifetimes. He recognizes all of these individuals in you. The reverse is equally true. You are not responding only to the Eisenhower part of his soul. You recognize all of the other reflections you have experienced, as well. You both have strong soul connections that have played out on Earth in various lifetimes, and it is the recognition of this closeness that draws you back together consciously at the present.*

*One final thing: Think of the individual soul reflections (soul rays) as part of the larger soul and not limited to a specific lifetime of character traits or patterns. The information each ray experiences is not restricted to that ray. Rather, it flows freely through the soul-center as one organic whole becoming available to all the other rays. An individual has in his **conscious** memory bank twelve lifetime experiences or rays. They did not occur in linear time, making the most recent ray—in your case, the Machaelle ray—the only receiver of benefits of these twelve lifetimes. They are occurring simultaneously and flowing to and from you at all times through the larger soul. You also have benefit of all the other rays, though they are not consciously fixed in the Machaelle memory bank. Be that as it may, they are still you and you are them. It is just that to fully live out the Machaelle ray, you need the specific patterning of the twelve* *lifetime rays you have chosen to be a part of your conscious memory bank. You do not lose all else that is being fed into your soul-center.*

I thought about this session for most of the day. While translating Hyperithon's words onto paper, I also experienced inside my body what he was saying. Consequently, I *felt* this simultaneous lifetime concept more than I intellectually understood it. And as a result, I was more comfortable with the notion that I (in one lifetime) died when I (as Machaelle) was in my mid-twenties.

On the following day, October 16, I connected with Hyperithon again to get information about a bad head cold that had descended on me overnight.

The cold you are experiencing is a clearing out and cleansing as a result of what you are going through with the Eisenhower opportunity. It is not a manifestation of blocking, which has been your concern about this cold. Note that you are releasing mucus easily, not "holding" on to it. When one's reality expands, there comes with it a certain amount of de-crystallization, re-arranging and cleansing. The old is making way for the new. The opportunity facing you is settling in nicely. The cold will not be severe, only inconvenient. You may take vitamin C to help yourself stabilize, if you wish.

He continued: *It is not your fantasy that you sense David with you constantly. Every time you open or direct your consciousness to him, you will find him there. This is not a new phenomenon to you. Every time you direct your consciousness to me, or to any of us who make up your conings, or any specific entity, soul or spirit, you will find us. The only difference now is that you have personal knowledge of David. You are able to visualize him in physical form, even see pictures of him and read about him. You remember him from his speeches on television when you were young. But these things do not change the rules or the circumstances. Those who open their consciousness to us and allow us to connect with them will always "hear" us in some fashion.*

As promised, the cold dissipated quickly—overnight, in fact.

Somewhere between blowing my nose again and sneezing one more time, I began to feel that I was entering a new phase of the so-called Eisenhower opportunity. This is all I could figure out on my own, so again I looked to Hyperithon for help.

We verify that you have entered a new stage. You are standing on an exciting edge of reality. We have already picked up from your thoughts that you wish to meet with David, face to face. It is this stage that you are now entering.

You are to link with him initially by using the vehicle of your connection during World War II. This vehicle is but a framework upon which you can establish a mutual starting point. It is something upon which both of you can lock in your respective focuses. But once the focus is comfortably established, you will both note a clear and distinct desire to change the scenario. You are each to allow that to occur. You both are reconnecting within a familiar framework—but as two more expanded soul reflections. Changes will need to occur.

October 18

I opened this session with Hyperithon determined to move forward—whatever that meant. He had already indicated that a face-to-face meeting with David was possible, and I was interested in doing just that. However, in this situation, I did not believe that "face to face" meant two people physically standing in front of one another. I assumed it meant that I would sense David's presence and see him through my inner vision. Up to this point, I had only heard David through my inner hearing. Hyperithon asked if I still wished to meet David directly. Without any hesitation, I said "yes." Although I was curious about the chance to join his "family," I did not think this required a "personal interview." I wanted to meet him because of the strong connections I had felt with him over the past couple of months. I believed that if I saw him, I would be able to better identify and understand these connections.

Hyperithon told me to go into the sanctuary, lie down and open a specific coning. I did just as instructed. As soon as the coning was opened, I felt a strong shift of energy inside my body. After about ten seconds, I sensed that I was no longer in the sanctuary and I opened my eyes. I found myself in the middle of a busy sidewalk. I figured I was astral traveling again, so I just stood there for a couple of minutes while I determined where I was and what I was supposed to be doing. I was quite calm because I had been through this drill before. However, I noticed that people were walking around me as if I was physically present. This was different.

A man walked right up to me. He was wearing a military uniform, and as he came closer I had a deep feeling that I knew him. He looked no more than fifty years old, and he walked with the ease and grace of a natural athlete. When he smiled, I knew exactly who he was. I had seen pictures of the famous Eisenhower smile before. He said, "Machaelle Wright?"

"Yes."

"I'm General Eisenhower. Come with me. I have a car waiting for us."

I asked, "Where are we?"

"London. Be careful, they drive on the left."

People kept stepping out of our way as we walked down the sidewalk. I could hear the sound of our footsteps—his *and* mine. We stopped alongside a parked car. For some reason, I recognized it to be a 1942 Packard. A younger military fellow snapped the general a salute and opened the back door. I didn't know what the protocol was about who should enter a car first—a general or a woman—so I hesitated. General Eisenhower gestured for me to get into the back seat first. Then he climbed in beside me.

That's when I said to him, "You know, they think you're dead."

He said with a smile, "Yes, well. Those press boys never get anything right!"

I looked down at myself and saw that I was wearing a military uniform. I assumed that this must be part of the scenario, like we were acting out a play and wearing period costumes, so I didn't question it.

"Can other people actually see me?" I asked.

"Yes, of course."

"Well, that's unusual. I've not experienced that before."

"Actually, you've not previously experienced what you are now doing. You're not astral traveling. We can only spend a few minutes together, then you will have to leave."

With that, the younger fellow got into the car, started it and pulled away from the curb. We drove less than ten minutes. In fact, we only went about two blocks. We stopped in front of what looked like an elegant hotel. The fellow opened the back door and both the general and I got out. He said: "You need to leave now. If you wish, we can meet here tomorrow morning at 6:45. I have a meeting I must attend in the morning, and you are welcome to come along on the ride. We can talk along the way."

"Fine. I'll be here." Then reality struck (a little), and I asked, "How do I get here?"

"Open that coning and tell them where you want to go. That'll do the trick. Now, you have to go."

I started to walk away, then turned around and asked, "How do I get out of here?"

"Walk down the street. It's all arranged. They tell me you'll just make a switch."

"Okay. See you tomorrow. Nice meeting you."

I turned away and walked down the street. I'd say I walked no more than two minutes, when I felt the same internal sensations I had felt while lying in the sanctuary. Within seconds, I could sense the sanctuary around me. I opened my eyes, and found that's exactly where I was.

I had no idea what had happened to me. I made notes about the experience. In fact, since coming back from Paris, I had kept notes of all the sessions with Hyperithon and my conversations with David. It just seemed like the thing to do. When I was finished, I left the sanctuary and continued my day. I didn't dwell on my fifteen-minute adventure because I had already decided I was going to do it again the next day. Perhaps with more information, the confusion would clear up and questions would be answered. Overall, despite my confusion, I felt comfortable with what had occurred, and, to my surprise, I felt quite at ease with General Eisenhower.

October 19

Early the next morning, 6:15 to be exact, I connected with Hyper-ithon to get set up for my appointment with Eisenhower.

He said: *We begin this session, prior to your second formal meeting with David, with a few more insights that might help you move through the experience with more clarity.*

You will not be acting out World War II, even though you are using the framework you experienced together during that time. The motivation for your current working partnership is not war. This time it is mutual growth in another context—a context that will become clearer to you shortly as you work together. We don't wish to spell it out because it is important that you allow it to flow into this experience naturally, rather than try to stuff purpose into the experience via preconceived notions.

I asked if the area of our working partnership would be comparable in intensity to World War II.

Yes, but on a different level. We see destruction as a force with a wide range of definitions. World War II demonstrated one area of destruction. There are others of equal intensity that are positive rather than negative phenomena. All aspects of World War II may be present to you again, but you may not recognize them since their dynamics will be so completely different. You will not be facing the horrors of war. You have already done that. But because of your discipline, you require life experiences and growth to encompass a certain amount of quality and intensity. Consequently, you can take on life from a broader vantage point. Don't expect this present situation to be different. This is what we mean when we answer yes to your question comparing your present working partnership with that of World War II.

With that, I was told to lie down in the sanctuary and open the coning. I "arrived" back in London just about a half block from the hotel where I was to meet the general. Once again, I was wearing a military uniform. I saw the general come through the door, so I walked quickly toward the hotel. As soon as I got to him, we exchanged greetings. He said he was glad I had decided to come. I told him I was too curious about what was happening not to come.

The car pulled up, and the same fellow jumped out to open the door. I settled in the back seat along with the general. He explained that we would be driving about two hours to a place just outside a small town called Hamet-on-Raven. His meeting would be short. He suggested that I might be more comfortable if I waited in the car during the meeting. I agreed. On the ride there, we talked about our names again. He insisted that I call him David, then he asked me about the unusual spelling of my name. I explained that it was the Hebrew spelling of the French name, and that I had been born into a Jewish family.

I spent a lot of the ride looking out the window. Once we got out of the city, the landscape looked similar to what I had seen during my travels in England. Although I did not recognize anything specifically—after all, I wasn't so familiar with England that I might have been able to point out anything anyway—I had no difficulty believing that I was indeed in England. I felt a general sense of recognition. I also loved what I was seeing. The fields, the beautiful fences, the small herds of sheep and cattle, the stone cottages. . . . It was all wonderful to me.

David's meeting took no more than half an hour. The driver, who up to that point had not exchanged any words with me directly, accompanied David inside. I stood outside the car for a bit and felt the sensations of the cool breeze against my face. I heard birds chirping in nearby trees and saw a few fly overhead. I looked at my reflection in the side of the car to see what my uniform looked like. It was a dark green color. The skirt was slightly A-line, and the jacket stopped at my waist and had brass buttons. I wasn't thrilled with the color, but the style wasn't too bad. I also noticed that my hair looked a little shorter and was less curly. When I got back into the car, I was convinced that I was as physically present in England as I normally was at Perelandra.

David and the driver returned to the car not long after I had gotten back in. David asked if I'd like to go for a walk along a nearby river with him. I said that would be a fine idea.

While walking, he offered me one of two apples he had "swiped" from the meeting. At first he was concerned about my stamina and how long a walk we should take. I assured him I was fit. Then I said something quite unusual: I told him I jogged about five miles every morning. This wasn't true. I've never jogged. However, my body felt like I *did* run five miles daily. The news seemed to surprise him a bit also, but he quickly said that he had forgotten about my jogging. He was surprised that I did it in the mornings, since we had already established on the ride out that mornings were not my best time of day. I figured that if he was confirming that I jogged, I must be doing it somehow—or it was a part of this scenario we were in. So I dropped the subject.

He asked me about my childhood. I gave him a thumbnail sketch, choosing not to go into detail. I remembered that my father had been in the Army during World War II. I briefly described Isadore's marriage to my mother. As I spoke, I saw (in my mind's eye) a square. The four walls were the facade where my parents put their energy. They made the facade appear normal to others, and everyone saw it as a "regular" marriage. Inside the four walls was nothing but black—a darkness that was created by the secrets they kept from themselves and one another in the marriage. Into that darkness, I was born.

I told David what I was seeing, then changed the subject by asking him about his childhood. He talked a little about his brothers and life in Abilene. He remembered his family as strict and strong, and his childhood as a lot of fun.

I began to tire—not physically from the walking, but more mentally. David suggested that I leave for Perelandra right away and not wait until we got back to London. I agreed. He asked if I wished to go on, to come back. I said "Absolutely." So we decided on the time and place to meet the next day. He then urged me to walk away from him. As I did, I felt myself shift—and when I opened my eyes, I was back at Perelandra again. It was after 11 A.M.

October 20

We met by the river. This time, David had driven there by himself. We walked for quite some time, talking about little insignificant things in our lives. It seemed like David was deliberately keeping the conversation light, so I followed along. What I noticed most was our ease together. There didn't seem to be a male/female barrier between us. I also felt that I was safe with him. We were just two friends who knew how to be together with ease and grace. Even the silences were not awkward. I found that if I relaxed and said what popped into my mind that I could recall small pieces of the past when we had known one another. But I had to really relax to do this and just go with whatever came into my head. It made the conversation somewhat disjointed because I kept dropping into completely different memories. He had no problem going along with whatever I was saying and kept encouraging me not to hold back.

He asked me how I was doing with understanding the situation I was now in. I said I had no idea what I was doing, only that I was somewhere in England walking around in a military uniform with a dead guy. Because there were no screaming headlines in the papers back at Perelandra about Eisenhower coming back from the dead and residing in England, I had to assume that the country I had visited in 1967 and the one I was presently walking in were not one and the same. By this time, David was laughing pretty hard. He appreciated my blunt description of things. He also said that the two countries were not one and the same, but cautioned me not to press this point.

He brought along two more apples, in case we got hungry. When he got them from the car, I teased him by asking if apples were all this country had to offer for food. He took it as a challenge and invited me to his "center" where I could have a decent meal and meet the others on his staff. I took this as a challenge and accepted.

We decided that I would meet him the next day by the river. He said we were only about an hour's drive from his place, and he thought "arriving" might be less disconcerting for me in this more serene setting as opposed to the streets of London. By this time, I was becoming concerned about "landing" on top of someone's head in London, so I agreed that the river made a fine meeting place. (I asked him why no one seemed surprised by my sudden appearances out of thin air. It seemed to me people would faint or something. He said that one of the easiest places for a person to "join in" is a busy city street. No one thinks that a person just appeared. There's so much activity and movement going on that they all think they simply had not noticed the person before.)

October 21

We met by the river at 4 P.M. and went for a short walk before driving to his place. Once again he drove the car, and, as promised, the trip only took an hour.

I couldn't see the house from the road, and when we arrived, David had to get out to open a gate at the entrance. The stone driveway snaked through a small woods. When we stopped in a parking area, I noticed that there were a motorcycle and several cars that were quite a bit more modern-looking than the one we were in. The house was a gorgeous stone, two-story building with a steep, sloping, natural-slate roof. I said to David that it reminded me of a lovely old English cottage. He explained that actually the house was comparatively new—a little over ten years old—but that they had it built to look like an older stone house. The front door was a work of art in itself. It was a large, beautifully-preserved wooden door with medieval-looking, black, wrought-iron hardware—and it was arched.

David asked if I was ready to meet the others. I was quite nervous, but I said, "Yes. It would be silly to back out now." Even though the door looked like it would need three men and a horse to move it, it actually opened easily and quietly. I walked into a huge room that was completely different in feeling from the outside of the house, which seemed dark and "tucked in" because of all the trees and bushes. I now found myself standing in a large, light-filled room with warm-white walls, wide-board wooden floors upon which lay several oriental rugs and, at the other end of the room, a black grand piano.

Almost immediately, a familiar fellow with dark hair, dark eyes and dressed in a military uniform walked over and greeted us—our "chauffeur." David introduced him as Butch. We shook hands and small-talked a little bit. I didn't know what Butch, or the others for that matter, knew about me, so I assumed the more "normal" role of a woman meeting a few people and put aside the fact that I had just appeared by a river from Perelandra, whose location in relationship to the river I wasn't sure of. At one point Butch asked me how my trip had been. I didn't know what he meant by that, so I said, "Just fine."

Shortly, we were joined by two other men, also in military uniforms. David introduced them as Mickey and Tex. I was invited to take off my jacket, if that would make me more comfortable, and join them by the fire for a cup of coffee. I had trouble getting the brass buttons on my jacket unbuttoned, so I gratefully accepted a little help from stronger fingers. They said something about buttons on a new uniform sometimes being a little stiff to work at first.

We sat in an area not far from the piano. It had two full-size sofas, three overstuffed chairs and a large coffee table—all of which were positioned around an enormous stone fireplace, complete with a crackling fire. I found the fire comforting. Mickey brought in a tray with a silver coffee pot, china cups and saucers, all the accoutrements one might need for coffee and a plate of small pastries. I found the coffee to be *really* strong—the kind that curls your teeth. So I just put the cup down and planned to let it sit for a while. Maybe once it cooled down a bit, it wouldn't taste so strong. Mickey asked me right away if the coffee was too strong. I tried to answer as nonchalantly as possible—I didn't want to offend anyone, especially over a lousy cup of coffee—but when I hesitated, he announced, rather gleefully, that he was going to make another pot, and rushed off before I could stop him. Then the others began kidding David and telling me that they had been waiting for someone with a little clout to complain about that coffee.

Apparently, David insisted that the coffee be made as strong as possible—like a Turkish espresso. They kept referring to it as "David's sludge." To get it the way he liked it, the coffee had to be boiled. No one else liked it, but he ignored their protests and insisted the coffee continue to be boiled. It was obvious that they felt confident that he wouldn't ignore me. I was a guest *and* a woman. I had the necessary clout. Before I knew it, Mickey was back with another pot and four clean cups, which he gave to everyone but David. We shared in the newly brewed, *perfect* coffee, and David kept his "coffee" to himself.

I asked who played the piano and was told no one. Then David and Butch confessed to dinking around a little on it, but it was nothing that any sane person would call "playing." They explained that they all felt that a home should have a piano in the "parlor" just in case someone should come by who knows how to play. This struck me as a little on the nutty side, especially since the thing in their living room was so big. Also, I was told, they had it tuned regularly. Obviously, these men were full of hope.

I have to say that it might sound to you that this living room was stuffed with furniture. But the room was so large that the piano and the seating area looked dwarfed. It was actually an open, airy room with just the right amount of furniture in it. The only thing I think was missing were pictures. There were no pictures on the walls.

The evening could not have gone more easily for me. There was such a strong sense of family among the four men, and they seemed to have no difficulty including me. The conversation was social and easy. I learned that the motorcycle belonged to Butch, and that it was a classic BMW that he had restored and kept in mint condition. We shared my scooter and his cycle tales with everyone. I suspect that we both embellished our stories a little.

The dinner was incredible. It was served in the dining room just off the living room. Although the room was considerably smaller, it was still large enough to easily fit maybe fifteen people at the table. I found out that Mickey was the "king of the kitchen." He did all the cooking and would not allow anyone to mess around in his domain. For our meal, he had cooked a large roast, potatoes au gratin and fresh green beans. For dessert, he had baked one of the most decadent chocolate cakes I had ever experienced. (He also baked the pastries that had been served with coffee earlier.) David had promised a decent meal, and he—and Mickey—had delivered.

By around 10 P.M., I began to feel drained. I assumed that I would have to go back to the river in order to leave, but David suggested to me privately that we go for a walk around the garden and that I leave from there. My exit from the evening with these men felt as graceful and "normal" as my entrance had been. I struggled back into my jacket, said goodbye, thanked them twenty or thirty times (and I meant it) and walked out the front door with David as if we were heading back to the car.

Instead, we walked down a narrow, winding path through a large garden with a lot of tall evergreen bushes that looked like boxwoods. A couple of times we passed stone benches nestled in among the bushes just off the path. I realized that we had circled around the house and were now in the back. From this vantage point, the house did not look at all like an English cottage, as it had from the front. Actually the place was very large and now looked more like an English estate. I mentioned to David that, despite the real size of the house, I still liked thinking of it as a cottage, which had been my initial impression when I first saw it. He suggested that I call the place "the Cottage." That sounded cozier and more in fitting with my evening's experience than calling it "the center" or "David's place," so I agreed.

When I told him how much I had enjoyed myself, he asked if I'd like to join them for dinner the next evening. Mickey would be cooking, of course. I accepted his invitation. He then suggested that I plan to "come in" at the spot where we were now standing. It was private, he assured me, and I could just walk around the path to the front door and come right on in. They'd all be inside. I said I'd be glad to try it, but he better give me the Cottage phone number in case I screwed up and end up wandering around London or along the river. He laughed and said that I'd be just fine. I took him at his word.

I walked down the path away from him. I have to admit that I was reluctant to leave. In less than a minute, I felt the shift occur, and then I felt the Perelandra sanctuary around me again. I opened my eyes and looked around the familiar sanctuary walls. When I checked my watch, I noted that seven hours had passed since I had "left" Perelandra.

October 22

I departed Perelandra at 5 P.M. for my evening at the Cottage. Much to my relief and delight, I arrived at exactly the spot David had recommended the evening before. All I had to do was open the coning, state my intent to shift to the Cottage and picture the spot. The whole process had to take less than thirty seconds. I arrived once again in my uniform. Actually, I was getting rather fond of the thing. It gave me a sense of stability knowing what I'd be wearing when I "dropped in." I stood in the garden for awhile and collected myself. This was the first time I had arrived without someone meeting me. I noticed that the sun would be setting shortly.* In the daylight, I confirmed that most of the bushes around me were indeed boxwoods. I didn't want to be late, so I didn't stay in the garden too long. I found my way along the path to the front of the house. I noticed that all the cars and the motorcycle were in the parking area—including the 1942 Packard.

Once I got to the front door, I hesitated because I wasn't sure I'd be able to open it. David had made it look so easy the evening before. I decided nothing ventured, nothing gained—so I grabbed the handle and turned it. I heard a solid clunk, and the door began to swing open. I just walked inside and said, "Hello?" David walked around the corner and answered, "Hello. You're right on time." I managed to get my jacket unbuttoned myself this time. After hanging it for me on the coat pegs on the wall next to the door, David asked if I'd like a "formal" tour of the place. At about that time, Mickey appeared with a mug of coffee for me, suitable for safely carting around on a tour. He also let me know that it was the "good stuff" and not the "sludge." I accepted the mug and went off with the two of them.

I was first taken into David's office, located just off the "piano end" of the living room. It was about the size of the dining room. Three of the walls were lined with bookcases. I noticed that most of the books were about the military, especially military history. He had a huge mahogany desk that sat on a big oriental rug. There were a few things on top of the desk, each (I felt) exactly placed. Overall, it was a precise and tidy office. Just to the right of the door was a small wooden table with a chess board set up on it. The pieces were moved around the board leaving the impression that a game was in progress. David explained that a game was always in progress. He

---

* Each level (planet) has its own unique relationship to the sun. Consequently, the time zones on our Earth are not the same as those on the Cottage level. The Cottage is just one hour ahead of Perelandra, but the men have set all their clocks to Perelandra time so we can coordinate our schedules easily.

and Tex played one another in ongoing games. Mickey told me that they never sat down together, neither one of them had the patience for that. They'd just stop on their way in and out of the office, look at the board, figure out whose move it was and move something if it was their turn. To give the games a little twist, they made small wagers.

I was next led to the kitchen. I had the feeling that I should be more honored to be in the kitchen than in David's office! It didn't look like it lacked anything. It had a dishwasher, large refrigerator, deep double sinks, a beautiful gas stove, double ovens, a *microwave* and plenty of counter space. It was a chef's dream. Mickey proudly showed me two coffeemakers—one, obviously brand new. He said that he had gotten the second one in town that day so that he could make a pot of the good stuff for all of us. David seemed to be taking the ribbing goodnaturedly and never wasted the opportunity to an-nounce that actually he was glad to have his "quality" coffee to himself. The older it got throughout the day, the better it was.

We went through the kitchen into another office. This one was about twice the size of David's. Three of its walls were lined with four-drawer filing cabinets. This was Butch's office. He and Tex were at Butch's desk working on something when we walked in. Butch explained that this was the information center where they kept all their records, files and necessary information. He also showed me a long hallway off his office where additional information was stored in filing cabinets. It was pretty impressive, but I had to wonder why a group of men who were modern enough to have a microwave didn't have their information computerized. I put my ob-servation in my back pocket and saved my question for later.

Before it was completely dark, we walked back through the living room and out french doors just behind the piano to a large stone patio. The patio steps led to the garden. From there I could see that the Cottage sat on a hill. Beautiful fields stretched out before us, and there were no houses in sight. David pointed out the golf course beyond the gardens to our left. I asked if he still golfed, and he enthusiastically said "yes." But he could only get Tex to go out with him. Butch and Mickey both hated the game. He asked if I played golf, and I quickly said "no." I had the feeling that had I not been emphatic, he would have pressed me into a golf game at some point.

When the five of us walked back into the Cottage, I noticed for the first time that the entire living room wall next to the piano was pane glass and that the french doors were a part of the glass wall. I had not seen that wall as glass before this.

We were then joined by another man, a younger man who looked to be in his late twenties. David introduced him as John and explained that John worked with them from time to time and periodically stayed at the Cottage for several weeks when necessary.

Once again we sat around the fire. They asked if I would like some wine. When I declined, Mickey brought in an entire pot of coffee for me. The others had the wine. We quickly settled into a casual conversation centered around what had occurred since I had left the evening before. I was struck by how much and how quickly I felt a part of this group. They were each quick-witted, quick to tease one another and quick to laugh. I noticed my guard coming down as the evening went on.

I had been there for about an hour when there was a knock at the front door. David got up to answer, and I had the impression that no one was surprised by the knock. The visitor was an older man in his late sixties. He was short and a little stocky, and as he walked with David over to where we were sitting, I thought I recognized him but I couldn't place him. David introduced him to all of us, and as everyone was exchanging greetings and shaking hands, my recognition grew stronger. By the time he shook hands with me, I knew exactly who he was—my father. Not Isadore, but a completely different man named Max. I had been seeing him in my mind's eye for over a week while I was doing my chores at Perelandra, and I had gotten insight that he was my father from another lifetime. I hadn't paid too much attention to this because the experience didn't seem to be "going anywhere." It was just a mildly interesting tidbit of information about some man from another lifetime. Now here he was standing before me. He must have seen that I recognized him, because he stopped shaking my hand and wrapped me in a huge bear hug. He kept calling me "Katie." From somewhere inside this man's hug, I took a shift and I dropped into Katie's life. I was now

Machaelle, operating within the memory of another person's life. When we let go of one another, we started talking about the "old days" with all the familiarity of two old friends who hadn't seen one another for awhile. I was so taken off guard by the moment, that the only way I could figure out how to get through it was to suspend my intelligence, relax and just float along with what was going on. At the same time, every fiber of my being felt at ease and grateful to be with Max again.

Max was quite the talker. He clearly had an Irish storyteller's streak in him. As I listened, I realized I *knew* these stories. We were not really father and daughter—at least not biologically. Katie's father died when she was five. She had been daddy's girl, so the death was an especially deep blow for her. The once bubbly little girl became withdrawn and shy. When she was six, Katie accompanied her mother to the local ice skating rink to pick up Seamus (pronounced: shame'-us), her older brother, who was having a lesson. She was sent inside the rink to get him while their mother waited outside. Without thinking, she walked across the ice to her brother who was half-listening to some pointers being given by his teacher—Max. He insisted that Seamus try a movement several times before leaving the ice and, while Seamus skated, Katie stood next to Max, as instructed. When Seamus left the ice to change to street shoes, Max talked to Katie about skating and asked if she would like to learn. She whispered a little yes. Max walked the two children to where their mother was waiting and talked over the possibility of Katie joining his beginner's class. He also suggested that Seamus be allowed to stop skating because his heart wasn't in it, and Max felt it was a waste of time and money to try to force a child into a sport that they didn't want to be in. The next week, Katie started skating classes, and Seamus was freed from them. Both were happy.

Katie was a natural on ice. She loved everything about it and quickly became one of Max's star pupils. She developed a strong bond with him, and he became her "new father." At the same time, Max opened his heart to her. Underneath her shyness a determined, spunky little girl gradually surfaced as the months went on.

Katie's mother suffered numerous financial setbacks after her husband's death. Within the first year, she talked to Max about need-ing to remove Katie from the skating program. Max would not hear of it. Katie had potential, and as much as he disapproved of forcing a child into a sport they didn't like, he believed in providing all the opportunity that a child could handle for a sport he or she loved and showed promise in. Max suggested that he take over Katie's training exclusively, at no charge. Skating and Max had so clearly benefitted her daughter that she agreed.

By the time Katie was seven, she was living with Max, attending the local school and skating during most of her free time. And she blossomed. Katie's mother, who had always been able to understand and get along with Seamus better than she did with Katie, gratefully deferred Katie's upbringing to Max.

As Max regaled everyone at the Cottage with his Katie stories, I found myself chiming in when a detail was missed or to add my own comments. I had no foresight about what I would say at any given time. Everything was just right there at the tip of my tongue. No one in the room questioned my seemingly endless knowledge about Katie and Max. This most "unnatural" scene was completely enfolded in "naturalness."

The men asked if "I" became any good as a skater. Max was shocked that they didn't know. "I" was a world class pairs skater and won the Olympic gold medal two consecutive times in pairs skating for England. Katie had presented Max with her second medal, which he happened to have in his coat pocket and took great pride in showing to everyone in the room. When I held the medal, I recognized it and felt I could remember the routine I had skated with John, my partner (not the fellow I had just met that evening), to win that medal. It felt like a long mathematical formula with num-bers and movement had dropped into my head.

By the time we were eating dinner, Max was insisting that I get back on the ice. He was completely focused on my physical condi-tion. David assured him that to do what I was presently doing, I had to be in top condition and that I had resumed a physical training program in preparation for this. I wanted to interrupt and ask what I was doing, but the conversation galloped right on. Besides, I also wanted to ask, "What physical training program?" But I had a feel-

ing that if I didn't interrupt, I'd find out. Sure enough, Max turned
to me at the table and asked,

"How many miles are you running?"

"Five to seven."

"Daily?"

"Six days a week."

"Situps?"

"Four hundred."

"Pushups?"

"One hundred."

"Daily?"

"Yes."

At the same time I was answering him, I was thinking, "This is
nuts. I don't do any of this. What the hell am I talking about?"
That's when several of the others at the table said they wanted proof
and challenged me to do twenty pushups right then. Without thinking, I got on the floor in the dining room and knocked off twenty
pushups without any strain. I figured I was in the midst of a
miracle!

Max left about an hour after dinner after nailing down a promise
from me to join him on the ice at the rink soon. (This was a brave
promise since I, Machaelle, did not know how to ice skate. I had
been pretty flashy on roller skates as a kid, but I didn't think that
was going to get me through this ice skating thing.) Not long after
Max left, I needed to leave as well. I was getting drained again. As
David walked me out to the garden "landing and launch pad," he
didn't say anything about the occurrences of the evening being unusual. Instead, he raved about what a great fellow my dad was—and
I agreed wholeheartedly. He asked if I'd like to join them for dinner
again the next night. I accepted without hesitation.

I opened my eyes in the Perelandra sanctuary and checked my
watch. I had been gone six hours. I lay there for a while wondering
who I was, but I couldn't get a handle on that mystery—so I tried a
pushup. I struggled through one, then left the sanctuary completely
confused but determined to return to the Cottage the next day.

October 23

I arrived back at the Cottage garden at 5 P.M. I stood there for a few minutes collecting myself. The sky was overcast, and there was a distinct fall nip in the air. I remember loving the feel of the cool breeze against my face.

Our evening was a continuation of the night before, with one exception. Max again joined us, but he brought along my (Katie's) brother, Seamus. I found out later that the men at the Cottage had encouraged Max to do this. When I saw Seamus, I immediately spotted a family resemblance. We looked like brother and sister. He gave me a hug and asked me what in the world I was doing in a military uniform. I told him I wasn't sure. He seemed to accept that as a reasonable answer. He called me Katie, too.

Just as with Max, I suddenly "knew" Seamus once he hugged me. I knew he was a musician and had his own band. He had hated skating, but he sure had a passion for music. He gravitated toward the piano in the living room right away—"just to check it out," he said. He pronounced it a "beautiful instrument" and, after a little urging (actually hardly any urging at all), he played several songs he had recently written. They had a Billy Joel flavor to them—or perhaps it's more accurate to say that Billy Joel's music has a Seamus Morgan flavor. At this point, I'm not really sure which is more "correct."

Seamus was as focused on his music as Katie had been on skating. His band rarely toured anymore, choosing instead to remain the only band to perform year-round, five nights a week, at the largest pub in the nearby village. (This place is actually just named The Pub.) The band was so famous that people traveled to The Pub from all around to hear them. Reservations were consistently booked three to four months in advance. This allowed all of the band members to stay in one place and have a life, while maintaining their musical standing with the public.

Max, Seamus and I entertained everyone through dinner with more family tales. At one point, Seamus talked about how Katie had been quite the source of income for him when she was eight years old. That piqued everyone's interest, so they got him to disclose all, over Max's objections. This led to Max's famous pencil-and-donut lecture—the world's worst talk about human sexuality.

It seems that Max decided that Katie needed to learn about the birds and the bees when she was eight. He admitted to putting much thought and research into the task before talking to her. On the Big Day, he held her in his lap while he showed her medical book pictures of the differences between men and women. Katie had showered with the boy skaters quite often, so this didn't surprise her at all. Then he moved on to the "female organ section" of the talk. For this, he relied on another medical book that had the female reproductive organs drawn on a series of color transparencies. Katie didn't give a hoot about female organs, but she was fascinated by those transparencies. She had never seen anything like that before, so she spent much of this part of the talk flipping the transparency pages back and forth and watching the picture change. It was during this time that Max explained the woman's menstrual cycle, and all Katie caught from what he had said was that at age twelve she would start bleeding from "down there"—"down there" was appropriately pointed out on a transparency.

Finally, Max moved on to the "sex section." For this he used a donut and a pencil as props, both of which had been carefully placed on his desk beforehand. When we got to this part at dinner, Seamus insisted that we could not continue without the right props, which Mickey cheerfully provided. In keeping with the tone of the entire talk, Max chose to describe the sexual act to Katie in the most straightforward terms he could. Katie listened intently, watching the pencil and donut movement. When it was over, she decided that this was the most absurd story she had ever heard. Nothing like this could ever happen. Max had to be lying to her, and this broke her heart. He had never lied to her before.

Max said, "It was terrible. Here she was on my lap with big tears rolling down her cheeks, and I couldn't figure out what was wrong. She wouldn't say anything and just left the office."

Katie then went to Seamus and told her big ten-year-old brother about the talk. After she got it out, she asked Seamus what he thought. He said he wasn't sure about all of it, but it sounded about right. Actually, he was quite happy about what she had told him. He had been trying to figure things out with his pals, and here was his little sister describing the whole thing!

That's when Seamus developed the great money-making scheme. He tricked Katie into telling his pals what she knew, saying that they might know better if what Max had told her was right or not. Unbeknownst to Katie, he then charged his pals an "admission fee" to hear the *real* facts.

By this time, the men were roaring with laughter while at the same time completely sympathetic about Katie's pain. They razzed Max unmercifully, which he took with a fair amount of grace. Even though we were all having a great deal of fun with this story, I sensed the men around me moving emotionally closer. I suddenly felt *protected* by them.

The evening ended with Max pressing me to set a date and time when I would come to the rink and skate. I agreed to October 25 at 3 P.M., the day after the next. I didn't think any amount of time would be sufficient for me to learn to skate in, so I might as well get this over with and prove to everyone that Machaelle Wright did not know how to skate. Maybe then I would learn just when I was doing all this jogging and physical fitness stuff.

The evening ended for me about 11 P.M. Once again I was invited back for dinner. When I told them that I was becoming a little suspicious about who they were going to introduce me to next, they assured me that it would just be the six of us.

When I got back to Perelandra, it was a little after 11 P.M. I tried another pushup—again, unsuccessfully.

October 24

As promised, we had a relatively quiet dinner with just the Cottage "family." By now I was feeling very much a part of this routine, and every day I looked forward to my evenings at the Cottage. An ease and familiarity had settled around us as a group, and I *liked* it. No one had yet asked me about my work, and I had no idea how David planned for me to fit into the Cottage work. I still didn't know what they did.

I asked a couple of questions about Max and Seamus—nothing that would explain how they fit into the picture. I just wanted to know if they lived close by. Seamus lived in the village, which was about fifteen minutes away, and Max lived on the other side of the village, about a half-hour drive. The rink where he trained was about forty-five minutes from the Cottage.

While we were talking, I realized that I had a lot of questions about Max and Seamus when I was at Perelandra. At the Cottage this evening, I seemed to always easily fall in and out of the "Katie picture," and those questions disappeared.

After dinner, as I was preparing to leave, David suggested that I arrive at the Cottage the next day at around 2 P.M. Someone would drive me to the rink for my 3 o'clock appointment with Max. I was curious what they would all do once they found out I couldn't skate, but I didn't say anything. I felt like this was going to be terribly disappointing to everyone. I didn't even have ice skates.

October 25

When I arrived at the Cottage, I was met at the door by Seamus.

"Hi. I'm driving you to the rink. The others will follow shortly."

Before I could say anything, he had me turned around and headed in the direction of his car.

Our time together during the trip was enjoyable and relaxed. I had slipped into Katie's life and found myself laughing about old times with him. Time passed quickly.

When we pulled into the rink parking lot, I recognized the building. I knew exactly where to enter and where the locker rooms were. Seamus told me that he would see me down at the rink, and I headed off to dress. I walked into the locker room and straight to locker number 1622. Across the locker door was a strip of masking tape with the name "Allison Brown" on it. That confused me. Then I realized that 1622 had been Katie's locker, but it was now assigned to someone else. I turned around to look for a locker with my name on it, and that's when I found a gym bag on the bench just to my right with "Machaelle Wright" handwritten on a piece of paper that was pinned to the bag. I recognized the writing to be Max's. In the bag was all that I needed to go ice skating—including skates. Everything was in good shape, but it was obvious that the clothes and the skates were not new. They had that broken in, comfortable look to them.

While I dressed, I felt a deep sense of familiarity about everything. I knew what to do, how to dress and where to go. As long as I didn't try to think about it, I could function effortlessly. I felt like I was two people. One knew exactly what to do. The other observed and was fascinated at what was being played out. I never lost either feeling, and they continued to function simultaneously. It seemed to me that the trick was to allow the feeling of familiarity to dominate and keep the feeling of wonderment and questioning in the background. If I did this, I believed I would be alright. I have to say, at this point I was not working myself up to being alright on the ice. My focus was just on getting properly dressed and finding the rink. These were the immediate challenges.

I walked out of the locker room with skates in hand, turned to my left and headed down a hallway that led to double doors. I walked through the doors, down some steps, turned to my left again and walked through another set of double doors. In front of me was an entrance that cut through rows of seats and led to the ice. Max was sitting on the right, waiting. With hardly a word between us, I sat down in front of him and began putting on my skates. We had done this together a thousand times. As I was lacing my boots, fear gripped me and I said, "I'm not sure I can do this."

"Of course you can. It's like riding a bicycle. It'll all come back to you as soon as you get out there."

"No. You don't understand. I can't skate."

"Don't be ridiculous. Lace up your skates and get out there."

I just looked at him. I decided I had gotten this far, I might as well keep going. The worse thing that could happen was that I'd fall as soon as I stood up on the skates. And if by some miracle I made it to the ice, I'd quickly prove that I was a woman who had a pair of ice skates on for the first time in her life. I felt certain that I wasn't going to be able to bluff my way through this.

Max began giving me instructions about what he wanted me to do to warm up. I listened to him as if I was actually going to get out there and do what he said. When he finished talking, I found myself standing on the ice. I had been so focused on what he was saying that, without realizing what I was doing, I had gotten out of my seat, walked to the ice, taken my skate guards off and was now standing on the ice. When he pointed for me to move out, I did just that. I slowly circled the rink while getting the feel for how the ice felt underneath my skates. It was an incredibly joyous, freeing feeling that, for a short while, left me with a lump in my throat and tears in my eyes. I gradually picked up speed as I felt my whole body move across the ice. Max let me circle the rink quite a few times, then he began telling me what he wanted me to do. By this time, I was completely focused on the feeling of freedom that I was experiencing and Max's instructions. Nothing else existed, not even my doubts.

Max gradually increased the degree of difficulty, and my body operated with a strong, familiar coordination with each new move or combination of moves. I had never before felt such clarity and organization in movement. At least, not with the body I had at Perelandra.

Before I knew it, three hours had passed. I didn't especially feel physically tired, but I was beginning to have difficulty holding my concentration and was having a problem completing some of the moves. Max stopped the practice and handed me my skate guards. For the first time, I looked into the seats and noticed all five men from the Cottage sitting there next to Seamus. It looked like a military invasion. They were pretty intense. I assumed it was because they were in shock. After talking to me for a few more minutes, Max joined the others while I removed my skates. I told them I would be back shortly, then headed to the locker room to shower and change clothes.

When I left the locker room, I ran right into David, literally. He was waiting for me just outside. He told me he had been sent to get me because they would be driving me back to the Cottage. Seamus needed to get to The Pub, and Max needed to stay at the rink to work with another skater. Several of the others had already left in one car. I was to ride back with David and Butch.

In the car, we got into a discussion about how it felt for me to be out on the ice again. I told them what an emotional experience it had been, and how I was grateful Max had been there to talk me through it. I didn't bring up my feelings of fear, shock and surprise, nor did I talk about my questions about being able to skate in the first place. For the moment, I simply allowed myself to sink into the joy of the experience. They talked about how good I looked on the ice and how content I seemed while skating. They also talked about my physical strength a lot. I felt they were just not used to athletic women. They were certainly used to athletic men because all of them looked to be in top physical condition.

After dinner, David asked me to have coffee with him in the living room. I didn't think much about the invitation until I noticed that the others were not joining us. We settled in front of the fire with our coffee—two separate pots.

About halfway through my first cup of coffee, I began to feel all of the fears and questions surface that I had about everything that had occurred over the past eight days. I talked to David about my confusion. I told him about trying the pushups at Perelandra and not being able to do one. I talked about how much the Cottage meant to me, and that I was beginning to have the urge to cling to the Cottage for fear that it might disappear from my life. As I spoke, my fears overwhelmed me, and I began to cry. I worked very hard to describe each fear to him, but my words were halting and inadequate. Every time I formulated a fear, I'd quickly see how ludicrous and inappropriate it was and throw it out before David could say anything. Then I'd address the next fear and go through the same process. David listened intently to everything I said, and spoke little himself. Basically, I was having this conversation with myself. One by one, I addressed my own fears. In the end, I resigned myself to the fact that whatever would be, would be. If my time at the Cottage was to end, I'd somehow be prepared for it. I would trust. This didn't make me happy, it just gave me more understanding and peace of mind.

When I finished, David looked me squarely in the eyes and said, slowly and carefully, "I promise you here and now, that you will remain personally connected with the Cottage for as long as that connection enhances your soul's growth."

Without hesitation, I said, "I promise *you* that I will remain personally connected with the Cottage for as long as that connection enhances the Cottage's growth and direction."

Instantly, I sensed that something important had occurred.

"Did I just officially become a member of the Cottage team?"

"Yes. You did."

That's when I heard applause coming from the patio. I looked out the doors, and there on the patio was a group of about thirty people—wispy people that looked like you could walk right through them—applauding joyously in approval and support of my new membership into the Cottage. I looked at David, who was at the time looking at these people and smiling, so I knew that he was seeing them also and that I wasn't hallucinating. Or we were both hallucinating. After about five minutes of applause, they disappeared.

I said, "Friends of yours?"

"Yes. Yours, too. Come on, let me show you to your room. You must be a little tired."

With that, he took me upstairs for the first time. At the top of the steps was a long hallway that veered off to the right. I estimated about eight or ten closed doors, which I later learned were bedrooms, that lined the hallway. He led me into the first room on the left—a large room (about twenty-by-thirty feet) with wall-to-wall off-white carpeting, a high ceiling, a fireplace at the far end, a bed, nightstand and lamp, dresser, several chairs and a small sofa that created a seating area, and a desk. The bed was already made up and the covers were turned back. There was also a small bathroom and walk-in closet that had another uniform just like the one I was wearing and assorted women's casual clothes—all in my size. I looked at David suspiciously.

He didn't give me time to put any questions into words. Right away, he took me to the room next door. "This," he said, "is the shower room." When I walked inside, I could barely believe my eyes. Before me was a large, sunken, serpentine-shaped pool that I estimated to be about fifteen-by-twenty feet in size. I teased him and said, "It looks like a lagoon." Around three of the sides were steps that led into the water, which looked to be about three-feet deep. The wall opposite where we were standing was natural rock. David pointed to a button that was recessed into the rocks on the right and told me that all I had to do was push it to start the water flow coming out from the rocks, if I preferred a shower. Except for the rock wall, the room was white. To my right were several stacks of white towels, and hanging on white pegs along the wall were six, white terry-cloth robes, each with initials monogrammed on the pockets in navy blue. I saw that the last robe had the initials MSW on the pocket.

I turned to David in amazement, and said, "You've known all along this would happen tonight!"

"I *hoped*. We weren't absolutely sure. You've always had the freedom to say 'no'."

He asked if I ever drank champagne. When I told him that I drank a little bit for special occasions, he suggested that perhaps this was just such an occasion and asked if I felt like having some champagne to cap off the evening. We went back downstairs. On the coffee table was an ice bucket chilling a bottle of champagne and two glasses.

We toasted the occasion, and that's when I admitted that I wasn't exactly sure what we were toasting. David said that in order for me to accomplish what was now before me, I had to make a commitment to the Cottage from the heart and soul. A commitment made through understanding and intellectual knowledge would not supply the strength, stamina and dedication I needed in order to address what now lay ahead. He also explained that the heart and soul commitment had to spring from inside me, and, to this end, it was crucial that no one at the Cottage do or say anything prior to the moment that would directly result in my commitment. I had to move from within, I could not be encouraged from outside. At the right moment, only he could extend the "invitation" for me to join. I asked if the skating had anything to do with this.

"Yes. You will need all the physical strength you can muster. By activating the skating, you've activated the physical strength that you'll need. But I don't think we should go into that now."

I agreed. I could tell I was too tired to listen. After one glass of champagne, I needed to go to bed. I verified that I was spending the night. I didn't want to assume this. David told me that now, as part of the team, I would be spending each evening and night at the Cottage, and that I would return to Perelandra in the mornings. I couldn't take in any more, so I excused myself and went upstairs to my new room.

David had said to let them know if I needed anything, but, after a quick check of both closet and dresser, I couldn't think of anything that they missed. I was impressed. I walked into the lagoon, locked the door, undressed and sat down in the water for a few minutes. It felt strange to be there by myself, yet it also felt like I had come home. (I was beginning to get used to having conflicting feelings.) I dried off, put on my very own monogrammed robe and returned to my room. By the time I hung up my uniform and finished getting ready for bed, I was exhausted. I think it must have taken all of three seconds for me to fall into a deep sleep.

October 26

When I awoke, I was quite surprised to see that I was still at the Cottage. I more than half expected to be looking at the Perelandra sanctuary. I noticed a small clock on the night table that read 9:15. I had no idea what the Cottage morning schedule was, so I quickly dressed in my uniform and rushed downstairs, assuming I was already late for something.

Mickey greeted me in the living room and invited me into the dining room for some breakfast. I kept him company by holding up the kitchen doorjamb as he prepared eggs and toast for me. By the time I sat at the table, the others had joined us and had poured themselves coffee. I was embarrassed to be late for breakfast, but they insisted that I should be getting as much sleep as possible and not worry about their schedule. Their main concern this morning was my comfort. Was the lagoon alright for me? Was the bed comfortable? Did I know there were extra blankets in my closet? Was the room too warm? Was it too cold? I felt like I had dropped into a gaggle of Jewish mothers. I assured them that I could think of nothing I needed, and I thanked them for everything they had already done. This last bit they waved off as if a bunch of men making sure a woman had everything she needed was nothing unusual.

By 10 o'clock, I felt certain I should be doing something. David suggested that I leave for Perelandra from my normal spot in the garden. He showed me a short cut through the living room and off the patio to the location, then told me to feel free to enter the Cottage through the patio door when I returned. Since I had been at the Cottage for such a long period of time, I wasn't sure if the leaving process was going to be "normal," or if I'd have to do something extra. David said that he felt there would be no change. In any case, I should try it and see if it still worked. I turned away from him and walked down the path into the garden. In less than a minute, I felt the shift. When I sensed the sanctuary around me, I opened my eyes. My watch read 10:20. Since it was daylight, I assumed that was A.M., and not P.M.

I left the sanctuary to find Clarence and to let him know I was still among the living. He was used to my being off by myself, but this had been an unusually long period of time.

As of September 1, Clarence was no longer working for Xerox. He wanted time to be at Perelandra, work on some small construction projects around the place and decide what he'd really like to do with his life. The commute had become tedious, and working on copy machines had become boring. The earnings on the money I had inherited from Isadore gave us just enough to cover our basic expenses, if we were careful.

I wasn't used to having Clarence around. In fact, I was used to having my entire afternoons and evenings to myself. I had developed an intense and focused daily schedule that didn't accommodate another person. So when he began staying at Perelandra all day, we quickly discovered that we bumped into one another a lot. The thing that saved us was separate bedrooms. This allowed me the privacy I needed to get information from nature for the research work, and now it would give me the privacy for my schedule at the Cottage.

Clarence was putzing in the kitchen when I found him. As I chattered on about nothing in particular, I realized two things: (1) It really was the morning after the night before, and (2) I was hungry. Clarence offered to fix me breakfast. As he prepared it—eggs and toast—I kept thinking about how I seemed to be surrounded by men making me breakfast. I wondered if I was going to start gaining weight. I also felt like I was quickly sinking into some twilight zone—except that everything around me at Perelandra seemed so normal.

While I ate, I told Clarence that I was going to need a lot of time to myself for a while. I didn't give him any details about why, because I wasn't sure how long I would be going to the Cottage, and I wasn't sure how much I should tell him about the situation. In the past, he had never questioned my need for privacy, and he was quite patient about my not talking about what I was doing. He knew that eventually, when I was ready to say something, I'd let him know what was going on. This morning was no different. I was relieved, because I wasn't sure how I was going to work this Eisenhower business into the conversation.

My major focus at this point was to see if it was appropriate and possible for me to leave for the Cottage from the comfort of the bed in my room rather than from the sanctuary. I called Hyperithon. He "cleared" me for doing the shift from my room. That's all I wanted to ask him, so I cut the conversation short, saying that when I had a little more time, I'd like to talk with him again. He didn't seem to take offense—in fact, he was his usual pleasant self.

By the time I finished doing my Perelandra work and eating an early dinner, it was 5:00 P.M. and time to go to the Cottage. I settled in my bed, opened the coning and visualized the Cottage garden. In just a few seconds, I felt the shift.

I stood in the garden for about ten minutes while I got acclimated to my surroundings. When I got to the patio door, I found David standing there, obviously waiting for me. He steered me into his office where a coffee tray was set up—with two pots, of course. I settled into a big chair, and he sat at his desk while he asked me questions about my day at Perelandra. We had talked for about an hour, when he looked at his watch and announced it was time for dinner. I admitted to him that, even though I had already eaten an early dinner at Perelandra, I was now actually hungry again.

"I'm going to weigh 800 pounds in a month, if I keep this up."

"It's okay. Don't worry about it. You're probably not eating enough."

I looked at him as if he were crazy.

When we entered the dining room, everyone was standing there waiting. The lights were off, and all I could see was candlelight, the sparkle of silver and the fresh white of a linen tablecloth. It was a special dinner to celebrate my joining the Cottage.

There were people in the room that I didn't know. Quite frankly, I couldn't see very well because the lighting was so dim. So I sat down where told—in my usual seat—with Tex to my left and David at the head of the table to my right. John was sitting across from me, and to his right was Butch. Beyond that, I couldn't really see too well. I was mostly struck by the festiveness of the candlelight, the silver and the linen. It was a beautiful visual combination.

Champagne was poured. I wasn't sure what to do. I had never been in a situation such as this. I thought I was in a 1930s movie and Bette Davis would be swooping in any minute. Then it hit me. I stood and restated the commitment I had made to David the night before. Only this time, it was for everyone's benefit. Everyone applauded in approval. Then the men from the Cottage stood, one by one, and welcomed me, each in his own words. I was deeply touched.

A fellow at the other end of the table got up, and I thought I recognized him. But I knew I had to be wrong, so I waited for him to speak. Sure enough, as soon as he spoke I knew it was Clarence. And it wasn't someone dressed up to look like Clarence either. It was the real thing. I knew this because of a little habit Clarence has. When he is in public and he gets nervous, he starts talking and won't shut up. At our partnership Mass, he gave the world's longest welcoming speech. Here he was, sounding just like Clarence. Finally, he got to the core of his toast.

"May we find the courage to eventually free ourselves to have the expanded life Machaelle has chosen. May she continue to teach me

so that someday I can open up more aspects of life to myself." Then
he raised his glass to me, "To our partnership."

Before I could raise a question or say anything to Clarence,
everyone took a drink of champagne, and the next toast began. Actually, this was the last toast. The man who was sitting at the other
end of the table opposite David stood. But I did not recognize him—
except for the fact that he had that wispy look about him and I felt I
could walk through him, if I wished.

He raised his glass and said, "A toast of gratitude for the sparks of
energy created by your commitment to this new life. May they continue to spread joy throughout the universe and serve to energize the
points of creativity existing in the universe."

As soon as he finished, I knew who he was—Hyperithon. I leaned
over to David and he confirmed my hunch. I was so surprised at
Hyperithon's presence and so taken by his toast that I forgot all
about Clarence for a while. Actually, what Hyperithon had said hit
me between the eyes. He was indicating that what I was doing with
my life affected the bigger picture. Now, *that* was a surprising
thought. I spent the first half of the dinner quietly thinking about his
words and letting them sink into my being.

I spent the rest of the dinner watching Clarence, who was having
a great time at the other end of the table and didn't seem to want to
pay any attention to me. I was also watching Hyperithon. I wanted
to see what it was like for a wispy person to eat. Could I see the
food go down his throat and into his stomach? Weird stuff like that.
(By the way—no, I couldn't see the internal workings of his diges-
tive system. I guess once he put the food in his mouth, it became
wispy, too.)

Shortly after dessert and coffee, Hyperithon and Clarence got up
together and began saying their goodbyes to everyone. Clarence and
I still had not had a chance to say anything to one another, and here
he was leaving.

I said, a little surprised, "Well, see you back at Perelandra."

He cheerfully tossed off a "Yea" and left the room with Hyperithon. So, there they were—my partner and some wispy space guy
going off together. Everyone else in the room was acting as if this
were the most normal thing that could be happening. I asked David

what I should say to Clarence when I got back. David told me that Clarence wouldn't remember anything. He would just probably be a little tired.

I said, "Was he aware he was here?"

"Not consciously. But we knew you'd want him here for this dinner, so we extended him an invitation, which he accepted, and then we arranged it."

He told me not to say anything about the evening to Clarence. When he was ready to know about such things, he would either ask me a question about something relating to the dinner or simply remember the event on his own. Since I couldn't pursue this in any direct manner with Clarence, I made a mental note just to find out how he was feeling when I returned to Perelandra in the morning.

By the time I got into bed, it was quite late. My final adventure for the night was the shower. I decided I'd push that recessed button and see what happened. Water streamed out over a rock ledge. It looked like a waterfall, and nothing like a regular shower. The water temperature could be adjusted by a small handle just left of the button. As I stood under the water, I felt an energy move through me. When I stepped away from the streaming water, the sensation stopped. As soon as I stood under it again, the sensation returned. It felt like my washing included some kind of a body balancing, and I had a funny feeling that I didn't need to use soap. In fact, I suspected that I shouldn't use soap, if I wanted the full benefit of this energy cleansing. I rinsed my hair without shampoo under the waterfall. When I finished, my hair had never felt cleaner. I made another mental note to check with the others in the morning about the practical matter of soap use in the shower.

October 27

I was up and dressed by 8 o'clock so that I could join the others for breakfast. They teased me royally about not sleeping until noon and, once again, told me I needed all the rest I could get. I was not to feel any pressure about their schedule. I accused them of pampering me to death. They informed me that they planned to ignore my protests.

By the time I got to Perelandra, it was 9:30—and I was hungry again. (This was nuts.) Over breakfast, I casually asked Clarence how he was feeling. He complained a little about being tired and said he didn't feel like he rested last night at all, even though he knew he had slept.

If I was from the Ozzie and Harriet School of Spirituality, I'd end the story right here. I'd tell you something about the Cottage work, say that all is well and that my life still includes the Cottage. But I'm from the Scuzzball School of Spirituality, and I promised you we'd get down and dirty.

When I made my commitment to the Cottage, I set off a chain of events that would forever alter my view of life, how I lived my life and how I physically functioned. The ramifications of this were enormous and like nothing I could ever have imagined possible. My life took on an intensity that, at times, I wasn't sure I was capable of enduring. In short, my commitment was the easy part. What I had to go through to fulfill that commitment was the challenge. It's this challenge that I want to share with you so that you can understand the *practical* implications of our commitment to expand our life.

What you understand about my life at the Cottage is what I understood up to this point. I had no additional information then that I have held back from you that would clarify what was going on. Whenever I have talked about the Cottage with others, they often express frustration and incredulity that I was not getting more information about what was going on and why. They always point out that, had they been in my shoes, they would have demanded information. But, since 1977, I had been trained by nature to suspend my rational intellect when faced with reality that was outside my framework of logic. Everything about the Cottage was outside that framework. I had also been trained by nature to allow action to play out, and to observe what happened as a result. There was so much action going on around the Cottage situation that was beyond my logic that I found the only comfortable thing to do was let it play out and observe. I felt confident, based on my six years of working with nature, that all the pieces would eventually come together, and I would have understanding.

I'm going to let you cheat a bit now by giving you some additional information about the Cottage, the world in which it sits, the Cottage team and what I'm doing to get there. I feel it will help you understand what I describe about my process as you read on.

The Cottage was built especially for David and his team, and is based on architectural plans drawn up by David. It is situated in England—the "England equivalent" of a country located on a planet that exists on a sister dimension within another reality. Its currency is English, like ours here. Its customs and social structures are very like our England. The general population speaks with what we would recognize as an English accent. David and the others do not feel aligned to this country, or any other country, in a patriotic way. Their work and their connection is global (regarding our Earth) and multilevel—in the broader perspective. But David has a personal history and a sense of home that began with his association with our England that drew him to locate the Cottage in its present setting.

As I've said, the level the Cottage and the "England equivalent" are on is a dimension of another reality within the band of form that is identical to our own in how it lives out the principles of form. It is a planet that is as large and as complex as Earth, but it is not our Earth. I once asked David why he chose to continue his existence in form. He said, "I believe there is a truth in form, and I am determined to fully discover it." After death and after his subsequent healing process, he chose to set up the Cottage office within this level, once again aligning himself to form as we experience it on Earth. All who work and live at the Cottage have the same commitment to functioning within this form.

There is an entire population living on the Cottage level. Many of them, like us on Earth, are born into and die out of the level. But there are people, like those at the Cottage, who live beyond time and age, and simply materialize into the level for a specific, and sometimes lengthy, amount of time. David once explained to me that the differences I felt between how people live life on Earth and how they live it on the Cottage level are due to one basic fact: The population on the Cottage level is more mature. The souls have lived in Earth-like form longer than we on Earth have. Consequently, they have addressed many of the problems that are just beginning to face us on our level.

The Cottage world *comfortably* recognizes people who associate with it by materializing in as adults for a specific period of time. At the Cottage itself, there is a fairly constant traffic flow of these visitors. If anything like this happened openly on our level, we'd either create a religion around these people or declare them aliens from space and lock them up before they poisoned our water supply or something. These kinds of interference can just wreck a person's schedule. They'd never get anything done! So these souls basically avoid our level.

Let me give you a specific example of how the Cottage level openly accommodates people like David's team. Those who are born into and die out of this level relate to money in much the same way you and I do on the Earth level. They do something to earn it. It's a specific and *finite* method of exchange. Each country, like our countries, has its own currency. People like the Cottage team relate to money differently. They have access to an *infinite* flow. They exchange it for goods and services based on precisely what they need. When I asked them how one gets into the infinite dynamic, they explained that it all had to do with a person's sense of self-worth, and that this is a different inner journey for everyone. Once an individual truly understood his self-worth, he automatically shifts into this dynamic. The bank in the nearby village accommodates both dynamics—finite and infinite. There are separate teller windows in the bank's lobby. The men at the Cottage all have simple checking accounts from which they can draw any funds needed. They don't have complex bank accounts for maximizing earnings because their money doesn't have to earn more money. They keep a record of what checks they have written, but that's just to keep themselves informed about how they are moving money. They don't bother subtracting amounts, and the monthly statement they get from the bank is to make sure the bank records of all their transactions are in order.

Also, everyone who lives at the Cottage pays local and national taxes. The men feel strongly that they are guests of this country and choose to participate in its governing structures whenever needed by their hosts. For example, they each have a valid driver's license and pay into the national medical system, even though they will not personally need this sort of medical assistance. They do not vote, however, because they say it is important that the people for whom the social and government systems were created—the born/die people—determine their own direction.

Although all the men at the Cottage are peers, they function in specific positions that create what appears to me to be a finely tuned team. Until I came to the Cottage, they went by the names David, John, Eric and Stephen. In order to recreate the necessary World War II environment into which I was to be received during those first days, they each took the nicknames of original members of David's personal World War II SHAEF staff: Tex, Butch and Mickey. Because they like the more casual, offbeat tone, they have kept the nicknames.

As might be imagined, the level of interaction among these men is "something out of this world." (Did she say that?) They express themselves clearly, precisely and calmly. But they also go through process together. I've learned that evolution goes on no matter what level of development you reach. As I began to settle into the Cottage life and rhythm, I felt out of place in this well-oiled, close, male community. But immediately, they reached out in extraordinary ways as individuals to fully incorporate me into the group. My work with nature was integrated with the men personally as well as within their work arena. They grappled with how I function, which is very different from the way they function. They are all masters of intelligence, intent and intuition. I think and operate more creatively and spontaneously. They put effort into learning how I function, and then made sure I had the environment that enhances that.

THE COTTAGE WORK

The Cottage men are all part of the White Brotherhood. Their focus is the government/military transition from the Piscean to the Aquarian dynamic. Their work is global, and it is multilevel to include government/military transitions that are occurring on other dimensions within other realities. They tell me that they combine the words "government" and "military" because, in reality, these two dynamics are connected—the military is the implementation arm of the government. They cannot be worked with as separate dynamics.

The Cottage is not involved in the consciousness raising work that most of us are more familiar with. A different White Brotherhood group works with all government/military consciousness-raising activities. I've learned that consciousness raising centers around public events that draw the attention of multitudes of people. The key to consciousness raising is public attention. This would include the anti-nuclear demonstrations, anti-war movements and the publicity surrounding events such as the shooting down of commercial airliners that accidentally violate a country's air space. These kinds of events attract people's attention worldwide, cause them to think and talk and, eventually, shift their philosophical positions.

The Cottage team addresses the government/military changes that must occur once a population's consciousness is raised. In essence, once we reach new understanding, how do we change structure and form to accommodate that understanding? The White Brotherhood assists us with these changes, and the Cottage team assists us specifically with government/military changes. Unlike the consciousness-raising activity, the Cottage work does not have publicity surrounding it. The team often works with individuals (via their conscious or unconscious levels) who are in positions to affect policy and institute change. They tell me they normally do not work with high-profile people because these people rarely create new policy and change. The Cottage team works with those behind the high-profile leaders—the ones who actually generate policy and set it in motion.

The men tell me that we on Earth have gone through an intense period of consciousness raising, starting in 1945 with the dropping of the atomic bomb. Once the bomb was dropped, conventional war, as was developed and practiced throughout the 2000-year Piscean era, became obsolete, and the new war that included nuclear weapons became unacceptable. Because of this, governments could no longer rely on war to gain for them what it had in the past, and so they needed to learn to deal with one another in new ways. Enough of us now understand this, and our government/military structures must shift to reflect the consciousness of the people.

THE COTTAGE TEAM

The men in David's team are all full members of the White Brotherhood. They have also lived complete born/die lifetimes in form and have a deep experiential knowledge of living through form and individuation, as we know it.

Tex (real name John): Tex, like David, is utilizing the physical body and soul ray that were established in a lifetime on Earth. At that time, he was a successful attorney and family man while he developed in the direction of his present position—a development that actually spans many lifetimes and associations with Earth. He has an exceptionally sharp mind that he says he was able to "hone to a fine edge" during his life as an attorney. At the Cottage, he comes up with all the questions. He is David's "chief of staff" and is particularly valued for his ability to challenge and ask the right questions. His job is to try to poke holes in their ideas and discussions. Physically, he appears to be in his early forties, is 5'10", has blonde hair, blue eyes and a light complexion. He loves golf and chess—and hot discussions.

Butch (real name Eric): Butch handles all of the office information. He has complete photographic recall. The reason they have not computerized, so I'm told, is because of Butch. A computer can't give them what Butch and his photographic recall can. He has a passion for his classic BMW motorcycle and spends just about every evening at The Pub, thoroughly enjoying friends and the music. He appears to be about thirty, has dark hair and dark eyes. He's shy about his recall talents—in fact, he never discusses it. Aside from this shyness, he's warm and fun-loving. He is not a golfer.

Mickey (real name Stephen): Mickey is a master of service. He completely takes care of the house and us, and expresses his heart through cooking and serving. He is a brilliant and valued thinker who gets pulled into meetings when they get stuck and need extra ideas. He has a passionate, loving relationship with food and expresses joy, celebration, home and stability through his meals. He's the only one I know who can walk into a room without creating even a ripple in the energy level. This means we can be deeply immersed in intense thought or conversation, and Mickey can enter the room, serve coffee and leave without impacting our focus. I have no idea how he does all that he does for us. He keeps us together and moving forward. He appears to be about thirty-five, but I'm convinced he's really an 800-year-old troll. He is about 5'7", has a slender build, dark hair and dark blue eyes. He has a strong, creative mind and, intellectually, he is closer to my style of thinking than any of the others. He loves to run and garden. He hates golf.

David (real name David): David is the head of the Cottage team—the one who sets the pace and makes the final decisions on direction. Also, he is the one who pulled the team together. He is in the clear position of leader, a position that is recognized both in and beyond the Cottage level. I would characterize his leadership as open and flexible. He functions in an intricate and equal weave with everyone in the team. He has an energy that I would characterize as *peaceful power*—a power that inspires stability and confidence. If I had to choose one word to define his heart, I would say "integrity." He appears to be around forty-eight. He's just shy of 6'1", nearly two inches taller now than before death. What hair he has is blonde, and he has a ruddy complexion and clear blue eyes. He's still an avid but self-proclaimed lousy painter. He loves golf, the outdoors and nature.

Hyperithon: A space soul and the head of the White Brotherhood Department of Science and Technology. He is a close friend of David's and a consulting member of the Cottage team, but he does not live at the Cottage. However, he comes to the Cottage frequently. Except for the one time when he was in his "formal," wispy White Brotherhood "attire" for my celebration dinner, he is in "regular" form when he visits. He is around 5'7", wiry in build, and has energetic, brilliant blue eyes that sparkle. He loves to laugh, and he especially loves good conversation over an equally good meal. Consequently, he loves to come to the Cottage.

John is another consulting member of the Cottage team who is still alive, well and living on our Earth level in the United States. On Earth, he is not conscious of his connection with the Cottage. His agreement to participate in the Cottage team has been made on the higher soul level. He has a position and an already developed expertise that make him a valued member of the Cottage team. However, on Earth he is a man who would not be attracted to reading this book and, if by some fluke he did read it, would think it rubbish. He is a traditional, conservative thinker who dismisses this kind of information as absurd—when he's here. He now spends about six months out of the year in a "split" existence. During this time, he maintains a normal daily schedule here and is completely unaware of his activities there. He will be joining the team full time once he dies. When he is at the Cottage, he uses a younger form of his present Earth body. Although he is in his late sixties here, he appears to be in his late twenties at the Cottage. He knows me well at the Cottage, but does not have conscious knowledge of me on the Perelandra level. The process he is using to participate in the Cottage is quite different than the one I am using. To be honest, I can't explain his process anymore than he can explain mine.

Machaelle (pronounced: Michelle): This brings me to what I am doing to get to the Cottage. It is called the Split Molecular Process. In order to participate fully and consciously at Perelandra *and* at the Cottage, my soul operates out of two separate, but related, physical bodies. Both bodies are from the same individuated soul system.* Both are soul rays of the same individuated soul. From the perspective of Machaelle, I would refer to Katie as another lifetime. She was actually born into the Cottage level, and she died at age thirty-six in a bombing raid during a war on that level. (All of Earth's sister dimensions have experienced war.) In her lifetime, she became an internationally recognized pairs ice skating champion, and Max was her coach as well as her "father."

In order for me to accomplish my goal to fully and consciously participate in life on Earth and at the Cottage, I needed two compatible bodies. Both had to be female, and they had to have similar

* See the Soul Rays/Lifetimes definitions in Chapter 1.

physical characteristics. The Katie body is 5'9" tall, weighs 132 pounds, has hazel eyes and dark hair. The Machaelle body is 5'9" tall, weighed 137 pounds in 1982, has hazel eyes and dark hair. The Katie body has short, *naturally* curly hair. The Machaelle body had long, straight hair—until August 1982 when I felt compelled to get my hair cut short and permed. The physical condition of the Katie body is superior to that of the Machaelle body because the Katie body is that of an athlete. This extra conditioning was essential for the Split Molecular Process (SMP) and was an important reason for involving that body in the process.

Those who have attempted to understand the SMP have tried to liken it to what they call "walk-ins." These are two completely different phenomena. A legitimate walk-in situation occurs when the soul from one body completely releases to another body and assumes a working relationship with the second body exclusively. (I have to say that I have not met a legitimate walk-in. I have met a number of people who claim they are walk-ins, but after listening to them for a little bit, they sound more like people who did not like their life, for whatever reason, and tried to assume the role of a new life and "new soul" in order to escape.)

There are actually two dynamics of the SMP that apply to what I am doing. The first is the SMP that occurs naturally every time we shift from one level to another through birth and death. In short, we have all done and will all do the SMP—if we have ever been born or plan to die. When we shift from one level to another, our soul equally divides (100–100 percent)* and shifts to the new level. In this way, we maintain a connection with all our pre-existing levels. Another way of saying this is that when we shift to a new level, our soul does not withdraw from the originating level. It divides and is now appropriately present on both levels. What I am now describing

---

* This really is a 100–100 percent split of the soul and not a 50–50 percent split. In a 50–50 split, the originating soul energy would be reduced by half, and the new split soul energy would also be half its normal functioning reality. In a 100–100 split, both soul forces maintain full capacity. The 100–100 percent split also occurs in microbiology among some organisms that enlarge, bulge and expand in size and/or shape. Then they separate, divide or *split*. The result is that one cell becomes two cells, both of which are usually identical.

is the driving phenomenon that occurs during manifestation that moves a reality from one level to another. During manifestation, when an energy is to shift levels, the SMP occurs and this results in the shift.

This dynamic as I have described it usually happens during what we call "vertical movement" within an individual soul ray. For example, when we are born, our soul moves from a different dimension to the Earth dimension, and we take on form as we know it. Perelandra and the Cottage level are on "sister dimensions" within two different realities. In order for me to *consciously* live at Perelandra and at the Cottage, I had to make a "horizontal" shift—that is, I had to shift from one dimension in one reality to a different but identically compatible dimension in another reality. The movement was horizontal. Had the movement been vertical, I would have shifted from the Earth dimension of our reality to a dimension that functioned with different expressions of the laws of form either in the same or another reality. The movement would have been "up" or "down," but not "directly across."

To pull off the horizontal shift between these two sister dimensions, I had to utilize two bodies. One would be "stationed" at Perelandra, and the other would be "stationed" at the Cottage level.

Because of free will, I could not just "phone up" Katie and tell her I wanted her body so she better vacate it. In order for me (Machaelle) to receive custodianship of that body, she (Katie) had to decide on her own, without enticement or pressure, to continue evolution by shifting the refracted soul energy from that body system and returning it to our soul (the larger, individuated soul that we share), where it could once again become part of our larger soul mix. I'm not aware of Katie's process in all of this. Those who assisted her do know, and someday I'll sit down and ask about her decisions. Obviously, she decided it was appropriate to return to the individuated soul, a decision that I honor for her extraordinary courage, independence and commitment to life. At the precise moment of my first SMP, she shifted back into the individuated soul, and I took over soul and sole custodianship of that body. The one soul, known as Machaelle, was now responsible for two separate bodies.

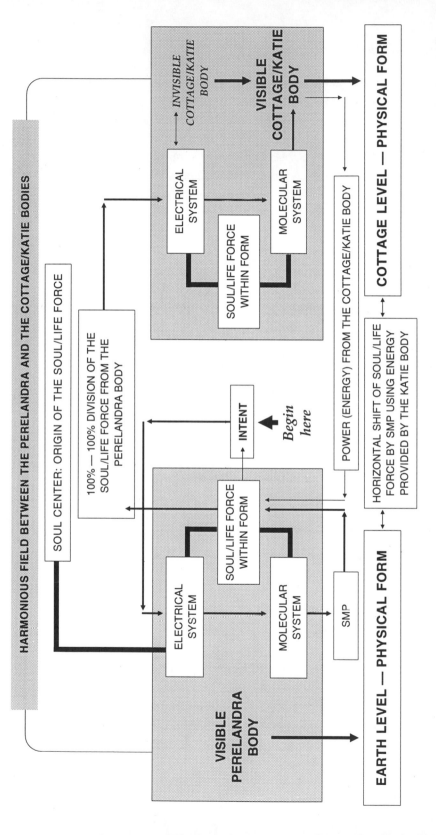

SPLIT MOLECULAR PROCESS BETWEEN THE PERELANDRA AND THE COTTAGE BODIES

This chart shows the shift from the Perelandra body to the Cottage/Katie body. The shift from the Cottage/Katie body to the Perelandra body follows the same pathway, but in reverse. However, the power (energy) for both shifts is supplied by the Cottage/Katie body.

To help you understand the SMP, I'll share Hyperithon's session when he explained it to me. Perhaps his words and the SMP chart on the facing page will make it clearer for you.

Each shift that a soul or life force moves through on its path to form, as it is experienced on Earth, is done through the use of the Split Molecular Process. The life force does not "leave" any one level for the next. It does the equivalent of the SMP from one level to the next, then does the process again, from the new level to the next—and so forth, until it reaches full form as you know it. In this way, all life force, no matter what level, maintains its link with all other levels it has experienced. The SMP is, therefore, a fundamental reality within all life force.

*Now, with regard to the Cottage, there is an unusual twist to the process. You are shifting your life force or soul force **horizontally** from one dimension to a fully compatible sister dimension in another reality. The pairing of your two bodies was truly tricky. You have two complete and independent systems that, although related within the same individuated soul system, needed to be as complementary with one another as possible. The two forms had to be as close to identical as possible. This is because the physical appearance of the body itself is directly related to and aligned with the makeup and expression of the soul force. Your soul or life force would not have found the form of a short, old, male acceptable. In fact, the soul would have repelled away from that form and remained within the Machaelle body as you attempted the SMP the first time. It is not that one is better than the other: It is simply that they are not compatible to the same soul-ray expression. So your two bodies had to relate physically in similar and compatible ways, thus creating a harmonious field between them.*

There is nothing I can use to measure or define the space between your two bodies. Nonetheless, it is an important physical reality that had to be addressed. Usually, measurement refers to time, distance and space within one dimension, and is not easily transferable between dimensions—unless they are sister dimensions. You are physically present on two sister dimensions that, like your two bodies, are related but separate and independent. However, that space between the two bodies had to contain a high degree of harmony or balance, and it is from here that you have increased the balance level to your present stability. Also, as you have integrated the Katie body, that stability has increased and improved.

*One other important issue with the physical bodies is that one had to be the "power plant" (if you will) during the process. This is because you do the SMP as part of your daily life rather than just at times of major transitions between levels. So, one body had to maintain the physical power necessary to move through the process on a regular basis, **plus** the relative power of the two bodies had to be compatible. Had the power been too different, it would have destabilized the bodies and the space between them. Although your conditioning at Perelandra is inferior to the Katie body, it is still within the compatible range of the Katie body condition. It was not difficult to pair the two bodies, and because of its athletic conditioning the Katie body was able to assume the power-plant role.*

*The SMP itself is activated by an individual's intent. Consequently, it is activated from within the individual's life force or soul. Within the physical body, that life force is anchored in form both electrically and molecularly. Just as all molecular systems contain the DNA, they also contain life force. The electrical system also includes an individual's life force. The electrical system functions as a bridge between the soul's life force beyond form as you know it and the soul's reality within that form—specifically, the molecules. An individual's intent resounds first within the electrical system. It then registers as direct action within the molecules. Life force, on any given level, can be **equally** divided once. Just as a person intends to take a step and then the corresponding muscles follow, a person can intend for the life force to equally divide and it will follow, as long as the intent includes the facility for receiving that life force once it is split. In your case, this is the second body. The split does not include the molecules. It only involves the life force contained in molecules. It is called the "split molecular process" because the split or division itself originates from the individual's molecules, not the electrical system.*

The life force in your electrical system in the Machaelle body

remains "untouched," which allows you to have a continuing connection and relationship between the two bodies whenever you are
at the Cottage. When it is time for you to enter the death process,
the life force will first split from the body molecularly and then
follow electrically. Once the life force has split electrically, the
Machaelle soul, within the Katie body, is separate and independent.

Regarding the Katie body: You draw the physical power for the
split from this body every time you do the process, no matter which
body you are moving into. When coming from Perelandra, the life
force is received first by the Katie electrical system. Prior to activation, this body is in a suspended state within the Cottage dimension,
but not discernable to the naked eye. It is most closely aligned to the
electrical level within physicality. Once your life force moves into
Katie's electrical system, it activates that body and shifts it into
"naked-eye" form as your life force reunites with the molecules. As
you know, this only takes ten to fifteen seconds. When you leave the
Cottage in the morning, the reverse is done, and the Perelandra
body is reunited with the incoming life force.

The body shift to the electrical state at the Cottage is simply an
option in the process that was deemed by all concerned, including
you, to be the most efficient way of integrating and co-existing with
the expanded reality of two bodies. Once you are at Perelandra, it is
not necessary for you to pull double duty by keeping both bodies
"up and operating," as it were. It would add more complication to
an already complex situation. In the preliminary meetings held with
you (beyond your consciousness), it was agreed all around that
maintaining the Katie body in a suspended state on the electrical
level while you were at Perelandra was preferable. It was also
preferable to maintain the Perelandra body in a quiet, but fully
physical state, while you were at the Cottage. Both states facilitate
the demanding and complex situation you took on with the two
bodies.

[Note: These preliminary meetings were held in 1981 to discuss
the possibility of my doing this kind of SMP and to prepare for the
shift as much as possible, if I consciously gave the okay later. The
meetings did not make my October 1982 decision automatic.]

Does this clear up the questions you have about the technical elements of the SMP?

Machaelle: Yes. However, if I talk about this freely, what is to protect people from trying it and getting into trouble?

Hyperithon: *Mostly ability and quality of intent. You never questioned the SMP because of your education and your experiences in the garden with nature—and with manifestation. For you, the process was a logical step that you only needed to trigger through intent. Others do not have this intimate education and experience. Their intent has built into it limitation based on lack of experience. Desire alone will not move them through the SMP.*

During my first days at the Cottage, up to the celebration dinner, I was not consciously aware of this new situation with two bodies. For one thing, the bodies are very close in appearance. At the Cottage, we have photographs of me (Machaelle) at three-and-a-half years and Katie at six. They look like they are the same child. As adults, we bear such a strong resemblance that we could easily be sisters, if not twins. I certainly noticed the differences in physical strength right away, but I attributed this to part of the mystery of being on the Cottage level and didn't think about it any further than that. Also, all my clothes at the Cottage are the size I would normally need for the Machaelle body. If I had suddenly been faced with a bunch of size 5-petite dresses hanging in that closet, and they actually fit when I put them on, I would have asked some questions.

There's one other reason why I didn't catch on right away: I'm not a "mirror person." Never have been. I can go weeks without looking at myself in a mirror. As a teenager, I once "abstained" for six weeks. It was my first Lent at the Catholic school, and I decided I would enfold the Jewish custom of not looking at oneself in a mirror during mourning (you're to think of the deceased rather than yourself during this time) as I prepared for the Crucifixion of Christ. So, at the Cottage, my natural inclination did not include rushing to a mirror to check myself out. Remember, the only time I saw my reflection during my first nine days on the Cottage level was off the side of the Packard that second day. All that did was basically confirm that I was standing there in a uniform.

Soon after the celebration dinner, the reality of these two bodies began to set in, and I had to deal with it. Here's where the challenge started. The difficulty with the Cottage body centers around the fusing of my Machaelle soul into an already developed body that had previously been fused with a different—but related—soul (Katie). The relationship one usually has with his body is that of a hand to a glove—the soul is the hand, the body the glove. There is a familiar and broken-in fit between them. At the Cottage, I was wearing a different glove that had been broken in by a different hand. This caused problems. While the Machaelle soul and the Katie body got used to one another, I experienced multiple physical problems in both bodies that had to be addressed. The three major issues were "shattering," "spasms" and cranial realignment.

I use the word "shatter" to describe what happened when my electrical systems in the two bodies experienced a massive short-circuiting. When this occurred, it felt as if my internal environment suddenly shattered, and electrical sparks were flying everywhere. It usually took the Cottage men one to two hours to balance both electrical systems and for me to regain my ability to focus.

"Spasms" occurred exclusively at the Cottage. The best way to describe them is to say that I would suddenly feel like I was internally vomiting. Really. In actuality, the spasm was occurring on an energy level, but it felt exactly like vomiting. After several minutes of riding it out, I'd be okay again.

These two reactions went on for about the first eight months, but they were especially prevalent during the first six months. I have noticed that, except for especially difficult reactions or times when I thought I would experience a reaction but didn't, I did not record in my notes how often spasms and shatterings occurred. To me this indicates that they happened so often that it was just part of my frequent, *common* process, and apparently, I did not deem it worth recording. Without exaggeration, I can fairly say that I dealt with spasms and shatterings three to four times a week during the first six months or so.

During the first year of this SMP, I worked on the Perelandra level with a chiropractor who I had gone to on a regular basis for several years prior to 1982. The challenges for the Perelandra body included learning to fully release the soul all at once during the SMP, rather than in quick stages, and dealing with the enormously heightened energy the Cottage experience was infusing into the Machaelle body. This created the need for cerebrospinal fluid (CSF) pulse balancing and structural realignment, especially with the cranials. All ten major cranial plates had to settle in a new, more expanded position and learn to contract and expand on the inhalation and exhalation in the new position. While I banged around with this problem, I experienced terrific head pressure and pain from time to time. This generally indicated that one or more cranials had jammed and were in need of adjustment.

The Cottage didn't just create physical challenges. I had the Katie-body cell memory to contend with also. Although the Katie life force was now a part of our individuated soul, the body still maintained cell memory of everything she and it had experienced as part of her development. Through physical cell memory, I had complete access to Katie's life experiences—which is why I knew how to skate and why I could easily reminisce with Max and Seamus. Ice skating and memories were seated within the body's cell memory. The Machaelle soul does not override or eliminate the Katie-body cell memory. This means that, while at the Cottage, I could recall Katie's experiences as well as my own. As part of my expansion, I had to figure out how to integrate my Machaelle abilities and life with Katie's abilities and life into one workable unit.

Basically, I was faced with the task of enfolding a whole new reality and a way of living. I had to change how I viewed everything and reinvent my life. And I had to do this by integrating a Cottage reality that I was *experiencing* that every therapist on the Perelandra level would have declared insane.

A suggestion: You might want to review the concepts and terms in Chapter 1 before reading on. Chapters 3 and 4 are the practical demonstration of those concepts, and a review beforehand might help you to better understand what you are reading.

RENEWER

SMP

Chapter 4

Those Jam-Packed
and Fun-Filled Days

The best way I can communicate what was required of me as a member of the Cottage is to show you the pattern and rhythm of how my involvement progressed on a day-by-day basis. My journal excerpts will convey the intensity but will also show how resolution came in manageable stages, not all in one intellectual and over-whelming lump. And by looking at the progression of different discussions I had with the men at the Cottage, you can see how effective the Information Policy was, and how information sprang from and wove into my daily routine. Also, you'll be able to see how many new and different concepts I was faced with nearly every day. When looking at the many different physical adjustments and changes I had to make because of this expansion, you'll notice that the pain or difficulty they created did not go on for lengthy periods, as one might expect in illness. Instead, I faced each physical challenge as quickly as possible and moved through them fast. This is one of the major differences between pain and discomfort caused by injury and illness and discomfort that is the result of an expansion of this magnitude. Finally, I think you'll see how the complexity of the two worlds that I took on settled into one, cohesive, integrated—and amazing—life.

My general daily schedule for 1982 was 10 A.M. to 4 P.M., fully at Perelandra, and 4 P.M. to 10 A.M., at the Cottage.

The pattern of eating, sleeping and working remained about the same as it had been during those first days at the Cottage. Since it was the fall and the Perelandra garden only needed to be put to bed, I was able to fully focus on the Cottage for long periods of time each day without neglecting my work at Perelandra. The journal notes that I have included in this chapter are those that deal with critical events, discussions and the pattern of my normal day-to-day schedule. I have also added information in brackets that I felt would help you understand the journal.

1982

October 27

John announced it was time for him to leave the Cottage. During a short walk with him in the garden, he explained that he leaves when he feels it's time, that it's not at all an intellectual decision.

I had a discussion with the Cottage men around personal power and glamour. The men pointed out to me that they have seen a change in my power since I came to the Cottage and joined their team. They feel I need to recognize and accept this new range of power, and that my personal sense of solidity and security in my new life in part rests on this. I brought up the issue of glamour and how I have seen others derailed by the glamour of finding themselves in a position of power. Basically, the power went to their heads. I wanted to avoid this trap, so I was focusing on my personal power as little as possible. The men said that many people who are perceived by others to be powerful have actually had their power dispersed by glamour. The glamour itself caused some people to construct the illusion of power around them, so that what we see is the image and trappings of power and not the real thing. When glamour is coupled with power, the power dynamic is self-directed and is often used for self-promotion. When a person has solid personal power, his life movements are based on what he knows about universal truth, and his focus is beyond himself. Most important, he is willing to shift his life movements as his understanding of truth shifts. Glamour takes away an individual's flexibility. But when an individual has flexibility, the men said, he has power.

October 28

While some of us sat around the fire talking, Mickey came in to tell David he had a phone call. When I said I was surprised there was a phone at the Cottage, they teased me: "Of course there's a phone!" I wondered aloud what phone company they're hooked up to. Bet it's not AT&T.

Thanked Mickey for (1) making sure I have everything I need in my room, (2) taking care of my uniforms and keeping them clean, (3) not making me drink David's coffee, and (4) making me feel so much a part of the Cottage. He said he considered it an honor to be part of the Cottage staff and that making sure we all had what we needed to function gave him pleasure.

John has left the Cottage.

October 29

Awoke early, feeling both alert and jumpy. Announced at breakfast that I felt like today was an important day, but I didn't know why. David seemed preoccupied at breakfast, but when I asked him if something was wrong, he said everything was fine, that he was just a little concerned about something. I didn't think I should pursue it any further.

When I left the Cottage, I got an intuitive hit that I should not close down the coning while at Perelandra, as had been my usual custom. I had the sense that I should stay in the coning all day and I followed my instinct.

Clarence and I met a close friend of ours for lunch. She had been out of town for five months and, of course, knew nothing about my work at the Cottage. [At this point, I hadn't even told Clarence.] When we were in the parking lot, about to leave, she asked what I had been doing lately. I told her I was going to spend the afternoon recording the progress of some sanctuary work. Uncharacteristically, she asked what it was about. (She normally did not want to know anything about my "sanctuary work.") I said to her, "I've made some serious shifts in my awareness that are as challenging to my life and how I see it as when I first began working with nature. They've been going on since July, and I'm now seeing some important patterns. That's what I'm recording."

I did not offer her any more information because I felt a time-and-place constraint—we were standing in a parking lot. Instead of letting it drop, as had been her pattern during the seven years we had known each another, she was now fascinated. She said she was headed to the Sherwin Williams store just up the street to check out wallpaper samples and, if I felt like it, I could go with her and fill her in while she looked through sample books. This felt inappropriate, but then she made a reasonable suggestion that overrode my initial hesitation. I could follow her in my car (Clarence and I had met at the restaurant), which would give me time alone to decide if I wanted to talk to her about it. If I pulled in behind her, fine. If not, she'd understand that I wasn't ready to talk about it yet.

I pulled in, deciding that I could probably give her the idea of what was going on without letting her know the whole story. I felt like it might be good for me to have a sounding board for some of my experiences. I still had misgivings about doing this in a paint store, but thought I'd give it a try.

We had the wallpaper section to ourselves. We sat side by side at a table while she looked through wallpaper books and I talked. I mentioned to her that this scene was crazy, but she suggested it was a good sign that she was looking at beautiful patterns—lots of creativity—while I talked. I didn't have a clue what she was talking about, but it sounded hopeful. She began flipping through large sample books. (Lucky for me she is a person who can do two things at the same time exceptionally well.)

I started rather clumsily. I was concerned about how she would react. Before long, she wanted the names of those involved. It was not like her to be so inquisitive, but she said it was frustrating for her to deal with so many unknowns. I gave her all the names, including Dwight D. Eisenhower. She was surprised that out of all people it was this person. We both agreed that our memories of him were that he was boring.

For two hours, I spun out the story. She asked a lot of questions. All the while, she continued looking at wallpaper samples. She rarely made eye contact with me, yet she was totally attentive. She seemed to fully comprehend the space/time thing I was dealing with. I told her about the Cottage in England and about my daily schedule. Then I told her about my commitment to the team and the dinner the next night to celebrate my commitment with everyone. Her immediate reaction was disappointment that I had not invited her to the dinner. At the end of the two hours, I had told her almost everything.

She said, "Well, you've certainly had a busy time. I'm not sure what to say now."

I teased her, "You'll probably just put this on the back burner and forget about it!"

"Oh, no. I want to be invited to the Cottage for a weekend."

I was floored, but the possibility of this happening made me laugh. We parted easily, joking about her spending a weekend at the Cottage in the English countryside.*

I left Sherwin Williams and immediately headed back to Perelandra. As I was driving, I began to feel sick and extremely exhausted. On my return, I felt compelled to get to the Cottage right away.

As soon as I walked into the Cottage, I was met by David, who seemed to be anxiously waiting for me.

"Are you okay?"

"I feel terribly fragile and exhausted. I don't know why."

He led me to a couch. "Here. Sit. Let me look at you. This has been very difficult for you. You've done a courageous thing."

I was confused. I didn't know what he was talking about. But I knew I was not in good shape. I had arrived at the Cottage feeling weak, and my mind was flying around the room at 100 mph. I kept replaying bits of my conversation with my friend as if I were an out-of-control crazy person. I asked David if he minded that I had said so much to her. He said, "Of course not. You were supposed to do this with her."

I still didn't understand. His entire focus was on me—calming, soothing and comforting me. He seemed deeply concerned about my condition. For the most part, he refused to let me replay what had

---

* My friend continued on to another wallpaper store in a nearby town. She told me later that she was followed all the way to the second store by a fellow in an old car with a new looking bumper sticker on the front bumper that read "Dwight David Eisenhower— I like Ike." While looking at more wallpaper samples, she saw a pattern that intrigued her, so she turned the page to read the information on the back. She found that this wallpaper pattern was from the boyhood home of Dwight D. Eisenhower. Later when she told me about these two incidents, she said they encouraged her to rethink what I had told her.

happened. He kept pulling me out of this mental state, which was really torturing me. I had a terrible time seeing him. My mind and my focus kept flying around.

I don't know if he knew what he was doing or if he was simply trying every trick in the book to help me, but he went through a progression of things that eventually restored my sensory system and my calm. Suddenly, I was his child. He whispered what he was saying to me. This forced me to focus on his words. Every time my mind jumped away, he'd bring me back. It seemed I could only remain in one situation for a short period of time. My whole body would start to feel jittery—like all my nerve endings were crackling with electricity. I had terrific head pressure and pain. Each time I tried to ask him what was going on, why he felt I had acted courageously, he'd just say that we'd talk about it after I was feeling rejuvenated. Meanwhile I was too drained. When he'd see me get physically restless, he'd do something—change rooms, take me for a short walk, make me change seats, make me change positions.... I couldn't stay very long in one place.

Finally, I could feel myself get calmer. The pressure was leaving my head, and I could stay in one position longer. I could see David again. That's when Mickey joined us with a pot of tea for me.

"How is she?" He was obviously concerned, too.

David said, "It drained her and she experienced some shattering. But she's okay. She wasn't damaged."

Mickey turned to me, "You did an amazing thing. We were all concerned." Then he softly touched my head.

I asked, "What did I do?"

David quickly said to him, "We're not discussing it until she's fully revitalized."

"Right. I'll tell the others she's fine. They're waiting now."

David turned to me, "What you did today was important, but I don't want to get into details now. I just want you to know you're strong and gutsy."

"I don't understand."

"Because of the physical state you are in, you were the only one who could do what you did today. We couldn't help you."

"Is this why everyone was so quiet at breakfast this morning?"

"Yes. We were concerned."

I could begin to feel my body relax more. Tex and Butch came quietly into the room to see for themselves that I was still in one piece. They said that I looked tired, but good. David said he felt I was "coming back nicely." It seemed everyone knew what was going on but me. But whatever I had done had resulted in my first shattering.

I noticed that my torso felt exposed and vulnerable, but having the men around me gave me a sense of protection. After about three hours, I needed to go for a walk, to move. I felt much better. My mind was calm, my body wasn't jumpy, my head didn't have pressure, and I was no longer trying to replay the afternoon. As we moved through the gardens, Tex, David and Butch decided now was the time for me to learn how to hit a golf ball. I received a half-hour lesson, given by all. It resulted in several lost balls and a lot of laughter.

Mickey cooked a special dinner in honor of whatever it was that I had done. Everyone continued to mother me. After dinner, Butch said that Seamus was coming over for a short visit. I asked him if Seamus knew anything about what had happened. He said no, it was just a well-timed visit.

October 30

I awoke feeling my strength had returned.

At Perelandra, I began my period. I called Hyperithon to ask how I am to handle having my period at Perelandra while I'm at the Cottage. He said that the menstrual cycle would be coordinated in both bodies, and he suggested that I talk to the men about it this evening. They could help me.

I wasn't looking forward to this discussion, but I felt I didn't have much choice about it. Hyperithon had indicated that they knew something about what I could expect, and I knew nothing.

When I got to the Cottage, I sat them all down and began.

"I would like to tell you something. It's a little hard for me to say this, but I have my period."

At that, they all started congratulating me and telling me that they already knew. I was taken aback somewhat. I was a thirty-six-year-old woman and had never experienced such a response over my period. It was truly strange. I asked, "Why is it wonderful and how did you guess?"

They said that on the Cottage level, the monthly cycle is special. It is considered a beautiful time for the woman. When she has her period, ovulates or becomes pregnant, she takes on an inner beauty that shines through. This glow is seen by her family who is then reminded of life and renewal. For them it's like spring: it keeps them in touch with creation. As men, and doing the work they do, they can easily loose sight of this. In short, my inner glow affected them all at the Cottage.

I said, "You make it sound like a celebration."

"It is."

Enough of the celebration—I had to get practical, so I asked: "Will I experience the same rhythm with my period in both bodies?"

They explained that the rhythm would be the same, but the flow might be different. At the Cottage, I could experience a lighter flow. They sounded like a bunch of experts, so I asked them how they got all this information. They said they decided when I joined the Cottage that they better become informed so they could help me when the time came. They thanked me for sharing my monthly cycle with them and assured me that it helped keep the Cottage in balance. I told them it was my pleasure. They also let me know that everything I would need for my period was already in my room.

For the first time, I felt proud to have my period; I actually saw something more than biological purpose. Several times when I passed a mirror, I looked at my reflection to check for the infamous glow, but I saw nothing. I figured it was a male thing—but I also wondered just how many people *could* see it. Was it something everyone would notice as I walked down the street? Or was it something only my family at the Cottage would see? I may be proud to have my period, but I wasn't too comfortable with the idea of shining like a neon sign for the world to see. The men kept assuring me it was a family experience, not a global one.

At dinner, Mickey served an amazing dessert—a cake in the shape of the Cottage! "It's a celebration, to all of us," he said. I was given the "honor" of cutting the cake. There was much discussion over who would get the chimney, which had the most icing. We ended up drawing cards for it—high card won, and so the chimney went to Tex.

October 31

At Perelandra. For the first time, instead of experiencing the usual low-level cramping, dread and feeling of being put upon, I was experiencing joy and a period with no pain.

I decided it was time to tell Clarence about the Cottage. I needed to start including him in what was going on. I made it sweet and simple, and let his questions guide me regarding what to say. I told him a little about the Cottage itself, the two bodies, the difficult work I had done in June and July, my suspicions about the connection between the Cottage work and Perelandra (although I wasn't at all sure about this), the Cottage team members, the military framework, my uniform and so forth. He asked many questions. He took the whole concept quite easily, saying that he felt I was having an experience like he had read about in a book (*2150 A.D.* by Thea Alexander) where a man was consciously experiencing two simultaneous existences. He was fascinated about the concept of my doing this and said he was happy for me. He immediately saw his role at Perelandra as physically "holding the fort down" while I was so deeply involved with getting the Cottage connection stabilized. He said he had no trouble with what I was telling him, mainly because he could see that *I* was absolutely clear and stable about what I was experiencing and saying—and, I had obviously kept my sense of humor.

I told him that I wanted to invoke the Information Policy with him, the same policy I was operating under with the men at the Cottage. I explained that, from this point on, I would not volunteer any information about my experiences. Instead, he would have to ask questions, and I would answer any questions he asked. This way, he would get the information that he was *ready* to hear, and I wouldn't be put in the position of trying to figure this out for him. Clarence felt I was being more than reasonable. And with that, we dropped the subject and got on with our day.

When I returned to the Cottage, David said to me, "Nice work." I

knew immediately that he was referring to my telling Clarence about
the Cottage. I felt only a little drained and quiet, but I could easily
hold my focus—and I had no sense of shattering or being disconnected. That's when it hit me, and I put two and two together. The
first shattering had occurred as a result of my grounding the Cottage
experience into the Perelandra body. I had accomplished this by telling someone at the Perelandra level (my friend, in this case) about
my life at the Cottage. With this, I consciously opened and activated
the Cottage experience into the Perelandra body and the Perelandra
experience into the Cottage body. The connection and fusion between the two bodies resulted in a shattering in both. When I told
David what I had figured out, he just smiled and said, "You got it."

We had three Frenchmen as guests for dinner. They were there to
discuss some business with the others, so I spent the rest of the
evening in my room. I discovered I had a balcony. My ability to
take in more details in my surroundings was expanding. I walked
out on the balcony and looked at the clear night sky.

November 1

After dressing, I went out on the balcony again. In the morning light
I could see the gardens below, the golf course to the left and the
gently rolling fields in the distance. Straight ahead, facing east (I
think), were more rolling hills stretching out for what seemed to be
miles. The balcony is about eight feet wide and the length of my
room. I also discovered that the wall of my room facing the balcony
is glass, just like in the living room. In my bedroom, I have drapes
that have been kept drawn, drapes that are the same off-white color
as my walls. When I brought up the issue of my new discovery at
breakfast, Mickey said that just yesterday he opened the drapes a
bit, thinking I might like a little more light in the room. He didn't
realize I hadn't known about the balcony or the glass wall. Apparently, in my struggle to adjust physically to the Cottage level, I
thought I was looking at just another blank wall. It had not
registered visually that there were drapes. Now I know. I wondered
what else I haven't seen yet.

At Perelandra. While I was getting ready to go to the Cottage, I
smelled a *very* foul odor in Clarence's bedroom. I assumed it was a

rotting rodent that one of the cats had dragged in. I told Clarence my suspicions, and he went on an extensive search in the bedroom for the offended and offending animal. He never found the thing, but he sure smelled it. He opened his window to clear out the stench, feeling confident that he would come across the carcass soon.

At the Cottage. Returned feeling a little drained from my Perelandra day. Had trouble calming down again. Also felt vulnerable, but that's usually the case when I first arrive. Today the confusion I have about exactly how I am "coming and going" in the Cottage and all the technicalities surrounding this surfaced in me, making it hard to complete my adjustment. Yet, I know it isn't time to take on technicalities—not yet. If I hold on, it will all smooth out for me. As soon as I walked through the door, David began working to help me get acclimated and to build my confidence back up.

I am beginning to feel a little guilty about his always having to give me his time and attention. But I had to admit to him that I can't seem to anticipate when I'm going to have a problem, and I also can't seem to pull myself together on my own. He spoke to me rather sternly about the fact that I still don't fully appreciate my dual role, and how I am in a unique position at the Cottage—one that they not only accept but respect and support. In David's words: "As you face all that is required of you to adjust to this new situation, you have nothing to apologize for and nothing to feel uneasy about."

We talked about how my sensory system is taking in more and more each day. He felt that my apprehensions and uneasiness about what I perceive to be a lower level of functioning stems from my not understanding or appreciating the full scope of what I have taken on. With all this said, I decided I would calm down a little—for now, at least.

Max joined us for dinner. He seemed to understand something about what I'm going through. For the first time, I was aware that he knew I'm also experiencing a physical life on another level. He could tell that I was a little tired, and I could feel gentle, unobtrusive love and concern from him. I assured him that I was fine—just adjusting (again) to being there. This opened up the conversation and he asked a few questions. He was interested in understanding what I was experiencing at Perelandra, so I gave him a sketchy picture of my life and work there—the garden, the animals, the woods, Clarence. He listened intently, but I could see the same sense of amazement about the Perelandra reality that I would expect to get from someone on the Perelandra level, hearing for the first time about the Cottage reality. How did it feel? What was it like? How did I do it? It felt right that I not go deeply into anything, so I explained to Max that I agreed with the men at the Cottage that I try not to "tear this thing apart" technically right now. I admitted that there was quite a bit I didn't understand, but I was sure it would all become clear eventually.

Although I knew everyone at the Cottage was aware of my work on the Perelandra level and supported me in what I was doing, they had given me a wide berth on the subject and had rarely brought it up. This new openness helped me. I no longer felt I couldn't casually refer to Perelandra.

The Cottage men presented me with a bicycle. I had mentioned the other day that I loved to go bike riding. They also picked up a couple for themselves in case I wanted company.

November 2

At Perelandra. Clarence asked what Mickey had served for dinner last night. I told him fish. Then I explained that the fish had tasted wonderful, but apparently (so the men told me) the cooking process creates a pretty awful odor that no one seems to appreciate. Then it hit us—was there some relationship between the foul odor in Clarence's bedroom yesterday and Mickey's foul-smelling fish? I told Clarence that I'd follow up on this at the Cottage.

At the Cottage. I related my bedroom-stench story to everyone during dinner. They all laughed uproariously. Seems Tex, David and Butch played a little practical joke on us. They figured out how to "exhaust" the fish smell out of their kitchen and into the house at Perelandra. They had not been sure what room they had vented into—they had hoped it would be the kitchen. Mickey was not in the least offended by any of this. He agreed along with everyone else that the smells were pretty bad. He said it had something to do with the reaction between the herbs and the fish during cooking. I said they had one hell of an exhaust system in that kitchen.

November 3

Awoke to my first rainy day at the Cottage. At breakfast, we got into a discussion about when I began to get information about David and what that was like for me. I told them about the funeral in 1969, the movie in June, the book, the three weeks of hell after I read the book, and finally reaching the point of knowing that I had to get insight on the situation or I would risk being damaged by the pain and confusion I was experiencing. Then I told them about my first sessions with Hyperithon, and the difficulty I had believing that someone like David would want to have anything to do with a little schmuck like me. I shared my opening process as fully as possible, choosing my words carefully. It wasn't easy for me to explain what I had been through.

David added how concerned he had been that I might say "no" at any point along the way. It had been important that I say "yes" to going on to the next step. In the meantime, he "paced anxiously." He wasn't sure that if the roles had been reversed, he would have been able to do the same. Everything up to and including my commitment had to be freely and consciously accepted by me.

Returned to the Cottage that evening and walked for about a half-hour in the garden. I crouched down and felt the coarse sand and pebbles of the path, picking up handfuls and letting it run through my fingers. Realizations and understandings began to stir in my head. For the first time, I saw the bird bath in the garden. I put my hand in the water and felt it splash around my fingers. I looked back east at the broad country vista and saw more stands of trees. I looked at the grey sky that was threatening rain again. I was now understanding more fully that I was really going through an adjustment period at the Cottage, and it was working. I was adjusting, and I was beginning to take in more of my surroundings. I realized that I had to keep moving in this adjustment time, and that my function and role as a contributor to the Cottage would clarify and become identified as I came out of this period. As I stood in the garden, I kept getting glimpses and snatches of how all of this was coming together.

When I walked up the steps to the patio, I saw Tex standing at the door waving at me. I focused on him and, for the first time, I saw him, actually saw him! All this time I could sense him, hear him, but I couldn't register him visually. I got so excited that, when I got to the door, I threw my arms around him and gave him a big hug. It was like seeing a dear friend for the first time after having been blind. I studied him: dark blonde hair, blue eyes, light complexion, my height, glasses.

Later at dinner, we all had a good time with my surprised reaction. It was a wonderful, exciting moment. Somehow, even in all the laughter, I was able to get more insight about the dynamics of my Cottage experience. Mostly, I finally realize, I'm taking in a vast amount of information and working hard just to process it. I haven't drawn too many conclusions from it yet, though.

I went on to tell the others how my sensory system is also changing at Perelandra. Unnecessary things were bouncing off me and simply not registering: TV, news information, conflict, the recent elections, stores, material things and so forth. Then I shared how frustrating it was for me not to be able to grasp what was happening at the Cottage. I talked about my frustrations, fears, sense of limitations and inadequacies. They fully focused on what I was saying while I poured out my feelings. I could feel myself work through the confusion, and I sensed a glimmer of order and hope. Suddenly, I said, "I know I'm working through something right now. But I swear to you—I swear—I'm going to make it. I'm going to do this. But I need your help."

That's when David spoke. He said that they had no doubt about my making it and pointed out the determination and strength they were seeing in me. He assured me that there was no question about their helping me in any way possible, but much of what I was doing was new to them, as well. My progress was fast—faster than they ever imagined it could be. Over and over, he assured me that I was not bogged down in any way, that, in actuality, it was quite the opposite. I felt like I was being urged on by the world's greatest cheerleader.

We talked about discipline and determination. I alluded to my real lessons in such matters, lessons that began when I was twelve. They asked me to explain what happened when I was twelve.

Slowly and carefully, I started the story of my childhood. I talked about my parents, our lack of relationship, their problems and divorce, their abuse of me and finally their abandoning me at twelve. As I spoke, I didn't get caught in a bunch of detail, but I gave them a full picture, nonetheless. I could feel myself *feeling* the pain, but I didn't cry. I didn't feel the need. But I could feel the pain. I spoke quietly, taking them through my attempts to reconnect with my father, his unstable second wife, my getting jobs to survive (beginning at age twelve), my years in Ocean City, Maryland, at the Academy and with the Catholic church. The task of surviving all of this gave me discipline and determination.

They thanked me for telling them this, and said they felt it was clear how I had developed my strength and courage.

Just then, three gunshots were fired by hunters into the Perelandra woods near the house. The noise startled me at the Cottage, and I jumped. At first I thought the rifles were being fired around the Cottage, but no one else had heard anything. That's when we realized that I had picked up sound from Perelandra and transferred it through the Perelandra body into the Cottage body. This was a new experience.

From time to time throughout the rest of the evening, I deliberately looked at Tex to make sure I could still see him.

November 4

Awoke full of vitality. The sun was out again. At breakfast, several of the men said they understood that I had written a book. I asked them how they knew so much about what I had done at Perelandra prior to my coming to the Cottage. They explained that the link I had with Hyperithon since 1980 was two-way. I may not have wanted to discuss anything with him for two years, but he could still monitor my work at Perelandra during those times. (When they saw my surprised reaction, they emphasized that he monitored my work only—nothing personal.) When he came to the Cottage for visits, he'd talk about the kinds of things I was doing with nature. That's how they first heard about me and my work. I thought, "Boy, small universe!"

I told them a bit about *Behaving As If the God in All Life Mattered* and offered to let them read the manuscript, if they wanted.

They said they'd like to wait for the finished product so they could take in the whole thing (the book, the design, the information) all at once. They gave me the sense that they didn't feel they had to look over my shoulder and that I was perfectly capable of doing my job and completing this project.

Somehow the conversation about books got us talking about historical books, and I confessed about my less-than-stellar past with world history. I told them about the two identical college classes I took. That took courage with this group. They teased me royally.

November 5

At Perelandra. Began to get insights about how my work with nature is seen by those at the Cottage as a disciplined skill that is somehow useful to them in their work. I saw that I would be working more with them in the technical area of grounding Cottage energy and in building frameworks with nature through which Cottage energy may flow and become grounded.

At the Cottage. I verified my insights with the men as soon as I returned. I talked to them about my surprise that they didn't already understand and work with the basic technical skills that they were looking to me for. They talked about the concept of expertise and teamwork. They said that if an individual could do all things, there would be no need to create and work in teams. A team is comprised of all the people with the different areas of expertise needed to accomplish a task or body of work. My skills do not fall into their areas of expertise. Although they were conceptually familiar with my line of work, they were not trained in it and looked to me to add these skills to the team. Also, I had the added advantage of being physically present on both levels. They pointed out that this would facilitate things enormously. But they quickly added that my first job was to completely move through the adjustments and changes needed to maintain one life in two separate bodies.

November 6

Every morning at the breakfast table, the men tell me what color I should be wearing. They say they see a color surrounding me, and each day the color changes. We played around with this a little, and

I found that if I stick something like a scarf or ribbon in my pocket that has the color of the day in it, I feel more stable physically.

Had a morning meeting at the Cottage on energy. Actually, it felt more like a debriefing designed for the men. I explained what I understand about energy technically. Through their questions, they got me to talk about the harmony and dissonance factor when one energy is added to another, and the different natural vehicles that can be used by the White Brotherhood to release information to those living on Earth. On this last issue, I used the example of an erupting volcano on Earth as a grounding device for such activity. Nature had already warned me about the appropriate location for fusing information energy to an actual volcano. If information in energy form is fused to the physical volcanic action right within the core of the eruption, the fused information would be incomplete or limited. This is because the volcanic action at the core is simply a "blowing-out" action and does not contain the real dynamics of the foundation of the volcano. For a full release of information energy, it must be fused deeply into the ground in a circle one to two miles out from the mountain just prior to eruption. From this location, the energy joins with the *full* volcanic action, combining with the foundation dynamics of the volcano itself. The information energy is then fully fused and fully released into the atmosphere at the point of eruption. It can then travel worldwide as part of the volcanic dust, thus making the information available to all.

The men asked me many questions about manifestation, and the mechanics of manifestation and grounding. Had I ever "lost" anything in the process? (Yes. I lost my focus and had to start over.) What did I know about de-manifestation, and what were the technical differences between the two, if any? (De-manifestation is the exact same dynamic as manifestation, only reversed.) What was the relationship between the form I might "create" in manifestation and my intent surrounding that form? (What is being manifested must be perfectly in line with a person's intent or the object will not manifest.) They asked me to talk about specific dynamics of energy within different kinds of structure, and the importance of maintaining clarity throughout all the work. Finally, we talked about different locations for grounding, and they asked about Perelandra's setup as a potential grounding point for the Cottage work. I said, "I think if Perelandra is used, it'll be a piece of cake with all the built-in nature balance. All I'd have to do is plug whatever you want grounded into Perelandra and just chug the thing on through."

At that, they cracked up and teased me about my fine use of technical language.

Evening. Talked about my use of flower essences* at Perelandra and how they seem to be helping me a lot lately. The men told me that many born/die people on the Cottage level use flower essences and that essences could be obtained in the village at the pharmacy in pre-mixed solution form only. The solutions were put together by the pharmacist based on his intuitive and intellectual sense of what a person needed. It was far from "scientific" and, although the Cottage men were curious about flower essences and what they could do, they did not like the seemingly haphazard way the pharmacist was using them. The system was too loose and made the men feel uncomfortable. So they never pursued essences.

They encouraged me to see if I could set something up with nature to shift my essences to the Cottage using the Split Molecular Process. They thought that this would enable me to have a fully potent set to use at both the Cottage and Perelandra. In short, the Split Molecular Process would split the second set off the first set, giving me two complete sets. I connected with nature and explained the situation, asking them if something could be done and, if so, what. Nature said this wouldn't be a problem and told me how to set up the split with them right then. I did precisely as instructed, and, in less than thirty seconds, I had an exact duplicate of all my essence sets from Perelandra—including finger-smudged bottle labels and the same amount of concentrate in each of the bottles that was in the Perelandra set. I tested them to make sure their potency was identical to the Perelandra-level essences. They were. Then I tested

---

* Flower essences are pattern-infused liquid solutions that work directly with both our electrical and central nervous systems. By taking the correct essences, we immediately balance the electrical system and stabilize the central nervous system. There are a number of different producers of flower essences worldwide. Perelandra began its own line of essences in 1985 with the Rose Essences. In 1982, I was using the Bach Remedies and essence sets one and two from the Flower Essence Society in California.

myself for essences, showing the men how to test using kinesiology and why this was superior to what the pharmacist was doing. I needed about four essences and felt an immediate balancing after I took them.

After dinner, they talked me into going to The Pub to hear Seamus and his band. While there, my knowledge of Seamus's love for music and even some of his songs surfaced. I just quietly sat back and enjoyed the evening.

November 7

Lately, I have been having a series of frustrating and frightening dreams, and I haven't been able to figure out what is behind them, so I had a session with Hyperithon while I was at Perelandra.

*In part, your recent dreams have centered around your frustration over not knowing all that is happening to you now. The dreams are pointing out that you are pushing your desire to know against the limits of your own timing. The fear dreams of falling from great heights to your death are related to a previous pattern that still exists from your life as the plantation owner. That is, the fear of being rent in two, of losing your mind while under severe pressure. Although we recognize that this adjustment time with the Cottage places you in a most unusual pattern of existence, it is **not** more than you can handle. Through your background and training, you are capable of taking on this dual reflection. The irony is that part of the training you have undergone to prepare for just such an opportunity was your experience of the complete nervous breakdown as the plantation owner. The breakdown helped you to understand the phenomenon of splitting in two so that you could understand Oneness.*

We suggest that you share the dreams and this information with the others at the Cottage. They are not aware of your plantation lifetime. By telling them, you will disperse the pressure you are presently experiencing, thus reducing the level of tension and frustration. But also by telling them, they will have a greater understanding about what you are dealing with and be able to support you more effectively through your adjustments. They very much want

to help you, to be by your side, to comfort you—but they need your
input to effectively do this.

Along with the dreams, I had also been experiencing flashes of
Cottage scenes in my head while I was at Perelandra. It was clear
that the flashes were of events to be "played out" in the near future,
not past events that had already occurred. Usually, I was faced with
the actual event the same day, once I returned to the Cottage. This
phenomenon had happened enough times that I felt I needed some
insight on what was happening, so I asked Hyperithon about it in
this same session.

You must remember that because of the greater degree of maturity
among its population, the environment at the Cottage is more con-
ducive to participation in a more expanded reality. Consequently,
what you experience infrequently within the Perelandra reality will
occur more frequently and with greater clarity within the Cottage
reality. You can project into the future at Perelandra, although this
is not one of your primary disciplines. In fact, you tend to pay little
mind to this phenomenon. But, in the Cottage environment, you can
project into the future more frequently—especially the short-term
future. The Cottage flashes you have been receiving lately are valid
projections. You have intuitively felt that you are not to play out
those flashes in your head in detail. This is good self-advice. To
allow yourself to totally experience the flashes will drain you. Cer-
tainly there is nothing wrong with identifying a flash—for example,
"seeing" that Max will come to the Cottage tonight with Allison and
ask you to help her with a physical problem. But to continue through
the flash to identify exactly Allison's problem and what you are to do
is too much of a drain on you. It would be like living three separate
existences instead of just two.

To conclude, you are activating bits and pieces of what you have
learned from several lifetimes into one, complex, two-body life. Your
participation at the Cottage and within the Katie body on that level
allows you to more fully express. So you can activate your skating,
your energy knowledge and the flower essences. Nothing is beyond
your control. Relax with these openings, and you will take consider-
able pressure off yourself. Allow the men at the Cottage to aid you.

Keep them as up to date as possible with your insights and what you are understanding. This is not a burden to them.

At the Cottage. I shared the information I had received from Hyperithon and the insight about Max coming over that evening with Allison, a six-year-old skating student of his. They knew nothing about Max visiting. He had not called them that day. Sure enough, after dinner, Max showed up with Allison. She had had a bad fall on the ice this evening, and her body was not relaxing out of the contracted trauma state. I tested her for essences and took her into the lagoon for about a half-hour. By the time we walked out of the lagoon, we were both more relaxed.

November 8

David returned the 1942 Packard to the fellow who collects antique cars and had been willing to loan him the Packard for a couple of weeks, and replaced it with a new car, the name of which I had not heard of before. With the addition of my life to their schedule, they felt another car was needed.

November 9

JAMFD: Just another mundane-fantastic day! Nothing out of the ordinary happened.

November 10 through 12

JAMFD times three.

November 13

Tex drove me to the rink to meet Max at 4:00 for some more work on the ice. While I was skating, I could feel that my moves had a different power, a different *direction* of power. The rotations in the jumps were initiated by the turn of my sternum and sacrum, and this motion transferred throughout my body effortlessly. The rotation for the jumps was internal rather than external, giving a new sense of quiet and ease to the jump and making the movement of the skates almost incidental. Max and I worked together on this for a couple of hours. I received two bad bruises as a result of some fairly spectacular spills. When Tex reported this to the others during dinner, I was once again surrounded by Jewish mothers. It sounded like they were under the impression that women didn't (or shouldn't) get bruises. I didn't let them get away with that kind of thinking without some good ribbing on my part.

November 14

After breakfast, the men gave me a thumbnail sketch of the work they are doing. They are examining all the individual strategies used in war over the past 2000 years (during the Piscean era) to see how they can be shifted and used as nonviolent strategies for global conflict resolution. The men call the shifting of these strategies "flipping the coin." Every strategy designed to be implemented within the context of war can be used just as effectively within the context of nonviolent resolution of government conflicts emphasizing teamwork, if their coin is flipped. Another way of saying this is that those strategies used during the Piscean era as the means for implementing and achieving government goals can now be used in the Aquarian era for achieving similar goals, but through nonviolent means and teamwork. Once the strategies are shifted, the Cottage team uses them as the components for new approaches, new tactics, and creates innovative, workable strategic packages—all within the context of teamwork. These packages are then released to individuals or groups to be used in specific situations on our Earth level.

This explains why so much study, reading and brainstorming goes on at the Cottage. It also explains the steady stream of visitors during the afternoons. Some of them are the original strategists. They are debriefed by the staff in order to better understand the subtleties of a tactic so that the full intent of the "coin" can be flipped. Coins that originated and were implemented in the Piscean era have already been grounded into the Earth's plane through both theory and action. By using these coins, the Cottage team ensures that their "new" strategy will not feel alien to those of us on Earth. Whether we participated in war or not during the past 2000 years, these strategies still feel familiar to us simply by the fact that they were played out on Earth and have become part of the planet's dynamic of reality. In short, the strategies are part of the planet's cell memory, and consequently, we will be more likely to accept the new directions. Had the Cottage created entirely new frameworks that did not have their foundations already grounded on Earth, we would have felt them to be alien and rebelled against them or rejected them outright.

My first reaction was to say, "This place is the Pentagon of the White Brotherhood!" I spent my day at Perelandra thinking about the enormity and complexity of the Cottage work. It was like a thick cloud around me that I had to let gradually seep into my being.

When I returned, I found a bunch of video tapes that Max had dropped off earlier. At breakfast, the men asked me if I minded their looking at the tapes Max had of Katie and John's competition performances. (Max had announced during one of the Cottage dinners that he had tapes of all practices and performances of his students— including Katie and John.) I was curious to watch Katie in action, so I gave the okay.

We watched about an hour and a half of performances. Max had spliced the tape together like an historical retrospective of John and Katie's skating career. As I watched, I could feel Katie's movements in my body. And I could anticipate the moves. In fact, I "knew" the routines. It was a fascinating experience. Then Tex put on a second tape, one that Max called "The Rise and Fall of John and Katie." This was an hour of spectacular spills that he had spliced together from both practices and performances. It was a little painful to watch. Max had attached a note to the video tape saying that he sometimes showed this to students who were going through periods of discouragement. They were able to see that even "the best had their bad days."

The tape included a serious fall that Katie had during a practice not long before their second Olympics competition. She was lifted over John's head when he ran into trouble, and she crashed to the ice. It was a nasty fall that resulted in excruciating pain and two cracked ribs. It was obvious on the tape that she was furious at Max. She wouldn't let him touch her, and she insisted on leaving the ice on her own steam. The Cottage men just looked at me and commented that stubbornness must be a soul pattern of mine.

We watched a third tape with more successful performances,

thank god. The TV had been set up in the living room, and I watched the tapes while lying on the floor in front of the fire with a pillow behind my head. After the third tape, I drifted off to sleep. In fact, I fell into a deep sleep. I began to relive Katie's serious accident in rehearsal that resulted in the cracked ribs all the way through to her performance at the Olympics. I relived the accident, the pain and the emotions. I could feel the taping that Katie had to wear around her chest to support her ribs. When she hit the ice, I became ice cold, even though I was asleep in front of the fire. I also cried out and began to sob. The men could not pull me out of the sleep. They saw that I was shivering, so they put a blanket over me and stayed with me as I finished the process. (At the time, they didn't know what was going on. They were operating on instinct.)

When I woke up, I realized a number of things about Katie's fall: (1) She considered it her fault because she had noticed a problem in that movement, and she let John and Max overrule her concerns. She had gotten angry because she felt they were not taking her seriously because she was a woman. So, instead of pressing her point, as she should have, she quietly steamed. (2) She did not want Max to touch her after the fall because she was so deeply angry at him for "allowing" her to get hurt. (3) She did not tell Max or John about the extent of her injuries. (4) She had a great fear of heights, especially any time she was higher than five feet off the ground or ice. She had worked against this fear throughout her skating career. (5) Her fears were even greater after the fall. (6) She knew that every time she landed from this particular move while practicing for and performing in that Olympics, she would feel tremendous pain, and she risked further injury. This, too, she kept to herself.

By the time I told the men what was going on, I was exhausted. But I had a clear sense that I had faced Katie's last demons, and that the trauma of this accident had now been released from the Katie body's cell memory.

November 15

Awoke feeling at peace, but fragile and vulnerable. Decided it was important to take it easy for the day at Perelandra.

When I got back to the Cottage, I asked Butch if he would mind driving me to the rink. Max was already there, but when I got on the ice I asked him not to disturb me. I needed to be alone. While skating, I went deep inside myself and quietly skated every move I could think of several times, all the while evaluating my body movements. I skated for two hours. That night at dinner I announced that I was deciding whether or not to continue skating. I was feeling that it might be time for me (and Katie's body) to leave the ice— completely. I asked for their input, and they said it was important that I follow my heart. If I felt it was time to stop, it was time.

November 16

Awoke feeling that I should stop skating. (1) After yesterday's evaluation of my body as I skated, I feel that my knees will begin to show irreversible physical stress if I continue. The Katie body has had, after all, many years of this physical stress. (2) Katie and I have reached all our goals. (3) Katie and I have paid all our debts. (4) Max and I are no longer coach and student. We are father and daughter. (5) I wouldn't be able to skate recreationally without periodically trying something dangerous just to prove I could do it. I know I have this in me, and it would frustrate me to feel that at age thirty-six, I needed to skate "reasonably and responsibly."

I felt calm about this decision. When I announced it at breakfast, I could tell they were breathing a sigh of relief, as well. Apparently, the potential for an accident had concerned them.

After dinner. They asked me how I feel about hunting and the controlled kills within preserves and other protected areas. This led us into a fairly lengthy discussion about animals and their relationship with humans, and animal death. At one point, I stopped talking in mid-sentence. They were all looking at me in such an intense way and listening so carefully that their attention simply overwhelmed me. I had never before experienced a quality of listening like this.

Tex pressed me on several issues. It was the first time I experienced his relentless probing. I matched Tex, challenge for challenge, much to the delight of the others. David explained that Tex is a master at finding and probing anything that even looks like a soft spot. I could tell there was nothing malicious in his challenges, but it sure made me feel like I really have to be on my toes around this guy. I think he was pleased that I didn't let him back me down.

In the course of the conversation, Mickey told me that he has noticed more wild animals coming around the Cottage since I joined. I told him I wasn't willing to accept responsibility for this!

November 17

Before dinner, I kept looking out the windows onto the patio. I said to Tex, "I think I hear something calling to me." After dinner, I felt compelled to go to the windows again. Just then, a little, dark ball of fur scampered across the patio right in front of me. I opened the door quietly and walked out on the patio. Immediately, the little thing ran over to me. I looked at it and realized, much to my surprise, it was a baby skunk. I estimated it to be about four weeks old. [I could make a decent guess at the age because I was familiar with baby skunks. Clarence and I had raised two de-scented skunks at Perelandra. We had gotten both skunks when they were five weeks old, and the one at the Cottage looked a little younger than that. The picture in *Behaving* on page 199 is of Louie, our all-white, albino skunk at six weeks.]

Two other things surprised me about the baby skunk at the Cottage. (1) All skunks are born during the spring, and this one had to have been born in October. I knew this to be most unusual. (2) England on the Perelandra level does not have wild skunks, and I was pretty sure that the same was true for England on the Cottage level.

I quickly got a banana from the kitchen and returned to the patio to see if the skunk would eat. I knew that, if given the opportunity, they could develop a real taste for banana. It eagerly ate small pieces of banana right out of my hand. While it ate, I began to feel I knew this baby from somewhere. That's when it hit me. It was the wild baby I had befriended early this summer at Perelandra. Our dog Elsa had discovered a den of baby skunks in the field just on the other side of the road from us, and she had barked until I came to inspect her find. There were five little ones, and they could not have been more than three weeks old. They looked hungry, so I watched for a while to see if the mother was going to return. When she didn't, I assumed she had died or had been killed. I put together a bowl of "skunk chow" and left it right next to the den, which was more like a little cave nestled in some rocks. When I returned early the next evening, the bowl was empty, and the babies looked like they were ready for more.

When I fed them, I made sure that I made as little contact as possible because I didn't want them to bond with me. I wanted them to remain wild. One afternoon, about a week and a half after I started feeding them, I found one of the babies on the bank close to the road, sitting belly up, human style, among some brush. When I approached, she didn't run. I discovered she was injured and couldn't move—she acted like she was paralyzed from the waist down. And she was covered with maggots. I suspected that she had been picked up by a hawk and then accidently dropped, breaking her spine. Despite all of her adversities, she was still feisty and determined to let me know she was in charge. But I knew she was going to die and soon. The skies were darkening for an afternoon thunderstorm, and I didn't think it was fair to let her die while she was being pelted by rain. So I fixed a box for her and took her to the house. I tested her for essences and moved her through the animal death process. She was feisty and sweet at the same time, and *I* ended up bonding with *her*. She died in the evening, and we buried her that night in the woods.

The other babies grew and left the den on their own. They even weaned themselves off of my homemade skunk chow before leaving. (Perhaps they were making a statement about my cooking.) By the end of the summer, I was so focused on the Eisenhower business that I had forgotten all about the skunks.

At the Cottage, the little skunk on the patio ate about a third of the banana. Intuitively, I had gotten that she needed help, but she must be allowed to remain free and not caged. I brought the men outside and introduced her to them. She wasn't shy at all. I told them her story, and how she and I went back a "long way."

The men immediately jumped into action. There was concern by all over her fate—especially from Mickey. They set up a box and a bowl of food just outside the kitchen door under a bench where she would be protected from the elements. I played with her a little, then settled her in the box. She was happy.

When we went back into the living room the men asked me, with mock concern, what else I had helped through the death process at Perelandra that might be showing up at the Cottage. With a straight face, I told them not much—just a camel, an elephant and two dolphins. Then I asked them if they'd mind enlarging the lagoon.

November 18

I went down to breakfast and found David intently looking out the window. I asked him what he was looking at. He said, "I'm not sure. I want to see what you see when you look out these windows." He talked about my impact on the Cottage, and how I have integrated my work within my own person and that I don't "just talk a good game." He said my presence at the Cottage is changing their entire environment and catalyzing changes in the men, including himself. Before I came, they understood something about the role of nature, but they had underestimated the influence someone could bring who has integrated nature into the very core of their being. Then, he asked me to look out the window.

"What do you see out there?"

"Life. God. And since I'm also God, I see family."

I tried to describe my life with nature—the joy, celebration and intimacy I experience. I questioned him about my effect on the Cottage environment. He said that even the walls inside the Cottage felt different. I suggested that this might be the result of what is called the Pan/Christ phenomenon—the coming together of the nature dynamic in its fullest with the evolutionary soul dynamic of the White Brotherhood. I suggested that my presence was grounding nature energy into the Cottage environment, which, up until now, had been dominated by the evolutionary human-soul dynamic. This could be expanding everyone's experiential ring-pass-not. Based on my experience at Perelandra, I told him that, whenever there is action, it is at its strongest, most vital, most stable when nature and the human-soul energies combine.

David said, "It's clear to me now that we need a better understanding of your work at Perelandra. Everyone here feels this. We're all experiencing the impact of your being here."

The impact of my presence at the Cottage is not something I myself feel since I have nothing to compare it with. But listening to David gave me the insight that I am to ground nature energy into the Cottage and help create a Pan/Christ or involution/evolution vortex. I promised him I would try to include them in my world. With that, we went to breakfast.

Evening. The skunk came out of her new wooden box (built this afternoon by Butch and Mickey) a couple of times for food early this evening, but she returned right away for more sleep. Mickey is diligently making sure she has everything she needs. I've told her that the best way to deal with these Jewish mothers is to ignore them and just carry on with her life. Mickey wants to name her Petunia. I think it's a perfect name for her.

November 19

At Perelandra. Got the hit to transfer to the Cottage the transcript of my 1978 talk to the Findhorn Community about my first year of co-creative gardening. David had asked me this morning what it is like to work with nature intelligences, and I think this transcript can answer that best. From Perelandra, I set it up with nature and did the Split Molecular Process with the transcript. We "landed" it on David's desk. When I got to the Cottage, he verified that he had gotten my "mail," and thanked me. Copies had been made, and they had all read it by the time I returned. Throughout the evening, we discussed my garden experiences and the principles I have learned from nature.

November 20

Slept twelve hours.

At Perelandra. An acquaintance from Findhorn brought a woman to meet me who has spent most of her adult life trying to deal with and get rid of five entities who have attached to her. She's been institutionalized several times and spent time in padded cells and on prescribed drugs. She claimed that the last entity finally released three weeks ago. Now she wants to be open to the "vibrations and communications" of nature intelligences. She asked to visit our nature sanctuary, and when she came out, she said she went through a healing process in the sanctuary. She feels that I am someone who can understand and support her opening process, *and* I am someone who has experienced this kind of openness and is "obviously stable and happy." From this she received encouragement and support. (I didn't tell her about the dead president thing.) I really didn't know what to believe about her story. I tried to convince her to spend time healing and exploring her inner process without feeling pressure to jump right into "cosmic service." I'm not sure she heard me. She's determined to press herself into some kind of "spiritual service" right away.

At the Cottage. I asked David if he had any information on the phenomenon of entities taking over or attaching to a person. I told him about my visitor at Perelandra and explained that entity attachment strikes a dissonant chord in me and goes contrary to my deep sense of universal love and my belief that we are all ultimately loved and cared for. In short, I just didn't think there were squads of spirit leeches floating around looking for unsuspecting humans to attach to.

David told me he had done a limited amount of research on the subject because they needed to know something about this phenomenon in relationship to their work. Since they often work with individuals on the Earth level while they are in a sleep state or semi-conscious, he wanted to know what the chances were that a person might feel "invaded" because of the Cottage contacts. He said that it is his understanding that "uninvited guests" will attach themselves to a person—but *never* without an indication or invitation from the person. The connections are never random. These people have relinquished their personal rights and have opened themselves to others within the context of victimization. Rarely are these connections dangerous in themselves, but because the "host" person is perceiving life from a victimization perspective, he *translates* his interactions with the uninvited guest within that framework. As a result, harmless interaction becomes frightening and overpowering because of two dynamics: (1) The connection between the unwitting host and the uninvited guest is inappropriate and will feel inappropriate in every way for the host. (2) The unwitting host is translating the experience through the lens of a victim, thus creating frightening interpretations of what is happening. The deep belief that we are loved and cared for and, therefore, safe sends out a clear signal that uninvited guests are not welcome. A person with such beliefs sounds an invitation for only loving, caring and respectful contact.

November 21

Slept ten hours.

Evening. Petunia ran toward me as soon as I came into the garden. Held her for a little while and talked to her about my day. Apparently she wasn't too impressed because she fell asleep in my hands, so I put her back in her den. I can tell that she's going through some kind of healing cycle. I feel that we have this in common.

November 22

After breakfast, Butch and Mickey asked if I would test all of them for flower essences. They were especially concerned about Tex who, for a couple of days, had been moving through some emotional shifts. I tested everyone, and Tex needed the most essences. The ones needed by the others were needed as a result of their support for and sympathy with Tex's process. As soon as I administered the essences to each man, I could literally *feel* his body shift. It was the strongest response to flower essences I have ever experienced with anyone—myself included.

Evening. Max invited us to attend a skating competition at the rink. We all thought it would be a good break. The competition was tight and boiled down to personal preference when it came to the judging. One of Max's pairs won the gold by a hair. I thought about how grateful I am not to have the pressures of skating competition to add to everything else I have to go through. Then I found myself laughing at the notion that I (Machaelle) could even consider competition skating! By the time I got into bed, I was wondering if I really could compete. I decided I didn't want to know.

November 23

At Perelandra. Clarence and I signed our wills at the lawyer's office. Now I feel like my life has some order!

At the Cottage. David and I went for a long walk before dinner. I notice that whenever I am alone with him, I can feel the deep link we have between us. I can relate to him with an ease that usually only occurs between two old friends who truly enjoy one another. It seems like the friendship that has spanned several lifetimes has simply continued uninterrupted. Whenever I try to think about this within a linear concept, I get confused and feel like I am stumbling around emotionally. As soon as I let go of the linear notion, I can once again feel that new logic, and our link makes sense.

November 24

Locked horns with Tex during breakfast. He got into another one of his pressurized word games with me. Generally, he begins by asking questions in a casual conversation, then the intensity escalates with his questions. Before I know it, I feel he has nailed me to the wall. I can usually feel the pressure building, but not soon enough to stop him. This morning I just got angry. I stopped him in mid-sentence and informed him he doesn't have my permission to play this kind of game with me. I'm not his toy. I didn't raise my voice, but I sure had him locked in an angry and intense stare. Although they said nothing and did not jump in to defend me, I could feel everyone else at the table supporting me, even quietly cheering me on. I left the dining room with feathers flying.

Evening. Spent a little time playing with Petunia in the garden. Her energy seems fully restored. When I got to the living room, Butch and Mickey met me with great smiles on their faces and called me "Rocky." Then Tex entered with bandages and slings draped all over him and waving a white flag! He apologized for the morning, saying that I was absolutely right to come down on him. It was clear that I had held my own, and they were pleased.

After dinner, they told me they could see the glow building before my period, which is due in a couple of days. I suggested that they were all weird, and that sitting around and watching my period-glow build was akin to watching paint dry. They ignored me. During the conversation, Butch asked me if I knew what it was like for a woman to have a miscarriage. I told him that I had had two (as Machaelle), and I spent a moment reaching into my memory to try to translate the feeling for him. Finally, I said, "It's like cruising down the highway at 50 mph, when suddenly someone jams the car into reverse without stepping on the brakes first. If you can imagine what that might do to the car; that's about what it feels like in a woman's body and mind."

They asked questions about this, and we got into quite a discussion about how it seems society in general, and men in particular, don't understand or acknowledge the seriousness of this event in a woman's life. For them, it was always a mystery whenever they heard that a woman had suffered a miscarriage. They could only feel sadness, and they could never figure out how to reach out to a woman in an appropriate way. Consequently, they held back.

Butch asked if I minded these questions. I told him that if they had been idle curiosity, I would have felt they were unfairly prying. He assured me that I was the only one they knew to ask these questions, and I assured them that I could tell the questions weren't idle curiosity. He said that this was something they had wanted to understand for a long time, and thanked me for my openness.

Later in the evening, when I was in my room, I decided I wanted to try to shift something from Perelandra using the Split Molecular Process that would make my room feel more personal. I connected with nature and asked if this could be done. When I got the go-ahead, I asked that my favorite, handcrafted corn-husk doll be shifted. We set up the proper coning, and in about fifteen seconds, I was holding the doll. I put her on my chest of drawers, then got ready for bed.

November 25

JAMFD

November 26

Returned to the Cottage in a shattered state. This is about the sixth time I've experienced shattering in the last two weeks. The episodes have not been as extreme as the first, but it still takes an hour or two to completely pull out of it. Plus, I still cannot pull out of them on my own. I have to rely on the others at the Cottage to help me refocus. Decided I will ask Hyperithon if he has anything that could be useful for me regarding this situation.

November 27

At breakfast, I was "warned" that they are expecting two visitors soon who may need to stay at the Cottage for several weeks because of some work they are presently involved in. I thanked them for the warning.

At Perelandra. Talked to Hyperithon about shattering. I was specifically looking for clues about how I can pull myself out of a shattering. He didn't mince his words.

The key that you are searching for is held by the others at the Cottage. They are the ones who can respond to and help you recover or "heal" from any shattering you might experience. Sometimes the greatest and strongest inner balance we can have is to know when to allow help to come to us. Your highly developed sense of independence has not yet fully opened to include the independence from self. This allows each of us to appropriately open to others. You fight this specific connection with the Cottage men. You see your need for them in this area as a weakness—when, in fact, it shows great strength. Accept the shattering phenomenon as a unique, a "beyond ordinary" experience in your life, and open fully to the Cottage men for help. You are good at helping others put pieces together but, as with many who have this talent, you do not allow yourself to avail yourself of these benefits from others. Your family (the Cottage) knows precisely what to do for you—both from what they have learned regarding shattering and from their intuitional instincts stemming from their love for you. They are aware that this will be a part of your reality as you go through this adjust-

ment and integration period, and it is now time that you understand this, as well. Let your family function as your family and expand your operating framework of independence!

This may sound strong and short to you, but we know that you communicate with clarity and respond best to this from others. You are accomplishing your adjustments and moving into your life at the Cottage with great speed. You are demonstrating your strength, agility, focus and determination. We urge you to have the patience and consideration with yourself that you would have for others.

At the Cottage. I had a little difficulty sharing Hyperithon's advice to me with the others. I knew this was going to give them "implied permission" to continue being Jewish mothers, as well as being the "shatter relief squad." But instead of kidding me, they quietly urged me to let them help me whenever possible. I guess I have begun my journey to learn independence from self.

Seamus showed up after dinner to "unveil" a couple of new songs he has written. I found out that David has given Seamus an open invitation to play the piano at the Cottage. I have the feeling Seamus will be stopping by frequently since he likes that piano so much, but I didn't tell anyone about my suspicions. I figured we were all even. If I have to unleash the Jewish mothers on myself, the least they can do is unleash my music-fanatic brother on themselves!

November 28

At the Cottage. Experienced another shattering when I got home. I didn't resist their help. Finally fell asleep on the couch in front of the fire. When I woke up, Mickey gave me soup for dinner.

November 29

Awoke to an unseasonably warm day. Sat out on the balcony and felt the sun's rays on my face. I could really feel a warm, healing sensation on my skin.

Evening. My night for a few questions. I asked if the people in the village know that the men in the Cottage are members of the White Brotherhood. David explained that some of them know and that others do not. Generally, it's a quiet piece of information that gets passed around by word of mouth among those people who might be interested. It is not something the Cottage men announce. In fact, they prefer to keep it quiet because they don't want any "folderol." I also asked why they are choosing to operate "in form." They said that they believe form contains an essential truth that they find challenging and exciting. It was as simple as that. With that, I changed the subject and asked no other questions. I could feel I didn't want to go any further.

November 30

We had a discussion at breakfast about these notes that I'm keeping. They suggested that I "talk to nature" and see about transferring a copy of the notes to the Cottage for safekeeping. They also urged me to continue the notes, saying that they felt my records about this two-level life were important. I told them that I thought the notes would be useless to anyone else but me, but that I would continue keeping them. If nothing else, they helped me to clarify my thinking and absorb what is happening to me.

At Perelandra. Had my first appointment with the chiropractor since going to the Cottage. I've been experiencing a strange head pain at Perelandra for about three weeks. It's not like a typical headache. It feels more like someone is pumping air into my head, and I'm feeling the pressure of too much air. I seem to be missing a relief valve.

I had to explain to the chiropractor a little about the Cottage if she was going to help me in any real and useful way. This made me a bit nervous. To my luck and surprise, she didn't blink. I think knowing me for over three years helped her not write me off as a lunatic. It also helped that we had established my "normal" pattern of what I usually needed when I visited her. Actually, I went to her for periodic maintenance, and generally I walked away with no more than a minor adjustment. On the whole, we both knew my body was strong and easily maintained its balance.

However, for this visit she had to adjust all ten major cranials, and I tested positive for Clematis [the Bach Flower Remedy for inability to hold focus], for stabilizing the cranials after the adjustment. She felt that the strain of translating everything that was happening to me took four times more energy than normal and resulted in my need for Clematis. My thyroid tested balanced, which indicated to her that the translations of my reality were accurate. Also my adrenals and liver tested balanced and quite strong. My pituitary, heart, pancreas and pelvis all tested weak. She did a pelvic adjustment that strengthened the heart/pituitary link and put both back on balance. She felt the heart/pituitary problem showed the intensity of my commitment and that it was a heart and soul commitment. My pelvis couldn't maintain alignment under the intensity of the commitment. The pancreas was strengthened to full balance with three supplements.

I told her about the trouble I was having with the shattering, and what I had to go through in order to come out of it. She suggested that I see her within seventy-two hours after a shattering, before the trauma crystallized in either body. And she recommended that I take Rescue Remedy when a shattering occurred.

In her opinion, all the adjustments pointed to a reshifting of my internal gears to a new balance. The cranials needed reshifting to handle the new intensity and flow of energy that I was experiencing. She said I looked like I was trying to catch six balls with my hands, but was only able to snag four of them as the other two flew by. (I've heard *this* before.) The effort was creating a "spasm" in the cranials, hence the need for Clematis. She felt that with the adjustments, I would be able to catch all six balls in a basket with ease. She assured me that she was doing only what my body was "asking for," and that she planned to let me take the lead in this. I was clearly operating in an area well beyond what was taught in chiropractic school, so she was going to follow my lead and not try to dictate a direction of her own. She felt that my need for only one minor spinal adjustment and one essence (for the cranials) indicated to her—beyond a doubt—that I was dealing with very strong energies from outside myself. Because of this, she had no trouble accepting the idea of the Cottage, and she was excited about what I was learning about the human body from my Cottage experiences.

I was relieved. I was also grateful to have the Cottage experience confirmed by another person on the Perelandra level. I left her office feeling that I had someone on Earth to help me hold and support this new adventure of mine.

At the Cottage. As soon as I walked in, everyone commented that I looked different—more solid, they said. More there. In fact, they were astounded by the changes. I told them about the work I had done with the chiropractor. We talked about the real and physical implications of my dual existence. I told them that I was excited about what I was discovering—the implications of my experiences on the human body, what must be done physically to accommodate these experiences and what must be done to maintain physical balance. Suddenly I saw an enormous learning opportunity being given to me. The men were obviously concerned about the "price I was paying" for my new life. They explained that this kind of dual-body challenge had not been taken on previously, so no one knew precisely what difficulties I might be faced with. They told me that everyone involved with the preparations for my taking on the dual-body life felt certain I could handle the adjustments and changes required. But they could only speculate on the details of what would be required of me to settle in and maintain balance, and the stresses I would need to deal with. Actually, watching what I'm going through is sometimes startling to them. In effect, I am blazing my own trail.

One change I wasn't too happy about: My vision at the Cottage is more vague than yesterday. Less is registering. The men felt that once all the chiropractic changes made in the Perelandra body finished shifting into the Katie body, my sight would be better than before.

December 1

They were right. My sight has returned stronger than ever.

At Perelandra. Went shopping all day with my wallpaper friend. Caught her up on some of the things that have been happening at the Cottage. She's urging me to change from writing these notes to dictating them, feeling that dictation would be less stressful on me. I told her I'd consider it, but I think I'm getting a lot of benefit out of writing everything down. It gives me a chance to review and reflect.

My friend told me that when she first saw me this fall in the restaurant, she hated my new hair style and could barely look at me.
The change was a total shock to her. But once I told her the Cottage
story, she realized she was seeing another person, Katie—and she
suddenly found she loved my hair. Odd.

At the Cottage. Caught the men up with the things I did at Perelandra. Asked them for their opinion about my friend's note-taking
suggestion. They lean toward dictation but urged me to do what is
most comfortable for me.

I noticed that my sight is returning even better than this morning.
It's more "complete," and I can see greater detail. It's as if my sight
depended more on the clarity in which things register in my brain,
not via my eyes. The cranial adjustments yesterday seem to be the
key.

Talked to them about a trip I have to take tomorrow on the Pere-
landra level to New York City. I'm concerned about keeping my
Cottage schedule. David suggested I just plan to come back to the
Cottage later, after I return to Perelandra. That was easy.

December 2

At Perelandra. Shuttled to NYC for a trustee's meeting regarding
Isadore's estate. Spent a full day in meetings with accountants and
my co-trustee, deciding the monthly budget each child will get next
year. Some of the budget requests from the mothers were outrageous, and only proved that greed was alive and well—and running rampant with Isadore's ex-wives.

"Phoned" David at the Cottage several times throughout the day
to let him know how it was going—as he had requested. It felt a
little strange to be in NYC on one hand and calling the Cottage on
the other. The lines of reality seemed quite blurred.

At the Cottage. Returned around 10 P.M. I was exhausted, but I
didn't shatter. Mickey served me soup because I insisted I wanted to
eat light. Everyone joined me, drinking coffee while I ate. We talked
about the day and had some good laughs over the goofy requests by
the mothers for next year's budgets. I went to bed right after I
finished eating.

December 3

Felt a sense of tightened energy around the Cottage. Left for Perelandra wondering what was going on. I figured that if they didn't tell me, it was probably something I didn't need to know about right now.

At Perelandra. As I went about my day, I got the insight that the two French visitors the Cottage men have been expecting arrived this afternoon. I also got the insight that I was to aid one of them, and I would know what to do once I met him.

At the Cottage. David met me in the gardens to tell me the guests had arrived and were upstairs resting before dinner. I told him I already knew they arrived. He asked if I knew who the visitors were. I said no, but I had "gotten" that I was to help one of them, and I would know what to do once I met him. David suggested I might want to rest before dinner also. Actually, I was happy to have some time to myself.

When I came down just before dinner, I found Charles de Gaulle sitting in the living room in front of the fire with David. They stood when I entered, and I walked over for the introductions. I have to say, I could not have been more surprised or nervous. The first thing I noticed about General de Gaulle was his height. He's a *very* tall man. He looked exhausted and aged—about eighty years old, I'd guess. I could tell he had an air of great power, but it was combined with a troubled heart and soul. David introduced us and we made eye contact for the first time. In fact, we couldn't seem to release eye contact. Suddenly, I saw the same shattered expression on his face that he had had the day of David's funeral. And I realized that at the moment David's coffin passed before de Gaulle on the Capitol steps, the general had a shattering insight. His power, vision and role in France had been limited by personal ego, and he had not served the country he so loved as well as he had thought. He has since lived in a private hell trying to deal with his discovery, choosing not to share it with anyone until now. David and the Cottage team were now giving him the opportunity to address and balance his role in France.

I don't think he consciously remembered seeing me the day of David's funeral. Perhaps if I had been standing in front of him with a bicycle, it might have jogged his memory. He said to me quietly, "You know, don't you."

"Yes." Yes, I knew about his hell.

Tears came to his eyes, and he sat down, staring into the fire. I sat down next to him.

David said nothing, but I could tell that he was quietly urging me to do whatever I had to do.

"I know I'm to ask you for help," said the general. "But I'm not sure what kind of help or why."

Despite his strong French accent, I was surprised he spoke English so well. In fact, with his pro-France reputation, I was surprised he spoke English at all.

As soon as he talked about my helping him, I understood that I was to test him for flower essences throughout his entire visit. I excused myself and got the essences from my room. When I returned, I said, "I think I can help you, if you wish."

"Please."

I explained flower essences to him and told him I felt they would help stabilize and support him electrically as he goes through his process at the Cottage. Much to my continued amazement, de Gaulle was open to my help in general and this help in particular. He kept saying he knew I was to help him. He tested for six essences in all, including Rescue Remedy, one time daily for his entire stay at the Cottage. When I administered them to him, I could feel the same dramatic shift in his body that I felt with the Cottage men. I suggested that he might wish to have a quiet evening in his room tonight. I sensed him to be open and vulnerable. He thanked me for my understanding and help, kissed me three times on my cheeks and left for his room.

Had a quiet dinner with David and Tex. Butch and François (de Gaulle's assistant/interpreter) went into the village together. David and I told Tex about the essence testing. They thought it was quite possible the essences solved the major problem they had anticipated with de Gaulle—how to get him to open fully. I feel the essences will support that process and take the pressure off the Cottage team to deal with the general on a psychological and emotional level.

They can focus on the military matter at hand now—if the essences really work the way I think they will.

After Mickey returned from taking dinner up to the general, he said de Gaulle was in good spirits and looking more peaceful.

December 4

Both our guests had breakfast upstairs. I could feel the others concentrating on the day ahead. Talked with David a little about the ego problem they were facing with de Gaulle. He explained that glamour and ego are neutral dynamics until they connect with personality. Then they can become negative or positive forces, depending on the personality. When negative, as in de Gaulle's case, they result in limitations around decisions and visions. When positive, they can result in heroic action. When the Cottage team studied de Gaulle's decisions and actions during World War II in order to identify his strategy, they kept running into a factor-x—something that obviously affected his role as leader. Finally, they realized they were looking at a strong ego/glamour dynamic. They studied the decisions and actions of de Gaulle's top men and found that they, too, had been limited by the same dynamic. As the leader goes, so go his supporting officers. For the work the Cottage needed to do, they found all of de Gaulle's strategies to be "unflippable." What they hoped to do now was have the general review all of his strategies, remove his factor-x and re-form the strategies based on new decisions without the influence of the ego/glamour dynamic. They expected that this was going to take everyone about four to six weeks to complete.

At Perelandra. It's the first Saturday in December. To David, this means the Army–Navy game. As per his request, I phoned him game updates throughout the afternoon. I told him that since I love football I wouldn't mind watching the game. Ugh. Army had no offense. They lost to Navy, 24 to 7. It was a terrible game.

At the Cottage. David met me as soon as I got home. The day had gone exceptionally well. De Gaulle is not fighting them, as they thought he might—he's only fighting himself.

I informed David that if I was going to be required to watch the

Army–Navy games, I wanted Army to have a better team. I had my standards. He was pleased to see that my allegiance was with Army.

General de Gaulle joined us for dinner and the evening. Actually, it was a pretty easy time. At dinner, he made a remark about the wisdom of my not drinking wine or liquor. Something about young women being much too frivolous about such stuff. I said, "My not drinking has nothing to do with a personal or moral stand. Drinking makes me vomit."

At that, as if on cue, the four Cottage men reached into their pockets and each pulled out a £10 note. Tex announced that Butch was the winner, and they all handed their money over to Butch. Unbeknownst to me, they had bet on how long it would take me to relax and say something outrageous to de Gaulle!

The general asked if I would join him in the garden for a short walk. While outside, he thanked me for my help. We talked a little about the process he's going through, and I suggested he may need more sleep because of it.

December 5

The general had breakfast in his room again. I must say, François, his assistant, knows how to remain out of sight. I've only seen him a couple of times since meeting him, and he doesn't join us for meals.

During breakfast, I talked about self-publishing *Behaving* and my concern about where I will get the funds to do it. They urged me to just move forward with the project and assume I'll get the answer when I need it.

At dinner. Congenial meal with David and de Gaulle talking about their war memories. Afterwards, de Gaulle retired early again. He was surprised at how much his energy was drained. I did a quick essence test with him to make sure nothing else was needed, but he tested clear.

December 6

Had a vivid dream about my mother, which I told to the others during breakfast. They added some thoughts about her that I had not considered before. They suggested that my mother's deep anger toward me stemmed from her feelings about her own mother dying during my mother's birth. They pointed out the fear my mother must have experienced during her pregnancy with me—all of it centering around whether or not she would survive the pregnancy and birth. On the one hand, she was probably frightened that I would "kill" her, and, on the other hand, she was probably deeply angry that I did not "kill" her. Had she died during childbirth, she would have "evened the score" around her own mother dying during her birth. They suggested that she was intensely angry toward me because I did not release her from her guilt about her own birth. Ended up thinking about this most of the afternoon.

At Perelandra. Went shopping and to a movie with Clarence. I decided I would bend the Information Policy rules a bit and told Clarence about the Cottage house guest. He had asked very little about the Cottage since our first discussion, and I figured this might be something he could relate to. He was impressed. In fact, he seemed more impressed that I had talked with de Gaulle than he was that I had talked with Eisenhower! I told him about what the men were doing together and how the flower essences seem to be helping a lot. He was surprised that anyone there would need essences. I had to remind him that process continues, no matter how much development we go through. It just never ends.

December 7

Got a little upset at breakfast because the men informed me (in a congratulatory way) that I was glowing. Since I don't have my period, it must have been the result of ovulation. I'm getting more used to them seeing this, but it's not something I feel comfortable sharing with Charles de Gaulle and his assistant. Again they assured me it was a "family thing" and that our visitors would not notice anything. I looked at myself in the hall mirror, but I still can't see any difference. I accused them all of being nuts and hallucinating.

At the Cottage. General de Gaulle looked especially drained tonight, so I checked him for essences. He needed two additional ones. He retired early for the evening. Later, the men told me that the day had been emotionally tough for him.

During a casual conversation after dinner with the Cottage men, I mentioned my trip to Paris at the fall equinox and the chestnut that appeared between my feet. David pulled a chestnut out of his pocket, and said, "You mean, like this one."

I looked at it and told him I thought it was very similar to the one I found. He asked me to split my chestnut so that we could compare them. Since it was just us Cottage "fellows," I set up a Split Molecular Process with nature right then. Sure enough, when we compared them, the two chestnuts were identical. David told me he's had his chestnut for years and used it as a "worry bead" while he thinks. I guess this is verification that when I called in the next cycle for myself during the equinox, I activated my coming to the Cottage.

December 8

Woke up this morning laughing. I had a dream about defeating General de Gaulle's underground unit by tossing hand grenades in the many bathrooms the troops were hidden in along Arm Pit Hair Canyon. When I told the Cottage men about the dream at breakfast, they congratulated me for my "great war victory." Got us all talking about dreams. Mickey says he dreams complete stand-up comedy routines. And he calls me the dream machine!

Before we left the breakfast table I was suddenly struck with a thought. I said to the men, "I've come home, haven't I."

"Yes."

December 9

At Perelandra. Spent the day Christmas shopping with a friend.

At the Cottage. Returned exhausted, but I didn't shatter. Noticed that the general looked like he was moving with pain. I tested him for essences and did two vertebrae adjustments on him. When I finished, he no longer had any pain. Boy, did I ever feel satisfied with myself.

December 10

My thirty-seventh birthday.

Awoke with a deep sadness triggered by a dream. Then I realized it was my birthday, and the sadness made sense, so I spent time this morning thinking about it. More than at any other time, I experience sadness on my birthdays. My mother was especially adept at striking out at me in anger at this time. She seemed to really hate the fact that I was born. After twelve, when I was on my own, she never again acknowledged my birthday. The memories made me cry, but I pulled myself together and got on with my day.

At breakfast, there was a card sitting at my place signed by everyone. Mickey said that Tex had checked around and gotten my birth date. There was discussion about whether or not I should celebrate two birth dates—Machaelle's and Katie's. The idea made me wince. It's hard enough getting through one birthday. It was decided that the "Machaelle fusion of soul to original form" was the important event in this situation, so December 10 will remain The Big Day. I thanked them all for the card. Their attention made me feel a little shy.

At Perelandra. Got hit with the birthday sadness again as soon as I came back to Perelandra. I felt empty. In fact, I felt like I was in a paper bag and couldn't get out. Tested flower essences, and needed eight!

At the Cottage. Returned feeling much stronger, thanks to the essences. When I got to my room, I received a sudden insight. I've always looked to others to give me acceptance and joy on my birthday. Now something felt wrong with that. I needed to switch the flow of energy from outside to inside. Suddenly, I realized that my birthday is a time for *me* to stop and recognize my own life that began with this day, and to consider all that this life has given me. As I thought about it, I could feel a sensation coming over me similar to what I have felt in the garden during the summer solstice. Perhaps my birthday is my own summer solstice—a time to reflect on the uniting of body and soul, and all that has come to fruition as a result. This excited me. My whole attitude changed about this day, and I thought perhaps I flipped the birthday coin. Eureka.

Had to work with the general tonight. He was in pain again. Adjusted three vertebrae along the heart line and tested him for essences. Whatever they are working on is hitting this man head on.

December 11

Evening. When I arrived at the Cottage, David met me at the door. As soon as I walked in, I was hit with a tremendous energy—like a bomb had gone off. I asked what happened, and David said it was an especially difficult day. The general was experiencing pain again. I had to again adjust the heart-line vertebrae. I could tell that he was holding on to his heart for dear life while he's going through his process. Had to test for a new solution to replace the one he had tested for the first night at the Cottage. Some of the new essences he tested for indicate that he is trying to integrate what's happening to him.

After the general went upstairs for a rest, I tested everyone else to see if they were reacting to any of the general's trauma. Each of them needed minor adjustments—the same heart-line vertebrae adjustment I had given de Gaulle, and Tex and David needed a couple of essences in addition. They were all working hard to support de Gaulle and his process.

December 12

I've been grateful that our breakfasts have been with family only and that our guests have chosen to eat in their rooms especially because it has given me a chance to talk about the many emotional issues that have been surfacing for me. My dealing with emotional issues makes sense to the others. It's making me weary. They feel that the Cottage level, plus the sense of safety I have with them, encourages it.

Returned home to a group of happy campers. They feel that they only need a half-day more with de Gaulle in order to complete their work together. The general and his assistant are planning to leave after dinner tomorrow evening. Everyone is amazed at how efficiently this work has progressed.

December 13

Got into a discussion at breakfast about physical conditioning. They explained to me that when each of them reactivated their body for the Cottage level, they chose the relative age for their body condition based on when their true power had first emerged prior to death. For David, this was fifty-two. When he entered the Cottage level, he was this age again. But this was simply a starting point. As each man moved through his personal process, the power clarified that much more and his body became more fit and agile, reflecting the internal changes. Although years can pass, they don't physically age because the body is so aligned to this personal intent. The bottom line of this for me is that Mickey could well be an 800-year-old troll, as I've suspected—he only looks like a thirty-five-year-old man because of his intent. It's all a facade!

David tells me that as Charles de Gaulle continues through the ongoing healing process that directly relates to his Earth life, he will strengthen and, at the appropriate time, he will align his body with the age when his power first emerged.

At Perelandra. The game warden knocked on our door to ask permission to track an eight-point buck through our woods. It had been wounded by a hunter, and the warden wanted to finish the job and end the deer's agony. I was affected by the gentleness and concern of this quiet man—not at all the stereotype I have of game wardens. I wished him luck. When he returned saying that he had lost the trail, I became worried about the fate of the deer.

At the Cottage. They did it: In eleven days they accomplished what they had originally thought would take thirty.

After dinner, I tested the general one more time. I cleared him from his Cottage experience, then asked if he wished me to check essences for his next step (whatever that was). I gave him a solution to take with him. He thanked me for my help, saying I made a difficult time easier. I realized I actually cared about this man, and I was sorry to see him go. He and François left by taxi. I didn't ask anyone where they were headed—I didn't think I wanted to know.

Mickey served a special celebration cake. David toasted our teamwork, especially the guts and courage it took to pursue de Gaulle.

December 14

Evening. Everyone had the day off—but me, of course. I have to come to Perelandra every day and to the Cottage every night. Both bodies need to be energized daily, and this can only be done while my soul is fully interacting with the body.

David and Tex spent the afternoon playing golf. Petunia wanted to trundle along but Mickey kept her back at the Cottage. She was such a good girl while we had the visitors. I was afraid she'd try to spray de Gaulle, but she basically ignored him. It could be that she's fallen in love with Mickey. She's learned that he's the keeper of the food, and she sticks close to him a lot. She's no dummy.

At Perelandra. Got an insight to make an appointment with the chiropractor for next Monday, December 20—which I did. I haven't a clue about why one is needed.

December 15

Made the mistake of questioning out loud if I might be leaning too much on the men while I go through my adjustment process. It was just a question. They jumped on me right away and accused me of not understanding. To top it off, they announced I wasn't leaning enough. I raised a white flag and called a truce.

At Perelandra. My cranials went out of alignment again. Tension and pressure pain returned in my head. I got depressed at having lost the alignment.

At the Cottage. As soon as I walked in, Tex noticed I was in trouble. I went to my room to take a nap. After dinner, while we were seated in front of the fire, it hit me that I had been assuming that my cranials slipped "backwards" to the old alignment. Perhaps they have slipped "forward" in an attempt to align differently and with *more* strength. The positive spin on things pulled me out of the depression. Tested for an essence solution to hold me until the visit with the chiropractor.

December 16

Feel we're getting back to normal now that de Gaulle is gone.

At Perelandra. Spent the afternoon with my wallpaper friend and talked about my head pain. Despite the cranial problems, she believes I've adjusted "remarkably well" to the Cottage level. I told her about de Gaulle's visit and my work with his structural adjustments and essences. She handled this well.

December 17

JAMFD

December 18

At my breakfast debriefing, I told them about last night's dream about a horse. This triggered a discussion about horses. I told them about Isadore training horses when I was young. He had strong friendships and connections with members and trainers on the U.S. equestrian team and began training me at age six for a future spot on our team. I rode every day, two to three hours daily when it didn't rain, until I was twelve. Each day I worked out in a ring, riding our different horses in a circle. Isadore rarely took me out on trail rides. I was training for the equestrian team, not for anything that might have been pleasurable. From this, I learned discipline. We compared what I had gone through with Isadore and with Max, and decided that the intensity and discipline that were developed were similar. The coaches were not. Max had maintained a deep and loving relationship with Katie, while Isadore rarely conducted a conversation beyond the fine points of horseback riding with Machaelle. The Cottage men decided I needed to learn to "go trail-riding and stop all that riding in circles." It was too rigidly disciplined. I handed them back the challenge of breaking my life-long habit—I already had enough to do.

December 19

Evening. Returned home feeling the need to be quiet. The feeling continued through the evening, and everyone noticed the change in me. I tried to explain it away by saying I was just coming down from all the focus and activity around the de Gaulle visit, but they didn't buy this. Tex kept checking my forehead to see if I had a temperature. The Jewish mothers were unleashed. They said they felt this was a different aspect of quietness than they were used to seeing from me. We'll see.

December 20

Awoke still feeling quiet and inward. Emotions were rising from someplace unknown.

At breakfast I tried to tell them what was going on. This brought up thoughts I had been having over the past few days about my life, the Cottage and all of them. Up until now, I realize I have held back five percent, feeling that this five percent would pull me out and save me if I suddenly discovered that this whole Cottage thing was the result of madness or fantasy—or both. But my recent experiences have brought me to the point of a *full* commitment. I now have no reservations. I have thrown away the reverse gear from my car, so to speak. I am 100 percent committed. As I spoke, I could feel the enormous implications of what I was saying. In short, it means that I am now certifiably insane as far as my society is concerned. I am an outcast. If they throw me in a padded cell, I will stay there for the rest of my life, because the Cottage and these four men are now fully integrated in the woven cloth that is who I am.

To the men, this explained my quiet. They urged me to talk out everything, to lay it all on the table.

I described my feelings of resignation about the implications of this integration. The good news is the integration. The bad news is that I am now undeniably certifiable by the society in which I live (on the Perelandra level). My emotions around what I was saying rose up, and I began crying. I told them that I had a deep fear of being harshly cast out. I had questions about how it would affect my life's work and the impact of my work on others. I felt like I was a lunar landing module getting ready to set down on the moon. But as I touched down, a bunch of emotional dust was being kicked up. I kept spinning in a circle, identifying all the dust and letting it work up. At one point, I touched anger—deep anger. I know, I see, that I am working within timing—that I initiated the Cottage work on one level during the fall equinox, and now, just twenty-four hours before the winter solstice, I was integrating this reality at a new level in my being. I felt the sense of outside timing pushing and pulling me to a place beyond my limits. I feel I'm being stretched to my limits, yet I feel that something is going to happen within the next twenty-four hours that will demand from me an even greater stretch. And somehow I'll be able to make that stretch—I'll be *expected* to.

Suddenly, I began to sob. I felt that all I wanted to do was scream to someone, to whoever was responsible for making me face this impossible stretch, "But what about *me*? What about *my* welfare?"

Just then, I heard a word in my head: *relax*. If I totally relaxed, the body and soul would effortlessly respond to the stretch. So I relaxed.

Instantly, my left eye began to more fully register images. It felt like it "popped" open. It felt wider and cooler. I had much wider peripheral vision in my left eye than in my right. It was so startling to suddenly be able to "see" out of the left eye, that I sat quietly doing eye movements to test my new sight (or was it insight?). David said, "I don't believe that in the middle of all this, you're sitting there doing eye exercises!"

I explained to them what was happening. When I completed the eye exercises, I returned to the questions I had raised earlier about the implications of my commitment. I told them I was simply going to stay with the work. Sitting in the middle of questions would never get them answered and, besides, they're all based on speculation. I had a feeling that as I move in this new commitment, the questions would answer themselves. I would just keep moving and simply let them work themselves out with time.

Just then, I drew back from this emotional experience and began to see humor. It's those little traumatic coffee breaks that add spice to life! I looked at everyone and calmly said, "So, how's your morning going?"

With that, we all had a good laugh. I ended up feeling integrated, strong and healed—but still a little open and vulnerable. I couldn't see any more emotional dust to deal with. I felt like I had climbed Mt. Everest. I was just glad it was over and enjoyed the stability I was feeling by being 100 percent committed to this work.

At Perelandra. My appointment with the chiropractor went well. I felt she needed to know more about the Cottage work so that she could understand the dynamics of de Gaulle's visit. She said she had been waiting for something to explain the depth of what was going on with me, and what I was telling her definitely helped. I also told her about the experience I had this morning. She was struck by the intensity of it. She went to work on my body, fully expecting my entire structural system to be blown. She found only the three vertebrae along the heart line misaligned—the same ones I had been adjusting all week for de Gaulle and the others. All my cranials and my pelvis were in alignment. All chakras and glands were strong, but my CSF [cerebrospinal fluid] pulses were still not strong enough to support the intensity of the energy coming in from the Cottage. She showed me how to increase the pulses myself. She also showed me a breathing movement designed to increase the CSF pressure, and said I would probably have to do this for as long as I stayed associated with the Cottage. Overall, she was stunned at how well my body was holding up under such intensity. She said, "This proves that when surrounded by a circle of love, a person can get through anything."

We discussed the quality of support I was getting from the men at the Cottage. She is convinced that this is a major factor in my holding alignment and balance so strongly during such intensity. She felt that in return I was functioning as the "in-house healer at the Cottage" and was utilizing everything I had ever learned about the body to benefit the others. We ended the appointment by agreeing that it is now time for us to get together to share work processes. She's anxious to hear about my essence work and observations on the Cottage level. She feels certain it will add to the body of information we have about essences from the Earth perspective.

At the Cottage. Returned tired, but confident about what had transpired with my chiropractor. I told the men that it appeared that I'm going to have to accept their role as Jewish mothers since it looks as if all that care and concern is important for my continued adjustments. They laughed and declared my chiropractor to be a true ally. It seems that I was the only one surprised by her comment about my functioning as the "in-house healer" at the Cottage.

December 21 — Heather Green

The men have been telling me every morning since my first week at the Cottage what color surrounds me. This morning they told me I was surrounded by heather green. Starting today I am keeping a record of my daily colors.

At Perelandra. Spent the afternoon preparing for the winter solstice. The men had asked me if it was possible to split the solstice Life Table* [see footnote on following page] to the Cottage, so I opened a coning to ask.

I first asked nature if it was appropriate to even consider such a shift. When they said that it was, I asked how they recommended I accomplish it. They said that because of the understanding I have of form and manifestation, and the care that is inherent in this kind of activity, my ability to use the Split Molecular Process for objects is fairly effortless. Certainly the SMP was much easier than the in-depth experiences I had had with manifestation. (I agreed with them on this.) Nature said we could shift the entire Life Table at one time. All I had to do was join with them in the shift/split and then hold my focus on the spot at the Cottage where the Life Table was to be "set." My focus would function as a directional and grounding dynamic.

The split of the Life Table took about five minutes. The men watched it "come in" at the Cottage, and I could feel their delight as it appeared. It was one of the most enjoyable, joyful experiences I've ever had with nature.

At the Cottage. When I arrived, the men asked me to explain the symbology of all the things I had chosen to place on the Life Table. They told me that when the Table appeared, the candle was already lit. Also, I noticed two brass candleholders with ivory candles on the Table that they said also arrived lit. I had not included these two candles on the Life Table at Perelandra, and I had not seen the candleholders before. They were a gift to the men from nature in recognition of their including nature in their lives in this new way. Actually, the candles were both a gift and a celebration.

At Perelandra. [The winter solstice: This is the celebration of the devic level within nature and its role as architect of all form. It is the earliest time in the nature year when the pattern of the cycle we activate during the fall equinox is accessible to us. Just after the solstice moment, I draw one or two cards (depending on what I am told) from the New Tarot deck. These cards give me clues about Perelandra's and my present cycle.]

I left the Cottage at 11 P.M. to prepare for the solstice at 11:39 P.M.

---

* Since the winter solstice is around Christmastime, I give nature its fair share of the season by setting up what I call a Life Table. On it, I create a nature setting of greens, nests, nuts, berries and birdfeather ornaments. I also include items from the garden and handmade crafts to symbolize the creative coming together of man and nature. For the winter solstice, the Life Table candle is lit, and at the exact moment of the solstice I focus my attention on the devic quality of life—the creation of the blueprints.

I felt I needed to be at Perelandra for this event. I planned a simple "ceremony" with Clarence in the sanctuary.

We sat quietly through the 11:39 period. Silently, so not to disturb Clarence's moment, I invited all the solstice energies to ground into Perelandra and myself, and I welcomed them in love and appreciation. Then, as instructed, I drew two cards from the Tarot. From nature, I drew the Renewer. From the evolutionary Christ dynamic, I drew the Deliverer. We went into the house, and I placed the cards on the Life Table.

> *The Renewer:* The Renewer reveals. The Renewer was former-ly the Death card. The Book of the Renewer also represents Death, for it is only through the gates of Death that the final mystery is revealed. Death is not necessarily physical death. The death shown here is absolute Death—or ego-death. It is the death that is the necessary prelude to re-birth. But only when Death is seen as an absolute can the birth into greater Being take place.
>
> The fear of death is so great that even the subconscious avoids it. But when the moment comes that Death is faced in all its awful majesty there occurs a transformation within one. One sees life from a different standpoint, from the standpoint of the ONE. For behind the gates of Death there is not an ab-solute void, but rather the ONE which is beyond the personal self and beyond mortality.
>
> In facing the absolute Death, the Seeker, kneeling within the crown and facing the skull, sees a skull whose eye-sockets form the symbol of eternal life. He sees the One Being. That and more.
>
> That is what the Renewer reveals. . . .
>
> With the Renewer the concept of Unity has progressed to the point where the Manifestation is united with that which lies behind and within the Manifestation: the One. It refers to the uniting of principles, or of God in man with the One Being.
>
> This can only happen when one has stepped through the gates of Death after drinking the cup of fire of the Deliverer . . . and thus Death, the Renewer, is seen as the cutting of the thread of Destiny, after which the Kingdom is opened.
>
> *The Deliverer:* Fire is the deliverer. . . . But what is this fire? Fire is death. Fire is that which burns all matter, leaving only

ash. Fire is that which purifies. Fire is Shiva. Therefore it may be said that fire is pure spirit. To drink a cup of fire is painful. The fire enters the young man's vitals: it consumes him.

The significance of the Deliverer Book is: That which is to come to Each. Deliverance is to come. It is to come through the fire. But this fire is not the fire of earth. It is electric fire. It is the fire of spirit.

Previously, the Seeker passed through the water in order to climb the path. Now, at the mountain-top, he must drink the fire. The water was baptism. The fire is initiation. Through the baptism of water in the tides of the Feeler he entered into the Maze; through the cup of fire drawn from the ignited torch of the heart he is delivered from it.

Initiation into Spirit is a further initiation than the initiation into Life and is a further step than entering upon the path. It is what is termed higher consciousness. It is the heart that is consumed and purified here. The flame of the heart has risen to great height in and through the experience of the previous Books—or through the steps upon the way. It has already been purified. But the paradox is that love itself must be sacrificed before one can rise to the next sphere or level. The blood of the heart must go, to be replaced by pure flame—or the electric fire of spirit. Attachment and devotion must yield to higher law if one would find liberation. . . .

Jesus said in the Garden, "O my father, if it be possible let this cup pass from me" . . . before he mounted the Cross, the symbolic T of initiation.

Yet the Seeker must drink this cup if he would attain eternal life.*

As soon as I put the cards on the Table (so to speak), I began experiencing a deep physical reaction: diarrhea, nausea, headache, a diaphragm in the tightest knot I've ever experienced and terrible pain throughout my back. After a period of just minutes, everything intensified. As soon as I could get into bed at Perelandra, I left for the Cottage.

---

* *The New Tarot* by John Cooke and Rosalind Sharpe. Copyright 1969 Rosalind Sharpe Wall and John Starr Cooke. Western Star Press. Out of print. All the Tarot definitions in this book are from *The New Tarot*.

At the Cottage. I began crying once I arrived. The pain was pretty bad, but I was also frightened. I tried to pull myself together, but after taking essences, everyone insisted I go to bed, saying we'd talk about this in the morning. I asked them if they knew something I didn't. When they said yes, I decided just to go to bed. I didn't want to hear it right then, but I was grateful to be surrounded by their protection.

December 22 — Brown

Slept late. When I went down for breakfast, the others were already into their day. They joined me while I ate. David told me that he had gotten a phone call from Hyperithon two days ago saying that the new foundation that I laid in place on that day by way of my commitment would be activated during the solstice. A large infusion of energy would enter my body since the foundation that I had laid was large. I would most likely have reactions, and all of this would be normal and expected—under the circumstances. I would need to heal and rest, and I would need time for the infusion to be totally integrated into my system's balance. My pain and reactions would disappear in two to three days.

At Perelandra. Returned with pain in my whole body. Just took it easy. I didn't say anything to Clarence because I didn't want him to worry.

At the Cottage. Returned with pain in this body, as well. Can't seem to get away from it. David gave me a little more explanation as to what's happening. He suggested that I look at the framework as a collection or grid of many squares. Each square is a different facet of what I'm activating. I'm choosing to lay in many squares at one time, and the quality of the process I went through two days ago allows me to do this. This framework is a tremendous addition in my two bodies. The result of all this will be a much broader base on which to operate in my work. They all felt certain my pain and discomfort would go away in a couple days. In the meantime, I needed to rest.

I retired to my room early. Mickey brought me soup for dinner, and the others looked in on me several times to make sure I was still among the living.

December 23 — Burgundy

Awoke feeling much better. When I went down to the dining room for breakfast, I found a porcelain yellow rose sitting on a piece of wood next to my napkin. The accompanying card said it was a small token of acknowledgment and congratulations for laying in the new framework, and it was signed by the four men. I placed the rose next to my corn-husk doll on my chest of drawers.

At Perelandra. The pain is decreasing, and I'm feeling stronger. But I noticed that I am clenching my jaw. It feels like I'm hanging on for dear life by my teeth.

At the Cottage. Return exhausted, but with just a slight body ache. My lungs felt cold, however. The Jewish mothers insisted I retire early and rest. They feel the chest thing is due to my resistance being down.

December 24 — Yellow

At breakfast, we talked about the male/female dynamics we all possess, and how in most partnerships the male looks to the female to supply the female dynamic and vice versa. In the new partnership, both people have both dynamics operating. They may learn refinements from one another, but they don't depend on the other to supply his or her dominant dynamic. As we talked, I realized that this is the most balanced group of individuals—male or female—I have ever experienced, and that these men can put most people to shame when it comes to caring, consideration and nurturing. What an odd twist in this day of feminism.

At Perelandra. Reviewed my notes on Monday's experience. It finally hit me how intense it was. I have been so involved with all the fallout that I haven't paid too much attention to the experience itself.

At the Cottage. When I told the others about my insight and thoughts about Monday's experience, my diaphragm immediately contracted into a painful knot. I could barely breathe. David called Hyperithon to find out if he knew what was going on. Hyperithon assured him I was fine, and that I had further grounded the framework by reviewing my journal notes and discussing my insights. He reminded David that this was an extensive process and that reactions such as those I was having were normal. He also said that I might have additional reactions tonight, once the Christ/evolutionary energy, triggered by Christmas, entered my bodies. At that time, the framework would activate.

Tested myself for essences to stabilize my diaphragm and prepare (as much as possible) for the activation.

At 5:30 P.M., John arrived. A surprise to us all. He decided to join us for the holidays. We launched into a family evening.

December 25 — Burgundy

Slept late, then had brunch with the family. I felt physically odd. My whole body felt like it was vibrating, like it was over-energized. I was spacey and I felt like I was floating. They assured me that I was probably adjusting to the huge infusion of energy I took last night and reminded me that the framework has been energized *and* activated. I tested myself for essences, which settled me down rather quickly. They wanted me to focus on something, saying that focusing my attention would also help settle me. So I regaled them with the only thing I could think of at the time—my tale of the night in 1970 when I went to a porno movie with a bunch of priests. I found out that out of everyone sitting at the breakfast table, I (the lone female) was the only one who had ever seen a porno movie. Now, that was a sobering discovery. I teased them, saying it was lucky someone in this team wasn't so naive!

Somehow, this all reminded them it was Christmas. (And they say my leaps are outrageous!) They had already told me that they don't exchange gifts. Instead, they have what they call a family day and just spend time together. I took them at their word, so I was quite surprised when they presented me with a gift. It was a small, nicely wrapped box. Inside was a gold dog tag with the inscription, "Machaelle Small Wright—If lost, return immediately to the Cottage. England." Several weeks ago I had told them I was afraid that when I die and leave Perelandra permanently, I would get lost in the universal ethers and not be able to find the Cottage. They said that was impossible because of the second body. My soul would have to automatically shift into the Katie body upon death of the Machaelle body. I told them I would take their word for this. It was clear that the dog tag was to make sure I got to the Cottage no matter what happened. I can't even begin to express how touched I was by the gesture and the gift.

At Perelandra. Arrived to spend as much of the day as possible with Clarence. We spent the afternoon and early evening with friends, joining them for a Christmas turkey dinner.

At the Cottage. They held up dinner for my return. I had not realized, until I sat down, that I would be faced with a second Christmas dinner—turkey twice in one day. It takes courage and dedication to get through two such dinners on the same day, even if you are feeding separate bodies. My Cottage body may have needed a meal, but my soul wasn't especially interested!

December 26 — Dusty Rose

At Perelandra. Conducted a flower essence session with a woman who had asked for my help. I was able to test her in new ways, thanks to my work with Charles de Gaulle. (I didn't explain this to her.) I encouraged her to contact me as soon as she feels an emotional/mental shift from her present pattern. This would indicate the need for a new solution, and we would not need to wait for the shift to reflect in her body before testing essences. I was pleased to see the benefits of my work at the Cottage extending to my work at Perelandra.

December 27 — Heather Green

Evening. When I returned to the Cottage, I shattered. Only this time, I experienced body pain and I was overwhelmed with fear. Cried. Everyone jumped into action, even John. It took about two hours for me to refocus and feel settled again. It's been a while since I've shattered so badly.

December 28 — Dusty Rose

John has brought up a problem he's having with a persistent golf slice that he can't seem to get rid of, no matter what he tries. He's asked me to look at his swing next to David's and Tex's swings, and see if I can spot what he (John) is missing. Apparently, he seems to feel I have x-ray vision when it comes to body movement and golf swings. I told him I'd give it a shot (so to speak), if he really wanted me to.

At Perelandra. Got insight that John is moving toward a significant energy release and major shift that could be triggered by my work with him around his golf swing. It will be important to make sure he wants to proceed. I should not be the one to initiate the session with him.

My jaw is still set. I can't seem to relax it at all. I can feel my teeth are clenched together.

At the Cottage. I felt deeply quiet throughout the evening. It was nice being with people who didn't feel I needed to be pulled out of this.

December 29 — Brown

Awoke still in a quiet mood.

At Perelandra. I felt I should open a coning to get information and insight about the process with John that I seemed to be moving toward. I was told John had an opportunity to begin working and functioning in more expanded ways, but to do this he had to go through a considerable release and physical shift. He was choosing to address this opportunity while at the Cottage. Although he was not consciously aware of what was before him, he was presently going through the preparation stage that would lead him to making the decision about whether or not he would accept this opportunity. As when I went through my early stages around the Cottage decision, John needed to make up his own mind without outside influence. I was simply to be available when he asked for my help.

I asked for advice about precisely how I could assist John. I was told that there was no pre-set process they could give me, that no one's process is pre-set. I was to move with John, supporting him, guiding him and responding to him as he chose his options along the way. I could not ensure ease for him. How he proceeded would be his choice. However, I could modify, simplify and make his options more efficient by utilizing my knowledge and understanding of healing principles. This would allow me to move with a greater range and agility within the structure of the process John was presenting to me. I was cautioned that if he chose to go through this challenge with me, I would most likely have to draw on every discipline I have to circumvent his intellectual blocks. The only practical advice I got was to aim for John to move through the process in one session so that he would have time to integrate the results while at the Cottage where he is surrounded by the safety and security of those he loves.

I was given one additional piece of information. I must not underestimate the positive healing effect my being a woman has on the men at the Cottage. They respond more openly and trustingly to my female energy, which has inherent in it a healing dynamic. This in itself will greatly assist the work I do with John.

At the Cottage. As soon as I walked in the door, John "reminded" me that I had said I would try to help him with his golf slice. This was my cue that he was saying "yes" to his opportunity. When he left the room to get a golf club, I told the others (I didn't *ask* them) to follow my lead with him. They agreed they would.

To start off, I asked David and Tex to swing the club several times. With this, I was able to see the fluidity of the swing plus the individuality in their motion. When I felt I had a good visual sense of the movements, I asked John to do the swing several times. It was immediately obvious that he was constricting the movement in his right hip socket, and this was shortening the swing and moving it in an arch that the others didn't have. When I pointed out what he was doing to the other two, I asked them to try to imitate his motion. The locked right hip socket produced a similar slice in their swing.

Using kinesiology, I tested key points in John's body for weaknesses. His pineal, solar plexus and adrenals tested weak. Structurally, two lumbar vertebrae and his right pelvis were misaligned. When I asked him to do the swing again, I could see that there was a limited rotation of the right thigh, and this was where the emotional energy to be released was being held. I asked John to lie on the floor, and I made the structural adjustments, which, in turn, strengthened the glands. I kept chattering about silly golf swings just to keep his mind off what I was doing and his intellect out of my way. When I began to work with his right leg, he experienced pain. While he protested a bit, I could tell that there were actually two blocks involved—one located in the right hip socket and the other on the right side of his neck. I gently moved his leg, and the energy began to stir. I asked John to visualize himself trying to push his shoulder against a large wall that was being held up by an ant. I already knew he had a terrific ability to focus and to visualize pictures that had no logic, so I was confident he'd be able to work with a wall being held up by an ant. I wanted this visualization to combine the reality of a big wall that he was trying to break through and the potential that this wall could fall because it was propped up only by an ant. As he got into the visualization, I could feel the wall fall and the energy move from his leg to his neck. I discovered that the neck was the major release point and that the leg rotation was the trigger. I asked him to push a second wall, but he hesitated. I immediately responded according to my gut instinct. I suddenly shouted his name and slammed my hand hard on the floor right next to his head. When he jumped, the wall fell, but he screamed out in terrible pain. I sat him up and held him tightly, encouraging him not to move and not to pass out. All this time, his hand was clenching the back of my neck. As his pain subsided, I suggested he let go of my neck.

I knew I had to do more work on the hip socket and help him learn to work the leg and hip in a new way. I slowly rotated his left leg so that he could feel the full movement and sense the rotation. Then I focused on the right leg and socket, making the rotation small in the beginning and gradually working to a full rotation as he stopped resisting the movement. Actually, I was amazed he was able to learn the new movement all in one session, even though I had already been told he could. It was a big leap for anyone to take.

I made him get up slowly and walk around the room a bit. Then I gave him two essence tests: (1) to stabilize him as a result of the emotional release, and (2) to stabilize his physical and structural changes. After all of this, he was anxious to try that golf swing again, so I said he could *if* he did it gently. There was no slice in the swing. I kinesiology tested him for any "post-process" work. He needed to not play golf, sleep as much as he wanted and do only light exercise for two days. With that, he thanked me and went to his room for a nap. The whole process took two hours.

It wasn't until after John left the room that I realized how much we had accomplished and how short a time we did it in. Amazing.

December 30 — Heather Green

Awoke thinking about various Perelandra garden chores. At breakfast, the men asked me if I would use the Split Molecular Process to shift the garden layout chart and any other chart information I have so that they can have a clearer idea of what I'm talking about in our conversations. I agreed to set up the split with nature.

John slept through breakfast.

December 31 — Slate Blue

For the first time, the men hesitated giving me my color for the day. When I asked them why, they said they could see the color, but they couldn't believe it. It was slate blue. I didn't see any significance in this, other than the fact that I had not worn any shade of blue since coming to the Cottage.

When I returned to my room that evening, I found a slate-blue velvet jumper and ivory silk blouse laying on my bed. The color combination struck me as being extraordinarily beautiful, and the velvet and silk combination gave it a deep and rich look. When I put the outfit on, I felt enfolded in an energy of familiarity and comfort.

At dinner, everyone commented on the colors. I told them about how the colors made me feel, but I had no idea what it all meant. No sooner had I gotten those words out, I heard inside my head "white robe trimmed with a certain shade of blue representing the lama." It only took a few seconds for the significance of that statement to sink in. Prior to "leaving home," some 5500 years ago, to begin a series of life cycles on Earth, I had been presented with "my colors": slate blue and ivory. Now I had come full circle, had activated all that I needed to activate and was being presented with the colors again.

I sensed I was to get up and go out on the patio, so I excused myself and walked out the patio door. Outside was a large group of those wispy souls, applauding, celebrating and telling me congratulations. I had gone completely through my passage. The souls surrounded me and I was overwhelmed. All I could say was "thank you." Just beyond them were some lights—the light of nature joining in the celebration. The moment humbled me. I felt myself surrounded by love. After about twenty minutes, the souls and the lights gradually disappeared.

That's when the Cottage men joined me. They said they had known this was coming and that they had been told to have the colors ready. Their surprise was that it came so soon. This was the sign that I had fully integrated and activated what I began just two weeks ago. The odd thing is that after all this, I still wasn't sure what had been activated and what it all meant. I only knew I was standing there in new colors.

I spent a quiet evening with my family, letting what happened sink in. They suggested I now take one week off to rest and relax. I have to admit that the idea sounded appealing.

1983

January 1 — Slate Blue

Wore the slate blue and ivory combination again. I feel I need to let the colors integrate more into my system. The men announced at breakfast that this is my week of R&R and that no serious discussions with me would be allowed. They also got me to agree to rest when they told me to rest. I am to lean on them more, and I'm to start doing it this week.

Took a nap before dinner. I can feel the exhaustion rise out of my body as I relax.

January 2 — Heather Green

Despite the R&R week, we slipped into a discussion about how a strong religious upbringing can lay the foundation and open the door to spiritual thoughts and realities at any point along the way (including post-death), even if the person does not participate in religion in his adult years.

Later I returned to the Cottage exhausted. I feel like I'm deeply in a hole, and I wonder if I'll ever recover my physical stamina. The men urge patience.

John is recovering nicely from his shift. He's preparing to leave the Cottage tomorrow. After dinner, he and I walked in the garden and he thanked me for my help, but he admitted he was not sure of all that went on. He only knew he felt better than ever.

January 3 — Brown

John left early this morning, long before I woke up.

I had a dream within a dream. I was asleep in my bed at the Cottage, dreaming that I was asleep in my bed at the Cottage. Had trouble finding the reality level I was actually on and waking up out of the dream. I felt like I was trying to climb out of an anaesthetic state.

At breakfast I suggested that Petunia might be interested in all the history the men know, and perhaps they might talk to her about it. David said he had already tried, but she doesn't want to remember past yesterday. Tex said this was a problem, since history is nothing more than a succession of yesterdays. No matter what, Petunia wasn't impressed. She just yawned them away.

Evening. Returned feeling strong, then within fifteen minutes I sank. The color drained from my face, and my body and head ached. In fact, I was in pretty bad pain. The men jumped into action again, eventually pulling me out of the shatter after about an hour. Once I felt restored, they talked me into sitting in the lagoon for awhile.

The Cottage feels empty without John. When he leaves, I find I need to reorder my sense of the Cottage balance.

January 4 — Ivory

Afternoon. I asked David, if he had to do it over, would he consider running for president again. He said that under the *same* circumstances he would, and that he did not regret his decision in 1951. We then talked about the differences between the leader and the pioneer. He explained that the men at the Cottage were leaders, and that a leader is someone who is one step out in front of the pack and has the abilities needed to move the pack forward. The pioneer is way ahead of the pack and by himself. He clears the path, but he doesn't lead because there's no one around him to lead.

January 5 — Burgundy

At Perelandra. Drove my wallpaper friend to Winchester to pick up her car from the shop and got caught in an ice storm. While waiting out the storm, I told her about the leader/pioneer discussion we had yesterday. She suggested that a person who chooses the role of the pioneer forfeits his or her right to support from others. She said that by definition, the pioneer is a loner, and to look to others for support is asking too much from others.

At the Cottage. The men immediately noticed my weariness when I got home. I told them about the ice storm and the conversation with my friend. They became quite angry, pronouncing her "dead wrong." I was surprised at their reactions, but they said this is precisely what they are trying to work through with me. They want me to lean on them more, not remain self-contained. I was to reach out to them for support, and I was to forget what she had said.

January 6 — Yellow

Afternoon. The men asked me if I did anything during my day at Perelandra that was dangerous, risky or even mildly unamusing! I assured them that my day had been quiet and uneventful.

They talked to me about an article they read today about the creative mind. They feel that I have a creative mind, and it is important for them to clearly understand what this means if I am to function as a full member of the team. Understanding how I operate will allow them to give me what I need in order to operate well.

After dinner. My back began to spasm with deep, sharp, localized pain—it made me double over. Tex stayed with me while David made a phone call. When he returned, he said that I was going through more adjustments, and that I would probably continue going through them for another week. I was doing fine, and I needed to relax. I felt discouraged at being in pain again.

January 7*

Awoke with more pain—this time in the solar plexus and head. I decided I'd sit in the lagoon for awhile to see if this gave me some relief. Actually, it was a good move. I fell asleep sitting in the water and, when I woke up, I had no pain. (Lucky for me the steps are such that I can sit on the lower one and easily lean back against the upper one, fall asleep, and not drown.) When I left the Cottage, I promised everyone that if I ran into trouble at Perelandra, I'd return home early.

Evening. Felt frustrated. I want to break out and feel strong again. Instead, I need more sleep and rest.

Went for a walk along the golf course with David. We circled around to the Cottage, walking along a small path leading through the woods. At one point, we crossed an arched bridge that spanned a small, fast-running stream. It reminded me a little of the arched bridge I used to stand on to receive lessons from the monk. As we walked along, I told David about my experiences with the monk and some of the lessons he had given me. He asked if I'd be willing to share my experiences with the others. I agreed to do this, but not tonight—I was too tired.

* When the daily color is not listed, it is because I forgot to record it in my journal.

January 8 — Heather Green

Afternoon. Got into a discussion about football. Talked David into teaching me how to throw a football—which he will, as soon as they buy the necessary football.

Talked about age again. David said that, during the war, he was fifty-two and looking ahead to his older years. Now he's "fifty-two" again and looking ahead to years of strength and vitality. He sees fifty-two as the hub of his wheel, which gives him the greatest access to all the different spokes of his life. This gives him an excellent base to build upon.

January 9 — Dusty Rose

Evening. Talked about the problem of people on the Perelandra level trying to pull me into defending David, his life and policies once they find out who I am working with. The men are quite concerned about this and had actually discussed the potential problem even before I came to the Cottage. I told them I had already run into the problem. Recently when I told a friend about my Cottage life, she immediately responded by calling David stupid. She *demanded* that I find out why he ruined the Oval Office floor with his golf shoes. (This was why she called him stupid. She knew nothing about his life except this one fact that she had gotten from a book.) I hadn't said anything to the men about the remark because it seemed too insulting to pass along. David is concerned that I not get caught in the cross-fire of people's criticisms of him. We decided it is best to use the greatest of discretion when telling others about the Cottage, and that if I should get into any cross-fire, let David know right away so he can give me the correct information. He feels that information is the best way for me to keep my equilibrium.

January 10 — Ivory

At breakfast. There is no vegetable garden at the Cottage. When I asked about this, they told me they were deferring the garden to me after I get there full time. [The term "full time" means dying on the Perelandra level, when my soul will shift to the Katie body on the Cottage level permanently.] David and Mickey both want to assist me in the garden, but said they were afraid I would be too much of a demanding task master. I assured them I would be fair—perhaps even gentle!

January 11 through 13 — Yellow, Heather Green, Burgundy
JAMFD times three

January 14 — Yellow
David flipped the D-Day coin. He felt it was important to do this by himself. They were having a little trouble with the flip, but then they realized that David had to add his personal emotions as a dynamic to all the decisions surrounding the D-Day strategy. This he did today, and the coin flipped, he said, four different ways.

January 15 — Burgundy
We took a break, and several of us went out to dinner at a little Italian restaurant in the village named Nino's. Excellent food.

January 16 — Dusty Rose
While I was at Perelandra, I "phoned" updates of the football play-off games to David.

January 17 — Yellow
Admitted to myself and to the others that I have been coughing at Perelandra since early December. Today I realized that the cough isn't just from the stress of the Cottage experience—it is also from the painful and closed process Clarence is going through to find himself.

January 18 — Heather Green
The men got me to talk about the pressures at Perelandra more. They encouraged me to step aside and let Clarence find his own way regarding himself and what he wants to do. Interestingly, they said that they have all wanted, at different points in their lives, the kind of help I have given Clarence, but this is the first time they've considered the cost of such help to the person giving it. Now they're seeing the other side of the coin. I realized that the best way out of the wall I feel cemented in is to focus on the Perelandra work only. It's time for me to start getting the information about this year's

garden anyway. The men are pressing for me to split all my garden information so that they can follow our discussions better.

At dinner. Small talk about the men's knowledge of current events on Earth. They explained that what I read in the paper and magazines are nonissues to them. They are more concerned with undercurrents and dynamics that do not make the news. I accused them of subscribing to *Timeless Magazine.*

January 19 — Ivory

At Perelandra. My cough is improving. When I'm at the Cottage, I don't cough at Perelandra at all.

Evening. Butch announced that he and Nicole [the singer in Seamus's band who Butch has dated for several years] have decided to be friends, not lovers. The decision has taken pressure off them both. He explained that their relationship works best when they are close friends and deteriorates when they move closer.

January 20 — Burnt Orange

Found out that Tex is an astrology buff. The others say it appeals to his intellectual side. He started out doing research to disprove it; now he's quietly hooked. He doesn't talk about it with the others too much, but he's done a chart on everyone—which prompted me to ask if he had done one on me. He said yes, and it shows that I'm tenacious and stubborn. I faked surprise and pain that such a thing could be said about me. The others joined in by asking me where in the world I had been hiding this part of my personality.

January 21 — Burgundy

At Perelandra. I'm feeling that I need to tell close friends about the Cottage. This is now a major part of my life, and it feels strange to be keeping this information away from them. The Cottage experience has changed the balance in all my friendships and, without the information, the relationships don't really exist because the people don't know who they are relating to. So I wrote a letter to two friends living in Europe describing the Cottage, its work and the physical challenges. I worked on the letter all afternoon, and I think I did a good job. By the time I finished, I had terrible pressure in my head and waves of pressure were running through my body.

Got caught in a strange cross-fire at a dinner Clarence and I had with friends. I looked for an opportunity to tell them about the Cottage. They already knew something was going on, and I had a feeling they were anxious to hear. A discussion of the most recent Redskins game [Washington's football team] came up, and I told them I had won a football pool on that game at the Cottage. Then I let them know a little about what was going on. The husband immediately pounced, saying that I didn't have a right to hold back this information from them, that it was silly for me to want to protect myself from them. He seemed to be saying that I was insulting him if I didn't freely talk about personal areas of my life with him. This made me mad. I told him no one except Clarence, the chiropractor, my wallpaper friend, and a few others knew anything about this until after the Christmas holidays, when I made my 100-percent commitment to the Cottage. Before that time, I felt it was no one else's business, including his.

At the Cottage. Returned shattered. We're all quite calm about the shattering drill these days. Once I was able to focus, I told them about the dinner and how the husband had responded to the Cottage information. When I finished, David said, "He's a child. That man's a child. He doesn't have the maturity to understand your complexity. You're putting more effort out to him than he's capable of appreciating and understanding."

The others quickly agreed. They all encouraged me to see him as an emotional child and to deal with him accordingly. They especially encouraged me to stop putting out effort he can't appreciate. Their advice was strong and matter-of-fact, and this startled me. They had a deep concern about my getting inadvertently hurt by him—and anyone else like him.

January 22 — Brown

Awoke in terrific spirits and with no pain. Rested. I was looking forward to the NFC championship game between the Redskins and Dallas. We set up a direct link between the Perelandra TV and David, using me as the conduit, so that we could broadcast the game directly to David. He could hear the TV broadcast through our connection. It was as if I was functioning as a radio for him. He, in turn, gave updates to the others.

At Perelandra. Great game—Redskins 31, Dallas 17. I could tell David was "on the other end" and keeping up with the game. Sometimes I got so excited and loud, he couldn't hear the play, but it wasn't a problem since there were so many replays.

At the Cottage. All four were waiting on the patio for me. There was a lot of kidding about the game. Butch and Tex bet £10 each on Dallas. David, Mickey and I got our £10 back plus a three-way division of the £20. I'm up almost £17 now in the football pool, if I have it figured out correctly.

January 23 — Yellow

At breakfast. One question popped into my head, so I asked the men. "Can we stay in form for as long as we want without risking limiting ourselves?" Yes, form is a state, not a limitation. That's all I wanted to know, so I switched the conversation to the AFC championship game today. I picked the Dolphins over the Jets.

At Perelandra. Set up the broadcast again to David. Dolphins 14 and Jets 0.

At the Cottage. I'm making a fortune on these football games.

January 24 — Ivory

At Perelandra. Spent several hours in the garden working on the strawberry row. *Loved* being there—solitude, peace, cows, horses, dogs, beauty.

At the Cottage. The men talked about how much more at peace I look after a day in the garden.

After dinner, I asked David if he was still in contact with Mamie. He explained that their relationship ended when he died, that they had done everything they were supposed to do together, and now she was continuing her own life and developing her own strengths. I again asked if he remained in contact with her, and he said "no." This would be inappropriate and unnecessary for them both.

January 25 — Heather Green

JAMFD

January 26 — Brown

Morning. Another difficult Katie memory surfaced. I can't remember what I was talking about with the men at the time, but I do remember it was insignificant. Suddenly, memories surfaced about Katie helping her best friend get to the hospital just after the friend had been brutally gang-raped. I described everything that rose in my mind—the hospital, the doctors, Caroline's hysteria (name pronounced: ka-ro-leen′). Katie had to remain with Caroline while she was examined. The rape caused a great deal of internal damage. I worked the entire process through by talking about everything that was surfacing. Katie was never able to cry about this experience because she insisted on remaining strong for Caroline. As the experienced surfaced now, I cried, and as I cried, I felt the release and balance occur in me. I especially released the fear of the violence. It was a strong experience, but it efficiently moved through. I found out that the men already knew about this part of Katie's history and had hoped I wouldn't need to deal with it.

At Perelandra. Felt the need to be quiet and finish balancing the Caroline/Katie experience in the Machaelle body. Spent the afternoon in the garden alone. Very healing.

January 27 — Dusty Rose

Felt a little drained. The others think it's because of the Caroline experience yesterday, and they urged me to rest. I promised I'd do just that, and I rested as much as a person can who has to hold up two bodies on two different levels.

January 28 — Yellow

Clear dream: A friend and I walked into a high-quality gift shop located on a beach. I had hoped to buy a bathing suit, but they weren't in stock yet. I noticed a wind chime hanging, and I touched it. It made the *perfect* sound—the sound I've been searching for over many years: perfectly clear and clean in tone. I considered buying it, but was suddenly struck with a question. Now that I've finally found the perfect sound, can I make a commitment to have this sound in my life forever? The wind chime would always be ringing. If I couldn't hold the commitment, the sound would change in my ears from perfection to irritation. I have a responsibility to this perfect tone. Then the dream shifted. My friend suggested I buy a small oriental rug that had caught my eye. She said it was quite valuable, but she didn't have the money, and I did. It cost $500, but she said it was worth $12,000. Its colors were blues and cream white, and the center picture was of the Shiva. It was one of a kind, so I bought it. I put the rug on the floor beside my bed, my bed in the dream. The blues in the rug perfectly matched the slate blue cover and dark blue duster. The match was visually striking.

When I told the others about the dream, they didn't say much, except that the rug and wind chime were important. They're obviously waiting for me to "get it."

January 29

JAMFD

January 30 — Heather Green

Super Bowl Sunday. Hooked up the game with David. Terrific game: Redskins 27, Dolphins 17. I returned home and discovered all four of them had bet on the Dolphins, giving me a total of £60 for the day. I accused them of throwing their bets so I could "earn" some money. They assured me they would *never* intentionally throw a bet. But now they know to pay more attention to my analysis of the teams. I've proven myself to be more accurate than they had anticipated.

January 31 — Burgundy

JAMFD

February 1 — Burnt Orange

Talked about the concept that quality of work is directly proportional to the quality of the relationships among the team members doing the work. The men have put considerable effort into stabilizing their relationships, and from this they can do their best work. My presence has added a new dimension to this process, and they feel that it has upped the quality and potential quality even further.

David and Tex let Petunia accompany them around the golf course. They said that several times she was so oblivious to what was going on that they almost teed her off!

February 2 — Ivory

A rainy day at the Cottage. Slept late.

February 3 — Yellow

At Perelandra. Shuttled to New York City with Clarence to discuss the tax strategy for Isadore's trust. It looks like we'll have to pay half of the trust out for taxes—something I don't understand since this is money that Isadore already paid taxes on. A day of accountants and lawyers, and a lot of discussion about strategy. I'm getting better at following what's being said in these meetings. When I finish, I should get an honorary accountant and tax law degree.

Returned to the Cottage late and ran the legal maneuvers on the trust by Tex.

February 4 — Heather Green

Awoke hopping mad about the tax business. I felt I needed to make a statement of some kind and not just pay this tax lying down. I know that most of it will go to the damn defense budget, and that really angers me. I considered sending the tax check to Reagan, requesting that I be allowed to have this money funneled to social programs and not defense (similar to conscientious objectors requesting alternative service).

When I shared my thoughts (and spouted off my anger) with the others at breakfast, David calmly stated, "It's not a sound strategy. It will get you nowhere, and it will give you nothing." They suggested that I need to balance the act of paying all this money out for something I feel to be useless and destructive. When I asked them what I could do to balance it out, they told me to use my work and life. It's all I have. At first I just stared at them. Then it hit me. Whatever money I must pay out in taxes, I can use the equivalent in energy toward getting my work out and changing the consciousness of others in a direction that is *opposite* what the money is being used for. In essence, the government will be donating that money to Perelandra via energy! This released that sense of powerlessness I had been having over the tax issue. I talked about what I came up with as a result of their suggestion. David said, "Now *that's* a strategy. That one will work for you."

At Perelandra. I decided it was important to do something symbolic at Perelandra to ground my intent to change the dynamic
around the tax payment. I did this rather simply by sending my accountant (and co-trustee) a card, indicating to him my change in
attitude around the money and tax.

At the Cottage. After dinner the men talked about their struggle to
keep from "taking over" the things I have to face. They'd like to
charge in, rescue me, protect me and make my life easier. We
decided that the imposed Perelandra/Cottage separation is a good
thing for them because it forces them to let go of previous ways of
expressing concern and to work things out with me as an intelligent
peer instead.

February 5 — Dusty Rose

The focus on my work at Perelandra is causing me to be preoccupied while at the Cottage. The men encouraged me to relax
about this; they said that it is natural to be preoccupied, and I
shouldn't fight it. They don't feel a distancing from me.

February 6 — Brown

Awoke from a magnificent dream: Off my room was a high, arched-
ceiling sunroom with large panels of glass rising three stories to a
dome of triangular glass panels. The room's floor space was small—
about ten-by-twelve feet. I looked out to see a beach and ocean only
about twenty-five feet away, and I saw that a storm was blowing up.
One wave came over the fence along the beach and crashed into the
glass wall about six feet up. There was a terrible force in the wave,
and I could see much foam and swirling sand in the water as it
crashed against the wall. I wondered if the wall would hold another
such crash. The water drew back to the ocean. But when I looked
out again, I saw a *huge* tidal wave coming at me. It was going to
engulf the whole structure I was in. I realized there was nowhere to
run because it would be impossible to outrun this thing. I decided to
stay where I was and experience the tidal wave. It kept coming—a
huge wall of water. The full wave hit the glass wall with great
power, but not chaotic power. The wave's impact against the wall
forced the wave to crest over the dome. From within the glass room,

I was totally encompassed by the wave. The only reason the walls weren't caving in was the glass dome that was structured to "lean" in the direction of the cresting wave. For a second, I realized that if the dome should break, I would be buried in a mound of safety glass. I actually saw small bits of glass raining down on me. Then my attention was drawn to the base of the wave. That's when I saw the *heart* of the wave's power—the place where the forces met in a vortex of power. From this, the water shot up the side of the wave (wall) to form the crest. I felt privileged to witness the heart of the wave, and it gave me enormous exhilaration and a feeling of power. The water receded into the ocean, and I could see the next tidal wave forming its wall. I watched as I became engulfed again. I awoke feeling engulfed in power.

At breakfast the men's discussion centered around the question: Would you stand there and watch the wave, knowing it could kill you, or would you try to outrun it?

February 7 — Yellow

Afternoon. I could feel electricity in the air when I got back. Mickey told me that David and Tex "went at things tooth and nail" today— an exhilarating but intense day. I asked if there were any dead bodies. He explained that these things usually just roll off everyone's back, and if something doesn't, the ones involved always make sure everything gets settled. Later, David explained that each man can have a strong position, and it's good none of them will give in easily. Usually, good work comes out of these hot sessions, which are most often between Tex and David. I asked the others what they do when it gets hot. Butch ignores them, and Mickey finds something to do at the opposite end of the house!

February 8 — Heather Green

Even though the men have said they want to see *Behaving* after publication so they can experience the book in its final form, they have been most interested in knowing about the production process I'm going through with the book. At their request, I showed the men slides I had chosen at Perelandra for possible covers for *Behaving*. We all seem to like the same handful of slides.

February 9 — Ivory

After dinner. Tex and David discussed the need to slow down and give Butch a break from work. They plan to play golf tomorrow and take several half-day R&R's.

February 10 — Brown

At Perelandra. Had a private Feldenkrais lesson.*

At the Cottage. Returned exhausted and with head pain. I explained to the others about the Feldenkrais lesson and how this work affected the body and brain. David asked, "Why are you putting yourself through this now?" I talked about my deep feeling that the human body is meant to move well, and that any block in the body is a block in the soul's ability to reflect through the body. This seemed to make sense to him. Once I took essences and a nap, the head pressure went away.

February 11 — Dusty Rose

Awoke late, to a wet day with hard, pounding rain.

At Perelandra. We have 25 mph winds and a foot of snow. The weather service is calling it a blizzard. Spent four and a half hours choosing pictures for the *Behaving* text.

At the Cottage. Exhausted.

February 12 — Yellow

After dinner. We sat around the fire while the men watched my period glow increase and change. I'm still slightly uncomfortable with their focus on this. Again, they talked about how my period reminds them of their creative side, of change, of life cycles and rhythms. These are all aspects that they, on their own, don't easily connect with. I had to admit that the sense of rhythm and renewal was important to my well-being. After listening to them, I decided I wanted to *gracefully* share this part of myself with them. Before going to sleep, I made the decision to give them each a yellow rose to let them know I now willingly include them in this. Decided I'd ask Mickey tomorrow morning where the village florist shop was.

* A Feldenkrais *lesson* was private. The *class* was taken with a number of other people. I usually took both weekly from the fall of each year to early spring.

February 13 — Burgundy

When I woke up, I found four yellow roses in a crystal vase on my dresser. Nature had heard my decision and acted on it. I was struck with the clarity and closeness of my connection with nature at the Cottage. I presented the roses to the men at breakfast and told them that I had decided to accept this connection between us. The gesture touched them. They said it was the first time they received flowers without being sick! I could tell they were intrigued with how I got the roses. I just smiled and said nothing.

February 14 — Ivory

Third morning of dreams filled with frustration.

At Perelandra. Spent a quiet day working on the book slides.

February 15 — Burnt Orange

JAMFD

February 16 — Yellow

At Perelandra. Another private Feldenkrais lesson.

At the Cottage. Needed to take a nap.

David had lunch with Max who is going through a crisis. He realizes his career as a coach is coming to an end, and he is now faced with the future. David tells me that the only thing I can do for Max is support him as he goes through his decision making—let him know I am with him and love him. They've invited him to have dinner with us this Saturday.

February 17 — Ivory

At breakfast. We all talked about the heightened pressures inherent in my dual-body, multilevel life as opposed to their linear lives, where they developed, went through the death transition and *then* expanded their understanding about reality. Taking this kind of expansion *before* death creates added pressures. (Even I'm willing to concede this point.)

February 18 — Heather Green

At Perelandra. Working up my nerve to call a friend who works at National Geographic for help with self-publishing *Behaving*.

February 19 — Heather Green

At breakfast. They asked me what kinds of things I might want from Perelandra for my office at the Cottage, once I join them full time. So far, the only things I could think of are my garden notes and the *Encyclopedia Britannica* (which serves me as a starting point and springboard for my work with nature).

Evening. Max joined us for dinner, and we had an easy evening. While I was sitting on the floor in front of the fireplace looking at some of Max's papers, I silently asked the Deva of Fire to tone down our fire so sparks wouldn't shoot out on the papers. The fire lowered immediately. When I finished reading, I thanked the fire for its cooperation, and it returned to its original level of activity. I assumed no one saw me do this, but I was wrong. Once Max left, they told me they had noticed what was going on, but they didn't know what to say.

February 20 — Burnt Orange

At breakfast. They brought up the fire "event" from last night. I questioned if I should do this kind of thing in front of them. I wondered about the appropriateness of it. But my partnership with nature at the Cottage is both more "casual" and more dynamic than at Perelandra. I'm not sure why. I don't think it has to do with the partnership itself. Rather, I think it has more to do with a difference between the two levels. The partnership just works with greater ease on the Cottage level. It's as if the general population on the Cottage level more easily accepts the reality of my working partnership with nature than the people living on the Perelandra level. The men said that I must continue my relationship with nature in front of them because it's a part of me, and this is my home. (It sounded so obvious to me as they said these things to me. I was surprised I hadn't figured it out on my own.) They just need to get used to things changing before their eyes. Mickey said these things have made him loosen up his sense of reality and form around the Cottage. After listening, I told them I would continue my special relationship with nature there until I get an indication from them or nature that I should stop. Immediately after saying this, a yellow rose in a vase appeared in the middle of the table. We laughed. This was my validation that nature approved my decision, and it was a little test for them about just how comfortable they would be about things changing and appearing before their eyes.

February 21 — Yellow

At Perelandra. Spent the afternoon with my wallpaper friend. She's convinced I may need to stop going to the Cottage at some point because I won't be able to keep up with this schedule for the next thirty years. The possibility alarmed me. The Cottage is too much a part of my life to even consider such a thing now.

At the Cottage. The men reacted to my friend's comment. "That's ridiculous. All this work and all these adjustments just so you have to stop?" They assured me this was not in the picture unless *I* wanted to stop. I was relieved. My visit with her exhausted me. They urged me to make an appointment with the chiropractor to be checked out.

Our guinea pig Millie (at Perelandra) passed on. I realized this when she appeared in my mind's eye while I was at the Cottage. I put her through the death process and, with nature's help, shifted the essences she needed to her. It was easy to work with her.

February 22 and 23 — Ivory, Dusty Rose

JAMFD times two

February 24 — Burgundy

At Perelandra. I saw the chiropractor, and my pelvis and sacrum were misaligned. The sacrum was "way out." I also needed several cranial adjustments. I did not need any essences—she tested me four times to make sure. She announced that the support I'm getting from the Cottage must still be working. I told her about the cough I've been experiencing at Perelandra since December. For that, my adrenals showed slight stress. She strengthened the adrenals with supplements, and I tested I needed one essence for the cough, as well. She suggested I come in more often while my Feldenkrais teacher is working on my pelvis and hips. I can't afford to have the hips misaligned while dealing with the Cottage. Just before I left, I asked her to test me kinesiologically while I asked a silent question: Am I a physical member of a team headed by Dwight David Eisenhower, thirty-fourth president of the United States and Supreme Commander of the Allied Forces in Europe during World War II? The test result was a clear, strong positive.

At the Cottage. Felt revitalized and strong.

February 25 — Ivory

Mickey asked me to essence test a close friend of his, Elizabeth, who is in pain.

February 26 — Brown

Evening. Worked with Elizabeth in my room. She needed extensive adjustments and a number of essences, and I could sense a major issue that is operating as a block in her right now. I talked with her about this. She asked me to talk to Mickey about the work I had done with her. I told her I would.

February 27 — Heather Green

Evening. Mickey met me at the door to say that Max was there and in pain. He had taken a bad spill on the ice. I checked him right away. He's bruised his sacrum. I aligned his pelvis and tested him extensively for essences. He needed several for stabilizing the sacrum and pelvis. It's hard on me to see him in pain.

February 28 — Yellow

Evening. David spoke to Max this afternoon. He's much better. Also, he has come to a decision about his future. He will retire after this season, and he's going to buy the rink. This way, he keeps his hand in skating without the pressure.

March 1 — Brown

Worked with Max again. The pelvis is holding well, but he needed different essences.

March 2 — Ivory

At breakfast. Shared with everyone about my frustrations around getting the ball rolling at Perelandra. For one thing, I'm having trouble working around Clarence's unfinished projects. After a moment's thought, David said to me, "I give you four days to get the ball rolling." My reaction to this challenge was fire. How dare he challenge me this way. Yet, at the same time, I could feel my energy lift and collect. He just smiled, and said, "Everyone needs to be challenged sometime."

At Perelandra. Focused myself and busted through the day.

March 3 — Burgundy

At Perelandra. Worked on this year's garden information. Also, I called my friend from National Geographic. We mutually decided it was best to meet in May about *Behaving*. I can feel the Perelandra ball really rolling now.

March 4 — Burnt Orange

Spent the night drifting between realities in my dreams. In fact, I had trouble finding my reality and pulling out of the dreams. Disconcerting. I decided that perhaps I was adjusting some more and it was best if I just concentrated on getting through the day. Sometimes the most comforting thing I can do is wake up and get on with my day.

March 5 — Yellow

Slept long and deep.

At Perelandra. Spent four and a half hours doing essence work with a couple who is preparing for the birth of their first child. It's particularly touchy because they have already experienced one stillborn birth and two miscarriages. Tested the baby for the essences she/he will need during birth and immediately afterwards. Also, the baby tested strongest when surrounded by the colors yellow and green. The parents will make sure those colors are in the receiving blanket. All in all, it was an amazing experience for all of us. It was obvious that the energy has shifted in the mother and the child in preparation for birth.

At the Cottage. Told the men about my essence work. We considered the implications of having an essence practitioner working in a hospital's obstetrics and nursery sections. I also talked about the need to have essence practitioners available for terminal patients, especially during the death process. The implications of this kind of essence work are staggering.

March 6 — Heather Green

At Perelandra. A "public" day. I dealt with a lot of phone callers. Also worked on a lengthy, written session with nature.

March 7 through 10
Brown, Dusty Rose, Ivory, Yellow

Feeling deep frustration, but I was not sure why.

March 11 — Heather Green

Four hours of sleep. I awoke crying, feeling terrible pain. Around 6 A.M. I could feel myself come out of the darkness, and I lifted to a new level of calm.

At Perelandra. Met my wallpaper friend for lunch. Talked to her about the frustrations I've been having. She declared her support for me in this and said if I needed to get away this weekend, just call. She'd meet me anywhere. I was surprised and touched by her caring.

At the Cottage. They said I returned looking better than I had in days. I told them it must be the effect of the support I had gotten from my friend.

After dinner. We talked about emotions, and I asked them what in the world they did to remain so emotionally calm. (They had already told me that, prior to death, David was known for his "explosive" temper. Yet I had not seen any evidence of this at the Cottage.) They talked about "the walls," a name they've given the process people go through after death. There is an intense healing period that goes on right after the transition, and it is directly related to all of the issues that were responsible for their death or needed to be faced at the time of death. Coming through the walls can take some people the equivalent of many years. But it must be done, because this is the process that puts closure on the person's pre-death life. As a person comes through the last of his walls, he is freed from restrictions and constrictions. For many, the walls are primarily emotional issues. Once the last of the walls are eliminated, a person is able to express himself where he wishes, when he wishes and in exactly the manner he wishes. There are no restrictions. Each one of these men have been through many walls, and each one is able to express emotionally as he wishes.

March 12 — Dusty Rose

I can feel a deepening sense of sanity enveloping the five of us, but I can't explain it any further than that.

Mickey talked about some difficulties he's having in his relationship with Elizabeth. After their ten-year relationship, he feels she's pulling back from him and putting up blocks. I was both touched and impressed by his openness about this.

March 13 — Slate Blue

At breakfast. Mickey announced that he and Elizabeth have mutually decided to switch from being lovers to friends. As he talked, something did not ring right to me. Suddenly, it dawned on me that she might now desire a lesbian relationship. I said, "This may be out of left field, but do you think Elizabeth is a lesbian?" The question stunned them all, but I could tell things were now making sense to Mickey, and he felt I was onto something. I felt an undercurrent of pain in him as we talked. He left the table early to spend time thinking, I presumed. I was puzzled by his reaction because I knew he would not think any less of her for her sexual preference. It wasn't his style, nor was it consistent with his heart.

At Perelandra. Got information about what I was to do for Mickey as he moved through the wall that was facing him and that Elizabeth was catalyzing.

At the Cottage. David met me at the door. I said, "I'm going to take Mickey over the edge. Don't stop me once I start." He said I had their support, but I could tell he was concerned about what I was going to do.

When we all got together, I asked how everyone was. Mickey admitted he felt anger, and that he hated the feeling. He wished he could let it go. That was my cue. I began taunting and irritating him a little. I said things to him I would not normally say to anyone. I could see he was getting angrier, so I escalated my taunts. That made him even angrier. I needled him more. He got *very* angry, but he was trying to control it. I worked him to a high intensity. Finally, I was standing in front of him and challenging his manhood. Then I brought up Elizabeth. That was the last straw. Without thinking, he slapped me hard in the face. This was what I was told this afternoon to expect, so when I saw it coming, I relaxed my head as much as possible so that it would move with the blow. It was still hard. (I saw David stop the others from jumping in and interfering.) Slapping me shocked him. I knew he would never raise his hand to anyone, and especially not to a woman. But I also knew I had to push him to do something that was *completely* out of character—a challenge to his integrity and heart—so that his release could be triggered. As soon as he hit me, the blood drained from his face. He screamed he was sorry. I put my arms around him, and he let out the deepest scream I have ever heard. Then his body began to tremble. I continued holding him while he cried. It suddenly occurred to me that the others were probably going to kill him for slapping me! I held onto him while he pulled out of it.

I could feel that the others also had released emotions. My taunts and his pain hit them where they too were vulnerable. In less than fifteen minutes, Mickey was calm, and we could all tell the pain and anger were completely released from him. He was at peace again. The intensity of the release surprised us—especially Mickey. We sat down again and talked about what they felt had happened for each of them. Each man dealt with his sense of manhood and manly balance. Lesbianism was not the central issue for any of them. It had simply been a catalyst. As we talked, I could feel everyone and everything settle down. We had really gotten through this. David said it was a hell of a good thing I warned him when I came in! We all tested for flower essences.

We went out to dinner together. The men wore their dress uniforms, and I wore my slate-blue jumper. What a fivesome. The men radiated. I could feel that we were much closer as a unit. We had a toast: "To us." They were most complimentary about my role as a punching bag.

March 14 — Gold

New color: gold. The men were as surprised as I was. I asked the obvious, "This is fairly significant, isn't it?" Yes, they said, but they would not tell me why. I was going to have to get that on my own.

At Perelandra. Drove Clarence to Dulles International Airport and saw him off for his own ten days in Paris. This is his first trip to a non-English speaking foreign country alone. I had urged him to go by himself because I thought the change and challenge it presented would shake him up and help pull him out of his lethargy about life. He left nervous, yet excited.

At the Cottage. As I was walking in from the garden, I got an insight about the gold color. It symbolized a gold chain that I had seen form inside me last night after working with Mickey, a gold chain that links me to the Cottage for eternity. The idea banged in my head. At once I felt joy and terror. What does this mean?

The four of them were waiting when I walked through the door. From the shocked expression on my face, they could tell I had gotten it. From the delighted expressions on their faces, I could tell they were all very pleased by this turn of events. They confirmed my suspicions right away.

March 15 — Gold, again

JAMFD

March 16 — Dusty Rose

At Perelandra. The solitude is allowing my two realities to fuse more.

The essence baby was born: a daughter, nine pounds and six ounces! Mom, dad and baby are doing fine.

March 17 — Ivory

The Perelandra ball is rolling quite nicely. I really feel like I'm leaving home in the mornings to work at my office.

At the Cottage. Mickey met Elizabeth for lunch. He feels they've created a stronger friendship and bond than ever before. She's nervous about exploring her new life and she's actually leaning on Mickey for support. He told me that they plan to have lunch together frequently. Life goes on.

March 18 — Burgundy

At Perelandra. Strained a back muscle. Had a private Feldenkrais lesson to release the stress.

At the Cottage. They are all surrounding and protecting me because of the back strain. They're feeling a little frustrated that they can't take the pain away from me the way I can take it away from them.

Went to bed early.

March 19 — Yellow

Awoke feeling much better. I can tell the muscle is on the mend.

At Perelandra. Worked on garden charts. My muscle continued to improve all day.

March 20 — Gold

[Spring equinox: At this time, devic patterns are released to and energized by the nature-spirit level. On personal issues, it is also the transfer of energy and the shift of intent from planning to action.]

At Perelandra. Had a long session with nature regarding the equinox.

At the Cottage. Exhausted to the bone, so I took a two-and-a-half-hour nap. I checked with nature and found that I could experience the equinox moment from the Cottage instead of going back to the Perelandra sanctuary. During the moment, the gold cord activated, and my hands tingled slightly from the activation. I was grateful the moment was soft and gentle.

March 21 — Gold

At Perelandra. Had a grueling trip to New York City to deal with the trust tax payment. The gold cord has allowed easier access by "phone" between the two levels. Since I was traveling alone and Clarence was out of the country, I had to check in with the men several times throughout the day. The bottom line for the taxes: We're going to have to pay the government fifty percent on money that has already been taxed. Amazing.

At the Cottage. Returned exhausted. Glad to get to bed and to put this day behind me.

March 22 — Ivory

Slept late.

At Perelandra. Accepted a workshop date for May 7 in North Carolina—much to my surprise. The gentleman from North Carolina and I tentatively decided on a one-day workshop on nature and gardening.

March 23 — Yellow

Slept long and deep. At breakfast we talked about wishes and dreams. I told them about a long-held wish of mine to someday have a place setting of "sunshine" dishes for breakfast. I dreamed of having morning coffee and breakfast on very bright, cheery, flowered dishes. I was convinced it would brighten my mornings.

Evening. I tried to skim over my day with the men, but they pressed me for details. They explained that they knew I wasn't deliberately holding back, that my self-containment made me "unpracticed" about sharing such things. It was important to my balance that I talk. I thanked them for their diligence.

March 24 — Dusty Rose

Gave them a copy of my first nature garden reading for the season, as per their request. Their interest in the garden surprised me. I could feel that it was honest interest and not at all patronizing. Yet I couldn't understand why they would be interested in simple garden readings that deal with mundane issues in planting and fertilizing. Their genuine interest both touched me deeply and puzzled me.

March 25 — Burgundy

When I arrived at the breakfast table, I found my place set with beautiful, bright, flowered dishes—my sunshine dishes. A gift from the men. The dishes really did make a difference!

At Perelandra. Had a wonderful, peaceful day in the garden.

March 26 — Heather Green

The men called a Cottage R&R day. David and Tex met Seamus this afternoon at The Pub for lunch.

March 27 — Gold

At breakfast. Asked them to explain what they knew about me prior to my coming to the Cottage. They spoke eloquently about my work and my determination. They had tried to get a book on my work with nature, but they found nothing. That's when Hyperithon told them that I had a book in the works. They had known for some time that there was a fifth position to be filled at the Cottage—the "grounder." My work, combined with my direct connection with the Earth level—I'm still alive and functioning on the Earth level—made me a front-runner for the position. The question was whether or not I would accept the position and all that it entailed. They then went on to tell me how much they were surprised by my quietness about my work when I first came to the Cottage. Once they saw how my presence changed the Cottage environment, they realized I'm not one to sit around and talk about the work—I just do it. They also realized I wasn't used to sharing it with others, and, if they were to find out more, they'd have to draw it out of me.

When they finished, David said, "You're not comfortable with this, are you?"

"No. It's a bit like taking cod liver oil. It's good for you, but it tastes lousy."

I knew I had to hear what they were saying. Somehow, I knew that listening to their impressions about my work would give me a new level of confidence and result in my opening to the work even more. I am to let the pendulum swing wider. It's just that I'm so much more comfortable thinking about myself as one little gardener who is interested in learning from nature about gardening. This relatively modest understanding feels manageable, even reasonable. What the men are pointing out feels too significant to cope with. I realized I have hidden behind everyone's perception of me on the Perelandra level as the "cute girl" doing her "cute little garden work." When I brought this up this morning, they pointed out that when others inappropriately make my work cute, it is a strategy, a tactic. If someone doesn't want to hear something, they can just shoot it full of cute. In their eyes, it would then be rendered powerless.

At dinner. Seamus and Max joined us. They got me to explain the concept of working with nature intelligences within the areas of ice skating and music. Both Max and Seamus grasped the concepts easily and well. A fun night.

March 28 — Gold

At Perelandra. Spent a wonderful day in the garden.

At the Cottage. It's the anniversary of David's death. I asked him if the day means anything to him. No, it's part of his past and is not important now. He sounded very clear about this.

March 29 — Dusty Rose

At dinner. Several of us went out to Nino's for dinner. A very nice break.

March 30 — Ivory

At Perelandra. Had a private Feldenkrais lesson. She worked with my left leg, left ankle and foot connection. When she struck a new alignment that felt totally alien to me, she told me to just stay with that feeling and let the emotions come to the surface while she held my leg in the new alignment. For about a minute, I had no impressions. Then the word "fear" rose in me. I stayed with that and started getting flashbacks—then I began to cry. I *experienced* scenes from my childhood and felt the hostility of the world bombarding me from the left. I felt myself cringe, and my entire left side braced for this broadsiding. To let go of the left side meant that I no longer needed to brace myself. My teacher continued holding my leg as I went through this, then asked if I wanted to go on. I said, "Of course." (I had gotten this far. I certainly didn't think stopping or turning back would help me.) She moved my leg in the new alignment again, and again I cried, experiencing all the emotions. We went as far as we dared, not wanting to overload my body with input. The new alignment made my whole left side feel uncomplicated and agile—and more relaxed than I've ever experienced.

Clarence returned from Paris. When I picked him up at the airport he seemed happy, but I couldn't tell if the trip actually helped him to turn his personal corner.

At the Cottage. Shared my Feldenkrais experience with the men. I was able to describe my emotions to them in greater detail than I have in the past. I felt certain this would help the changes in the Machaelle body settle in better.

March 31 — Ivory

At Perelandra. Went shopping with Clarence, which took some of the coming-back-together pressures off both of us. He's decided to go back to work and seems relieved about the prospect. He admits he's been floating for the past months. Paris helped.

April 1 — Yellow

Sleeping long hours into the mornings these days.

At Perelandra. Made a schedule of things I wanted to do this day, and I stuck to it. I told Clarence he needed to stay out of my way.

April 2

JAMFD

April 3 — Dusty Rose

At Perelandra. Easter. Had a good talk with Clarence, which resulted in our recommitting to our partnership in light of the changes the Cottage has created.

At the Cottage. We had a wonderful Easter meal. I thought about my uneasiness during Christmas, and how I felt a little like an outsider. Now I feel very much a part of this family.

April 4 — Ivory

At breakfast. They asked me to explain, after I come to the Cottage full time and have the benefit of hindsight, what going back and forth between the two dimensions was like for me—the cost, the pressures, the challenges. They feel they only see a portion of what goes on. We all think that once I have the benefit of hindsight I will understand more fully what this experience has been all about.

April 5 — Burgundy

At Perelandra. Had another private Feldenkrais lesson and worked more on the left leg and pelvic alignment.

At the Cottage. Returned feeling vulnerable and out of focus. I felt the need to touch things and focus on feeling what I was touching. I tried to explain to the others my frustrations and fears about what it's like to be out of focus. It brings up my fears about reality and illusion and my frustrations about not being able to verify anything about the Cottage on the Perelandra level. They got me to admit that I need to see the chiropractor, and that feeling out of focus indicated an alignment problem. Just coming to this conclusion helped me focus.

April 6 — Heather Green

My focus was much improved when I woke up this morning.

Evening. David spoke with Max today. My dad is working with the nature information I gave him. He's even taught himself to do kinesiology! He's excited about the discoveries he's making and anxious to apply them to skating and the quality of the physical properties of the ice at the rink. David feels the discoveries have given him a lift and a sense of excitement about his future. Max is not talking about the specifics yet because he feels vulnerable about entering this new world. I said I could certainly understand that.

David went on to tell me that, for the first time since Max and I have reconnected, Max is seeing me as Machaelle and not Katie, the girl he coached for so many years. Now he's afraid of losing his daughter. Will the switch from Katie to Machaelle mean that his daughter no longer exists—again? David urged him to come for dinner more and to be with me more, and he assured Max of my love for him. David said to me that if Max hasn't made a move on his own in a week, he'll get him to the Cottage himself.

I asked David how in the world Max (and Seamus, too) was prepared for seeing me—especially since everyone knew Katie had died in a bombing raid. David explained that all of the important preparation work for both of them was done on the unconscious. When the foundation was completely laid, David approached both men and spoke to them about what I (Machaelle) was preparing to do, who I was, my relationship to Katie, how I would be utilizing her body and why. Although the concepts were new to both men, the foundation that had been laid allowed them to hear and comprehend.

It was felt that because of the critical roles they played in Katie's life, a similar relationship now would be helpful to me. Once this was understood, and once they each agreed to helping me, it was up to us to meet as we did and allow our relationships to develop naturally.

I was relieved to hear all of this. Why Max and Seamus were responding to me in such a loving and warm manner was a mystery to me. Of course, my response to them has also been a bit of a mystery.

April 7 — Brown

At Perelandra. A frustrating day. Can't get an appointment with my chiropractor until Monday, but I can get one tomorrow with her partner. I decided I needed to go sooner, not later. I'm feeling frustrated about being so tied to my chiropractor.

Worked in the garden shed sharpening my tools. Very pleasant.

At the Cottage. A small, technical problem cropped up when I returned. I came into the garden during a driving rain storm. I didn't know about the inclement weather until after I got all the way in. It had been raining at Perelandra as well, and I wasn't sure if the rain I was sensing was a Cottage illusion caused by the Perelandra reality. It wasn't an illusion. By the time I got to the patio door, I was drenched. I ran in, and one of the men said ever-so-calmly, "Don't you check the weather before you come in?" We all had a good laugh. However, the upshot is: I will come and go from my room from now on.

April 8 — Yellow

At Perelandra. Had an excellent visit with the different chiropractor. He knows *nothing* about the Cottage. He adjusted three cervical and one thoracic vertebrae. My sacrum and both temporal plates (cranial) were also out. He said it was most unusual to find both temporal plates out. Took a bit of doing to get them aligned again. He showed me how to test for and do sacral and pelvic adjustments for myself. I tested for one flower essence for the cervicals. He felt that the fact that all my adjustments were not emotionally based made it obvious to him that I am dealing with strong energies outside myself. That's the second chiropractor who has said this to me. And this one knew nothing about the Cottage. A strong verification.

At the Cottage. My focus was much improved. Seamus joined us for dinner. I could tell I was less Katie and more Machaelle for him tonight also. He asked a lot of questions about my "other life" at Perelandra.

April 9 — Dusty Rose

I asked David if he missed "playing" that leadership/statesman chess game. No, even though he can play it, and he enjoys a good game with worthy opponents, his goals are different now.

April 10 — Ivory

Evening. While I was in my room, Elsa (one of our dogs at Perelandra) walked in! She had spent all day close to me at Perelandra, and now there she was. I immediately became concerned, fearing that somehow I had accidently triggered her shift. And I was worried about what this was going to do to her physically. She bounded right over to me. I connected with nature and was told that it was fine for her to be there. Nature had set this up for *her.* We went downstairs to meet everyone, and she seemed perfectly at home in this new house. She won everyone over immediately. They think she has intelligent eyes. She made out during dinner, everyone sneaking her bits of food from their plates. After dinner, she settled by my feet. I watched as she slept and thought about the irony of being outdone by a dog. She seemed so at peace with everything. I had a feeling she didn't care how she got to the Cottage or if these men were supposed to be dead. Later in the evening, she got up and walked across the room as if she knew exactly what she was doing, and disappeared right before our eyes. I hoped she was now fully back at Perelandra and that she wasn't chasing someone's cows on another planet.

April 11 — Gold

At Perelandra. Elsa was fine and showed no signs of insanity. I talked to her about my morning at the Cottage. She also showed no signs of interest.

April 12 — Burgundy

At breakfast. During a conversation about battlefields, I raised some questions: What effect does a battle have on nature at the battle site? Does nature withdraw from a battlefield? Does the battlefield heal? Does nature choose sides during a battle? Does it even understand what's going on? What was the relationship of war to the devic patterns of the two countries involved? As I reeled off the questions, I saw Tex jot them down, saying I may be onto something. David said that when I come full time, he's going to give me those questions and some of his own to work on. I had this terrible feeling of work piling up at the Cottage, and I haven't even died yet. Seemed unfair!

At Perelandra. Called my friends in Europe. They did not respond to a letter I wrote them over three months ago about the Cottage. When I talked to them, they seemed most receptive about what I was doing. The wife said she'd write me this week, for sure. They sounded genuinely happy for me, but also overwhelmed by it all. It would have been nice if they had responded to my letter.

April 13 — Heather Green

JAMFD

April 14 — Brown

At Perelandra. Spent the afternoon in session with nature about the garden. I sent a split of the session pages to the Cottage, as per their instructions.

At the Cottage. Returned to find Tex and David reading my session. They were interested in the detailed fertilizing information nature had given me. They're also concerned about the amount of work I'm doing to get the garden up and operating, and frustrated that they can't "pitch in" from time to time. I reminded them that it is a seasonal crunch. In June and July, the garden work is manageable again—until the August and September harvest madness.

April 15 — Dusty Rose

JAMFD

April 16 — Gold

At Perelandra. Spent five hours taking a workshop on developmental movement. The focus was on the development of the head and spine movements from newborn to six months. The workshop was attended by mostly professional dancers, therapists and physical therapy teachers. I got a clear understanding of the intensity of development a child goes through the first year. It was an interesting insight into movement.

Had dinner and went to a movie with Clarence and some friends. I really wanted to be at the Cottage instead of sitting with a bunch of extremely noisy, popcorn-crunching, soda-slurping people trying to watch a movie dealing with subtle human emotions.

At the Cottage. Exhausted. While I ate a late dinner, we talked about the workshop. They were especially interested in the child development information I got from today's workshop.

By the time I got into bed, I could feel the physical effects of the workshop in the Katie body.

April 17 — Ivory

At Perelandra. Windy and extremely cold. Worked on the cold frame transplants. Still felt vulnerable from the workshop—my head and neck were sore, and it was hard to get comfortable.

At the Cottage. I noticed golden light all around me as soon as I got in. At first I thought it might be a sunset effect, but when I checked out the window, I saw that it was too early for a sunset. No one else saw the golden hue, but they didn't think that meant I wasn't seeing properly. Perhaps it's another adjustment.

Told David about a convention being held in Washington this past week for survivors of the Holocaust and their families. He asked me my feelings about it, in light of my Jewish background. I told him that, as far as I knew, everyone in my family who was not already living in America died in camps or were killed during the war. David talked about what it was like for him to inspect a concentration camp in Germany. The faces, the eyes, the malnutrition and the death all burned in his memory.

April 18 — Yellow

Seamus joined the men for lunch. He said he was working hard to deal with my dual life, but he felt he would eventually get a handle on it. That was all they would tell me.

April 19 — Heather Green

At Perelandra. Got fertilizer information for all the flower gardens and had a devic session about bees and wasps. When I was finished, I split the pages to the Cottage.

At the Cottage. They have been pressing me a bit to make sure I keep good notes about the garden work. They are confident that at some point I'll have the opportunity to get the information out to others.

April 20 — Brown

At Perelandra. Had a private Feldenkrais lesson, then visited with "my essence baby." She's chubby, and her mom says she's content and quiet. I held her for just a moment, and it felt like I've known her for quite a while!

Planted, fertilized and "essenced" the thirteen evergreen bushes that had to go into the garden. The wind calmed and the day ended beautifully. I actually didn't want to leave the garden. Wanted to just sit and take it all in.

At the Cottage. The men took an R&R afternoon. David and Tex played golf, and they got Max to join them. He had played when he was quite young and has decided to take it up again. Tex says he plays quite well, considering he's so out of practice. It's obvious he's a natural athlete. They said Max has a "unique" swing, but it's effective.

April 21 — Gold

At Perelandra. Clarence and I had dinner with a couple of friends who showed me a picture book of restored log cabins. I spotted "my cabin," a one-room, beautiful cabin with a porch. I asked my friend [whose line of work was restoring and building cabins] how much that one would cost. He said about $19,000. My mind started clicking like crazy—a one-room cabin with a loft out by the garden. The idea felt heavenly. My own little place facing the garden, rolling farm land, open skies—and giving me solitude.

At the Cottage. By the time I told them about the cabin, it was clear the idea was quickly growing into a passion. They cheered me on, saying they felt it was a fine idea.

April 22 — Ivory

Awoke with my mind still on the cabin.

At Perelandra. I asked Clarence how he would feel about my having a cabin. He admitted that last night he thought it might drive us apart, but now he realizes it wouldn't. It's my dream and has been for years—so why not? He said having my own place might help me to more easily juggle my complex life. We walked out into the woods to locate possible sites. I connected with nature, and we were led to a location right on the edge of the woods, directly facing the garden. It has a beautiful view.

April 23 — Gold

At dinner. The men and I talked about times of significant change in our lives. I told them that the Cottage experience was the third time in my life when every aspect of reality I held got tossed into the air and had to be reevaluated, redefined and reset. The first time, when I went out on my own at twelve. [The first time was actually a form of the ring-pass-not experience, but I have never considered it as such. It was more like a trial-run for the other two, more full-scale experiences. I consider the first experience just one child's lousy luck. Some may argue this point and could justify tagging it "ring-pass-not." As the one who had the actual experience, I choose to call it a trial run.] The second time, when I opened to and began working with nature intelligences. The third time, the Cottage. We decided my stubbornness and humor were what kept me going at these times. (I suggested it was just my humor. I informed them I didn't accept that I was stubborn.)

April 24 — Brown

At Perelandra. Got hit with a crisis of reality. Who can say any of this (nature and the Cottage) isn't crap? I could just be crazy, and perhaps I've invented it all. Perhaps it's all in my own mind.

At the Cottage. They were not surprised or shocked by my crisis. They feel it's healthy for me to question everything and assured me that, given the same circumstances, they would question it too. At that moment, I couldn't imagine how I would get out of this crisis. It amazed David, given my feelings, that I came home to the Cottage at all today. That's when I realized I have a drive deep inside me that keeps me coming back to the Cottage, no matter what—a most inexplicable drive that is stronger in me than anything. With all the doubts and challenges I've dealt with, I haven't once hesitated to come home. My recognition of that drive was verification in itself.

I went for a walk through the woods and ended up down by the little bridge. I sat down near the water, resting my back against a tree, and dozed off. When I woke up, I was out of the crisis. I felt like a new person—vulnerable, but new.

April 25 — Yellow

Slept eleven hours. At breakfast, they announced that they feel certain the cabin is being "urged on me" by my influential friends [nature], and that I have nature's total support for this. They felt I should not be surprised if everything goes smoothly with the cabin construction.

At Perelandra. I decided to test the Cottage men a little and have a session with nature on the cabin. Their pronouncements were verified. Nature is inviting me to become a permanent part of the garden environment by including my personal living space in that environment. This will symbolize a new level of my relationship with nature. I spent the rest of the afternoon working on the cabin design.

At the Cottage. I told the men their announcement this morning was verified and showed them my design ideas. They like the simplicity.

We all got an ice cream attack in the middle of the evening—a sudden "hankering" for banana splits. We invaded the ice cream parlor in the village.

April 26

JAMFD

April 27 — Ivory

At Perelandra. A crazy day. A Feldenkrais class, followed by lunch with my wallpaper friend, then a trip with her to Front Royal. Came rushing back to Perelandra and spent several hours with the essence baby and her mom. Then Clarence and I had dinner with the cabin contractor friend and his wife. Our friend looked at my cabin plans and said he could build it for $17,000. Clarence said he would do the electrical wiring, and I said I'd do the exterior painting. He said he'd have the cabin ready for me to move in by September 31.

At the Cottage. They're all convinced the cabin construction is going to be a good experience for me because it's so right.

April 28 — Gold

At Perelandra. Showed another friend the cabin plans. She said her husband would be happy to do the exterior painting and floor finishing for me. [His profession is house painting and floor finishing.] I told her I'd talk to him about job cost. She informed me he would be insulted if I tried to pay him, that this would be his way of doing something for us after all we've done for them. Nice.

Spent long hours in the garden. Hard work.

At the Cottage. Told the men I feel like all my friends are doing the cabin for me.

April 29 — Gold

At Perelandra. Spent much of the day in the garden alone.

At the Cottage. Dinner at Nino's.

April 30 — Dusty Rose

At Perelandra. Had a nature garden session and got the go-ahead to begin planting. I'm spending longer hours in the garden and returning to the Cottage later.

At the Cottage. Everyone is rallying around me as I get cranked up for the spring planting. What a difference their support makes.

May 1 — Heather Green

At Perelandra. Spent all day in the garden, working until my body could no longer stand the strain.

At the Cottage. They had a surprise for me when I got home. They've purchased adjoining property for my garden and nature work when I come full time. I had mixed emotions. On one hand, I was thrilled, and, on the other hand, I was too damn tired from my gardening day to care. They seemed to understand.

May 2 — Yellow

At Perelandra. Feldenkrais class in the morning and the garden throughout the afternoon.

At the Cottage. At dinner, they talked about their commitment to support me and not try to mold me to fit their lives. I have a valuable service to perform that is equal to their own, and they feel a responsibility to support that and not detract from it. I talked about how much their support is affecting me and my work, and how they had turned around all those years I had spent alone supplying my own support system, encouraging myself to go on. They support my very being, and this has enabled me to open and move with greater ease in more expanded ways. I can feel myself blossom and shine, and all because they've taken over that role of supporting me. They give me strength and confidence—and I'm learning to lean. (At which point, they all chimed in, "Slowly.") My moment with them made me cry.

May 3

JAMFD

May 4 — Ivory

At Perelandra. Decided to take a break and go to Manassas Mall by myself. I stopped by the bookstore and was immediately faced with a large display for a new book with David's picture on the cover. I've deliberately stayed away from any books about David since reading that one last summer. I've had a feeling that other people's opinions about this man would not be helpful to me. But I felt drawn to buy a copy of this new book: *Hidden-Hand Presidency* by Fred Greenstein.

At the Cottage. David saw no problem with my reading the book by Greenstein. He was already aware of its content and felt it was a fair study.

May 5 — Burgundy

Woke up about 3 A.M. with sharp cramps and chills. Tested essences and took what I needed. Everything calmed down enough for me to get back to sleep.

At breakfast. The men think my physical glitch this morning had to do with the coming workshop jitters.

At Perelandra. Finished reading Greenstein's book. It verifies the character and personality of the person I've met—except for that temper business. I guess death and plowing through a few walls can do wonders for a fiery temper. At least, that's what David tells me.

May 6 — Yellow

At Perelandra. Clarence and I traveled to a house just outside Chapel Hill, North Carolina, for the workshop. We stayed in a huge earth home with a huge atrium in the middle. Elegant "working conditions," except that one hears every sound and conversation in the place because it is insulated by all that earth.

At the Cottage. Had no trouble getting home. Earlier I had asked nature about what to do, and they assured me I'd get to the Cottage easily. Actually, it was an easy shift. But I was tired from the car trip and keyed up about the workshop. So I went to bed right after dinner.

May 7 — Slate Blue

Left the Cottage early so that I could be "in one piece" in North Carolina and prepare for the workshop.

The workshop went well—much fun was had by all, as they say. We had about twenty people, and they asked me to come back and give a follow-up workshop in the fall. I told them I'd think about it.

At the Cottage. I may be able to easily shift back and forth from different locations on the Perelandra level, but it doesn't make me comfortable doing it. I like being at Perelandra. I was happy to get to the Cottage, eat and go to bed.

May 8 — Heather Green

Returned to the earth house for a leisurely late breakfast and the trip back to Perelandra. I was anxious to return to my Perelandra home base.

At the Cottage. A "congratulations-for-a-job-well-done" dinner at Nino's with everyone.

May 9 — Gold

At breakfast. We talked about different teaching styles. When the men have taught, they have tended to be studied, prepared, directed, aware of every move by everyone in the room. My style is experiential in its approach—fluid and intuitive. We agreed that both styles are successful, just different.

At Perelandra. Garden planting.

May 10 — Dusty Rose

At Perelandra. Spent a full day working in the garden. Five baby birds hatched in the garden shed.

At the Cottage. Discussed my need for privacy in the garden. I told them I felt it might be difficult to work well if I felt I was being watched from the Cottage. I didn't want to be everyone's matinee entertainment. They agreed with me and decided the garden will be walled! Then they asked if they would be allowed in. Told them I'd think about it.

May 11 — Heather Green

At Perelandra. Another full day in the garden. Got a phone call from a friend from England who is traveling in the States and wants to visit Perelandra with her boyfriend tomorrow. I felt trapped into saying yes, but I was terribly disappointed. I had hoped to spend the day uninterrupted in the garden before fulfilling a commitment to help other friends with a house tour this entire weekend. I felt like the rug was pulled out from under me. I can't seem to get good blocks of time in the garden, and this is *very* frustrating.

At the Cottage. They say I'm too accommodating, and I need to learn to say "no."

May 12 — Burgundy

Woke up with the idea of asking my friend and her boyfriend to stay at Perelandra a few days to help me in the garden shifting the outer band of mulch from hay to pine-bark chips. It's a big job for me alone, and I could sure use the help. My decision to ask them for help lifts a weight off my shoulders.

At Perelandra. My visitors enthusiastically agreed to help me.

May 13 — Gold

At Perelandra. Full day working in the garden. All three of us worked steadily and for long hours hauling off hay and hauling in pine-bark mulch. We needed to use both the tractor cart and the pickup truck, and managed to complete two-thirds of the job.

At the Cottage. The men urged me to come home in the evenings whenever I could make it and not feel pressured to keep a regular schedule—especially during this gardening time.

May 14 — Dusty Rose

At Perelandra. While I fulfilled my commitment to work a friend's house tour, my house guests finished shifting the mulch in the rest of the outer ring. I had to admit I was glad to sit rather than haul.

Someone I hardly knew called from Toronto to ask if she could visit for five days beginning next weekend. I told her no. It felt good.

May 15 — Ivory

At Perelandra. After a late breakfast, my house guests left to continue their trip, and I finished my house-tour commitment. My house-tour friends were appreciative of the time I gave them and offered to "pay us back" by giving *Clarence* two afternoons in the fall to help him with a building project. Clarence accepted right away. Since I was the one who had put in the time and effort, I had hoped they would offer to do something for my cabin—especially since the man was a cabinetmaker. But they didn't, and that was that.

At the Cottage. Returned home feeling much gratitude for my life there.

May 16 — Gold

Had a very vivid dream experience. I was taken by a monk in a monastery through several stages of experiences that led up to a final stage. This last one was so gentle, and it left me with a deep sense of peace. I knew I had been through something important. The monk couldn't believe how gentle the experience had been for me. He took me back through a couple of stages so that I could do them over. Then he took me through the final one again. Everything checked out. I had gone through all the stages. That's when he said I could leave the monastery. The exit was elaborate—through labyrinth-like hallways—and I needed to be led out by another young monk with keys. I exited through big, arched, wooden doors. When I got to the street, I was in Paris. As I walked down the street, I received insight that I had been through the initiation of Black Death, and that this was a major experience. Yet no one around me knew what I had been through. Suddenly, I saw a long reception line of, what looked to be, important people—and they were waiting for me. I started down the line. Each person put his hands on my shoulders and kissed me on both cheeks. I didn't know who they were, but I felt their power and position to be much greater than mine. Finally, at the end, was David. He put his hands on my shoulders, kissed me on both cheeks and said, "Congratulations."

At breakfast. The men were familiar with the Black Death initiation. They started to explain it to me but stopped themselves, saying it would be best for the insight to come from within me. I felt fine with this.

May 17 — Dusty Rose

At Perelandra. Tried to get to the last Feldenkrais class for the year, but the truck battery was dead (I left the lights on yesterday).

I was drawn to look at *Hidden-Hand President* again. It struck me, as I leafed through it, that the man being described had so much vital energy—physical and intellectual—that he often paced during meetings. He *needed* to move. Yet I know he is now able to sit absolutely still for long periods of time. The change intrigued me, and I felt there was something for me to learn here. David is prone to explain it away by saying either that it is intent or the benefit of death.

At the Cottage. I talked to David about my thoughts. We decided his changes have to do with focus, a redirection of energy flow from an outer mode to an inner mode, which is accomplished through intent. The energy flow has shifted from outer action to inner action in such a way that spending hours in one position is still physical activity for him. We realized that this is related to when athletes visualize their movements and physically feel they have fully practiced, even though they haven't moved.

David got excited about this conversation. He feels he can apply it to his golf game—something he hadn't thought of before this—and asked me not to tell the others what we talked about.

May 18 — Heather Green

Evening. Tex announced that David shot a hole-in-one and that it was on the hole he said he would make it on! Apparently his game is much improved—and overnight. Tex demanded to know David's secret weapon. I'm not saying a word.

I am now beginning to get insight about Black Death. Black is the absorption of all color = all. Death = transition. Black Death is the transition of all things, all characteristics, all talents within an individual. It is the moving of all parts together at one time up the spiral.

May 19 — Brown

JAMFD

May 20 — Burgundy

At Perelandra. Spent the afternoon planting annuals. While working out by the garden shed, I noticed one of the baby birds out of the nest, standing on the rafter. They were all watching me work and seemed quite calm. Over the two weeks, they have become quite used to my presence, and I've thoroughly enjoyed their company. As I planted, all five babies took off and flew for the trees—all at the same time. I wasn't ready for the "children" to leave the nest.

May 21 — Gold

At Perelandra. Worked on the slides for *Behaving.* Decided to move the book through the publishing process myself.

At the Cottage. When I discussed my book decision, they felt it was a good idea. They wanted me to know they support me in this and are behind me all the way. They feel strongly that the timing is right to get this book out. David in particular felt he might be able to help me through the publishing labyrinth since he had published several books on the Perelandra level prior to death.

May 22 — Ivory

At breakfast. We tossed around loads of goofy ideas for the book— and we laughed a lot.

May 23 — Slate Blue

Awoke from another amazingly vivid dream: I was at Perelandra and I was visited by a gnome. This was the first time I had experienced a nature spirit in traditional form. I was digging a drainage ditch around an area in the garden that had standing water while several other people watched me dig. When I looked up, I noticed the gnome standing at the other end of the garden. Everyone rushed to him, trying to touch him, "pet" him. He somehow remained just out of reach. He was calm and tolerated their hysteria well. I tried to convince the people to pull back, but they wouldn't listen. The gnome and I walked away together, and he thanked me for helping with their land, saying that now they wouldn't have to leave. I said, "Did you know I teach others about you?" "Yes, of course." I asked him if there was anything he would like to change about what I was saying to others. He replied, "No, nothing. We especially appreciate your emphasis on action—love in action." Right before me, he took love energy and fused it to what all the people had been doing with him—seeking to adore him. I watched the love become powerless. He then fused the love energy to action, and I *felt* a tremendous power.

He asked me the time. I said, "It's 10:15." I noticed he was wearing a gold watch that looked to be an antique. I also noticed it was running and read 10:15. That's when I realized he didn't know what 10:15 meant and had hoped my answer would clear it up for him! It was obvious from his reaction that it didn't.

I asked him, "What would you do about the warring nations?" He looked straight at me. "Well, first I'd get the best pilot from each of the warring nations. Then I'd get them each a house in Bethesda and give them each $1 billion. After a prescribed amount of time, I would see which one had improved his life the most and increased the money the most. That person would be the winner. As Emily Bowlin has said, this is the person who believes his soul lives on forever and lives his life accordingly."

I sensed the gnome fading and I woke up.

I shared my dream with the others at breakfast. David felt the warring nations solution was ludicrous, but said they'd consider the principle behind it. Perhaps there was something there. As for the dream itself, they felt it was an indication that the Black Death was activating. How they came to this conclusion, I don't know.

Evening. Dinner at Nino's for several of us.

May 24 — Yellow

Awoke in the middle of the night with terrible leg pain near both hip joints. I spent about a half-hour in the lagoon, then headed back to bed and to sleep. In the morning, my legs were fine.

May 25

Got another lecture on the need to pace better and not drive myself so hard. I don't have to make the same mistakes they have made, they tell me. I told them I heard them, but I won't be able to do anything about it right now because I'm too busy! They informed me they don't back away from challenges.

May 26 — Ivory

Awoke in the night with a bad fever. I sweat it out in the lagoon. When I told the others about it at breakfast, they felt it was probably more Black Death reactions setting in. It's too bad I don't fully understand what's going on with this Black Death business.

At Perelandra. Good day in the garden. Worked until late.

At the Cottage. For the first time, I returned to the Cottage wearing something else besides my uniform. When I left Perelandra, I was so tired that I thought about how nice it would be to arrive home in my cotton nightgown. When I got in, I was wearing that nightgown. I don't know why I haven't thought of trying this before. I guess it's because I'm only just beginning to explore this dual life, to expand and experience the possibilities a bit. I laid down immediately for a short nap, then dressed for dinner—slacks, not my uniform. How normal can things be?

May 27 — Heather Green

At Perelandra. An excellent day in the garden. I planted nasturtium plants in the outer ring of two sections. It's much easier to transplant, especially in the pine mulch. Finally, I have all the glitches with that outer nasturtium ring solved. Putting in forty-three plants per section happens to be perfect spacing. (Nature must know something!) I can feel I'm developing a head cold.

At the Cottage. Returned wearing casual clothes today. I'm getting good at this.

May 28 — Brown

Developed a high fever in the night. Sweat it out in the lagoon. When I woke up (in bed) this morning, the fever had broken.

At Perelandra. The cold is well on the mend. It seems like breaking the fever at the Cottage turned the cold around at Perelandra. Worked eight hours in the garden. I finished planting nasturtiums in the tomato patch and the last garden section. I wanted to get as much planted as possible because we're expecting rain.

At the Cottage. Totally exhausted. It was hard to hold my focus, hear and see. Very frustrating. I excused myself and went back to my room for a nap. While I slept, I slipped into a "delirious" state. I couldn't find reality, and I didn't know if I was at the Cottage or Perelandra. The fever had returned, so I pulled myself out of the bed and sat in the lagoon where I slept for two hours. When I awoke, I was fine again. Mickey insisted I have soup in my room. Everyone was in high Jewish-mother gear.

May 29 — Brown

I awoke feeling fine.

At Perelandra. The contractor is ready to start my cabin. He still feels my design is good. Clarence began clearing the site today. Nature has placed it where only small trees need to be removed.

May 30 — Ivory

Another early morning of high fever that broke again when I sat in the lagoon. The men feel the fever is directly related to the Black Death adjustments. By morning I was fine—again.

At Perelandra. Clarence spent more time clearing the cabin site.

At the Cottage. An uneventful evening and night.

May 31 — Gold

At Perelandra. At the men's urging, I went to the chiropractor. Both femur bones were out. She worked with me on a self-adjustment technique. The left side of the pelvis was slightly out, but this was directly related to the femur problems. The T-7 [thoracic] and C-2 [cervical] vertebrae were misaligned and two major cranial bones were stuck in the inhale position. This was allowing heavy amounts of energy in all the time and causing my eyes (at Perelandra) to have constant white flashes of light. I needed no essences, but she tested that I will need them and should begin to test myself daily. This was unusual. My endocrine system was strong, except for slightly weakened adrenals. In all, she felt I was in excellent shape, considering my life and the Black Death fallout I've been going through. The cough, that has now been going on for six months, is what is stressing the adrenals and is caused by the strain around what has been happening with Clarence and not the Cottage.

At the Cottage. Returned to find the men anxious to find out what happened with the chiropractor. I realized that they have been concerned about the "mysterious" Black Death fallout. For a bunch of Jewish mothers, they know how to remain calm when they want to.

June 1 — Burgundy

Feeling anxious about starting the publication process for *Behaving*.

At Perelandra. Called my friend at National Geographic, and we decided to get together at her house on June 10 to talk about the book and decide on the pictures to be used.

June 2 — Dusty Rose

They've gotten word that John may be returning soon. They should know shortly.

June 3 — Apricot

New color. Awoke feeling alive and ready for action.

At Perelandra. Worked in the asparagus bed all afternoon. Got rained out, so I returned to the Cottage early.

June 4 — Gold

Felt a deep contentment throughout my morning.

Evening. I had a terrible physical shattering when I returned. Mostly, I got sick in the stomach. Right after taking essences, I had an insight about Perelandra centering around my partnership with Clarence that brought a new clarity and lifted a weight off me. I realized that the daily essences I had been testing for since seeing the chiropractor had prepared me for this insight. Amazing.

June 5 — Gold

The men are urging me to take one day a week off and to do things for myself that day. It sounds appealing, but I told them I would consider it only after the garden was settled.

At Perelandra. Worked more leisurely in the garden.

Evening. Took a three-hour nap. Max called just to check up on me and to make sure I'm okay.

June 6 — Ivory

They're still pressing me to take off one day a week. I feel certain I'll do this once the garden is in.

At Perelandra. Actually, I'm becoming *very* content in the garden, and I can feel myself beginning to hit quite a stride in my work. I can tell that I am shifting and my work is shifting. Everything is taking on a new significance. I can't put my finger on it yet, but this new level of contentment and confidence sure feels clear.

At the Cottage. Had coffee with several of the men on my balcony when I got home. I shared my thoughts with them about the changes I'm feeling in myself and my work.

June 7 — Gold

Mickey asked if it would be possible for me to split food from the Perelandra garden for their use. He was especially interested in having some strawberries for tonight's dinner with Max and Seamus. I told him I'd check with nature.

At Perelandra. Got the okay from nature to split any food we wished, and we set up a process for doing the split right into Mickey's kitchen. While picking the strawberries, I realized the difference in my harvesting attitude as a result of their enthusiasm toward the garden and its produce. Until now, this has always been a weakness in my work process. I'm interested in the research, not the harvest. Consequently, I put less focus and care into the harvesting. I've had little reason for feeling interested since I'm not cooking [Clarence does all our cooking], and there has been little enthusiasm by anyone else for the produce. Now I feel enthusiasm, caring, excitement and appreciation. The Cottage input has shifted my interest and focus, and I could tell today that I felt more joy and care about the harvesting. Now the Cottage has a direct impact on the garden, and I can feel a greater, clearer connection between the Cottage and Perelandra.

At the Cottage. Took a nap before dinner. The evening was most enjoyable, with much laughter and many stories. Both Seamus and Max can really spin a tale.

June 8 — Heather Green

At breakfast we talked about space souls and how their activity and intentions are so misunderstood on Earth. They explained that a "space soul" or "space brother" is a human being who is in form and capable of accessing, acclimating to and working on many levels. When I looked at them funny, they assured me that using the Split Molecular Process did not mean I was a space soul. I was relieved. Space souls use just one body.

June 9

I was a bit distracted throughout breakfast. I'm getting revved up for tomorrow's meeting with my National Geographic friend.

At Perelandra. Another long day in the garden. The soil is still extremely wet from all the rain, and it's taking a long time to work it and plant.

At the Cottage. Had a long talk with David about soil. I told him about thoughts I had from nature around tilling mulch and sand into the soil this fall. It would be a big job. David suggested that if this is necessary, perhaps I could till just the rows and not the paths. That way I won't have to remove all the hay from each section and I'd only have to open one row at a time. As we talked, it dawned on me that, for the first time, I was actually talking to someone (human) about the nuts and bolts of this garden. What a new experience!

June 10 — Yellow

At Perelandra. Focused on my friend and *Behaving*. While I was picking strawberries for her, an actual whirlwind picked up bits of straw mulch and surrounded me in a gentle, joyous shower of straw. It's time to get the book going.

I had not seen my friend in several years, yet it only took an hour and twenty minutes to get to her house from Perelandra. I would describe her environment as a "creative mess." One room was the "bird room" where she keeps various birds—without benefit of cages—while they heal from injuries.

Back in the winter, I had sent a copy of the manuscript for her to read, but I quickly discovered she had not read it at all. So I explained a bit about the book. She launched into a speech about birds being the "real people," and people being the most destructive creatures on Earth. She accused me of putting man above nature and asked me what the difference was between me and any other religious fanatics who believe they know the truth and believe they never make mistakes. Somehow, I was able to diffuse her accusations by telling her how important mistakes are in my work and how much I learn from them.

I was uneasy about my friend's reactions, but I felt she was the only one who could help me get this book published. After dinner we went through the slides, and she was a different person. She was open, creative, and had terrific ideas. I felt she was the best designer for *Behaving* and would do the book justice.

At the Cottage. I returned to the Cottage from my friend's house because I was spending the night there. I was exhausted. When I told them about her challenges, they wondered how an old friend could question my integrity like this. I too was confused a bit by this, but I still felt her sense of professionalism would keep the balance needed for *Behaving*.

June 11 — Apricot

It was hard to hold my focus at the Cottage while I was still at my friend's house. This wasn't at all like my experience in North Carolina. The men asked me to call them as soon as I was on the road back to Perelandra.

Perelandra level. My friend and I had a leisurely breakfast at a nearby restaurant and talked about old times. It was an easy conversation, and I feel a lot better about her working on the book than I did last night.

The drive home was tough. As soon as I got on the road, I felt like I had been run over by a truck. Actually, I had been run over by my friend's extremism.

At the Cottage. Tex and David still question if she is the one to design the book and help me go through the publishing process. I feel certain the key is her professionalism. I also feel a tremendous weight has been lifted from my shoulders to have entered the final stage of the book.

June 12

John returned to the Cottage today. Having him back is like having the whole family together again for all of us—myself included.

June 13 — Gold

At Perelandra. Had a long day in the garden. I worked through the afternoon sun and heat and, at one point, took a cold shower with my clothes on!

At the Cottage. I returned and crashed. Took a long nap before Max and Allison arrived for their "appointment" to have Allison checked for essences. She's on a solution for three and a half weeks.

John has gotten right back into the Cottage routine.

June 14 — Brown

The men spent the rest of the afternoon catching John up on what has been happening while he was gone.

Max and Seamus joined us for dinner. There's an especially strong friendship forming among John, Butch and Seamus. I've begun calling them the Merry Marauders.

June 15 — Apricot

They had a big golf game today with John, Tex, David and Max.

At Perelandra. I spent a couple of hours in the garden, then drove to town and treated myself to lunch. Topped off the big excursion with a haircut.

At the Cottage. No one will tell me who won the golf game!

They are pressing me to talk about the garden more. Tonight I got a lecture on the value of batting around ideas. They consider this a valuable tool and use it frequently for coming up with new and different ideas.

June 16 — Ivory

Evening. Left Perelandra early because I just felt like taking a break at the Cottage. After dinner they warned me about the possibility of an upcoming "energy conference" that they may want my input on. It's good they warn me about these things.

June 17 — Gold

Awoke with a deep sense of peace that stayed with me throughout the day. My earlier insecurities about being so different from these men and my fears about trying to keep up with their extraordinary minds have quietly dissipated. Now I can feel security in our differences.

June 18 — Dusty Rose

This was a day spent on male/female relationships. We now have the first American woman (Sally Ride) in space, and I've been amazed at the idiotic and biased press coverage she's getting. They ask her stupid questions. I'm a bit startled at how far the old male/female thing has not come, as though the last twenty years haven't existed.

At Perelandra. Clarence watched the space shuttle launch early this morning and talked about the ridiculous coverage of Sally Ride.

Among other things, it seems she's a bad housekeeper, and the press won't get off that point.

Clarence and I went to our bank to talk about the loan for the cabin. The male loan officer totally disregarded me throughout the entire time we were there. He didn't even shake hands with me. As far as he was concerned, I might as well have been a potted plant. This couldn't have been more fitting for the day. On top of it, there was a photography show by a local National Geographic photographer set up around the bank. Every time I looked over Clarence's shoulder, I looked right at a photo of David sitting between Kennedy and Truman at some formal function. I kept remembering a talk we had this morning at the Cottage about reality and illusion. I'd look at the idiotic loan officer and then at the photo and wonder just what was reality and what was illusion here?

June 19 — Dusty Rose

At Perelandra. Clarence and I had an intrusion this morning—some fellow just had to stop by unannounced and discuss his spiritual life. He had heard about my work from someone—he was never clear about who. He's one of those "intense seekers" who like to sit around talking about seeking—intensely. I tried to give him encouragement. He stayed three and a half hours, declared me a new age scientist, then left. He managed to thoroughly waste our time and drain me.

At the Cottage. I had a long discussion with John about how I handle my Cottage life and experiences on the Perelandra level. We agree that for now it is probably best that this kind of thing is kept quiet. Had the intense seeker known about the Cottage, I would never have gotten rid of him today.

June 20 — Heather Green

When I awoke, I felt extremely restless. I took essences, but I was never able to settle down. I decided when I got back to Perelandra I would get away for awhile by myself.

At Perelandra. Had a nice time at a mall. I enjoyed my solitude among the crowd and had a good time just looking at things. Just the R&R I needed.

When I got back, Clarence handed me a letter from my friend at National Geographic. She wrote that she could not do the layout of my book. She finds my theology/philosophy "potentially dangerous" and me "a fanatic." I think she lumped me in with Hitler and James Watt! She wrote something about "the most destructive and goriest moments in history" were merely for the sake of a civilized-sounding philosophy. She considers mankind untrustworthy and feels he should not be encouraged to trust his subconscious.

I found her letter to be ludicrous and sad—and it hurt. She admitted she still hasn't read my book and that she was basing her judgment on our discussion of June 10. (I didn't think my explanation of the book and my work was *that* bad.) I'm sad for her because of her obvious and complete dislike and distrust for mankind in general. How sad it must be to feel this and to live with it every day.

In the four-page letter, pages two and three outlined everything I'm going to have to do to get this book published. She even gave suggestions as to the best layout and design. This, added to all the information and comments she made on June 10, has given me confidence that I can get the book published myself, and do it well. She's also going to go through the slides I left with her and red-dot the ones that, in her professional opinion, are publishable. She's doing everything but making editorial decisions as to where to place them. I'd just as soon do this myself anyway. I've got a good idea of what needs to go where. I feel good about taking complete charge of the book.

She also suggested a printer that National Geographic uses—and it's located in Rockville, Maryland just a block from where Clarence is now working. [He got a job with a copier company.]

Clarence didn't have much of a reaction to my friend's letter. He did verify that the printer she referred to was indeed near his office.

The men at the Cottage made up for Clarence's apathy. They pronounced my friend cruel and her letter outrageous. Now they understand, they say, why I was in such bad shape when I returned to the Cottage after dealing with her. They're glad she's not working on the book. Actually, I'm now glad also.

I checked for essences and tested that I didn't need anything.

June 21 — Ivory

[Summer solstice: This is the time for celebrating the result of the whole natural process of the cycle that began with the fall equinox—the devic pattern successfully and fully fused into form with the active assistance of nature spirits and humans. It is the celebration of the coming together of all levels, and I experience it as a celebration of joy, sunshine and laughter within all realms of nature.]

At Perelandra. I left the Cottage right after breakfast to prepare for the solstice. I had a session with nature, which I split to the Cottage. Then I picked strawberries, cleaned the sanctuary and put the solstice bows out. This year's solstice colors are gold and white. I split one bow to the Cottage for them to arrange with a candle.

At the Cottage. They put the bow and candle on the living room coffee table. Just before the moment of the solstice, I could feel my body electricity increase. I thought about what we've all come through together and what we've accomplished around this split business and my split life. At the moment of the solstice, I saw the Cottage and Perelandra connected by a broad shaft of light. When I opened my eyes, I found a large bouquet of white daisies with golden centers—the solstice colors for this year—on the table. David said that apparently my influential friends wanted to get in on the celebration. I felt nature was acknowledging what we had accomplished since the fall. We had champagne and David toasted: "To the solstice and the lady who brought it to us."

June 22 — Gold

At Perelandra. A good maintenance day in the garden. Pulled hay in on the rows to conserve yesterday's rain. I wrote my National Geographic friend a note thanking her for the publishing information and suggesting that the next time she disagrees with someone, she might consider resisting the urge to ram her foot down the person's throat and, instead, simply say she disagrees.

At the Cottage. Now they're trying to teach me the fine art of puttering. They think I should putter around Perelandra more. We decided to take a break and "putter" our way to Nino's for dinner.

June 23 — Yellow

At Perelandra. Clarence called the printer and set up an appointment for me to talk to them about the book. He says he feels it would be best for me to always deal with the printer myself rather than use him as a go-between. He won't have the time. This means I'll have to drive the four-hour round trip myself. The book ball is totally in my lap.

June 24 — Apricot

JAMFD

June 25 — Burgundy

At Perelandra. Needed to do something simple and physical, so I mowed. Clarence worked more on clearing the cabin area. I finally got a letter from my friends in Europe in response to telling them about the Cottage. They accept the Cottage, but they are working hard to understand how I'm going there and why.

June 26 — Gold

I had trouble holding my focus at the Cottage this morning. This is surprising, since the mornings are usually my easier times.

Shattered when I got home. The shatter squad pulled me out of it in less than an hour. Max joined us for dinner. He's still calling me Katie, and it looks as if this will be my Dad's favorite name for me no matter which of his daughter's souls he is addressing.

June 27 — Ivory

Morning. It's still hard to hold my focus. My thoughts are scattering everywhere, like electric flashes, and I'm missing parts of conversations.

At Perelandra. I spent two hours in the garden. The electric company man came to discuss the electric line to the cabin. It will be underground. Finally got my representative at the printer on the phone, and we decided it was best for me to see her tomorrow in person to go over the book printing. I called my chiropractor and made an appointment for Thursday [June 30]. It was terribly hot and humid, so I returned to the Cottage early for a little relief.

I went for a walk, accompanied by Petunia. She's full grown now and full of herself—which is a dangerous thing to say about a skunk. And she's become a valued member of the Cottage. Each afternoon she comes into the kitchen for treats from Mickey, then she waddles into David's office, bangs over his trash can and digs around for the cookie he's hidden in there for her. It's a ritual that I think everyone is afraid to change since, as David says, she wields a little power around there because she's not descented. They let her go with them when they play golf because, they tell me, her presence keeps the foursome in front of them moving! It was odd to think that it was only a year ago that she was living in the field across from Perelandra. During our walk, she tried to get to know one of the neighboring cows and her calf. It was cute.

June 28 — Slate Blue

My appointment at the printer was an absolute success. They can do the whole job. We threw around some ideas, and I made some decisions so that now they can give me an estimate of the cost. They showed me samples of the text from *Behaving* that someone set in different fonts while we were talking. What a rush to see my own words in print. Everyone there was quite friendly and seemed not only willing but eager to work with me. I will work with their layout artist on the design and layout of the book. I left my manuscript with them so they can start getting it into galley form right away. My representative is bright, energetic, pleasant, amiable, direct and easy to talk to. I left there feeling high and with the strong conviction that this is the book's *best* route. The book and these people seem compatible. I'm looking forward to learning from them throughout the publication process.

At the Cottage. I was excited to share with David about the book and my feelings about seeing my words in print. I also told him how I had some hesitations about whether or not this book is worth printing and how print adds such authority to words. He gave me encouragement around getting the book published and talked about his similar feelings when he saw his own words in print the first time.

June 29 — Burgundy

At breakfast the men got me to talk more about what my focus difficulties feel like and about my sense of frustration. I'm not even sure of what I've eaten the last few days. Talking about the frustration brought me to tears. I was relieved to tell them about the pressures, but, at the same time, I felt like a failure. They worked hard to get me to see that this has nothing to do with failing. It's just more adjustments. I've got to remember that I'm doing something unusual. Their words buoy me up, but I'm still spacey as hell.

At the Cottage. David made a few phone calls and found out this afternoon that when I opened the new Cottage/Perelandra connection at the solstice, I took a shot in the head with energy, and this is what's causing me problems now.

June 30 — Yellow

My chiropractor worked with me for two hours. Both sides of the pelvis, the sacrum and L-5 [lumbar] were out. The L-5 problem was holding up my period. C-1 was way out and twisted. And the entire left side of my cranials needed adjusting. She said I looked like I had been in a cosmic crash. The summer solstice shot was more than I thought. She had difficulty getting a CSF pulse to the left side of my head and difficulty realigning my cranials. As she worked she kept saying: "I've never seen anything like this." The left side of my head is the seat of understanding, and she says I must not work so hard to understand, especially since everything with my work, Perelandra and the Cottage is now settling so well. She insisted that I relax and let it flow by me more.

I needed four essences, all having to do with intensity of work. Her testing showed that I must do two essence tests daily and that I must do separate tests for each body. This is what's needed to complete the adjustment I'm going through on the left side of the head. Also, I must think about the definitions of the essences I test for because they will give me the proper input to the shift. And I'm to do all of this for two weeks.

No new supplements were needed as part of the daily regime,

however the adrenals needed two supplements just to get jump-started again. My root chakra was weak, and after a bit of testing, she found out this was due to a conflict between the imaging of the Perelandra/Machaelle body and the Cottage/Katie body. The Katie body tests more "correct" for me. Also, when the men think of me, they image only the Katie body. Although I see both bodies, I most-ly image the Machaelle one. This conflict of imagery causes my root chakra to drain in the Machaelle body. She said I am to solve the problem by riding a bicycle at Perelandra for twenty minutes two times weekly, while clearly imaging the Katie body. I told her she was nuts, and she told me to just do it.

She asked me if I could split to the Cottage from her office, and I said I'd try. She held the CSF pulses in my head while I did the split. I stayed at the Cottage for about five minutes, then came back. She was still holding my pulses when I "arrived." She said that while I'm actually doing the split, I have no discernable CSF pulses. As soon as I got to the Cottage, the pulses returned strongly and in a different pattern than they had been prior to the split when I was just in the Machaelle body. Once I got back fully to the Machaelle body, the pulses returned to their original "Machaelle pattern." She also said that, by far, my pulses were stronger while I was at the Cottage. I could tell she was amazed by all of this and excited. She said: "It's *very* clear you're working with two separate bodies."

At the Cottage. I arrived in much better condition. We had an easy night, talking about nothing even remotely significant—once I told them about what had happened with the chiropractor.

July 1 — Heather Green

David opened a discussion at breakfast that resulted in some tem-porary but major changes. I agreed to the following:

1. He is going to take over my journal notes for the entire month of July. I am to write nothing. He will debrief me daily about what has gone on.

2. We discussed what was easy for me (focusing one-on-one) and what was hard (focusing on everyone all at once when I first get home). They want to work with me and not against me, and plan to adjust their interactions with me accordingly.

3. I am to take my one-day-a-week off beginning next Wednesday.

4. I am to visit a friend of mine who has invited me to her house near the ocean, and I am to stay as long as I want. Even though I will still need to return to the Cottage every night, it will be good for me to have a break from Perelandra.

5. I am to talk to them more about what is going on at Perelandra, especially the pressures, so that they can help me keep my balance. To assist, they will question me more about specifics. They are urging me to draw on their life experiences more for help.

6. I can continue doing my weekly garden sessions, but I am not to enter a new stage of intensity with the nature work until the end of the summer or early fall. They feel certain that if I just say something to my influential friends about this, they [nature] will be happy to work with me.

So I enter a new stage. No writing for one month. Freedom. Goodbye!

July and August

My month was so successful, that it was extended for an additional month. During this time, the cabin construction got underway, and I continued with the general maintenance and work with the garden. I visited my friend at the beach for a week and loved it. I was able to shift back and forth to the Cottage from her house easily. Nature did not introduce anything new in the garden. However, I worked with nature to develop the two-week flower essence process, which I started during this time and continued for about six months. I didn't plan to do something this intense, it's just that I kept testing for a new process as soon as I got out of the finished one. As a result, I unloaded a lot of internal baggage that had been interfering with my desire and goal to live a smooth and easy Cottage/Perelandra life— and the Two-Week Flower Essence Process was "born."

Several things happened during these two months that were significant enough for me to remember. I received back the letter I had written on September 16, 1982, to my friend at Findhorn. It had been forwarded between Findhorn and Australia (his home country) six times. Finally, the people at Findhorn sent it back to me. When I reread it, I was particularly struck by my description of my sabbatical year and the prediction that, once I returned from Paris, I would be moving into the new. (I have to be the master of understatement.)

On July 28, I visited my chiropractor once again. (David and I agreed that I would keep my own notes on her work.) I told her I had slight head pressure and that I constantly saw an inner light that was not at all like the inner flashes or visual shattering I was used to. I was fairly able to hold my focus during conversations, but my mind drifted, especially in the mornings. I had pain in my right hip socket and right ankle.

She adjusted the left cranials: occipital and interior temporal. The sacral adjustment released the psoas (pronounced: so'-as) on the left, which also aided the occipital adjustment. I needed no spinal adjustments. My neck stiffness was due to the occipital problem. She realigned my right foot, pulling it "out," and tested that the foot did not need taping for additional support. The right femur/socket pain was caused by ligament stress. I was actually trying to hold the femur in the socket—as if my leg would just drop off if I let go! The sacral adjustment took the pressure off the femur/socket. My adrenals tested strong, and I needed additional supplements: B_{12} and zinc. I did not need any essences!

She asked me to split to the Cottage again while she tested some questions.

- Was the left cranial essence process now complete? Yes. Was any follow-up needed? No.

- She surrogate tested through the Machaelle body to the Katie body to see if the Katie body needed any supplements. It needed no essences or supplements, but it needed extra protein—thirty-five grams extra daily. She said this sounded logical to her because I had already told her that we "locked" the Katie body in one week after the skating was activated—meaning that the Katie body, like the men at the Cottage, does not age. When we did this, we also locked in that metabolism, and I must maintain an athlete's diet at the Cottage.

- Regarding the pelvic realignment that's occurring as a result of my "bicycle/Cottage-body focus therapy": Is this alignment proper for me at Perelandra? Yes. Will this alignment free up the sacrum and allow it to function properly, in light of the two-body challenges? Yes.

• She then asked about the daily color I wear: Was it effective for the Cottage body? Yes. For the Perelandra body? No. That's how we found out there were actually *two* colors I was supposed to be wearing each day—one for the Cottage body and a different one for the Perelandra body. The one the men had been seeing tested for the Cottage body. My chiropractor told me to ask them if they were picking up a second color. If so, I was to test to see if that was the Perelandra color.

When I got back to the Cottage that night, I asked them about this. As it turned out, they had been seeing a second color all along but had ignored it, thinking it was an insignificant mind trick on their part. (I told them to shape up or I was going to fire them. They promised to do better.) When I tested the second color the next morning, it was indeed the color ribbon I was supposed to be wearing at Perelandra. The two colors functioned together to stabilize the bodies and the electrical field between the two bodies. As a result, I felt a dramatic strengthening in both bodies.

Behaving was moving through the publication paces at full steam during this time. A number of unusual things happened. The first woman who was typing the manuscript for galleys got so inspired by what she was typing that she quit her job—something she had been wanting to do for some time—and set out to do something she really loved for a living. The second woman who worked on typing the manuscript thanked me for helping her release (via the book) a terrible fear she had been keeping inside for over five years. On the day that the *Behaving* galleys were to be printed, the galley machine printed out *only Behaving*. No other galleys would print out. This meant that *Behaving* could leap-frog ahead of the other books on the production schedule and thus be published on time. The book designer stopped screaming "shit!" every time he got frustrated over a design problem and began screaming "If you don't behave, the Carrot Deva is going to get you!" instead. The color photo for the cover was stripped in three-and-a-half days and not the usual three-and-a-half weeks. Everywhere I went in the building, I kept hearing comments about devas and nature spirits, and the people working the printing presses asked to meet me. It was an amazing time for me.

The last big thing I can remember about this time is some work I did with John that had to do with the "energy conference" I had been warned about. John was getting ready to leave the Cottage, and they wanted him to act on some information while on the Earth level. This required that I work with him at the Cottage to shift that information, in one complete package, through his subconscious to his conscious, making the information fully available to him on the Earth level. I set up a procedure with nature, and we did this work in about an hour one afternoon. I have no idea what the information was. My job was to help John shift it, not understand it.

September 1 — Heather Green (Cottage)/Ivory (Perelandra)
I'm taking back the notes. My vacation from them has been healing and freeing, and I come back to them with a new attitude. I'm going to try to keep them simple. The basic patterns are now set, so there's no need to continue recording daily rhythms unless there's a change.

The Cottage work over the past two months has been tricky, intense and demanding. On top of that, their attention, focus, support and concern for me over the past year has been ever-present. We're all relaxing a little now because my life is settling in nicely.

September 2 — Yellow/Brown
At Perelandra. Hectic. The cabin now has a completed deck and porch, and the windows are framed in. I sat on the deck late this afternoon and watched a flock of Canadian geese fly by. It was a magical sight.

September 3 — Gold/Heather Green
The Cottage is on R&R. They're working half days, playing golf and getting out to the village in the afternoons. David made a huge pot of *his* soup for lunch, a full-bodied vegetable soup. He got use of the kitchen by bribing Mickey with something. They won't tell me what. We all had dinner at Harry's [a pub-like restaurant in the village], then we went to The Pub to hear Seamus.

September 4 — Apricot/Yellow

JAMFD

September 5 — Dusty Rose/Ivory

We talked about their operating from one framework (the White Brotherhood) and living in another (the Cottage level). The men have specific attitudes, purpose, "rules" and guidelines, but they are guests living within a different system. They seek to act responsibly and with sensitivity in the English system without compromising the guidelines they live under, and they feel that getting emotionally wrapped up in a system that they are not a part of is a useless waste of energy. Their lives are more on the universal level rather than a local level like the Cottage in England. David said that for him to become president of a country again would be a step down from the scope and impact of his present work.

September 6 — Brown/Yellow

I had a restless night and a keyed-up morning. At Perelandra I had to go to New York again on trust business. I guess the flight made me think about death, and that made me ask some questions about the nuts and bolts of my death process. I discussed this with the men, and I learned: Because of the Perelandra/Cottage connection, they'll know when I "plan" to transition and will be with me immediately. This is also the case even if I should get into an accident situation. They know what to do to help me through the process. All I have to do is connect with them, but I'll probably "bump" into them connecting with me. They tell me my process is completely covered and should be smooth and easy in light of what I know and what I've experienced already. All I have to do is focus on feeling and experiencing it. They will be with me every step of the way. I decided not to insist on knowing every last detail of the process, deciding I would trust them to lead me through it well. But just knowing how I need to respond once the process begins has put me most at ease.

In NYC. There's a minor upheaval. The lawyer who has handled our trust legal issues since Isadore's death was fired last week by the head of his firm. My co-trustee suspects embezzlement. All of us are stunned. Our straight-arrow attorney, canned. We immediately made

sure he didn't mishandle our trust and, as far as we can tell, all is
well. His fellow-lawyers are covering up his "alleged" illegal action
for the sake of the firm. Nice bunch. Love that integrity. I suspect I
was picking up on this problem last night and this morning, and
that's why I had such a restless time.

September 7 — Ivory/Gold

At Perelandra. Got a phone call from the lawyers in NYC. I struck
an understanding and agreement with them about their policy to
protect and back their ex-lawyer's work for our trust. I had to play
off male egos and, worse yet, lawyer egos. This is the only time the
lawyers have chosen to deal directly with me, and it's only because
I wasn't rolling over about this "alleged" embezzlement issue. They
had to diffuse my questions and concerns to make sure I wasn't a
loose cannon, so I ended up in a conference call with several of
them—including the head of the firm. Of course, I know they can
probably steamroller me any time they wish, but it's still fun to see
them go through the facade of acting responsibly toward me.

The blue-line proofs for *Behaving* will be ready tomorrow.

September 8 — Burgundy/Gold

At Perelandra. I picked up the blue lines. Now *Behaving* is in "book
form" with pictures inserted. It's an exciting moment for me to see
this. The next step: press proof and printing. The book should be
published in less than two weeks.

The chiropractor and I decided to try something new. She wanted
to work on both bodies, so Max was at the Cottage primed and
ready to do any Cottage adjustments on me that she surrogate-tested
through the Machaelle body. David was also present. He didn't want
to miss this.

First, she checked the Perelandra body. Everything was fine, except the right pelvis was misaligned. She didn't do the adjustment
right then because she wanted to see how the split would impact my
Perelandra body as it was. When I did the split, the pelvis automatically aligned. That so amazed her, she asked me to come back and
do it over again. (We found that I could hear her while I was at the
Cottage if my intent was to hear her.) I said to the men, "Excuse

me," then headed back to the Perelandra body. As I came in, my pelvis went out again. When I went back to the other body, the pelvis automatically aligned again. She was impressed with this. While making the shift, the CSF pulses responded as they had the first time she monitored them several weeks ago. The PB (Perelandra body) cranials were fine. The two-week essence processes I've been doing have been quite successful. PB cervicals 3 and 4 were slightly out and easily adjusted. No adjustments were needed on the Cottage body (CB). When she tested for supplement changes, the PB tested fine, but the CB tested for more protein—ninety grams total daily. I'm to take a protein supplement twice daily at the Cottage rather than trying to eat ninety grams of bulk—which we decided would amount to about half a steer each day. She tested that ninety grams of protein at the Cottage was what is needed for that body's metabolism, plus for the Perelandra body's stabilization during the split shift. Protein strengthens the muscle fiber, and she felt that I am now deriving my sense of being physical from the Cottage, not from Perelandra. To her this makes sense. That's where the bulk of my physical life is and I'm more physically focused at the Cottage. She feels that at Perelandra, I'm more "light," which is why the essences are working so well on the PB. The physical "feeding" for the transition process comes from the CB, and this transition (plus the CB metabolism) needs ninety grams of protein. She feels certain that the protein stabilization at the Cottage will stabilize the muscles holding my alignment at Perelandra. She also feels that my body weight changes in the PB when I shift to the Cottage—the PB becomes lighter.

It was an extraordinary session, and it again physically verified what I have been doing. It was tricky holding myself open and focused at both levels simultaneously, but it was possible. She's clear that we're working with two separate bodies that create a balance between them. They don't "bleed" into one another because balance is an integral element in this. She has a clearer innate feeling than I do about what the SMP is all about and how it functions. Together we're uncovering the nuts and bolts of this process. From now on, she will automatically check the balance of both bodies, and she asks that Max be available to give any adjustments on the

CB. (Max is most eager to be part of this team and was a bit disappointed today when no adjustments were needed on the CB.)

After I shifted back into the PB fully, she checked me again. The CSF pulses were *very* strong and the cranials remained aligned. This is the first time this has happened in about a year, she feels. She also adjusted my pelvis. She and I were both pleased with today's work.

At the Cottage. Max is urging me not to go back into Feldenkrais once the class starts up again. My teacher doesn't understand that she's dealing with a two-body system, and today's work with the chiropractor showed him how important it is for anyone touching me to understand this. He's convinced that, under the present circumstances, Feldenkrais is no longer right for me. He has made me promise to talk it over with him if I decide to resume classes. Right now my inclination is to only take the class with the other students just to keep my Perelandra body moving and not take any private lessons.

September 9 — Apricot/Heather Green

My first day of the extra protein. Mickey is mixing the powder in orange juice, which he gives me at breakfast and again when I get home. This evening, while I was sitting with Tex and David, I suddenly sensed an expansion in my head beyond anything I've experienced before. I felt more space in my head, no pressure and my vision widened. I could also feel my heartbeat resonate throughout my body. I relaxed with these comforting, enjoyable sensations.

September 10 — Gold/Gold

At Perelandra. "Attacked" the blue lines, looking for any errors.

September 11 — Dusty Rose/Brown

At Perelandra. Spent the day on blue lines and picture proofing. Whenever any doubts surface, I lean heavily on David's assurances that this book should be published.

September 12 — Yellow/Apricot

At Perelandra. Took the blue lines back to the printer. My corrections will be completed by Wednesday afternoon. I need to return

Friday for the cover proof and check the negatives for the blue-line corrections. Monday is the scheduled press day. I'm quite nervous about the book's publication. I know I'm starting a new cycle with this and making myself more vulnerable by going public.

Evening. Something was wrong with the protein powder. When I drank it, I spasmed. It's been a long time since I've spasmed.

[I experienced spasms for about the first six months at the Cottage level. Although they were uncomfortable—I don't think anyone enjoys feeling like they are heaving—they only lasted for a couple of minutes. Compared to the shatterings, this was a snap. No one had to jump into action. I only had to wait out the spasm, and then I could continue whatever it was I had been doing. It happened so frequently during those first months and was such a comparatively simple thing to deal with, I never bothered to record when they occurred—until this day, when the spasm was so unexpected and out of pattern.]

Mickey checked the can and found that the expiration date was yesterday, but we think something else must have been off. He made a new mixture from a new can, and it went down smoothly.

September 13 — Gold/Ivory

At the Cottage. Had another painful release that only took about fifteen minutes, this time from my left hand. I have no idea what released, but I guess I didn't need to carry it around any longer.

Mickey served a beautiful end-of-the-summer celebration dinner on the patio, and Max and Seamus joined us. I felt fine from the release, just a little vulnerable.

September 14 — Brown/Heather Green

David called Hyperithon to get his advice about the possibility of my staying home a full day now and then. The bottom line is that I can do this, but I should not do it often—in fact, I should do it most sparingly. Both bodies need the full presence of my soul daily in order to maintain their proper balance.

At Perelandra. Ah, just an average day in a split life. Drove to the printer in Rockville, stopped at the bank, had lunch in Warrenton, discussed cabin issues with the contractor, then went to the Cottage.

I tested that I am to take essence solutions for one week for all the little glitches on my left side. They're all connected, and I sense I am clearing them out for the fall equinox. I started tonight.

September 15 — Gold/Gold

JAMFD

September 16 — Apricot/Heather Green

At Perelandra. Checked the final proofs for the book cover. We go to press Monday.

At the Cottage. The extensive essence process is working. All the glitches on the left are either gone or considerably better. But it leaves me feeling vulnerable.

September 17 — Ivory/Dusty Rose

JAMFD

September 18 — Yellow/Gold

At Perelandra. Spent the day brushing the exterior of the cabin with a wire brush to prepare it for staining. Then I picked tomatoes.

At the Cottage. Exhausted. I had dinner with several of the men at Nino's. I remembered that one year ago tomorrow, I left for Paris. David told me tonight that, for those ten days while I was in Paris, he was told there would be no contact with me. I had to be totally alone and detached from Perelandra and him in order to make the free decision as to whether or not I would enter the next stage that would lead me into the Cottage. They were not told about my decision to continue until I was on the plane heading back to Washington. I told him that's when I actually made my conscious decision to continue—on the plane.

September 19 — Brown/Heather Green

At Perelandra. The book is still in "stripping," and it will probably be printed tomorrow. It is a three-day process: printing, ink drying, binding. I cleaned the cabin. I'm not good at waiting.

September 20 — Ivory/Gold

At Perelandra. Now they say the book will be printed tomorrow. I'm climbing the walls. I processed some tomatoes, then drove to

Manassas to get a biography about David that has just been published—and that David is now reading. He respects this biographer and feels it's an honest attempt to present a clear picture.

David says that leadership is an art form, and it's never too late to improve. Sometimes good biographers have insight that can lead to change or improvement, writing something he (David) has not thought about before. He's always on the lookout for improvement. His leadership now is trickier because he's not visible to most of the people he works with on the Earth level, and he's often not part of the consciousness of those he's leading either. Mostly, he works with people on their subconscious level.

September 21 — Gold/Gold

At Perelandra. Rushed to the printer for another cover proof. We're trying to decide the exact color mix on the cover photo. Now it looks like the text will be printed starting Friday and finishing Monday. It will be folded and cut on Tuesday, and bound on Wednesday. I'm no longer holding my breath.

At the Cottage. I worked on the essence solutions—I'm testing seven glitches altogether. I sometimes wonder if this will ever end. It still tests that this is in preparation for the equinox, but I continue to be left in the dark as to what is going on.

When I finished taking the essences, I suddenly felt light-headed and I could feel my cranials shifting dramatically. I thought I might be passing out, so I laid down on the bed. Then I sensed that all I had to do was lie still and let whatever is to happen, happen. For two hours my body shifted and adjusted, one area at a time. I maintained my focus on the sensations. Finally, I felt the process had completed and that the shifts had taken place in both bodies. I got up and walked around the room a little, and I could feel definite changes. I was in a new alignment, but I didn't know why.

After dinner the men asked me to test them in preparation for the equinox. Each one of them needed several essences, which was not the normal pattern for them. In fact, they rarely need essences. I asked nature to give me insight about what was going on. Immediately, I saw a grid touching into each of our soul levels. The essences were to clear out anything that might prevent it from seating properly. The grid would settle into the soul level after being called in by us at the equinox and, as we move through the year's cycle, the grid will move through various levels that will result in full grounding. By activating the year's cycle in concert with nature's cycle, we automatically connect our grids to the "grounding rod"—nature. For me, the grid has to enter both bodies and, in preparation, both bodies needed to go through simultaneous shifts and releases to allow it to integrate securely on both levels simultaneously.

September 22 — Ivory/Ivory

I received word from nature that we were to begin the equinox today at 10:42 A.M. and continue it tomorrow at the same time when it is actually scheduled.

I opened the equinox coning, and we each silently called in the new cycle. (I must admit that, for the first time, over the past week I experienced hesitation and second thoughts about this when I considered the upcoming new cycle. I think the drama of last year's new cycle has made me a little gun shy! When it came time to call it in, I took a deep breath and plunged ahead.) At the moment of the equinox, I saw a grid slowly and gently enter my soul level. It moved through that level, then split (like the SMP) into two, and each grid entered each body. They moved through to the feet, then from the feet into the ground. Both grids then met in a middle space between the two bodies and rejoined, becoming one again. It moved up through my soul level and rose to the top, moving to a place just above. There it exploded like fireworks into many sparkling stars.

When we all compared notes, the men said they only felt a slight shift. I just looked at them. Some of us were underachieving here. We celebrated the equinox and our "team grids" with dinner at a fancy restaurant in the elegant hotel just outside the village. Butch offered a toast, thanking me for bringing new opportunity to them and making such a difference in their lives.

September 23 — Ivory/Ivory

We set up again for the equinox, each of us silently calling in the new cycle one more time. This time, I was to audibly lead them through the visualization of what I was seeing occur. A circular grid formed over each man's head. There were two over my head, making six grids total. I saw a lighted white candle appear just below the middle grid. They moved into a semi-circle, giving the appearance of a menorah. One by one, a stream of white light moved out from the flame and touched the grids, connecting each to the flame itself. The grid radiated light when it was touched by the stream. After each was lit, their light intensified, and all six grids radiated much light. Then a green light began at the base of the white candle and moved slowly up to the flame, creating a soft-green candle. The light moved into the flame and, one by one, entered the six streams. It traveled up each stream to the grids, infusing them with green light. When all the grids were changed, the whole picture was green. The grids shifted back over our heads then moved slowly through us from our heads to our feet, then settled in our chest areas—and we each finally had our grids.

I realized during the visualization that this was clearly a Pan/ Christ event. The evolutionary Brotherhood Christ energy work was done yesterday and was symbolized with white light. We had called for the next cycle, and this triggered the formation of the grids. Today was the igniting of the grid by nature and its green light.

This time, everyone saw what was happening and felt the grids move through them. As usual, they seemed to know something about these grids—certainly a lot more than I do. I feel the grids have moved us onto a whole new level of teamwork together, but I don't have a sense of the specifics. Actually, it's such a strong feeling, I don't think I want to hear the specifics yet.

At Perelandra. The printing of the book has begun!

September 24 — Yellow/Heather Green

At breakfast. Talked to the men about my feeling that there is something for me to share with others about my growth and experience, coming from the nonviolence/anti-war movement to the point of discovering the existence of the "Pentagon" in the White Brotherhood. This journey has certainly shifted my consciousness around the military, and I feel it might help others to do so as well. They listened carefully to my thoughts and reasoning. What I was saying had merit, but they were concerned about my vulnerability in going public. I, on the other hand, questioned the potential invasion of their privacy. I told them I only recently understood how deeply I was being changed and affected by this new understanding of the military, and I sensed it was time others began to understand these things also. We decided to test the waters at the workshop I'll be giving in North Carolina next weekend. If the feeling is right, I will talk about this aspect of the Cottage.

Evening. Returned exhausted. I was not feeling well at Perelandra. At the Cottage, I felt drained and had a cramping stomach. From the Cottage, I did separate essence readings on each symptom and felt immediate changes. It is now obvious to me that one key to maintaining my balance lies in the liberal use of the essences. As soon as I feel myself go off, I need to check the essences with both bodies. I'm beginning to feel the meshing of the two bodies into one balanced whole. It's tricky, and all this focus on my glitches sometimes gets to me, making me feel emotionally "untogether." The men disagree with me constantly, saying that they see strength maintained through the pioneering of new "medical" processes, and they keep reminding me of my unique life and its stresses. Sometimes I can't tell if they're cheering me on or beating me up!

September 25 — Brown/Ivory
At Perelandra. The cabin roof is now painted, and we've bought the woodburning stove.

September 26 — Gold/Heather Green
At Perelandra. Had to go to the printer to make a decision on a flawed picture. Their touch-up was fine, and I told them to run it. The book will be bound on Wednesday. I can pick it up on Thursday. I go to the workshop on Friday. Talk about deadline hugging!

September 27 — Heather Green/Heather Green
At Perelandra. The text printing is complete.

Chiropractor appointment. First she tested and cleared the Perelandra body. I had a pancreas/thyroid break. It's only the second time in six years I've had this. I also showed a potassium deficiency and needed a T-7 adjustment (T-7 = liver, *pancreas*, spleen). The pancreas/thyroid break is caused by the pancreas weakness. The thyroid tests strong. The occipital: the "sides" were uneven, and the adjustment was made by stabilizing the sacrum. The sacrum tested okay and with *no stiffness*. (This is only the second time she's ever seen the sacrum respond like this with someone who normally has a "tight" sacrum. This was most surprising to her.)

The Perelandra body needed supplements for five days, four times daily. The pancreas/thyroid break is tied to the next cycle that we called in on the equinox. She tested that the coming workshop will be part of the grounding. The pancreas is now stabilized until after the workshop.

When I shifted to the Cottage body, I laughed as I became physical and blew out my right pelvis in the Katie body. It automatically readjusted as I "collected" myself. My thyroid tested weak and needed essences for rebalancing. The pancreas/thyroid break was multilevel. Max adjusted my sacrum a little, and my chiropractor could feel that adjustment in the PB.

Information that resulted from her questions:

- The Cottage protein level is now fine.

- I should not do Feldenkrais until after my cabin is complete. Then I can do private sessions *only* if my teacher is willing to work with me while I have a simultaneous connection with the Cottage body.

- I have not needed to warm up at the Cottage when I do something physical. This is because the body is reverting back to that metabolism we all have as children—the ability to move without the need for warm-up. Children's muscles are always ready for movement and maintain a high metabolism.

- She noted that it's easier to kinesiology test me when I'm at the Cottage.

- She checked David's "phone hookup" to me for any draining: no draining. I'm holding fine. He can now call me any time while I'm at Perelandra.

Then we decided to experiment. Would the Perelandra and Cottage bodies function in tandem to create a surrogate link between levels? We set up a surrogate test, connecting David (then Tex, then Max) to my chiropractor by linking them at the Cottage with the Katie body, and to my chiropractor, who tested that link through the Perelandra body.

First we tried David. At the Cottage, I focused on my touch with him, then felt our connection through my body and saw it "touch into" the PB's left arm. Her test on my left arm was strong—we had a successful hookup. She asked me to cross my legs at the Cottage: the connection broke. Then I crossed my legs at Perelandra: the connection broke. Finally, I crossed my PB arm over my head: the connection really broke fast.

I activated a coning and held my connection with David within the coning: the connection strengthened. In fact, it was much stronger than the first connection. It's clear that the coning stabilized the connection.

With David lying on the floor, I scanned his body first with my right hand only: no response. Then my left hand only: no response. Using both hands: a strong, positive response. As I scanned his entire body, she applied pressure to the Perelandra left arm. Everything tested strong until I got to the left leg, thigh and pelvic area where my PB arm went weak. I stayed on those areas while she tested several things and received insight. Although he has physically healed from problems he had in those areas during his lifetime, he is only back to "square one." He's ready to move from square one and out of the cycle. This will complete the process. To do the job, he only needs essences. She tested him, and he needed just one. This deep balance of his left leg will ensure that he won't "trip off" into the cycle again.

Max: I suspected more work needed to be done with his sacrum. The scan registered weakness in the lumbar, thoracic *and* cervical regions. She tested specific adjustments needed for every area. It was a complicated situation. I got the gut feeling not to adjust him at all, but to put my hands on his sacrum and focus energy through his entire spinal column to the head. She told me to try it. I did this two times, then she tested the spine again. Everything was now strong except for the thoracic area. I moved energy through that area again. Then it tested strong. It tested that the weakness we got from my first scanning didn't deal with structural misalignment. Rather, it was registering areas where CSF was having difficulty moving through each of the high curves of the spine. The flow needed to be regulated. She suggested he walk after this session to keep the sacrum more fully activated.

Tex: Everything tested strong during the scanning, except the prostate—which tested a strong weakness. He only needed one essence to strengthen it. As with David, this began the process of moving him from square one out of a cycle.

We could barely believe what we had stumbled onto. I said goodbye to the men at the Cottage and shifted fully to the Perelandra body. After all of this, my chiropractor only charged me for the work she did on the Perelandra body. What a champ.

At the Cottage. Max joined us for dinner. He says that after his walk he feels strong and young—"like the juices are moving."

September 28 — Yellow/Apricot

At Perelandra. The cabin process has been slowed by a sheetrock strike. I feel I'm in a logjam. I decided to take things in hand and break through the jam by asking the contractor to call around the area stores for sheetrock.

September 29 — Gold/Yellow

At Perelandra. The logjam is broken, and we found enough sheetrock to do the cabin job. The contractor picked it up today.

I picked up 3,000 copies of *Behaving* and had a wonderful moment at the printer. I gave a copy of the book to everyone who had worked on it, and then we had a massive book signing. I signed their copies, and they signed mine. We all felt great about the book.

At the Cottage. I split six copies of the book and took them with me to the Cottage where I gave them out. David was surprised and pleased by the book's dedication. They each made me sign their copies also. I felt silly.

We had a surprise dinner for the successful completion of *Behaving*. It was a very special night for me. I could feel the support and celebration of my family.

September 30 —Brown/Ivory

At Perelandra. Clarence, a friend of ours and I drove to North Carolina for the workshop. We carted along a carton of books—just in case.

October 1 — Gold/Gold

We had only nine people in the workshop. I asked them what their expectations were, and they all said they wanted "advanced work." Then some guy asked a question that required that I talk about the Cottage in order to answer it. I couldn't believe it. I ended up spending the whole day giving a Cottage workshop. I talked about the things I've been learning, new ideas, concepts and life experiences. They showed special interest in the walls (a post-death process) and my process of getting back and forth—and that notion of prosperity and limitlessness. They especially wanted to hear about that one. I'd say it was a good day.

At the Cottage. They were genuinely touched that these nine people cared about the Cottage work, even to the point of asking what they (the workshop people) could do to assist the Cottage team.

October 2 — Brown/Ivory

I had an uneventful trip back to Perelandra, and I was happy to leave for the Cottage from there again. The men at the Cottage gave me a bouquet of red roses to thank me for handling the workshop so well. (David had been included in the coning and monitored the workshop the entire day. He was able to fill them in on everything that happened.) I was touched by their gesture. They asked me to split a carton of *Behaving* home. It turned out to be no harder than splitting a single sheet of paper.

October 3 — Apricot/Yellow

David had lunch with Max and gave him a copy of *Behaving*.

October 4 — Gold/Gold

At breakfast. The men are finished reading the book and asked a few questions this morning. Mostly, they were interested in the lessons from the monk on the bridge. They wanted to know in detail what the monk's lessons were and the kinds of things he emphasized.

October 5 — Heather Green/Heather Green
At Perelandra. Mailed out books to the people who had ordered prior to publication and sent out over thirty copies as gifts to people I know. I also set up a simple recordkeeping system so I can keep track of sales.

At the Cottage. Returned not feeling well again. I had pain in my left hip joint and leg, plus there was pain around T-7 and head pressure. I was so angry at feeling low again that I decided I'd lay down and work on myself. I made adjustments in both bodies using energy and shifting my focus back and forth to each body. It was an interesting experience and gave me excellent results. I stabilized the work with essences. It all took about an hour of intense focus, but I got up not feeling any pain. The men said I looked a hundred percent better than when I first arrived.

Butch gave a copy of the book to Seamus today.

October 6 — Dusty Rose/Heather Green
I got another pep talk about not looking at my downtime as weakness or failure, and remembering I've taken on a most difficult and taxing challenge. My adjustments do not mean my health is weakening or deteriorating. They are reasonable for what I am going through, and I should not be so impatient with myself. This is hard to get into my pointed brain because it's not how I'm used to thinking about health. Society and the medical establishment have taught me well that a symptom is a sign of illness or imbalance, that we are physically weak in some way. I keep thinking my need for adjustments implies a weakness in me, and I can't afford to be weak now. The men are trying mightily to turn my thinking around by pointing out that my symptoms are simply part of the adjustments that are part of the process I am going through. One would think I could get this. Intellectually, when I am not in pain, I do. As soon as I feel pain, I'm back in the old pattern of thinking. The men must be getting through to me, however, because I admitted they were right and asked them to keep working on me about this.

October 7 — Ivory/Heather Green

At Perelandra. Spent the afternoon at a mall buying kitchen supplies for the cabin. I had a lot of fun.

October 8 through 10

JAMFD times three

October 11 — Brown/Brown

At Perelandra. I had another appointment with the chiropractor.

Perelandra body: She gave me a sacrum "phase 1" adjustment, which was exactly the correction needed for what I saw last week when I worked on myself. T-7 was "coaxed" back into alignment by a C-5 adjustment. I needed no additional supplements, and my CSF pulses were fine. The occipital was slightly out but adjusted automatically with the sacrum work. My pancreas still needs some occasional stabilizing with supplements.

Cottage body: The pelvis slipped out on entry again. She had felt the last time I visited her that I was entering in the wrong room at the Cottage, but she didn't say anything about it. Today we tested that I should enter in the lagoon because the minerals in the rock wall would stabilize my entry. These minerals could be duplicated in any other room in the Cottage, and they would have the same effect on me. For now, I'll just use the lagoon. The thyroid is still not fully stable, and this, she believes, has to do with my opening up at Perelandra about the Cottage work. I'll need to go through some adjustments for this. (I'm thrilled.) My protein was okay, thank god, and my body needed no structural adjustments.

The men feel that I don't get enough sleep, but I tested that this is not detrimental at this time. When I move to the cabin, I'll eliminate the Perelandra disturbances and strike a better sleeping rhythm.

Scanning David: His left leg process is complete, and he is out of the cycle at square zero. (He told me this morning that he now realizes that even though his leg no longer was a problem, he still had had thoughts about it being limited. Now he feels there is nothing there to "hang his thoughts on." That must be what square zero means—the release of any energy that might even hold thought.)

Max: His sacrum tested weak, but the rest of his spine and head tested strong. We "jump-started" his sacrum, and it tested strong again. He just needs to continue walking as often as possible.

Tex: His essence process is complete, but more work is needed on the prostate. He tested for four supplement tablets for healing and strengthening the prostate. (I split these from her office.) Then he's to wait five days for healing and test for a second essence process.

October 12 — Heather Green/Heather Green

I had an insight to try something with Tex for his prostate weakness. I had him sit down opposite me, and I held both his hands. We didn't talk, I just held his hands. In about two minutes, I felt energy pulsating rhythmically from him into my hands. First it came into my left hand, then my right. I could feel strong static in the energy. I got the insight that this was the "radio" energy that was transmitting from his prostate. I continued holding his hands, and about three or four minutes later the pulsating energy lost its static. After another three minutes the pulse gradually softened and eventually smoothed out. At that point, I felt a gentle, even, smooth and comfortable energy. Then, as I held his hands, I asked him what he most wanted to do right now. "Hug you." I stood up, and he held me for over five minutes. I could tell it was difficult for him to let go, and he admitted this to me, as well. I encouraged him to just hold on and stay with the feelings. He said this was a different experience for him. When I felt his softening stabilize, I took his hands and we sat down again. He was calm and open. We broke away from this gentle, delicate process between us by drinking coffee.

At Perelandra. I received more insight about Tex's process. The pulsating energy was the prostate energy. At first it was masculine in feeling. He needed to connect with me to receive female energy that, in turn, served to regulate and smooth out the prostate energy. Sexual issues were not involved in this. Rather, it was the masculine/feminine energy balance in the prostate that was the issue. This includes his relationship with women in a nonsexual but loving manner. It is this issue that Tex had been dealing with prior to death and that resurfaced when he began taking essences two weeks ago.

I called my chiropractor for her thoughts about what happened this morning. She agrees with my insights and feels that my work regulated Tex's prostate energy and activated his female hormones.

The supplements she had given him helped his prostate go through the physical strengthening that was needed before the female hormones could be activated and balanced. He also had to complete the shift of his mental concepts around sexuality and women, which were acting as inhibitors, distorting the prostate energy before everything could be regulated.

She felt this process was exciting and promising. (1) It shows that the prostate imbalance is the physical manifestation of an imbalance in men's relationships with women and their not knowing how to love women nonsexually. This could be a lead to treatment of prostate weakness before it manifests into something physical. (2) It points out the potential of balancing energy between men and women via the reproductive organs. The prostate and the ovaries have the same regulating function. This explains why the men at the Cottage are relating so strongly to my period and ovulation. They feel a regulation and balancing occur in themselves, which is then translated in their heightened sense of creativity during these times.

At the Cottage. We all had a long talk about Tex's process, my insights and what the chiropractor said. It made sense to them. This discussion gave me an opportunity to ask them questions about something I had been thinking about for awhile. From the beginning, I never felt sexual energy from them toward me, and, although Mickey and Butch had long-term relationships with women, the others did not include sexual relationships in their lives—that I knew of. Also, Butch and Mickey seemed quite comfortable recently about switching their relationships from lover to friend. I admitted that I never felt more loved, safe and respected by men than I do by them. In fact, I've never come close to this experience. How did they view sexuality as it pertained to themselves?

The bottom line for them has to do with coming through the walls. By definition, this process creates deep balance—including their male/female balance—and allows them to make honest lifestyle choices that enhance their souls. This means they don't look to or need a woman as a lover to supply elements in their lives and being that might have been otherwise missing prior to coming through the walls. Consequently, they are free to relate to women without a sexual barrier. Their choice whether or not to express themselves sexually has to do with what is right for the present time on a soul level. Once made, these choices—which can range from not having a personal relationship with women to a deep and loving marriage—do not create a struggle or yearning in them because they are soul choices.

[This explains the ease I felt in these men. It also explains how a group of men could be so gentle and nurturing toward me. They once asked me, in all seriousness, if I ever wished for female companionship while I was at the Cottage. In actuality, the answer was no, but I was afraid that, if I had said yes, they were going to rush right out and rent me a female companion! At the time, their question surprised me because it was not something I had thought about at all. I told them then that I didn't feel overwhelmed by men. Now I could also say that they have such a strong male/female balance, I just don't feel anything is missing in my life with them.]

Seamus joined us for dinner. *Behaving* has opened the Machaelle side of his sister to him. He found the story of my early years difficult to take and kept saying he wished he had been there for me. I was touched by the brotherly protection I felt from him.

October 13 — Yellow/Apricot
At Perelandra. The cabin has hit another snafu. The contractor's presence is needed. The windows are still not in, one interior wall is moldy and lumber needs to be ordered—and the contractor's phone is out of order.

October 14 — Gold/Gold
David's birthday. They don't celebrate birthdays in elaborate ways—Max took the men to lunch at Harry's. The others won't even tell me their birthdays, which leads me to believe they weren't born at all—they were hatched or something.

October 15 — Heather Green/Brown
At Perelandra. The cabin windows are in.

October 16 — Dusty Rose/Dusty Rose
JAMFD

October 17 — Heather Green/Heather Green

At Perelandra. I became an official member of the cabin construction crew today—actually, I was the wood gopher. It helped to do something, since I'm so impatient about moving in.

October 18 — Gold/Gold

The first anniversary of my SMP and coming to the Cottage. We had a celebration dinner at Nino's.

October 19 — Apricot/Apricot

At Perelandra. I spent some "unofficial" time with my chiropractor. She asked me about some nature work I was doing with battlefields. Right about then, she said she thought David was trying to get in touch with me. I checked it out and, sure enough, he was waiting for me to finish talking before "ringing through." He wanted to join in on the battlefield discussion. In fact, he would like my chiropractor to go to the Gettysburg Battlefield with me to do the battlefield work there. He also wanted to be included in the coning once we were there so that he could work directly with us. Actually, he plans to function as tour guide with the chiropractor, while I concentrate on doing the nature processes. This development was a surprise to me as much as to her. He suggested we do it sometime in February or March when the ungodly cold weather will assure us there won't be many other people around. She happens to be a Civil War buff, another surprise for me, and she said she would be pleased to be a part of this adventure.

October 20 — Heather Green/Brown

Evening. While sitting around the first fire of the season, we got in a discussion about integrity and how important this is to all of them. Most of the men learned about integrity from their parents. When they asked me where I learned it, I had to think a minute. My parents were woefully lacking in integrity. Then it hit me—I learned it from my parents, too. They showed me what the lack of integrity could do to a person's life, and that was a valuable lesson for me to see.

October 21 through 23
Yellow/Ivory, Brown/Brown, Apricot/Apricot

JAMFD times three

October 24 — Ivory/Dusty Rose

At the breakfast dream-debriefing, we had a lot of fun with another one of my crazy murder mystery dreams. A lavender-and-blue rose bush, a key, a body that couldn't be found, a huge hotel, my missing loafers and the question: Why is a particular European sect stronger in strain and heritage than their American counterparts? David suggested that the key belonged to an Oldsmobile that was parked behind a cactus in the western novel he was reading. It's obviously there for my getaway!

At Perelandra. A busy cabin day.

At the Cottage. We talked about tomorrow's first anniversary of my commitment to the Cottage. I told them what a 180-degree stretch this has been to my reality. I have such a deep feeling of confidence, satisfaction and accomplishment for having made this journey, and there's much I've learned about myself. I also told them about my surprise at seeing how much my presence has positively impacted them.

October 25 — Gold/Gold

I awoke with a feeling of celebration and accomplishment that lasted throughout the entire day. The men said they wanted to have a "formal" celebration dinner for my anniversary tomorrow evening, the one-year date of last year's formal dinner. I thought it was a bit much, but they insisted. We had a quiet, simple dinner together tonight and continued our conversation from yesterday about the past year's events. I can't believe I have been at this for a year.

October 26 — Ivory/Ivory

At Perelandra. Drove with friends to a rock shop in the suburbs to get a quartz crystal "slab" for the cabin. I had received insight a week ago that I was to do this for the cabin.

At the Cottage. I talked about the new quartz, and David asked to see it. So I split it to the Cottage. Later, I had the feeling that I was to let it remain split. In fact, I should have it in my room, making a strong connection between my room and the Perelandra cabin.

When I came downstairs after dressing for the special dinner, I was met with my first surprise—John. He came home especially for the occasion. Then Max and Seamus arrived.

The dining table was again set with white linen, silver and candles. I noticed I was able to see it much better than a year ago. As we sat, I had another surprise—Hyperithon. This time he wasn't in his white, wispy "outfit." In fact, he looked like a normal human being. He said he had come for two reasons: (1) He wanted to be part of the celebration; (2) He wanted to collect the kiss on the nose I had promised him after some good news he gave me in a session several weeks ago. I immediately walked over and kissed him on the nose. He was holding my crystal that I had left on the coffee table after showing it to everyone, and he placed it in the middle of the table, saying: "This should be here tonight." We all agreed it was a nice touch.

Tex was asked to be the spokesman for everyone for the toast. In essence, he talked about the joy my presence has brought to them and the love they have come to feel for me.

I was speechless, really, so we just sat and had another one of Mickey's amazing dinners: duck à l'orange with all the fixings and an outrageous chocolate pastry for dessert.

I knew I wanted to make a toast, but I didn't want to use champagne. Since I don't normally drink, it felt like champagne wasn't the appropriate vehicle for me to use. I considered contacting nature for help and giving everyone a white rose. While I was debating the propriety of this, Hyperithon leaned over and quietly said to me, "Do it." (Apparently he can read my mind, so I better watch my p's and q's around him!) Encouraged by Hyperithon, I said to them all (aloud): "I'd like to show you my love and gratitude, but I'd like to do it *my* way." With that, I connected with the Deva of the Rose and the appropriate nature spirits, silently told them what I'd like and set my focus on a single white rose. Simultaneously, a single white rose in a crystal glass bud vase appeared before each person, including me. While I was focused on the devic and nature spirit levels, I could feel the eagerness and joy from nature to be part of our celebration. Everyone was touched, and I felt a special closeness with my influential friends.

When I looked at the roses, I knew something more should be done. My attention kept getting pulled to the crystal in the middle of the table. It crossed my mind that it would be appropriate if the roses were permanent. This would symbolize my commitment to the Cottage more than a dying rose that would soon have to be thrown away. I also wanted to give these men something permanent as a reminder of how I felt about them. Again, Hyperithon said, "Do it. You're the only one here who can do it." (This man could be dangerous.) I got up and walked to the center of the table. Then I created a circle around the crystal with the roses—there were nine in all. I connected with the Deva of the Rose and the Deva of the Quartz Crystal and told them what I wished. Then I followed my instinct. I moved my hands around the circle of roses and lightly touched each one. Then I held my hands on either side, like I was cupping the circle. I asked that the energy of the quartz crystal enter the form of each vase and rose. Immediately I saw the energy enter the bottom of each vase and move slowly up—through the vase, the stem, and then the flower. As the energy moved completely through the flowers, the petals exploded in the air just above the now-crystal rose. It was as if the quartz crystal energy "pushed out" the flower energy. At the explosion, I once again felt an extraordinary sense of nature's joy and celebration. I quietly gave everyone back his newly created quartz-crystal rose and vase, making eye contact with each as I handed it to him. I let each man connect with my consciousness. When I handed Hyperithon his rose, he said, "You did beautifully."

This time *they* were speechless. Finally Max said, "Does she do this kind of thing often?" Mickey appropriately announced that now was the perfect time for coffee.

The celebration continued through the evening. The roses stayed on the dining room table until each person left the Cottage or retired. When Hyperithon left, I walked him to his car. He told me he looked forward to our work together this winter. Of course, I didn't have a clue about what he was referring to.

October 27

When we compared our roses during breakfast, we noticed that each one is slightly different. We talked a lot about the "rose routine," and I told them how honored and moving it was for me to participate with nature on this.

At Perelandra. Had lunch with my wallpaper friend, who is back in the area after having been away the last five months. We talked for two hours. In the process, she managed to insult or attack everything I had discovered and built upon this summer. She ignored my anniversary at the Cottage and finally announced she didn't wish to talk about the Cottage because she wanted to "keep it light." Also, she was insulted that I didn't autograph the copy of *Behaving* that I had given her at lunch.

At the Cottage. When I told them about my lunch, they declared my friend to be crazy—and that was that. After I took essences, the color returned to my face (they said) and I felt calm.

October 28 and 29 — Ivory/Brown, Yellow/Yellow, JAMFD times two

October 30 — Heather Green/Ivory

At Perelandra. Worked all day in the cabin, cleaning and getting it ready for the final inspection. I feel like I'm preparing for a damn final exam. I resent the idea that some stranger is coming to tell me it's okay for me to live in my own cabin. What an invasion.

At the Cottage. John is preparing to leave tomorrow. He says that on the Earth level he's becoming more consciously aware of and open to the reality of his trips to the Cottage. In short, he's starting to get the idea that something's going on. It will be most interesting to see if he'll ever find his way to Perelandra before dying.

October 31 — Dusty Rose/Ivory

John left in the early morning hours. He doesn't like drawn-out goodbyes. Once again I can feel his absence in the house.

November 1 — Brown/Brown

At Perelandra. Passed the final inspection. My wallpaper friend stopped by to give me ideas about how to stain and/or paint the cabin windows. Our time together went much better this time.

Got a call from some fellow who has read *Behaving*, asking if he could visit and talk to me about the book. I'm going to meet him for lunch in town on November 19.

November 2 — Gold/Gold

David looked tired and upset about something at breakfast this morning.

Evening. David told me that for the past few days he's been having disturbing flashes in his memory. Without warning, different scenes he witnessed in the concentration camps during the war surface—the degradation, the bodies (both alive and dead) and especially the eyes of the people looking at him as he passed by to inspect conditions. He's never shared his feelings in detail about this experience with anyone, choosing to keep the horror to himself. He's also never experienced the memories flashing before him like this. He was reluctant to talk to me about them because of my Jewish background, but I suggested that now is probably the time for him to talk about it and that this is what the flashes are all about. He said he'd think about it.

November 3 — Apricot/Apricot

At Perelandra. Scrubbed the cabin floors for six hours straight to get them ready for staining.

At the Cottage. Exhausted. David took the day off and went off by himself for a long walk. He looked like a new man when I got home, and his spirits were up again.

November 4 — Ivory/Ivory

At Perelandra. Met with the contractor and gave him my shelving designs, which he said he'd work on this weekend. He told me how much he's enjoyed working on the cabin and that it was an easy job for him. The whole crew loves the design and working at Perelandra. He said that the other night while shooting pool, one of the guys talked about how easy I was to work with and how much they liked my sense of humor. By the time the contractor finished telling me all of this, I felt I had been awarded a gold star.

At the Cottage. Tested for four or five different essences for each body, which surprised me. I received insight that this is a link-breaking time for me as I prepare to move into the cabin.

November 5 — Brown/Apricot

At Perelandra. Another day of cabin focus. The floor is stained; the woodstove is on the pad; the chimney cap is installed. It was a magical moment for me to see the floor stained.

November 6 — Gold/Gold

At Perelandra. I painted the utility closet while Clarence finished setting up the stove and started the first fire. Yesterday, when one of the guys climbed up to install the chimney cap, he found a 1983 penny that had been pressed into the cement at the top of the chimney by the stone mason. I'm told it means good luck.

I sat alone for awhile in the cabin and stared into the fire. I feel like the heart of the cabin is now activated.

My meeting in town with the fellow who wants to talk to me about *Behaving* has been switched to December 10.

November 7 — Ivory/Ivory

At Perelandra. I started what looks to be a long job of staining the windows and trim in the cabin.

At the Cottage. David and Tex are still working on finding a missing piece they've been looking for over the past couple of weeks. They feel they're about to find it and are focused on the job.

November 8 — Brown/Apricot

At Perelandra. We're all in the final cabin push. The well was begun today, not without incident, however. The driver wrapped the big rig around a hickory tree, and we had to chain saw the tree down to free the truck. Got the construction crew to sign a plaque that I'll hang in the cabin: This cabin was built in 1983 by...

November 9 — Yellow/Apricot

At the Cottage. David and Tex thought they found their missing piece yesterday. When they tried it out today, it indeed held up. I can feel both of them are relieved. I haven't a clue about what this is all about. I've decided that if they don't volunteer the information, it's probably not important that I know. I do know that this was a big piece that affects a number of issues.

I'm feeling frustrated about the cabin. The final work is going slowly, and it's all building up in me.

November 10 — Brown/Apricot

JAMFD, as long as I consider spending all afternoon in the cabin staining trim normal.

November 11 — Ivory/Apricot

The carpenters are finished in the cabin!

November 12 — Heather Green/Apricot

Stained window framing and trim.

November 13 — Yellow/Apricot

Stained window framing and trim.

November 14 — Apricot/Brown

Stained window framing and trim.

November 15 — Apricot/Apricot

Stained window framing and trim.

November 16 — Yellow/Yellow

Another good cabin day.

At the Cottage. The men have been most supportive as I've gone through this intense cabin period. However, they called Hyperithon at one point to find out if he felt I was putting out too much effort right now—they were told I was doing fine. They're just supposed to encourage me to get as much sleep as possible. My health and energy level are holding up fine. I'm actually going through a period of feeling normal. It's wonderful watching the season move into my second winter of this expanded life of mine. And now, with this physical balance, I'm feeling great calm and peace.

November 17 — Gold/Ivory

At Perelandra. I'm still working full tilt on the cabin—I'm aiming to move in Saturday.

While working, I suddenly felt a sadness about never having experienced a good father/daughter relationship. I even cried a bit. Then I remembered I was dealing with the wrong father—Isadore. I/Katie had had a beautiful relationship with Max, and I still do. This experience made me feel how difficult it is to maintain an equal balance between the two levels of my life now. When I thought of "father," I automatically thought of Isadore and lost the balance within my expanded life. With it, I lost my loving relationship with Max. My Perelandra life, from which I spring, has a stronger "hold" on me still. I sense there will be a day when this will no longer be so, where my various life facets will be connected and balanced. Then, when the subject of father comes up, I will automatically think of Max.

November 18 — Apricot/Apricot

At the Cottage. Started my period tonight while we were sitting around the fire. Max had joined us for dinner, and this was the first time he noticed the glow. At first he thought he had had too many scotches, but everyone assured him it was just me!

I needed to work on his sacrum again tonight. He had an emotional release while I was working that had to do with his fear of the future. He's going through such a big change in his life right now. I had a feeling this was the last release needed, and his sacrum would move easily from this point on.

November 19 — Ivory/Ivory

Moved into the cabin and spent my first night there! The full moon cast light across the field beyond the garden, and I hardly needed to turn a light on to get around in the cabin.

At the Cottage. I talked about how nervous I was to finally move into the cabin. It's such a big step into the unknown. However, I noticed when I arrived home that shifting to the Cottage was effortless. Moving to the cabin has made a huge difference. I guess this verifies that it was a good step to take.

November 20 — Gold/Gold

I didn't sleep as long as they had all hoped I would. I was anxious to get back to the cabin and continue settling in.

November 21 — Gold/Ivory

I've noticed that I'm sleeping deeper and more peacefully now that I've moved into the cabin—just not long enough.

At Perelandra. My energy was a bit low, so I practiced puttering. It's obvious these last few weeks of focus on getting into the cabin are now catching up with me.

November 22 and 23
Heather Green/Heather Green, Apricot/Yellow

JAMFD times two

November 24 — Heather Green/Heather Green

Thanksgiving.

At Perelandra. Clarence and I had a nice, quiet, enjoyable time together. He made a full turkey dinner. It was good to feel the pressure of the cabin construction off both of our shoulders. He says he's feeling fine about having his own space, and that it gives him more freedom. I was pleased to hear him say this because I had been concerned he might hate the changes once we actually made them. Up until now he's been most supportive about the cabin but, once I moved in, I was afraid that might have changed.

At the Cottage. They had a crazy day. Golf with Seamus, Max, Tex and David. It was the first time Seamus has played. They said he did quite well and had a natural swing. Petunia went along to keep score—and the foursome in front of them moving.

We had a fun family dinner. Mickey outdid himself.

November 25 — Ivory/Ivory

At Perelandra. My job for the day was to connect David to the Army–Navy game. I knew Army was in trouble when, after four minutes of play, Navy led 21–0. But then Navy got complacent and Army woke up a bit, and we had a decent game. Also, Army replaced their quarterback after four minutes into the first quarter— good move.

Clarence and I had to leave at half-time for a dinner with friends in Washington, Virginia. I left the TV on to see if David could still hear the game without me in the room. Just a mile from Perelandra, he totally lost the sound. Obviously, I need to be around for any broadcasting. The final score: Navy 48–Army 13. I'm glad I missed the second half.

Dinner with our friends was okay. There were twelve of us altogether. Nothing interesting or meaningful was said. I missed being home.

November 26 — Apricot/Apricot

At Perelandra. Bought twelve bushes for landscaping the porch and deck sides of the cabin.

At the Cottage. David's flashes have returned. He keeps seeing eyes, especially the terror in the eyes. He still has a tremendous reluctance about talking about all of this with me. Rather than describing what he saw, he talked about the feelings it evokes in him—man at his worst, horror, disbelief at what man had done to man, hollow eyes. Especially the hollow eyes.

November 27 — Brown/Brown

After much coaxing, Max spent the night with us at the Cottage. He slept late and eventually joined us for a late breakfast. It was a nice feeling having him with us. David talked him into staying for golf.

Evening. It's been one week since I moved into the cabin. It seems like I've been there forever. However, I still haven't hit a schedule of calm because workers drift in and out doing last-minute stuff. I look forward to the time when everyone will be gone and the place will truly be mine.

November 28 — Gold/Gold

At Perelandra. Made a decision to try the Feldenkrais class for three weeks when it starts up again, then I'll decide if I should continue after that. I feel like the class might still offer some answers and breakthroughs.

At the Cottage. I bounced my decision off the men. At first they seemed positive, but as the evening wore on, they expressed reservations. Since the teacher doesn't understand anything about what I'm working with, nor does she give any indication of wanting to understand, the men are concerned that there might be the possibility of my blowing the good balance I've maintained these past few weeks. I told them I feel I have to try it before I can make a good decision.

November 29 — Ivory/Ivory
At Perelandra. The Feldenkrais class wasn't a complete success, nor was it a complete failure.

At the Cottage. I felt head pressure as soon as I got in. I tested essences and the pain released immediately.

November 30 — Apricot/Apricot
Completely wiped out. I felt okay at the Cottage, but, as soon as I got to the cabin, I felt out of it. I tried raking and leveling the road by the cabin, but I had to stop. I didn't even have the energy for writing notes. So I returned home early and took a nap. The Jewish mothers descended. They're afraid I might be getting the flu, and, because of my circumstances, they feel it might hit me harder.

December 1 — Brown/Brown
At Perelandra. I'm still dealing with workmen. I'd like to put out the cabin crystal, but it tests I should hold off until after the workmen are finished and after my appointment with the chiropractor Saturday.

December 2 — Gold
[For a couple of weeks, the colors of the small ribbons I wear have been the same for each body. From this point on, I will only list one color when they are the same.]
JAMFD

December 3 — Heather Green
Perelandra and chiropractor's appointment.
Perelandra body: She adjusted the left pelvis, L-5 and one cranial. The sacrum and pituitary tested weak. She used point stimulation to

strengthen and balance the sacrum, and a zero balance technique for cervical and head balancing. She felt strongly that all of this was the fallout from Tuesday's Feldenkrais class.

Cottage body: No adjustments, no essences and no nutritional weaknesses. Everything is holding strong. It tests that Feldenkrais is not applicable or necessary for that body. Feldenkrais does have useful information for me, but I need to apply it differently now.

When she monitored my CSF pulses as I made the transference to the Perelandra level, she felt three distinct rhythms: the Cottage rhythm, the transference rhythm and the Perelandra-level rhythm. Once again this amazed her.

December 4 and 5 — Gold and Dusty Rose/Ivory

JAMFD times two

December 6 — Yellow

At breakfast. I tried to remember another time in my life when I've felt this deeply happy, content and peaceful. There have not been any. I feel my base is now securely in place, and my life is in order. Any two-bit psychiatrist would look at me and declare me totally insane, but look at how happy, peaceful and stable I am. Amazing.

At Feldenkrais class #2. It seemed to go well, except that my energy drained as the day went on and I tested for Rescue Remedy.

At the Cottage. Max joined us for dinner so that he could check up on how I was doing after the class. The Cottage body checked out fine.

December 7 — Brown

At Perelandra. Went Christmas shopping with my wallpaper friend. Our conversations were light today, but what was especially different was that I did not feel the need to talk to her about the Cottage. I was perfectly comfortable *not* talking about it—whereas before, I felt compelled to talk about it. My Cottage life is normalizing.

December 8 — Apricot

At Perelandra. The big day. I thoroughly cleaned the cabin from top to bottom—spit-and-polish order. Around mid-afternoon I opened a coning and got ready to put out the crystal. (The other crystal was already out in my bedroom at the Cottage.) I felt the cabin joining the garden environment and felt the celebration within the nature kingdoms as they officially received it. Man and nature had united to create the cabin—nature supplying all the materials and man supplying the design and know-how to work the materials into a cabin. I placed the crystal in the south window, and I formally presented the cabin to the universe, to Perelandra and to the garden. I felt a tremendous connection form with the Cottage, and I saw light at both ends of the connective channel.

December 9 — Brown/Ivory

JAMFD

December 10 — Ivory

While I slept, Mickey sneaked in my room and put a vase with a dozen yellow roses on my chest of drawers that was from everyone for my birthday. I find that this year I'm quite peaceful about this day.

At Perelandra. Had my lunch meeting in town with the fellow who had read *Behaving*. What he said about how the book impacted him verified that it was right to have the book published.

December 11 — Gold

JAMFD

December 12 — Brown

At breakfast. They asked me how difficult it is for me to juggle Christmas in two places. I told them it's a bit pressing, but that I felt it was important to keep a balance between both levels as I go through the holidays. We kicked around some ideas for making it easier for me. So far, we haven't come up with anything significant.

At Perelandra. Got my first inquiry about the book from a bookstore. It's magical watching *Behaving* move on its own. It's all being done by word of mouth.

At the Cottage. The men took me out for a belated birthday dinner at Harry's. My lunch appointment in town on the 10th had drained me, so they decided to postpone the dinner until tonight. We had fun. An easy, relaxing time.

December 13 through 15 — Burgundy, Brown, Gold
JAMFD times three

December 16
At Perelandra. Planted the twelve bushes around the cabin.

At the Cottage. When I returned home exhausted, it finally hit me that exhaustion must be more than a physical phenomenon. It has to be a soul state as well, therefore transferable from one body to the other when my soul switches.

December 17 and 18 — Ivory, Gold
JAMFD times two

December 19 — Dusty Rose
The men decided they were not going to put up a "cheesy little tree" like last year. My Christmas baskets have inspired them. They went into the village, en masse, picked out a huge tree and bought new decorations.

December 20 — Brown
At breakfast. I told them how frustrated I feel about wanting to ask them questions, but having to draw back because it would take too much focus on my part to hear a complex answer. They try to make sure they're not overloading me with information and to help me hold a balance in this by keeping their comments as concise as possible. They reminded me that we have a lot of time ahead of us and we don't have to rush to tell one another our stories and thoughts.

Perelandra and a chiropractor appointment. I told her about some sensory "flashes" and "altitude drops" I've been having in both bodies lately. These are different glitches than I've heretofore experienced. She feels I'm entering new shifts and that I'm "through the door but not yet into the room."

Perelandra body: She adjusted L-5, which, in turn, had been throwing the sacrum slightly off. I had a tightened left psoas and needed one cranial adjustment. The L-5 problem is tied to a problem I've been having with my period.

At the Cottage. Max was present and ready to jump in as soon as he was needed. I needed no adjustments, my nutrition was fine and my endocrine glands were strong. I needed one essence that was linked to the problem I'm having with my period.

My period at Perelandra is not in perfect sync with my period at the Cottage, and this is indicating a problem. Normally, a major hormonal shift occurs two days prior to the period starting. Something is jamming my nervous system around the period (L-5 area) and pulling L-5 out. The jam is causing cramps, and the hormonal shift is pushing to get through the nervous system. The Cottage body is adjusting to the situation by showing stress in its nervous system, and that's why it needed the one essence. From now on, I'm to check to see if L-5 is out two days before my periods begin. This won't be hard because my glow begins building two days before I start, and the men can tell me when the glow first appears. If L-5 is out, I'm to adjust it. At the same time, I'm to test for essences. This will tell me what is causing the "short" in the nervous system.

Regarding the coming change/shift: My new glitches are just the beginning symptoms. No special preparation is needed, and she and I will be able to make the necessary adjustments when the need arises.

Once again, she checked the SMP by holding my CSF pulses through the transfer to the Cottage. I started with strong Perelandra pulses, then the transfer pulses were imperceptible. They didn't pick up again until I was in the lagoon looking at the rocks. She felt my process had smoothed out quite a bit over these many months and was probably facilitated as much as possible. In order to do the shift, there is a tremendous collection of energy and focus just prior to the "blast-off." The blast-off is where there's a protein drain. Also, she says it's clear it's more challenging on me to get to the Cottage than leaving the Cottage for Perelandra.

At the Cottage. Max stayed to help decorate the tree. They were all concerned about my CSF pulses and the lift-off cost, but I reminded them that over the fifteen months that I've been doing this, I've only strengthened. In fact, I've gotten stronger all around. I've not weakened or deteriorated in any way. They admitted they understood the shift was not damaging to me, just taxing. For me, the knowledge of the lift-off cost brings home more clearly what I'm doing, and this makes me feel a little vulnerable. Perhaps I'm humbled by it all.

The tree is lovely. It's over seven feet tall and has been *carefully* decorated. Max half-complained about how "damn picky" they all were about the decoration placements. Since I'm doing the solstice table by myself, I was only allowed to watch and advise.

December 21 — Yellow

At Perelandra. Another day of focus just to get through it all. I put together the Life Table, which fell together easily. Around 3 o'clock I called David to tell him I was ready to shift the Life Table. We decided it would go in the same spot as last year. I set up the coning, and, when it was time to do the shift, I felt the coning intensify. I held my focus on the table, and again it shifted as a whole. The others watched it come in at the other end. This time, the job of transferring the table left me a bit drained. I could feel it as soon as the shift was completed. I sat in front of the table at Perelandra for about twenty minutes while my energy restored.

At the Cottage. I received the insight to draw the Tarot cards tonight and have them sitting on both tables for the moment of the solstice (5:30 A.M.). The men decided they would light the table candle at 5:30 and leave it lit the entire day.

I opened a coning and got my instructions: draw three cards from the Major Arcana. Shuffle the cards after each draw, cut them and then pick the card on top in my right hand. The first card: Hanging Man. Second card: Reverser. Third card: Way-Shower. Then I was instructed to set up the coning so that it created an energy vortex around the Life Table for the entire solstice day. As each of us come to the table throughout the day, we will move into the coning and open to the information that each needs to have from the three Tarot cards.

> *Hanging Man:* The Hanging Man is the Redeemer.
> The dilemma expressed by the Hanged Man of the older Tarot is being resolved in a new way. The Hanged Man was helpless. A rope noosed his right ankle and, being hung upside down, he could physically do nothing to extricate himself from his seeming plight. He needed an outside agent to cut him loose or he was doomed.
> The Hanging Man is also in a dilemma: he is hanging

others. As the Hanged Man was trapped physically, he is trapped morally, and he is weighted down by the two figures dangling from his outspread arms. His sole salvation is by redemption, an enormous feat, involving the entire seeming outer world.

The Hanging Man represents the Christ state. This involves the balancing of all opposites by permitting all to flow through him. To do so, he stands on man's ultimate creations. These structures signify man's highest aspirations and man's digging into the depths, the dredging of the unconscious. He does not touch the earth directly; he is balanced precariously upon the dual realm of ideas and ethics.

The Hanging Man's body forms the five-pointed star—perfected man. He is inspired despite his dilemma. He is aware of a different—or cosmic—order, in which higher laws are involved. The Hanging Man stands not only as a balancer but as a bridge, a mediator, and by this very token a sacrifice. The redemption lies in the effort to bridge, reconcile and bring together the seeming opposites.

He knows infinite consciousness and infinite unconsciousness simultaneously, yet he cannot move forward until the male and female sides of his own projection are going in the same direction, no longer divided, but in Unity. Unity alone produces redemption.

The Hanging Man is reversing the polarities in order to achieve unity.

He awaits his place in the heavens, but he knows he shall never attain it until every living entity is redeemed. Redemption is a universal act. His responsibility is stupendous but self-ordained.

Compassion might be termed the essential nature of the Hanging Man.

And his animal nature is in line.

He is one who, through self-salvation, has arrived at the state of redeeming all those around him—a tremendous responsibility as demonstrated by the Book of the Hanging Man.

But the responsibility is first of all to Self—for only thus can universal redemption be accomplished.

The Reverser: The androgynous figure of the Reverser, formerly Temperance, is at once the simplest and most meaningful

Book in the entire Tarot projected by the Nameless One.

The Reverser stands upon the ground but the landscape is of no importance except to indicate that the figure is upon the earth, not in the sky.

He is the son who has become his own father and mother, and he is also the Sun.

The figure of the Reverser represents a birth. It is a birth of a new consciousness. This new consciousness depends upon the correct channeling of flow.

The Reverser is the awakened One who has heard the cock's crowing.

From the left hand of the Reverser descends the stream of fire. The water, received in the right hand, is channeled through the Reverser's body and thus is transmuted to the descending stream of fire in the left hand. This says that the Reverser has become the downpouring cup of light or fire, the Holy Grail, the essence, the elixir.

The fire is purification, initiation and the purified fire of the heart.

The fire that descends as a flow from the left hand of the Reverser is, however, not the mortal fire of earthly burning. It is the electric fire that resulted from the drinking of the cup of fire of the Deliverer which transformed the human heart into the shimmering heart of the Speaker.

With the Reverser, the fire descends to earth as a constant sacred stream. This fire is the nameless, indescribable elixir. It is the Divine. No words exist for this state. It can only be experienced by those who have come to it.

The Reverser correctly channels flow.

The Reverser is the converter. Even as the flow of water can be harnessed to produce electricity, thus functions the Reverser.

The Reverser, above all, is a statement of the coming uniting of principles of the One in Man, or the Self, with the One Being: or God.

It is the birth of the Divine.

The Way-Shower: The Way-Shower announces a breakthrough. True vision is its essential message now—Singleness of Purpose, to enlighten by letting the flow of blessings rain down. The Ancient One is directly participating, guiding mankind into a new realization and dimension. He opens the way to a promised land—the Completed Man that is to flower in the many during this coming cycle.

The letter G, which is represented here, states that the Center of the Self has been found and from that center, like an arrow, Singleness of Purpose shoots forth.

The Way-Shower Book is a golden book—at once a promise, a fulfillment of a hope, and the statement of a breakthrough in consciousness. That which is above pours down, golden, upon that which is below. The way is showering; and the way is being shown.

Now the eyes of the Star are directed toward the earth, flooding it with light. Soon the sleeping city will awake. It will hear the heralding of the cock.

At Perelandra. Northern Virginia was hit with a terrible ice storm, and Clarence couldn't get home tonight.

December 22 — Ivory

At the Cottage. I set my alarm for 5:15 A.M. to get ready for the solstice. I felt everything had been done last night to prepare for the moment, so all I had to do was open the coning and stay awake. Not long after 5:30, I fell back to sleep.

We had a family dinner at Nino's to celebrate the day.

December 23 — Burgundy

JAMFD

December 24 — Yellow

At Perelandra. The wind chill factor dropped the temperature to 35 degrees below zero. The solar heating in the cabin kept the place absolutely toasty. I spent the day inside catching up on my notes.

At the Cottage. I took a long nap when I got home. I seem to be sleeping more lately. When I went downstairs, John greeted me! He's returned for the holidays.

December 25

A day of juggling between Perelandra and the Cottage to make sure I covered Christmas on both levels. It takes a little focus, but I managed to pull it off. The men put no demands on me.

December 26 — Yellow

I had a dream about having a baby, a daughter. I feel something has been born in me and that I'm in the process of change right now. Also, the essences indicate something is changing.

December 27

Seamus and the band will be giving a benefit concert for the children's wing of the hospital on Friday. (I didn't even know there was a hospital.) We're all invited. He needs an extra percussionist for the concert, and Butch has agreed to take on the challenge. He's gone into a crash course with Seamus to learn the music, and his photographic memory is serving him well. The challenge has put quite a sparkle in his eyes. David tells me Butch does this kind of thing every once in a while—takes on something completely new for the challenge. I admire his courage to just stir things up for the sake of stirring.

December 28 — Burgundy

I made a decision about Feldenkrais. I am not going to be able to work directly with my teacher on the two-body business. She simply doesn't want to deal with my situation and seems most pleased to be out of the picture. So I will be working around her.

December 29 — Gold

We had a discussion about my wallpaper friend. She and her husband have been insulting to me since their return this fall. I think there's a good possibility they both think I'm insane. The Cottage men feel that, at the very least, the two have been thoughtless and rude. Lately she has tried to shoot me down whenever I've brought up some new thing I've discovered as a result of my Cottage work. She doesn't seem to have a sense of celebration about my life.

December 30 — Yellow

Butch left early to work all day with Seamus on the music for tonight. Nervousness is beginning to settle around him.

The concert was packed with over 3,000 people. An amazing evening. Afterwards, Butch was most pleased with himself, but announced he doesn't want to do this again. It was too much pressure.

December 31 — Gold

I woke up sick as a dog at Perelandra *and* the Cottage: terrible headache, stomach turning, muscles hurting, body cold. I sat in the lagoon for awhile and called Hyperithon from there. He told me to just move through it with essences. There was nothing special I needed to do. I went back to my room and started the essence testing. After a bit, I fell asleep for about an hour and a half. When I woke up, I had no symptoms! I felt weak, but okay—like I had the three-and-a-half-hour flu. By this time, the others had been alerted to the problem and David had called Hyperithon, as well. Apparently, this is part of my change process. I'm ahead of schedule on this, as usual, and it has caught everyone off guard. Again, I'm thrilled.

The question was whether or not I could get through this enough to be able to accompany Clarence tonight to dinner at a fancy restaurant with friends. He was really looking forward to this evening. I got a chance to tell him about the problem this afternoon. He was supportive and said that if I didn't feel up to it, we wouldn't go.

My strength built throughout the day. I stayed at the Cottage on the couch in front of the fire, taking naps about every hour or so. By 5 o'clock I felt like a new person. I left for Perelandra and attended the dinner with Clarence. And, what a dinner! I kept my menu.

- First course: A caviar tasting of fresh Iranian Beluga, Sevruga and American Salmon Roe (not my favorite course)

- Second course: Gravlax of local Rainbow trout with mustard dill sauce

- Third course: fresh black truffle soup with shiitake mushrooms

- Fourth course: Salade Tiede with fresh foie gras, smoked duck breast and black-eyed peas

- Fifth course: Champagne sherbet with Chambord

- Sixth course and the entree: Rosettes of lamb tenderloin, Sauce Choron and french beans with almonds

- Seventh course: cheeses

- Eight course: Your choice of dessert—white chocolate mousse; Chocolate-pecan grapefruit tart; fresh New Zealand raspberries with Crème Anglaise; gateau de deux chocolats glacé or white chocolate ice cream with hot, dark chocolate sauce. [I had the raspberries with Crème Anglaise.]

- Ninth course: Tuiles des Amandes

- To toast the New Year: A glass of champagne and framboise

I made it through the entire meal, and I didn't feel like throwing up once.

1984

January 1 — Gold

At Perelandra. I received a call from Dottie (my mother) wishing us a happy new year. She sounded sluggish on the phone, but I think she was sober.

At the Cottage. Talking about the phone call from Dottie led the men to ask me if I didn't drink because of what alcohol did to her. My reasons for not drinking are complex. Early on, her alcoholism certainly played a part in my decision not to drink. I didn't want to risk falling apart by trying to escape in booze. But at this point in my life, this isn't my reason. I have clear, stable feelings about myself—my direction, happiness and work. These are strong feelings, and alcohol is just not part of that reality. The men told me that they consider alcohol to be something they participate in with a "light touch." I have to admit that, despite all the celebrating we do, I have not seen any of them drink more than two glasses of champagne.

January 2 — Brown

A big golf day for John, Seamus, Max, Tex and David. Seamus showed off his new clubs. It looks like he's planning to get serious about the game. I think he truly enjoys being with this bunch of men.

At Perelandra. I moved my office into my old room at the house. Everything fits better in the larger room. Clarence built shelving in the closet for extra storage. The office has a nice feeling to it now.

January 3 — Ivory

At Perelandra. The Feldenkrais class started a half-hour late because the teacher decided to wait for people who never showed up. I had to leave on time because of an appointment with the chiropractor. This resulted in my leaving without the teacher demonstrating a move on me that she had showed all the others. She was clearly frustrated at my not being able to stay longer, and I was totally pissed at her.

When I got to the chiropractor's, I warned her I was fighting mad.

This is the first time I've gotten checked out by the chiropractor right after a Feldenkrais class. She's been wanting to see the effects of Feldenkrais on my structural alignment for some time now.

Perelandra body: All four points of the pelvis were out, and the sacrum was tilted and stuck. My CSF pulses were very light. I had a B-vitamin deficiency, which she straightened out by giving me one B-supplement tablet right away. Also, C-7 was out. She adjusted the pelvis and sacrum, and immediately the cranials misaligned. I had been holding their position against the pelvis/sacrum problem and, once adjusted, the cranials "relaxed" and popped out.

Cottage body: She monitored my CSF pulses during the split process. Again I started out with a medium, steady rhythm at Perelandra that immediately dropped to nothing during the split, then began to pick up again and get strong when I looked at the rocks in the lagoon. The Perelandra pelvis went out slightly during the split process, so she adjusted it. The CB alignment was fine, and the endocrine glands, CSF pulses and nutrition were all strong. But I did need two essences.

The results of her testing showed that the body stress at Perelandra and the essences needed at the Cottage are mostly linked to the problems I've been having with my wallpaper friend. I've been dealing with her personal pressures on me ever since her return in October. This, combined with the issues I've been having with the Feldenkrais teacher and the clash between the direction of the classes and my situation, has caused some real problems. The PB is taking the brunt of the physical stress, and the CB is feeling the emotional fallout that is resulting in the need for essences there. My chiropractor put her foot down and said I must deal with the situation as soon as possible. I can no longer let this ride. In short, my body can't handle the stress any longer, and I must say "enough" to my wallpaper friend, and I must decide what I want to do about Feldenkrais. I'm on an essence solution up to and just after the talk with my friend. ·

While I was at the Cottage, I could tell that both David and Max were deeply concerned about me. I asked Max to have dinner with us. I wanted to test him for essences to make sure he wasn't being affected by all this. And I'm sure he agreed to join us for dinner so that he'd have a chance to check on me and make sure I wasn't getting hit any harder by the situation.

As soon as I got back to Perelandra, I called my wallpaper friend and made an appointment to see her. Unfortunately, we can't get together sooner than Thursday. So Thursday it is.

At the Cottage. By the time I got home, the men knew about the problem I was having with my wallpaper friend. I tested everyone for essences, and they all needed Rescue Remedy. I couldn't help but feel the support they were giving me—as if their need for Rescue Remedy was a compliment.

January 4 — Brown

At Perelandra. I "rejoined" the Life Table at Perelandra and took it down. As I worked, I thought about what I was going to say to my friend on Thursday.

We have overnight guests who arrived this afternoon: mother, father and nine-month-old baby. The baby is beautiful, happy and extremely goodnatured, which was really lucky because she kept vomiting all the time. If she had been cranky to boot, the situation would have been tough. The parents explained that her allergies have been acting up since they've been on the trip. Our dogs were in seventh heaven. With her vomiting all over the place, they think the baby is a crawling food factory. We quickly learned not to jump into action when she threw up, and let the dogs have first crack at it. This left us little to deal with, and I think the baby relaxed more since she felt she was useful (at least to the dogs) and not an inconvenience to the adults. On a whole, the guests have given me a good break from my wallpaper-friend problems.

At the Cottage. John has decided to stay for an additional week to continue working on a project.

January 5 — Gold

I awoke tense and preoccupied about my talk with my friend. David says I have much more tolerance and patience in these matters than he would have. But he supports my effort to confront her and still attempt to keep the friendship.

At Perelandra. Had breakfast with our guest. The baby threw up one more time, thus endearing her to the dogs forever. Once they got on the road, I left to see my wallpaper friend.

We talked for two and a half hours. She seemed to be upset about something, so I let her talk first. Once she stopped, then I began. I told her that she has treated me strangely since her return in October. She agreed and said it may not be me causing the problems. It may be the pressures in her own life. I explained my position fully and told her she had to back off. I had enough pressure without being her punching bag.

She said she understood my loyalty was to the Cottage. When I asked her straight out if she considered me insane, she responded no. She said I was traveling down a life road that she recognized as existing, but she has made the decision not to travel herself. She knows this road exists, but she doesn't understand it and questions if I might be moving too quickly. I told her that she can't compare my movement on this road with her life experience. The two are too different, and it's like trying to compare the proverbial apples and oranges. I feel my movement is the right pace for me, in light of what I'm doing.

I talked about her lack of celebration around the achievements and joys of my life and her seeming need to shoot everything down. As an example of what I was talking about, I used her reaction when I gave her a gift copy of *Behaving*.

She said she would try to be "less careless" with me. I told her I would try to immediately point out when I felt she was coming at me and shooting me down.

When we parted, I felt the friendship was still intact. I had used as much care as possible to get my points across. She said she had not felt I attacked her. I said everything I wanted, and I left feeling much stronger about my own position and direction.

At the Cottage. Returned drained and exhausted, so I immediately took a long nap.

When I told them about the conversation, they said they felt it went much better than they thought possible. They also said I looked clear and relaxed.

January 6 — Ivory

JAMFD

January 7 — Dusty Rose

At Perelandra. Did not feel well, like I was fighting the flu. I had head pain, body chills and no appetite. Despite this, I got the hit to do the 1984 moon rhythm calendar for the garden. The process was effortless, and I was glad to have my mind focused on something. I had to split the calendar to the Cottage. They like to keep track of the Perelandra rhythms throughout the growing season.

At the Cottage. Returned not feeling well. First I took a nap, and then I checked essences. It looks like I'm still processing the exchange with the wallpaper friend. A lot of release and repair essences were needed.

Max joined us for dinner. I could tell he wanted to make sure I was alright—I didn't tell him about the essences I tested for earlier. We had an enjoyable evening by the fire, and we convinced Max to spend the night. Frankly, I thought he looked quite tired and wondered if his sacrum needed pumping again. I decided I'd wait and let the chiropractor check this Tuesday.

Max has bought the skating rink. David talked him into buying it and putting the ideas he's had all these years for better skating conditions into effect. This is what's helped him get through the retirement crisis, and it's also why he's been so interested in learning how to "listen to ice intelligences" these past few months. Recently he's been busy overseeing the renovations, and this is what's tiring him.

January 8 — Ivory

At Perelandra. A day of football—which I broadcast home to David.

At the Cottage. When I got home, I found David quiet. At first I passed it off as a result of the "tedious work" he had been doing in the office while he listened to football. However, as we talked about the games, it came to me—he saw the eyes in the concentration camps again. He was still reluctant to talk about it, but this time he was more willing to describe the pain he felt. It always happens without warning. I suggested that I test him for essences, especially for his reaction when he sees the eyes. He tested for a strong solution of four essences, and he's to take a dropperful after each episode. As soon as he took the solution, his whole face lightened.

After dinner, we got into a discussion about family homes. It's clear that, even after death, David's family home is still the one in Abilene, and he still has a sense of roots there. I, on the other hand, have no family home. The irony of this wasn't lost on me. He's "dead and gone," yet he still has a family home on the Perelandra level. I am alive and well there, and I have none. Reality turns inside out again.

January 9 — Gold

At Perelandra. I drove to Madison, Virginia, to buy a bird bath heater. While at the store, I picked up a mug for Clarence and a cotton woven rug that had perfect colors for the cabin. The rug was made in the Shenandoah Valley in Virginia by the Mennonites.

I took our dog Elsa with me on the trip. I've felt close to her lately. She loves the cabin and spends much time with me there. I sometimes talk to her about the Cottage and tell her how much I'd like it if she came there after she is finished at Perelandra—if that's what she wants, of course. The men feel she should return a few times and go for walks with us so she'll have better information for making her decision! It wouldn't surprise me if both our dogs came to the Cottage once they leave Perelandra. I've felt for some time now that this could happen, but I didn't want to think about it too much, in case it was just wishful thinking on my part. I'd rather have the surprise than the disappointment.

At the Cottage. I received a gift from everyone: a football. They had to have it "imported" in from the United States (the U.S. on the Cottage level). I got my first lesson on how to throw the thing. It's going to take me a while to get used to the feel of it.

January 10 — Heather Green

At Perelandra. I'm still unclear about what to do about the Feldenkrais situation. Just stopping the classes and private lessons doesn't feel like the thing to do. So I've decided to continue them until I get some more clarity on the matter. I arrived early for today's Feldenkrais class and insisted that the teacher do the movement for me that I missed last week because I had to leave on time. It took less than five minutes, and I was happy. I felt I finally got my full lesson from last week.

For the three of us who were present last week, the teacher gave us a "practitioner" lesson on working with another person more effectively when we are paired off in class. It was an excellent lesson for me. In essence, we were taught to support the person's direction, letting them initiate the movement. Their body chooses the direction it needs to go in. Once the direction is established, the one assisting suggests (through the hands) options to the movement. It is important never to force the body in what we think is the "correct" direction. We had a dramatic example of this. The teacher was trying to get one woman to move her head in a specific way while lying down. The woman automatically arched her upper back away from the floor, and she couldn't even begin to move her upper back and neck. I held her upper back *up*, where it wanted to be. Then the teacher moved her through the movement, which she could now begin to do. Once I released her back, it flattened to the floor more. So it is important to let the body go where it wants, then give options to ease the body out of the old patterns. I felt the effectiveness of this sensitivity clearly while I worked with my partner.

Chiropractor appointment. Perelandra body: *No adjustments!* No essences were needed and my nutrition is fine.

Cottage body: During the split, the Perelandra pelvis went slightly out. She questioned what was going on and found out the pelvis was slightly out at Perelandra to begin with, but it didn't show up during the testing because it was so slight. The split pulled it out further. The pelvis goes out during the split whenever I'm fatigued. It goes back in while I look at the rocks and adjust to the Cottage. Consequently, no specific adjustments are needed. I just have to give it the time it needs. (She thinks around fifteen minutes of adjusting to the Cottage is all that's needed.) Cottage testing: all okay!

- My period is due in two days and she tested that L-5 is fine. No extra supplements or adjustments were needed. The chiropractor was amazed at this. (Usually women need supplements and/or adjustments near the time of their periods.) We both feel this is the result of my new attitude about my period, thanks to the Cottage.

- She asked if we could get actual CSF pulse readings through me for the men at the Cottage, but we can only get their effect on *my* CSF pulses. The CSF is not part of the nervous system. It is a simple fluid/pump system and can't be surrogated.

- Can I use visualization to "prime" my sacrum at Perelandra? (I need to be able to do this alone.) Yes.

- Regarding my wallpaper friend: The situation is cleared out for now. But she will continue, at times, to be a problem. I must keep my direction straight. She has no understanding of what I'm doing.

Scanning Max: His sacrum needs priming. I'll do this when I get home tonight, then check him for essences.

Scanning John: This is the first time he's been tested, so she gave him a regular checkup. He checked out fine. We then asked some questions: Do my adjustments on John affect him on the Earth level? Yes. Has his golf swing on Earth improved? Yes. Are these adjustments helping him prepare for his death transition? Yes. Is his attitude and understanding about reality beginning to change on the Earth level, and are the adjustments facilitating this process? Yes. Is he (on the Earth level) conscious of these changes? Yes, but he doesn't understand their origin.

The chiropractor said she could feel a definite difference while testing John, and she could tell his situation at the Cottage is different from the others, including me.

At the Cottage. Everyone is quite relieved I'm back on track. I talked to John right away because it occurred to me on the way back to Perelandra that this was the first time he had experienced my "buzzing in and out" of the Cottage. He assured me he was fine with this and that David had already prepared him this morning. He was pleased to be "allowed" to participate in all of this.

I primed Max's sacrum and checked to make sure the pumping was fine. Then he turned over on his back for me to test him for essences, but I couldn't get a clear essence test. I got the insight that the sacrum situation returned when he turned over. I needed to place my right hand on the sacrum and my left hand under his neck and hold them in position while the sacrum equalized and adjusted. After about one minute, I felt heat in my left hand—Max felt it too. I held my hand in place, and after a few more minutes, Max released a buildup of energy that he had been holding in the sacrum area. This was what was interfering with the sacrum swing. I continued moving the energy out through my hands and then moved it on out of the Cottage and released it to the next appropriate level. As I continued holding his sacrum and neck, the heat equalized under both hands. I held him a little longer just to make sure everything had stabilized, then I checked him again for essences. This time the test was clear.

The essences centered around trusting women. Before I worked on him, he had said he thinks he's had this sacrum problem since he was about thirty-five, when he stopped skating and began coaching. That's how he remembers the timing. But this is also around the time of his divorce, and I'll bet he closed down because of that. Apparently, now it's time to open up again and begin trusting. When I showed Max the definitions of the essences, I saw that he understood what this was about. He gave me a knowing look. Ah yes, Max.

Max spent the night with us again.

January 11 — Apricot

I got a football lesson from David and John before I left this morning. I'm getting better. David thinks I'd be a better receiver than quarterback.

At Perelandra. Got hit with ice and snow last night, so I didn't have my private Feldenkrais lesson. What was particularly nice was my calm about this situation. I didn't feel like I was missing anything. I'm detaching. It was a good feeling.

January 12 — Yellow

I kidded David by asking why—with his love of soil and gardening, and his power—he doesn't take over or attempt to take over the Cottage gardening and land plans. He's been deferring all these decisions to me. He surprised me with a lengthy answer. For over a year now, he has watched me deeply affect, move and change all of them, and he has experienced changes in the Cottage itself. Yet I've not consciously set out to do anything. Rather, my power is in my ability to be, and its source is deep within me. When I arrived, he suspected such power in me, but assumed I would display it in ways similar to the men. When he first met me, I was so quiet about everything, he wondered where the power was. Hyperithon had already warned them to "hold on to their socks." But my quietness didn't jibe with this goodnatured warning. So he decided to sit back and watch me, and that's when he saw the source of my power. He saw the impact I was having on everyone and everything just by my being—and he has learned. He knows I see and approach things differently. If he tried to take over, he would learn nothing and see nothing differently. His love of land is too great to bypass this opportunity. This is my arena, and he's not going to take it over—that would be foolish.

When he finished, I just looked at him. Here I thought I had goodnaturedly pushed him into a corner, and I only succeeded in pushing myself into a corner. I tried to think of some witty comment, but I couldn't. So I said "thank you," and shut up.

At Perelandra. Worked in the cabin. The temperature outside was in the mid-twenties. The birds were especially happy about their heated water supply.

January 13 — Gold

At Perelandra. Met my wallpaper friend in town for lunch. I listened to her talk about her life and said nothing about the Cottage or my life. I was quite relaxed about this.

I have had an experience at Perelandra several times now. I see myself alone with a woman. Usually we're outside shaking out small throw rugs. While we're talking, she tells me something she's waited many years to say to someone. It's a secret thought she has held, and she has needed to say it to another woman. After she tells me—the content of which I never get during the experience—I see the two of us laughing hysterically. I usually end up sitting on the ground holding my sides. I can't believe she has said this to me. And then the scene fades away.

At the Cottage. I told the men about my experience, and they are most intrigued. They won't let me pass it off as just fantasy.

January 14 — Ivory

At Perelandra. Clarence had to spend the night in a motel last night because of another ice storm. He returned to Perelandra around noon today, and he spent the afternoon installing a phone at the cabin.

At the Cottage. I had a long talk with John. He's getting ready to leave soon, and we have not had much time together. We talked about his frustration about his "two lives" being so separate. I urged him to let the two lives come together organically, let the growth and understanding occur in timing, and not try to blast through and force them together. The opening is going to have to come from within his Earth life. His Cottage life will only be able to support the opening. He asked my opinion of how best to initiate the opening, and I suggested that he begin to listen to his "poet side"—then act on what he hears, no matter how silly or illogical it may seem at the time. I feel John's poet side is the key to his opening right now. I also suggested that he respond to this poet voice *privately* for awhile in order to protect himself from others' insensitivities during this vulnerable time. He laughed and said, "I know what you mean."

He admitted he's having a little trouble breaking away from the Cottage this time. He feels the strong, positive effects of the Cottage stability and safety.

January 15 — Gold

JAMFD

January 16 — Gold

John left after breakfast. He didn't sneak off this time and actually gave us a chance to say goodbye.

I returned to the Cottage in late afternoon so that I could take a nap. [I can't sleep at Perelandra unless the Cottage body is activated in form and sleeping as well.] I ended up having a long nap and a vivid dream. In it, I told Peter Caddy about the Cottage, its work and David. I awoke from the dream feeling just as tired as before because of the effort I put out to tell Peter what was going on.

At dinner I told everyone about the dream, and David asked me to describe my relationship with Peter Caddy. I explained that I had seen little of Peter when I was at Findhorn, but we had reconnected during his numerous trips to the United States, and from this we forged a friendship.

January 17 — Brown

I had a dream about where the Cottage is located. From Perelandra, the Cottage is in an inward direction, not outward from Perelandra. Inward is also the direction of eternity, and the Cottage is in the direction of eternity. But then the dream reversed on me. I saw myself looking into the center of a circle at a hard, small center core. This core was physicality. When I turned my focus away from the core and literally turned around to look outward from the circle, I saw eternity.

At breakfast I told the others about the dream. They informed me I was on the right track. But when I asked them which dynamic was "the right track," since I seemed to have two opposite dynamics presented, they would only tell me to have patience. Blah.

January 18 — Dusty Rose

At Perelandra. My first real snowfall since moving into the cabin. It's beautiful. As the day progressed, I developed some pain in the right hip area. I tried to loosen the hip, but I realized I was dealing with a muscle injury caused by kicking the mulch pile yesterday to see how frozen it was. Stupid. Tested the essences and spent two hours on the floor working on relaxing the hip pain. I adjusted my pelvis, then I called the chiropractor to see if she could give me any further advice about what I could do for myself. She said the essence combination that I tested for makes sense to her, even though it is a most unusual combination for this situation. My healing process is more complex because of the two bodies. I should continue with the essences and check the pelvis several times throughout the day to make sure it holds its alignment. Then I'm to soak in a tub at Perelandra, and in the lagoon after I get home. If I'm not considerably better by tomorrow noon, this indicates more damage, and I'm to make an appointment to see her. We're both pleased at how I worked with this situation on my own.

She and I continued talking about the snow. She's been doing some cross-country skiing, and her description made something click in my head. Suddenly, I *knew* I wanted to cross-country ski. I had been wanting to do this for years, but always ended up waiting for others to say they wanted to do it with me. Now I'm going to break away from their indecisiveness and just do it myself.

When I left for the Cottage, I could tell the hip was definitely healing. By the time I got into bed at the Cottage, I felt like I had new hips!

January 19 — Ivory

I had a conversation with David after breakfast about consciousness. Out of the blue, I asked him where he took on consciousness. Without blinking an eye, he said, "Uranus." And that ended that discussion. I didn't know where else to go with it.

At Perelandra. Adjusted my pelvis again and tested for essences. Then I went for a walk in the snow, shoveled snow off the deck, fed the birds and thoroughly enjoyed my time outside. I laid down in the sun on a mat in the cabin and relaxed the hip again. The sun gave me a healing warmth. The hip is definitely improving.

At the Cottage. I took a nap and had another dream. It was a dream within a dream. In my dream's dream, I was "told" very clearly that animal death (meaning the death of the animal in man, his body) is the death of the ego.

At dinner I brought up the dream, and the men said the message was true if one understood ego. You don't become an entirely different person. Rather, you become an expansion of yourself. The "death of ego" is another way of saying the "benefit of death." The men are always referring to the benefit of death, something they have as part of their conscious experience and something that I have to look forward to experiencing. They're always saying that they understand something more than I do right now because they've had the benefit of death.

January 20 — Heather Green

At Perelandra. I drove to a mall and purchased cross-country ski equipment. I had a ball.

January 21 — Ivory

At Perelandra. I waxed my skis, following the instructions as best I could in the ski book I picked up yesterday. Then I took a deep breath, got the skis on and took off for a new adventure. I navigated the big field next to the garden three times. I must say it's an efficient way of traveling in the snow. It was quite cold, and Elsa and Jesse ran along protecting me from the neighbor's horses and cows. It was glorious. It didn't take long for me to find a rhythm. I don't know if I'm skiing correctly, but it felt good—and freeing. When I was finished, I felt like I had spent the day on the slopes! I returned to the cabin and checked the alignment of my pelvis again—it needed an adjustment.

At the Cottage. Regaled everyone with my big ski adventure.

January 22 — Brown

At Perelandra. "Hit the slopes" again. I'm much improved. I didn't fall nearly as often as yesterday. There's something magical about coming out of the cabin, hopping onto skis and hitting the open fields.

The Redskins lost the Super Bowl. It was a terrible game—so boring that David didn't want to continue listening to it. A game has to be pretty horrible for David to lose interest.

January 23 — Dusty Rose

I'm turning fanatical. I worked on ski movements in my head this morning. I feel like skiing has brought the Perelandra me closer to the Cottage me—like I'm integrating. All the ski talk is making some of the men restless to get outside. So they're playing more golf these days. They say the cold doesn't bother them, just the wind.

At Perelandra. Today I worked on executing turns without falling. The weather is warming and the snow is now old. Suddenly I'm aware of snow conditions. Now I must wait for new snow. The pelvis held well today—no adjustment needed.

At the Cottage. All of us had dinner together at Harry's. A good break for the men.

January 24 — Gold

JAMFD. Freezing rain and lousy road conditions allowed me to skip Feldenkrais.

January 25 — Heather Green

An important dream: I was in a classroom and part of the class. We were discussing nature and had been given the assignment to come up with new approaches to nature—to study, experiment and find new ways to work with it. I suggested that we just touch into nature's own intelligence. It would guide us in the new direction. My classmates' reaction was one of polite curiosity. Then we were divided into two groups. Each group was given a pumpkin. Our's was large and oval, with orange-green coloring and warts. I loved its homeliness. The others remarked that it was old. I looked at it, and thought, "No, it's young. They're not reading the pumpkin right."

We were given an assignment: What does this pumpkin say to us? The intellectuals in the group symbolized their own thoughts about the pumpkin by arranging things around it in a certain way. One by one, the students created a face of a $10 bill, with the pumpkin as the center of the bill.

I suggested that we were not hearing from the pumpkin. The others told me to open to it to see what I could get. I did just that. The pumpkin told me to bring forward six braids of specific colors that I was to get from the Native Americans in the group. Then I was to tie one specific color of ribbon on a finger of each of the remaining six members of the group. I was told that two of the ribbons represented the past: conscious and unconscious. Two represented the present: conscious and unconscious. And two represented the future: conscious and unconscious. I explained this to my six classmates. Then I got them to sway their bodies while looking at their own color. There was great power being transmitted to them from the color. Their hands began to move, and they gently wove their ribbons together. As they swayed to the other side, they wove the other way. In the end, they had formed a woven band of many colors. As they continued swaying, the band of weaving changed, and so did the colors.

The pumpkin said to me: This illustrates the natural law that nature automatically understands and works with. It fully recognizes the many levels of individuality, yet weaves them into one band of wholeness. Man doesn't know, understand or act within this law at all. And he must.

At breakfast Tex said he's been around many pumpkins in his life, but none ever said anything like that to him! In all, they felt like the imagery of the dream fit right into their feelings about the dynamic of teamwork.

January 26 — Gold

At Perelandra. Played "telephone tag" with David today. I tried to call him, but realized he was having lunch with Hyperithon at the time. So I pulled back. Hyperithon then told David I was trying to call. (He *is* dangerous!) David called me right back. This is nuts.

Clarence and I had a long talk in front of the woodstove at the cabin. He told me that as he's been watching my growth and choice of directions, he's started to see me as an individual rather than just a partner. He wonders what I think about these days.

January 27 — Ivory

I've been sensing a change around my translation process, so I followed instinct and I did my first coning session from the Cottage. It was a trial run to see if I could do this from the Cottage. At first I experienced spaciness and nausea. I received a "fine-tuning" adjustment during the session and felt a shift in my head. It seemed like the parietal bones at the top of my head opened wider. The session also worked best when David was in the room with me and functioning as the anchor—a job he seems eager to perform. It was awkward translating the session in writing, so I thought I'd try oral translation next time. Afterwards, David suggested I use a dictaphone. He also thinks it will be easier on me if I translate simultaneously into two dictaphones—one at the Cottage and the other at Perelandra. This way, I won't have to unnecessarily drain myself switching tapes and transcripts between levels.

It is easier to split something from Perelandra to the Cottage than from the Cottage to Perelandra. After experimenting with this, my perception is that the difference is the result of the mindset of the surrounding general population on the level that is receiving an object. If the general perception is that these kinds of things happen, the object is "received." It's as if it is moving into friendly territory. If the general population basically does not believe such things can happen, an abrasive-like layer forms that inhibits the transfer. So we're going to try to translate simultaneously so that I won't have to deal with the Perelandra-level abrasion.

January 28 — Gold

I left the purchase of the dictaphone at the Cottage in Butch's capable hands. At Perelandra, Clarence and I picked out a machine of excellent quality. It's perfect for my needs.

January 29 — Dusty Rose

At Perelandra. A friend of mine had suggested I call a woman about ideas on distributing *Behaving*. After talking to this woman today, I felt strongly that, for now, I am to develop my own book network and distribute the book directly. I am not to try to "sell" the book to distributors. I feel this direction (distributing directly) will pay off in the future and be useful for any future publications. (Did I say that?)

At the Cottage. I talked over my thinking with them, explaining my feelings and the deep sense that I am to move *Behaving* through a different labyrinth. They see nothing wrong with my approach, saying that the energy of the book is true, therefore it will move and I don't have to push it along.

Max joined us for dinner.

January 30 — Heather Green

JAMFD

January 31 — Gold

At Perelandra. I had an appointment with the chiropractor. I gave her a gift, a baby food blender that she had been looking for. I told her it was the Holy Grail cleverly disguised as a baby food blender. (Her daughter will be pleased!) She's ordered adjustment wedges for me so that I can stop using pillows for pelvic adjustments.

Perelandra body: I needed a pelvic adjustment that was related to the parietal bones and the shift they took during the Cottage session.

I also needed a parietal adjustment because, after the Cottage session, the Perelandra parietals "jammed" into the exhale position. No new nutrition and no essences. Everything is holding well.

Cottage body: A-okay! The parietals took the session adjustment beautifully.

Her testing gave us the following information.

- The psoas at Perelandra is tightening due to the pelvic action and not a kidney problem. Feldenkrais will help this.

- I'm going through a fine-tuning process in the heads in both bodies called a "parietal spread." The shift during the Cottage session was physical, as well as higher. But the process is completed, and there is no need for further checks. Everything is in place. This fine-tuning will help the split transition. I've needed the input from the many adjustments I've gone through over the past year and a half before this parietal shift.

- On translation session days at the Cottage, I need an extra ninety grams of protein. When David functions as the anchor, he is also to have ninety grams of protein plus twice his daily intake of carbohydrates.

- Right now, I do not have any comprehension of the intensity of the area I am preparing to enter via my coning sessions. It is a big step, and it seems like it will involve getting to the heart of matters.

- Most important, my chocolate and coffee intake are not interfering with anything.

I left her office with an ominous feeling. Now what?

At the Cottage. The men explained that they have been told about the direction I'm heading in. We all left it at that. I'm sure I'll figure it out soon enough.

Max had dinner with us and spent the night.

February 1 — Gold

At Perelandra. I had lunch with my wallpaper friend. Her attitude toward me has changed. Perhaps our talk really did help.

February 2 — Ivory

It's *the* day—the day we begin this new series of translation sessions from the Cottage. David told me several times that I can refuse this step, that I can say no. He assured me it would be fine if I decide I want to hold off. I told him he had to be nuts. After all this fanfare, I can't imagine saying no. Besides, it feels right and I feel ready, despite my high nervous state.

After breakfast, I set up for the session from the Cottage with simultaneous translation into the machine at Perelandra. David, serving as my anchor, sat to my left. I opened the coning as instructed and asked to connect with the intelligence I was to translate. Immediately, I felt a *major* shift in energy, so I concentrated on the task of an oral translation of what I was receiving. The session lasted for two hours, and, when I was finished, I had an introduction to the consciousness I was working with. Its energy was different than anything I ever felt before—yet deep and loving, as well. However, I didn't feel the bubbly joy I so often feel when I'm working with nature or Hyperithon. When it was over, both David and I were drained. I also felt down, depressed—like I had not translated well. David said he didn't know what to say to me, except that I was wrong. He felt the translation went well and that the information was "good, exciting and worthwhile."

We all had a quick lunch together, then I left for Perelandra. Butch said he would transcribe the tape this afternoon.

At Perelandra. I ate something right away, then headed into town. I still wasn't happy about the quality of the work I had done, nor was I clear about what I thought that quality was.

At the Cottage. Returned with my low feelings intact, so I just took a long nap. I dreamed about flying angels doing precision drill practice over Perelandra. I also had an elaborate dream about a singing, dancing, technicolor advertisement for a new beer. Actually, it was an old beer packaged in a new can that had a new technique for sealing the seam. I consciously decided this dream was nuts, and it was time to wake up. When I did, I realized I was no longer depressed.

At dinner the men told me that Hyperithon had called this afternoon to give his congratulations for a job well done. (He was included in the coning.) I'm beginning to see that the session was not a failure. In fact, when I read Butch's transcript, it read much better than I had remembered the session going. I actually didn't recall much of the session except the bumpy or difficult parts, so when I pulled out of it, I had no clear memory of the session as a whole— only the rough spots. I decided I must do another one as soon as possible and get over my case of nerves. We agreed to another session on Monday.

I did not get any indication of a name from the consciousness during the session, so I've decided to make it male and call him "Igor."

February 3 and 4 — Brown, Ivory

JAMFD

February 5 — Yellow

At Perelandra. Got a phone call from my chiropractor, and we set a tentative date for our trip to the Gettysburg Battlefield: March 7.

At the Cottage. After dinner I talked to Tex and David about an anger that is building up again toward my wallpaper friend. I don't know where the anger is coming from because she's not doing anything specific that I can put my finger on. They listened intently to everything I said. When I asked them for their input, they agreed that the anger was building because I was bending over backwards to accommodate her and others. Rather than hold my own position about my life experiences, I apologize to others for it by accommodating their position. I feel my position might offend them. The men feel my efforts to understand others are commendable, but this gets me into trouble when I relinquish my position in the process. I never need to apologize for who I am or where I stand.

As they talked, I could feel the tension leave me for the first time in over a week. They must have hit the nail on the head. If I wasn't able to give myself permission to stand my ground, they were. I could feel my attitude begin to change, and I could clearly see how I had given up my position for the sake of another's feelings or comfort. When I saw the dynamics of what I was doing, it made sense that I would respond by getting angry.

February 6 — Apricot
I awoke feeling nervous about the Cottage session scheduled today. I decided I just needed to get back on that proverbial horse.

Mickey set us up for coffee this time. The session went much better—maybe the coffee made the difference. I got the name for the consciousness: not "Igor," but "Universal Light." This time I felt more confidence and agility in my oral translation. David ended the session after two hours, right about the time I was experiencing a preposition poop-out. (I was spinning around in my head in search of the right preposition—and not finding it.) I came out of this session exhilarated. I felt good about the process, and we both felt good about the information. We were starving again, so we went downstairs and starting shoving in protein. Butch took immediate custody of the tapes so that he could do the transcribing this afternoon. He's too efficient for words.

There's such a difference between the feeling while doing a written translation and an oral one. They are two totally different dynamics, and it is clear I'm more trained in and used to transcribing sessions in a written format.

At Perelandra. Met a friend for lunch and went shopping at a mall with her. Not a good move. I didn't feel comfortable until we sat down at the mall for coffee. David and I agree that reading trash murder mysteries at Perelandra on session days is better for me. Or, doing *physical* gardening work. Although the men voted the trash novel idea over the garden work.

February 7 — Heather Green
At Perelandra. Had difficulty keeping my focus this morning in the Feldenkrais class because I was so bored. This is unusual for me.

February 8 — Ivory
I'm feeling overwhelmed and stretched at Perelandra. It was triggered by a call from an acquaintance asking if she could visit all next week. Feeling pressure to be a gracious "nice guy," I agreed to it, even though the new translation work is taking a lot out of me, the garden information is pressing in on me, and the Cottage notes are still taking a lot of time. I feel I need help, but I don't know

where to turn to get it. The men are encouraging me to get help, but I'm to make sure it's the *right* help. Just talking to them about this lifted me out of the depression.

Max joined us for dinner and gave me a box he had been keeping for some time. It was filled with Katie's things—several of her skating dresses, a pair of her favorite training skates and her two Olympic gold medals. He felt I should have these things now. I gave the first gold medal she had received back to Max.

February 9 — Gold

At Perelandra. I had another visualization experience with the woman who has been trying to tell me something. She's been coming to me in my mind's eye every time I've shaken out my throw rugs at the cabin. It's always the same scene: We're shaking out our rugs together (usually she gives me precise instructions about how to shake them properly—it all has to do with the snap), and she tells me something that I can't hear, but I react to it in the vision by laughing. This afternoon, while I was shaking out my rugs, she appeared again in my mind's eye—and this time, I could hear her. She's David's mother, Ida—only now she calls herself Elizabeth. I finally got the secret she's been trying to tell me—why she named her *third* son (David) after her husband. It's an incredible secret she's been keeping all these years, and one I won't betray by recording it in the notes. It's a wonderful story, and I feel honored she's chosen me to share it with.

She links with me when I shake my rugs because it's the one thing we do that we have in common—and the rugs were made by the Mennonites from the Shenandoah area. She was raised a Mennonite, and her family's home was in the Shenandoah in Virginia.

At the Cottage. I said nothing about my experience with David's mother. I have to decide if it's appropriate to share it with them. What if she doesn't want him to know about the contact or the secret?

February 10 — Ivory

I awoke feeling that it was okay to talk to the men about Elizabeth, so I told them about it at breakfast. Of course, David immediately asked me to tell him why he was named after his father. I let him know she would have to tell me it was okay to tell him—I wasn't going to break her confidence. This whole experience has really struck me about how much our lives extend beyond death.

Suddenly it hit me that Elizabeth wanted me to tell David about his name. When I did, he had to laugh. But it quickly became clear that the information deeply touched him. He said it was like her to say so much in one succinct sentence. She always had that ability to nail it all down in few words. He insisted that I contact her again and continue developing my relationship with her.

Although it wasn't easy, we pulled ourselves together for another Cottage session. Actually, I felt it was good for me to come into a session feeling scattered just to see what I had to do to establish a good focus. I never have any idea what Universal Light has planned, so I had to take a little extra time today to settle down and focus. I think if I had known the topic beforehand, I would have something specific to set my focus on—but then I'd lose the surprise element.

The session was on Gettysburg and the work I'll be doing there on March 7. It was a long session that set up the new battle energy release information beautifully.

I left for Perelandra right after lunch.

At Perelandra. Felt great—solid and grounded. I ate chocolates, read a good trash novel and took a walk.

February 11 — Yellow

At Perelandra. For the first time, Clarence asked about my sessions at the Cottage. He has known they were going on because I told him about it when we bought the dictating machine. So I described who I'm working with (Universal Light) and gave him an idea of the kind of information he's giving me. Clarence showed a great deal of interest in the information and asked to read a transcript when I get a copy typed up at Perelandra.

I finished typing transcript #1.

February 12 — Apricot

After breakfast, Max and I got another football lesson from David. That got us talking about personal competition, and I admitted I had a tendency toward killer competition. Max added insult to injury by agreeing with me much too quickly. David said his competition has shifted since dying, and now he's pulled back from "fierce competition"—especially in his golf. These days he aims for personal quality and fun.

At Perelandra. Elizabeth joined me for another rug-shaking session. This time she showed me the differences in rug quality. She likes my kitchen rug because it shakes clean the best. She showed me how I can put more wrist action into my shaking and get more rug snapping. She has no use for my bath rug that is made of synthetic materials. I find it a bit strange to be getting rug lessons from Elizabeth Eisenhower.

I asked her, "Did you ever just want to fly away on your rugs?"

"Yes, often. To far-off lands."

I was a little surprised by her admission, yet I could tell she wasn't complaining about her life. She was just sharing another secret thought.

David is convinced that this is his mother, and that she's found a friend. He's pleased for her and for me, and he is supportive of what's happening between us. He urges me on. I'm feeling quite stretched by the experiences. Just as I'm becoming familiar and at ease with one level, another one opens to me.

At Perelandra. Our house guest arrived. She'll be spending five days.

February 13 — Heather Green

At Perelandra. Our house guest, who happens to be a lawyer, is a little nuts. She immediately hit me with her conspiracy theories. According to her, World War II was fought over drug trading, and Henry Kissinger bumped off some woman who frolicked in the nude with Reagan and both of them were wearing dog collars at the time. Our house guest told me it's all true because there are pictures published in *Hustler* magazine. (Now there's a bastion of accuracy and journalistic integrity.)

At the Cottage. I told them the story about World War II and the other stuff. They pronounced it all garbage and had no interest in seeing the *Hustler* pictures my house guest said she brought along as proof. They're a little concerned about me and this woman's effect on me.

February 14 — Gold

Valentine's Day.

At Perelandra. Zoo world. A friend I hadn't seen for a while stopped by to tell me her partner is threatening suicide and running around with a loaded rifle in the back of his truck. He's crazed that she wants to end the relationship. Then there's the house guest who has still more conspiracy theories.

At the Cottage. As soon as I walked in the door, I could feel the sanity and stability of the Cottage. Oddly enough, their day was also intense, and centered around insanity. There is truth in war, they say. And there is also insanity. Much of their work is to distinguish between the truth and the insanity. Some days they don't know what end is up, and today was one of those days. I told them that if they needed a "little breather," just visit Perelandra for a couple of days.

We went to The Pub tonight because it's Seamus's last performance before the band takes an R&R for the next four weeks.

February 15 — Ivory

At Perelandra. The house guest's visit is dragging on. I'm tired of the conspiracy crap and watching her wheels spin. I took her shopping as a diversion. The moral of this story is not to be so accommodating when someone calls and says they'd just love to come spend some time at Perelandra. We're not a resort hotel.

February 16 — Dusty Rose

At Perelandra. The house guest is developing a heavy, depressive energy around her. She's got herself in quite a hole with her conspiracy ideas, and it is all self-imposed. She's thirty-three, single, child-free, has a career with a good salary and basically has the whole world available to her. Yet she's deeply unhappy. I'd like her to be unhappy elsewhere.

A friend visited, and I felt she needed to hear about the Cottage, to hear about the options in life. Everything I said made sense to her, yet it was all new. I could see it freeing her to understand a broader reality. It was amazing to watch. She was genuinely pleased for me, for my happiness, and she made me feel good about having shared my Cottage experience with her.

Talking to her about these things and not talking to my house guest about them gave me a new sense of freedom, clarity and purpose about the Cottage information. I don't have to keep it from everyone, nor do I have to tell everyone.

At the Cottage. For the past few days, I haven't needed to take a nap when I got home. It seems like I've had to nap every afternoon for months, yet I had never taken naps prior to the Cottage impact. Perhaps things are really beginning to even out for me.

February 17 — Brown

At Perelandra. I helped my wallpaper friend this afternoon and ended up feeling pummeled by her new-found frenetic energy.

Arrived back at Perelandra to find our guest parked (uninvited) in my chair at the cabin watching the "birdies" play in the bird bath. I wonder if it's against the law to shoot a lousy house guest.

At the Cottage. We finally located Seamus. He's been sleeping with his phone unplugged for the past three days. He's coming tomorrow night for dinner.

February 18 — Ivory

At Perelandra. She must have heard me loading the rifle. The house guest from hell left. Had lunch in town with Clarence to celebrate: We-Survived-the-Week. We agree that she was most unpleasant and amazingly thoughtless.

I worked in my office on the transcripts while Clarence gave the house a good cleaning. He even washed the dogs.

I'm getting that strong feeling that spring is coming and it's time for me to move outside again.

At the Cottage. No nap again. Max and Seamus joined us for dinner, and they both spent the night.

February 19 — Apricot

I did an Energy Cleansing Process for Perelandra while I was at the Cottage. It was a strong, clear process, and when I was finished, I could see light around all the different areas at Perelandra. The cabin had gold light, the garden green, the shed white, the sanctuary gold, the house white and the woods white. For the first time, I felt the need to ground myself after the process. I visualized myself walking down ten steps. When I stepped onto the ground (or when I thought I was going to step on the ground), I stepped out on ice instead and began to skate joyously. I'm not sure if this qualifies as full grounding!

At Perelandra. Typed a good copy of transcript #2 and started a Universal Light notebook for storing all this information.

At the Cottage. I arrived home feeling queasy; I had head pain and a fever. I did an essence test and got four intense essences, including Rescue Remedy. I have no idea what's happening now, and I decided not to think about it.

I'm feeling a deep sense of growth, stretch and development. It's a wonderful, exciting, awesome time for me—even scary. I announced to the men tonight that I'm much too young for all of this. They agreed.

February 20 — Gold

At Perelandra. It was unseasonably warm, and I really felt it was time to move. I cleaned and set up the cold frames in the garden, then organized the shed a bit.

February 21 — Gold

I had a great private Feldenkrais lesson. I "discovered" the inside "loop" of the pelvis. As soon as it was included in my sitting position, my whole torso relaxed into the sitting alignment. I now feel the pelvic shelf. My teacher and I suspect that my faulty alignment dates back to when Isadore taught me how to sit in a saddle, when all he really had in mind was the look he wanted. He didn't know what I was doing wrong to get that look. The fears I had about him and riding made me contract the inner pelvic area, and I just continued holding the area. This misaligned my entire structure slightly. When I left today, my legs were in a new alignment and moving more freely, my back and ribs had relaxed, and the pressure was off my neck and head.

February 22 — Ivory

It was a Cottage session day. We thought we'd experiment a little and have the session after I came home again—just to see which was easier for me.

At Perelandra. My wallpaper friend has made another amazing turnaround regarding my life and work at the Cottage. The quality of her acceptance has changed. Now she's supportive of my keeping these notes, saying they'll be invaluable if I want to write about this in the future. And she's much more open to the flower essences.

At the Cottage. It took a little while to shake out the cobwebs, but once I got going, the Cottage session cooked. Tonight's topic: The Law of Triangulation. When it was over, I felt a deep caring and love for Universal Light. His insights are really laying a new foundation of information for me.

My strength held up throughout the session, and I didn't have an energy drop at the end. Both David and I felt hungry but not exhausted.

February 23 — Heather Green

At Perelandra. I worked on the notes all afternoon. While I was recording my hastily scribbled short notes for 2/19 in the journal—I do this when I don't have time to write a full entry in the journal—it suddenly clicked that the essence reading for that day was connected with the pelvic adjustment on 2/21. I finally figured out why I needed those amazingly intense essences: deep fear, trauma, shock, extreme stress. This was what was holding up the pelvis, keeping it contracted. I had to release all of this before the pelvis could come into my awareness and drop into the correct position. This also explains the sudden, isolated feelings of illness on Sunday. I had felt there was no connection with anything going on presently in my life. Now it all makes sense.

I met with a couple of friends who have read *Behaving* and wanted to talk about it. I assumed I would not need to hold back when it came to the nature work I was doing. At one point they brought up the topic of the universe and their perceptions, so I talked about what I was learning from Universal Light. It may have been too much. They looked like I was blowing them away. When they left, I had the terrible feeling I had screwed up.

At the Cottage. The men feel I didn't screw up. They say I should take my stand and let others "come" to me. They've "never seen a teacher worth his salt talk down to students." Instead, the teacher makes the student reach.

February 24 — Yellow

JAMFD

February 25 — Heather Green

At Perelandra. Decided to do the new Battle Energy Release Process at Perelandra right after I arrived back. I just got the feeling to do it. I sat in the cabin in front of the double doors facing the garden and opened the coning. I could feel the importance of the Pan/Christ balance—working with man's emotions that are being held within nature. I set up the process as nature instructed and requested the release of the battle-related energy being held by nature. I was stunned at the continuous, white, steam-like energy rising from everything, everywhere. I had no idea this would be so dramatic. As the energy released, I had a physical reaction—a high increase in electricity in my body. I checked to see if the energy being released was somehow going through my body. No, I was simply responding to all the activity going on around me, and I was fine. The steam formed a thick white cloud, which I released to the universe once the cloud had finished forming. I watched the energy move away and felt it being received into the universe. I shifted my focus to nature and checked for any essences needed to stabilize it now that this energy had been released. I mixed the solution and put it inside the genesa crystal in the middle of the garden. When I turned around to go back to the cabin, I found a gold satin ribbon in the spiral path—a gift from nature. The process worked.

I felt I was to look at the garden soil. When I did, I found that the soil consistency had changed from heavy clay to loam.

I sat in the cabin for a long time feeling what had happened. I was overwhelmed by the amount of energy involved. I just sat there a bit stunned.

At the Cottage. When I told the men about what happened with the process, they expressed concern that I had done this alone. I told them I felt it was important to do it alone this time so that I have a full and clear understanding of what I'm dealing with. This is important when setting up a new process. They were not surprised at how much energy was involved because they know what happens both in battle and when preparing for battle. [Some of the Confederate troops rested on the land that is now Perelandra just before the Battle of Manassas during our Civil War.]

February 26 — Gold

At Perelandra. A warm day. I worked in the garden. The work was excellent, and the soil turned with ease. I was able to open the rows in one-third of the garden—usually a three-day job for me. It must be part of the difference due to yesterday.

At the Cottage. A good night's sleep gave me distance and perspective on yesterday's experience. The men have calmed down about their concern for me. They're extremely supportive, although every once in a while they still express concern about the intensity of the process.

February 27 — Dusty Rose

At Perelandra. A much colder day, so I did office work. It's possible that I won't have to fly to NYC tomorrow because they're expecting a snowstorm. I'm not disappointed.

February 28 — Yellow

At Perelandra. Trip to NYC was called off.

Clarence's interest has really been sparked by the Universal Light transcripts. Besides reading them, he's also helping me type them.

At the Cottage. They're going through an intense time in the work. I'm not asking what it's about. I have my own intensity to deal with. David encouraged me to shake rugs and talk to his mother—soon. He says I shouldn't be shy, and obviously she wants to talk to me.

February 29 — Heather Green

I awoke not feeling well and with a foreboding feeling about the Feldenkrais lesson scheduled this morning. I decided just to take a deep breath, move forward and see what comes up. Apparently I like to live dangerously.

At Perelandra. The Feldenkrais lesson was emotionally tough for me. She worked on the pelvic shelf again. Immediately, I began to cry. It was a difficult emotional release centering around fears and self-protection, stemming from my childhood. She worked slowly, moving me around the entire pelvic base so that I could identify all the areas. It was difficult for me to get the confidence to move onto the front of the pelvic base. When I left, I felt drained but I had a strong sense of emotional balance.

I received a note from the friend who I just told about the Cottage. She said she had two Eisenhower experiences after leaving Perelandra. On the car radio, during the drive back, she heard a tape of David talking about how people really want peace, and hoping that some day the governments will get out of the way and let them have it! Then, in a discussion she had with her husband that night, she was giving Jackie Kennedy the credit for the Kennedy Center. Her husband said this wasn't true. The first plans for it came from President Eisenhower. These two happenings gave her a sense of confirmation.

At the Cottage. I told them about my Feldenkrais experience, and the men reminded me that nothing stays on the back burner forever. These old fears had to come up sometime.

March 1 — Dusty Pink

At Perelandra. Had lunch with my friend who has the suicidal partner. He's stopped being suicidal and is now threatening her. I kept trying to get her to leave him, but she won't. So I told her if she needs a place to run to for protection, she can stay in our spare bedroom.

Transcripts #3 and #4 are now ready for typing.

I can't get the chiropractor on the phone. She hates the phone and won't return calls. Gettysburg is coming up and I don't know if she's still going. I told David I was thinking about going there on my own, but he's not too keen on the idea. He's urging me to continue trying to get the chiropractor. To bribe me, he took me out to dinner at Harry's.

March 2 — Ivory

At Perelandra. I finally got the chiropractor. The Gettysburg trip is set with her for next Wednesday. This ball is now rolling.

At the Cottage. I had a session with Universal Light. He gave me insight on the evolution of historic facts and more on Gettysburg. There's much excitement among the men at the Cottage about this session because it touches their work. They are not only aware of the changes that go on around history, they work with the nuts and bolts of those changes—they assist in the evolution of history.

I came out of this session feeling spacey, even though I felt the session went extremely well. Essences put me right back on track.

March 3 — Yellow

At Perelandra. Typed a good copy of transcripts #3 and #4. I'm almost caught up now.

My friend's partnership crisis is heating up. David suggested that I tell her to remove the firing pin from each gun in the house. I passed the information along.

March 4 — Brown

At Perelandra. A full afternoon of garden work: spread straw on the asparagus bed and pruned the old raspberry canes.

My friend is borrowing my truck tomorrow so she can move her partner's stuff out.

March 5 — Ivory

At Perelandra. It rained, so my friend couldn't move her partner's stuff out. He's quite nuts. She's moved in with us for the week. I keep thinking this is a turning point for her—if she survives it.

Elizabeth and I met over the rugs again. She connects with me as soon as I stand on the deck and start shaking them. (Luckily, once we're hooked up, I don't have to keep shaking rugs. This could get tedious.) I felt her gentleness, and there was a sense of a mother/daughter energy between us. We talked about our mutual love for gardening, and she surprised me by talking about my work. She's heard about it! We talked for a long time about the different things I am learning from nature. I wanted to ask her how she heard about me, but I was afraid of the answer. I told her about my trip to Paris and how I bought a cashmere sweater imported from Scotland as a "souvenir." She laughed, calling cashmere "fuzzy silk."

At the Cottage. David is pleased with this development between his mother and me. He says he can communicate with her, but not directly. She's on a different level from Perelandra and the Cottage, and she's with his father, David. I told him I already knew she was with David from our conversation this afternoon. I also told him I now understand why everyone in the family called him Dwight. Having two Davids around makes a conversation pretty challenging. We sometimes can't figure out which David is being referred to at the time.

March 6 — Ivory

At Perelandra. Spent the day preparing for the Gettysburg Battlefield trip tomorrow.

At the Cottage. Talked with the men at dinner about my feelings about tomorrow's trip. I admitted that I feared the proximity to the Eisenhower life on Earth might somehow challenge his existence in my life. [The Eisenhower Farm where he and Mamie lived during their later years is located right next to the battlefield.] There is still that little voice inside me that questions all of this, even though I have a deep belief and knowing that the Cottage and this man are quite real in my life. David insists that my little voice and the questions it raises are healthy. Running simultaneously with my fears about the trip is my belief that something will happen tomorrow that will verify everything.

I also told them that several people at the Perelandra level who know about the trip have said to me that I'll never get the job done because the area is huge—it will take me years. David suggested I not listen to them. He's going to be directing me around the battlefield tomorrow, and he knows what he's doing.

March 7 — Gold

Ash Wednesday: redemption and purification

The chiropractor and I got to Gettysburg by noon. It was a beautiful drive. As we entered the area, we found "Eisenhower" signs everywhere. We pulled into the main Tourist Center and parked the truck—the parking lot was empty. Right in front of the truck was a sign: "Eisenhower Tours." I said to her, "This must be where we start!" Next to the sign was a wooden map holder complete with *one* map of the Gettysburg Battlefield. I got the map and gave it to her. David had set it up for her to do the navigation around the battle-field with him while I concentrated on doing the processes with nature. When she looked at the map, she didn't have any sense about where we were to go until I opened the coning and included all of us in it. That's when she became connected with David, and the two of them started plotting out the route. When they finished, she declared David to be brilliant and told me he was using the towers around the battlefield. From the towers, I would be able to work with huge areas of land in all directions just by standing at different positions around the tower platforms. This was going to be easy and most efficient.

The first tower he sent us to was the Eisenhower Tower that over-looked his farm, Big Round Top, Little Round Top and the Peach Tree Orchard. I set up with nature and did the Battle Energy Release Process for every section or area of land that they told me to do.

We worked from a total of three towers and a small cemetery near Barlow Knoll. The final stop was at a large, empty parking lot at Cemetery Ridge. This is when the chiropractor took over. While we were sitting in the truck, she noticed a crypt in the middle of the cemetery that she claimed was changing size while she was looking at it. I accused her of having eaten too much chocolate, but she insisted that we should investigate. She led me through the cemetery to the underground crypt—we called it "the bunker"—where we were contacted by Dr. James Warren, the resident of the bunker. He asked to accompany my friend to her office where he could observe several techniques she worked with that he needed in order to assist other souls who had died during the battle. He had been a physician in a kind of MASH unit that had been set up near the battle. Both the chiropractor and I were quite surprised—to say the least. But she invited him back, and we even suggested he might like to ride along in the truck with us. Luckily, we couldn't see him. That might have been a bit much for us to take. I did suggest we might all stop at McDonald's on the way back and let Dr. Warren have a real present-day experience.

It took us a total of two and a half hours to do all the work. We had a sense that this was an initial cleansing of the battlefield and that I might need to return to fully complete the job. As we drove south and as we passed one major battlefield spot—The Ridge and the Copse of Trees—my friend wondered aloud about why that one spot had been missed in our work. She explained that this was where the deciding battle was fought and that it was a particularly fierce battle. She thought it odd that it would be missed or ignored. Since I knew nothing about the Gettysburg Battle or the significance of this particular area, I didn't say anything. I figured nature and David knew what they were doing.

By 5:30 P.M., my friend and Dr. Warren had been dropped off at her place, and I was back at Perelandra and then the Cottage.

At the Cottage. Spent the evening with the men, laughing and sharing about my day at Gettysburg and our adventures. They were all very pleased about what was accomplished.

March 8 — Ivory

At Perelandra. I feel a deep exhaustion that is no doubt the result of yesterday's work. I was glad not to do anything that required focus. Had lunch with my wallpaper friend and, other than her concern that I was still smiling after my trip, she had no interest in what went on.

I checked in with nature about Gettysburg and found out that they would like me to return in May for another phase of the work there—if I want to. Of course, I agreed to return.

At the Cottage. I was glad to be among family and friends once again. It can get a little lonely at the Perelandra level. David and the others are still excited about what happened at Gettysburg. It has had an impact on their work, but I'm not sure how. They were most pleased that I agreed to go back in the spring.

David has asked me to do an Energy Cleansing and the Battle Energy Release Process for the land on the Eisenhower Farm as a favor to him. He feels this will fulfill a promise he made many years ago when they first bought the property. He wanted to do everything in his power to restore the land back to its original state of fertilization and balance. I told him I'd be glad to do the processes and that I'd return soon to do them.

March 9 — Yellow

David convinced me to postpone the session we had planned today. I'm still tired from Gettysburg.

At Perelandra. I told Clarence a bit about the trip, and he asked to go with me to Gettysburg in May. He wants to be part of the process and see what I'm doing.

March 10 — Apricot

At Perelandra. I'm still having trouble focusing, so I ended up sitting in the sun and watching the birds.

At the Cottage. We talked about my Cottage notes, and I told them I was a bit disappointed I was not being more reflective about what was going on. They pointed out that when you don't have precedence, history and logic to bounce actions and events off of, it is difficult to be reflective. They feel that it is more appropriate that my notes be a collection of facts and not be reflective, and that I concentrate on recording facts for establishing patterns and rhythms right now. There will be time later for reflection about all of this.

March 11 — Ivory

A big mind-adjustment day, and it all occurred over breakfast.

I feel I am right on the edge of a new direction. I have much to say to others about what I'm learning from my life at the Cottage. After a year and a half of experience, growth and change, I now see I can share this with those who might benefit from it. I'm sitting on a ledge looking back at my preparation and ahead to a new level of sharing with others. I don't know when it will happen, but I know it will.

Nature is the base for what I am doing and what I have to give others. It is my core and the framework of this Cottage experience. I keep hearing the line from a session that was done three years ago: "You will pave the way to bring others to you so that they can understand their own freedom and release the karmic and emotional bonds that are limiting their creative abilities."

In short, today I felt an integration with all that I am doing: the garden, nature, the Cottage, Universal Light, the two bodies and so forth.

March 12 — Apricot

In today's Cottage session, the topic was again Gettysburg. Universal Light says the key word for the work there is "love." I received several visualizations during the session that allowed me to *experience* what was being translated. I saw the battlefield gridwork around Earth, and I saw key points in the grid, but I couldn't identify them.

When I was finished, David and I were both quite drained. I decided I would spend the afternoon reading a trash spy novel. Nature advised me to hold off on planting in the cold frame.

March 13 — Heather Green

At Perelandra. Snow and freezing rain—Feldenkrais was canceled. I worked with nature to get the garden information. There are *many* changes: the vegetable rotation, the division of vegetables, the position of vegetables in the rows and potatoes will not be planted. The center of the garden is changing with a major addition. Only nasturtiums are being planted in the annual band, and I think mixed annuals will be planted around the outer ring. I worked three hours on the information. There are so many changes that I feel I need to double-check the work.

March 14 — Gold

The men have informed me that they want to take full responsibility for their own essence testing and have asked me to give them a class so that they can learn kinesiology. We agreed that I am to continue testing any guests and any serious situations.

We discussed my return to Gettysburg tomorrow. They are concerned that the two-hour drive and the work will be too much for me, in light of all else that has happened this past week. But I want to go. I feel a strong pull to do this work. I've also gotten the okay from nature to do soil-balancing work for the Eisenhower Farm, and I'm most interested in seeing the results of the testing.

March 15 — Gold

I returned to the Eisenhower Tower and spent one and a half hours working with nature on the farmland. I tested that the land is divided into three pieces, and I worked with each piece separately. What was most interesting were the different needs for each piece.

After doing the work, I needed to go straight back to Perelandra. The work was a deep experience for me, and I just didn't feel like trooping around the town of Gettysburg afterwards. When I got back to the Cottage, David thanked me for helping him fulfill his promise. I could tell he was personally pleased.

March 16 — Ivory

At Perelandra. An insignificant day. (The men had convinced me to take an R&R.) I watered houseplants, went for a walk with the dogs and read my trash spy novel.

At the Cottage. At dinner I talked to them about some thoughts I had today. I had suddenly realized how much I needed these men in my life. I have resisted even thinking this because I was afraid I would be giving up the strength that comes from standing on my own two feet. Now I realize that my need for them isn't a sign of weakness or limitation. Rather, it's a strengthening of all that I am and allows me to move ahead in greater strength. This is a big shift for me. My words made them smile.

David had lunch with Hyperithon. He's being quite secretive and mysterious about their discussions. However, he seems excited about whatever they talked about.

March 17 — Heather Green

I awoke feeling like a new person. I gave the men a kinesiology lesson after breakfast. I must say, they had no trouble discerning positive and negative. I think this is what happens when people don't put up walls of resistance or believe kinesiology is too weird to work. It's amazing what mindset can do for you.

At Perelandra. Spent five hours rototilling! Returned to the Cottage worn out.

March 18 — Gold

At Perelandra. Spent the whole day in the garden again. I aerated and turned the soil of the second third of the garden. The soil composition is obviously different and is working up better than ever.

March 19 — Apricot

At the Cottage. It seemed like a year since our last Universal Light session and I felt rusty. The topics of this session were nature and Gettysburg, the Eisenhower Farm and David, and Perelandra and the coming equinox.

The Perelandra garden's center is to be changed in a rather dramatic way. I am to include a specific gem with the quartz crystal slab, and this gem will connect with the devic dynamic that is present on other levels of form beyond Earth. After the session, David said he was not surprised about the change. He feels I'm having the same shift at Perelandra that he experienced in his work as a result of our work at the Gettysburg Battlefield. Whatever was happening for Perelandra felt good to me, but I didn't know what it meant.

At Perelandra. I cleaned the garden center's quartz crystal and prepared it for the equinox.

At the Cottage. The men presented me with a beautiful bouquet of flowers. They explained the symbology of the arrangement they had chosen: white daisies with gold centers for the spring equinox and five yellow roses for the special things I've accomplished or gone through in the last ten days:

1. The Gettysburg Battlefield work
2. My new perspective on my work: sharing my experiences on the Cottage level to help free others and restore them to their creativity
3. The Universal Light sessions
4. The Eisenhower Farm work
5. The shift of the garden center at Perelandra

There was also one white rose to symbolize me. It was quite an overwhelming gift.

March 20 — Ivory and Slate Blue (both levels)
Spring equinox: 5:25 A.M.

I set my alarm for 5:10 and prepared for the equinox. At the moment of the equinox, I felt a strong wave of energy wash through me, and I saw the garden at Perelandra take a shift.

At Perelandra. I spent time in the center of the garden—in fact, I was drawn there. Then I went to a Feldenkrais class, ran a bunch of errands in town and planted transplants for the garden.

At the Cottage. A family dinner at Harry's in celebration of the equinox. Both Max and Seamus joined us.

March 21 — Ivory

At Perelandra. A stormy day with driving rains kept me in the cabin. I checked the garden information, and it tested out okay.

Clarence said he's feeling better about himself these days, even happy. I must say, he's looking better than he has in a long time.

March 22 — Apricot

At Perelandra. Had a strange day with two friends who spent a considerable amount of their time grousing about their lives. As I listened, I realized I had nothing in my life that I wanted to grouse about.

March 23 — Ivory

JAMFD

March 24 — Yellow

At Perelandra. Spent the afternoon rototilling. Without thinking, my attention kept getting drawn to the center of the garden and the new changes. It reminded me of this multilevel, most wonderful life that I lead. I can feel that I'm truly making a 180-degree turn in my life.

March 25 — Apricot

The men have decided that I should have a cabin, not unlike the one at Perelandra, in the garden area at the Cottage. Get this—it will give *them* a place to sit when they visit the garden during the cold months and a kitchen for making *their* coffee! Oh yes, and it will be convenient for me, too.

At Perelandra. I filled in the large garden chart and sent a copy to the Cottage so that they'll know what's being grown where. They reminded me that the chart will make it easier to keep up with what's going on at Perelandra.

I was struck today by how much the men consider me a part of their family. I actually mean something to them. Today I started seeing my Cottage life with new eyes.

March 26 — Gold

The weather is starting to break at the Cottage, and I'm already looking forward to sitting out on my balcony and drinking coffee.

The Cottage sessions are now moving more smoothly. I think the decision to do them weekly has helped me fine-tune the translation process. I don't get jammed with a bunch of different directions coming at me at once. But David and I are both still feeling quite drained afterwards. I'm hoping this smooths out more.

At Perelandra. Spent the afternoon working in the woods around the cabin.

March 27 — Brown

My morning thought: What if "coming to the Cottage full time" means that, instead of doing the Split Molecular Process from Perelandra and moving to the Cottage, I shift and do the split from the Cottage and move to Perelandra. This has some interesting possibilities.

At Perelandra. A cold, raw day—so I stayed in the cabin and worked on the notes. It's a bit overwhelming to look at everything that has happened these past two weeks. It was good to read the notes and think about all of it again.

At the Cottage. The men have been putting in some intense work for about a month now. They tell me this doesn't indicate there's trouble anywhere—just that they are doing some "delicate work."

March 28 — Ivory

At Perelandra. Another rainy day, so I spent the day in relative relaxation. I listened to music, read and sat by the fire watching the rain and the birds. I was going to get the fertilizer information, but nature told me not to get it until after raking the mulch into the rows. This way, nature will know what the complete makeup of the rows are and can give me the fertilizers that are needed after everything has been taken into consideration.

Clarence and I had dinner with my wallpaper friend and her husband. The Cottage was not mentioned (both of them know about it now) until it was time to leave the restaurant. The good news is that I felt no desire to talk about the Cottage with these people tonight. Ignoring the subject felt okay, and I didn't feel any pressure to have my life accepted by them. I do feel, however, that what I can share about my life at the Cottage was/is more interesting than anything that was talked about tonight. More and more, I can see how interesting and different my life is, and I find it fascinating to watch other people, those who know something about the Cottage, try to ignore my life and my work. That in itself is interesting to observe.

March 29 — Heather Green

I had a terrible night. There was a raging storm going on at Perelandra—high winds, driving sleet, thunder and lightning. The tin roof on the cabin was making quite a racket. The noise was so great that it was impossible not to hear it, even though I was at the Cottage at the time. The sleet banging against the windows frightened me the most, I think. Part of me couldn't understand what the hell I was so frightened about, and the other part of me was just plain scared. I finally got to sleep around 3:30 A.M., but then I kept dreaming about things that created feelings of deep apprehension.

During breakfast, when I talked about my night, I started getting insight about my being in bomb shelters during war. I "saw" flashes of light and heard the structure rattling from the impact of the bombs and debris. I described to the men what I was seeing, and they agreed that my description of the storm and my insight were both consistent with what one can experience in a bombing raid. I had also experienced an odd change in atmospheric pressure last night during the storm that they said was similar to what happens when bombs go off. Since Katie died in a bombing raid, I guess I needed these fears to surface. I'm hoping this is all I need to do with it. I only needed a total of three essences.

At Perelandra. I had an excellent private Feldenkrais lesson, then I had lunch with my friend who is going through the partnership crisis. Actually, she's surviving it—and so is he.

I spent the rest of the afternoon drifting mentally. I ended up doing next to nothing because I couldn't focus on anything. So I watched the birds at the feeder and the weather fly by.

Storm report on the Perelandra level: Thirty-six tornadoes touched down in the Carolinas. Sixty people are dead and thousands are homeless. The barometric pressure traveling up the east coast is the lowest in recorded history. An intense cold front and an equally intense warm front have collided right where this low pressure was centered in the Carolinas. Two people died in Washington—hit by trees. There are six inches of snow in the northern Washington suburbs and two feet of snow in New York City.

At the Cottage. I had to take a nap. Several of us got into more discussion about bomb-shelter memories. David said I'd have to be a "damn fool not to be frightened by the sound of bombs exploding around you."

March 30 — Gold

A day of tremendous change, shifting and growth. It began at the Cottage. I expressed frustration at seeing the men speak around me and not being able to hear them because my sensory system is overloaded. And I'm frustrated that we leave so many conversations for later, when I come full time.

I want to have freedom to choose what I do and don't hear, like I have at Perelandra. We can all close down and not hear something. But when I do this at Perelandra, it's not frustrating because I know that, if I desire to hear, see, touch and taste, I can. I have control (for the most part) over my sensory system in that body. At the Cottage, I'm still learning and activating the full range of function in my sensory system, and often I don't have the freedom of choice— or if I do, I don't have the technique down yet. I have the desire to take in everything, yet I can't.

The men reminded me that I must go slowly. I am one soul with two bodies and two complete sensory systems that are dealing with input from two separate lives. My soul must learn to deal with this massive amount of input. The men admit that perhaps they have been over-cautious with me and not said things that they could have. There have been judgment calls, and they have chosen to err on the side of caution.

To satisfy my desire for details about what they are doing, they explained that they are now working on Torch, the North African campaign during World War II. They are breaking down all the events and strategies, "re-doing" the whole operation without the mistakes. This is not an emotional strain on David because long ago he accepted the mistakes he made during this campaign, but the work they are now doing is, all the same, more intense than they had expected. They explained that they are only now concentrating on World War II, after having broken down the strategies of the previous wars and battles, because World War II was laid on the foundation of all previous battles. Piscean warfare culminated in World War II, and it was important to get a working knowledge of what occurred previously and how the coins flipped prior to tackling World War II.

They said they could see that they can open up more with me, but they wanted me to understand that my role in the Cottage does not include having an expert working knowledge of warfare and government. This is their role. My contribution centers around my developing relationship with nature. I am to develop with nature the processes needed for them to accomplish certain goals with their work, and I am to continue my research with nature so that new avenues in this area can be opened and made useful to the Cottage and those on the Perelandra level. In short, my focus needs to remain on nature and the co-creative research project we call "Perelandra."

They went on to tell me that they were supportive of my feelings of frustration about not being able to take everything in as I would like to. They have tried numerous times to project themselves into my situation in an effort to understand what I'm going through and have found it overwhelming. They suggested that I share my feelings and fears about all of this with them. If nothing else, they can help me maintain balance. Again they brought up the two-body business and how difficult a situation it is. I must take things in slowly and allow the adjustments to occur in good timing.

At Perelandra. I arrived feeling a stronger balance. And I realized that they were right about my needing to talk to them more about how I'm feeling about whatever is going on.

I worked all day in the house potting up thirty-two *dozen* transplants—a repetitive task that promotes thinking. I found myself wondering how three intelligent people—my wallpaper friend, her husband and Clarence—can go through meals with me and ask no questions about my nature research, Cottage life or Eisenhower. Every time we go out to dinner together (about once every two or three weeks), they ignore my life, as if it doesn't exist for them. We talk about copier machines or exterior paint, or real estate sales or gossip about the locals. The situation not only astonishes me, it makes me angry.

At the Cottage. I talked to David about my thoughts. He said, "You don't understand that others don't know how to relate to your life. They don't know what to do with it and they don't know what to do with you. You and your life threaten their belief systems. They have no wherewithal to take in what you say, and your words just bounce off them—your life bounces off them. They must reduce you to a level where they can relate. They must 'average Joe' you."

People need to ask the silliest, most mundane things because it's the only way they can relate. I won't be able to change this for them, and no amount of convincing from me can change this. Only they can make the changes, and they will do it only when they want. It's a waste of my time for me to try to change it for them. I must stand my ground, stop bending over backwards to accommodate their belief systems and let them adjust to me. It's their problem, their limitation—not mine. I need to let them average Joe me all they need, but I am not to posture myself in their limitations.

As he talked, I could feel the pressures that had built up this afternoon dissipating. I think I felt a coin flip inside me. His insight was amazing, yet so simple. I just need to let it sink in.

David feels that what I dealt with this morning is an indication that I am ready to take in more and that I'll have fewer hearing blanks. My sensory systems can feed more into the soul. I hope he's right.

March 31 — Ivory

Awoke with severe pain in a wide band around my mid and lower rib cage. It was so severe I could hardly breathe—I could only wait it out. I had a strong intuitive feeling that this was the physical release related to the mental shifts made yesterday. Eventually the pain subsided, and I went back to sleep.

When I told the others about the pain, they became concerned and solicitous, and urged me not to overdo it at Perelandra. They also agreed that I sure have this habit of hitting things head on.

At Perelandra. At breakfast with Clarence, I told him about some of the changes that are going on at Perelandra. I also told him about the problems I've been having accepting that my life is so difficult for others to relate to and what David said on the subject. Clarence agrees with David. He says he supports me, but has no idea how I do what I do—it's beyond him. He only knows I do it. Actually, the conversation left me feeling a sense of our partnership. It's the closest I have felt to him in a long time.

I worked six hours with Clarence in the woods between the house and the cabin piling fallen trees and dead limbs. We transformed the area into a beautiful space.

At the Cottage. I arrived home so tired I was punch-drunk. I had to take a nap. David and Tex were still going on about my morning's chest pain. Butch and Mickey were out with Seamus helping him have a last blast before reopening at The Pub. He's going to be performing five days a week now, not six. (David says his pacing lectures—those pesky comments he makes about slowing down—have been absorbed better by Seamus than me.)

April 1 — Brown

JAMFD. It's Sunday, and I pretended I was going to lull around in bed all day, drink coffee and read the *New York Times*. Sometimes these little mind tricks can help.

April 2 — Gold

We had a Cottage session: Today's topic dealt with the dynamics of the Cottage team.

At Perelandra. I worked to get the nursery plants in around the cabin. I received a terrific, well-thought-out response from a woman in New York City about *Behaving*. It was just the lift I needed. I was feeling overwhelmed with work today and needed a boost.

At the Cottage. I'm in my spring schedule now and am returning home around 6 P.M. instead of 4 P.M. We took Seamus out to dinner to cap off his sabbatical. He returns to The Pub tomorrow night. Dinner was wonderful. I could not ask for a more terrific brother.

April 3 — Ivory

At Perelandra. I had lunch with my wallpaper friend. She asked me about the Cottage, and we had a good time talking about my life there. She seemed most at ease with the conversation.

Worked all afternoon in the garden. Planted a Peace rosebush in the outer ring, several blueberry bush replacements and did a shallow tilling of the rows to help the soil dry out better.

At the Cottage. Tired.

April 4 — Apricot

At Perelandra. I had another good private Feldenkrais lesson—this time connecting the rib cage with the pelvis. Then I spent the afternoon in my office working on the Universal Light transcripts. I *must* do something to ease up this lengthy transcription process. I've asked several people if they would like to take it on as a part-time job, but they either can't or they don't have the typing skills. I don't know who else to turn to. I can't have just anyone type these transcripts. I've decided to have Clarence investigate buying a word processor for me. I know nothing about computers, but I feel this will offer me what I need to make the job of transcribing reasonable.

At the Cottage. My discussion with Tex, David and Mickey about computers got us talking about Butch and his incredible memory. During his life before death, Butch was married and had two children. His wife couldn't relate well to this gift of his, and, although there was a love relationship in the beginning, her inability to relax around his gift eventually distanced them. The children were "normal" and also didn't know how to relate with him. Overall, the situation made Butch sensitive about his gift and this is why he is reluctant to be open about it. They tell me he enjoys my teasing him about our different gifts: his great memory and my extraordinarily lousy memory. David says Butch is able to work best when he has been given a "loose rein" and full freedom. You can't hold his head tight at all—he says Butch and I have this in common.

April 5 — Ivory

At Perelandra. Thinned cold frame seedlings and typed transcripts.

I had a revelation regarding the transcripts today. I realized that the act of typing them grounds the material through me, making it more usable. The typing is the tool for the grounding. Now all I have to do is figure out how to accomplish this more efficiently.

April 6 — Heather Green

At Perelandra. Spent the day in the garden shifting straw and topsoil between the rows in the third (untilled) section. All the rototilling I had done in the other two sections was undone by the recent heavy rains. It's my fault. I should have asked nature for a tilling timing. Instead, I jumped the gun. Now I have asked nature, and the scoop is that I need to aerate it all again, then till when I'm ready to plant. That way I won't fight the rain. I'll learn.

At the Cottage. We got into a discussion about sexuality, and they came up with a wonderful definition of sex: Speaking through form without words.

April 7 — Ivory

At Perelandra. Clarence went in search of a computer. I aerated the garden rows. Nature confirmed that today I am to leave the aerated rows untilled until planting. Then till, fertilize, lightly till again to work in the fertilizers, then plant. I feel like I'm finally understanding this soil process. 1984 is the Year of Soil.

As I worked, I kept feeling the presence of Elizabeth Eisenhower "next to me." I did not "tune" into her because, to be honest, I was tired from the physical work and I felt I couldn't focus.

After the garden work, I took a short rest, then shook out a cabin rug. Elizabeth connected with me immediately. She understood my not being able to have the time to shake rugs lately—a mother who raised six sons knows these things! I sat on the cabin deck in the cool early-evening air, spending just a moment with her—two busy women stealing a little time together. She confirmed that she was connecting with me earlier in the garden. We both agreed that we enjoy gardening better than rug shaking and decided to spend time together in the garden tomorrow.

April 8 — Yellow

At Perelandra. My physical energy was not as high as yesterday, so I chose to do more gentle work. This allowed me to spend one and a half hours connected with Elizabeth. We had a wonderful time together. While working the soil, I spotted a small, almost-clear quartz stone. It so caught my attention, I knew I couldn't just leave it. I checked with nature and found I was to shift the stone to Elizabeth on her level. So I set up the process just as nature was instructing me to do, and shifted the stone to Elizabeth's hand. She was delighted and asked me how I did that. It felt absolutely right that she be connected with the garden. She has such a great love for soil and gardens.

At the Cottage. I had intended to go home and tell David about my time with his mother. Instead, I immediately went into a process and began feeling drained, with nausea and terrible head pain. I felt like the rug had been pulled out from under me, so I took essences and laid down on the bed. A line kept playing over and over in my head: I love my life more than life itself.

Eventually, I was able to go downstairs for a cup of tea, and that's when the others got me. I explained what was happening and told them the line I kept hearing. I admitted that the line had been coming up in my head for several days, but I had been afraid to think it, let alone say it. David asked me why I was so afraid to say it. I told him I didn't understand the feeling I was having around the words "more than life itself." My work with nature all centers around life, and it feels like blasphemy to say "more than life." David expanded my definition of life by saying that life defines the state of all individuation. It alludes to existence within boundaries. Beyond life is that state of no individuation or, to use my term, the Void.

Suddenly I realized I *could* say I love my life more than life itself. I love it beyond life, where all becomes One, as well. As I said this to them, the pain in my head released, the nausea dissipated, and my energy returned. Apparently, my resistance to saying this, even to myself, was really blocking me.

April 9 — Gold

I awoke with a vision: As the result of the process yesterday, the tuning fork connecting the levels of my life at the Cottage had released and was now ringing clearly. The newly released tuning fork touched the Void and moved my connection from the Void through the levels to the physical, and each level was vibrant, intense and in balance. I have truly blown open the doors in this Cottage life. This is a moment equal to the connection of the gold cord and the grid.

In the Cottage session, Universal Light immediately congratulated me on the freeing of the tuning fork. He used the opportunity to discuss triangulation on a more personal level between me and the Cottage.

At Perelandra. I felt a bit disoriented and couldn't work in the garden, so I went to town just to get out. My friend-in-crisis visited just after I got back to Perelandra. She's still in crisis.

At the Cottage. Everyone has read the transcript of the session and congratulated me—including Max, who had stopped by for a quick round of golf. We had a great family dinner.

April 10 — Ivory

Awoke with a severe case of tuning fork afterglow.

At Perelandra. Worked all day in the garden and got a "call" from Elizabeth. We're using the stone for our connection now instead of the rug shaking—we're both pleased with the change. We talked about *Behaving*, which she has read, and I asked her if there was anything in it that she had trouble with. I expected her to bring up some of my nature experiences, but she said she could relate to the nature intelligence idea easily. She had difficulty with my childhood. We talked about that for a little while, and I assured her I had come through those years fine—in fact, they gave me the discipline I needed for the nature work. Then we talked about the book-writing process itself. She has a high regard for books. I'm still not asking her about how she got my book. I'm assuming David (her son) got her the copy somehow and, if he wasn't the one responsible, I don't want to know about it. The potential answer here seems too big for me to handle right now.

At the Cottage. I received insight after I got home to change the outer ring in the Perelandra garden. Instead of planting annuals, I am to plant rose bushes—a 300-foot ring of roses—all different colors. The men feel this has to do with the shift the garden took at the spring equinox and that the roses might signifiy the anchoring of a stronger, more stable energy.

April 11 — Gold

In the evening the men told me they completed the work on Torch, and they seem most relieved to have this one under their belts. They're going to back away from office work for a couple of days, just to take a breather. David is going to putter, Tex might get away for a couple of days with Max, Mickey is planning to work some in our gardens, and Butch plans to get out a lot on his cycle. They have talked me into not working on the transcripts or doing any Universal Light sessions for the next three weeks. It didn't take much arm-twisting.

At Perelandra. Opened a garden coning and verified the rose bush information. The rose ring is now possible because of the recent spring equinox shifts and the battle energy release. Once the bushes are planted, I will feel an addition of age, stability and new grounding in the garden. (Roses are old in history.) I am to order forty-four bushes that, when added to the Peace Rose already planted in the outer ring, will bring the number of roses to forty-five. I shall order them tomorrow.

April 12 — Apricot

JAMFD

April 13 — Ivory

At Perelandra. We got hit with another terrible thunderstorm with heavy rains and hail along with wild thunder and lightning. I wasn't nearly as frightened as I usually am during these things. Perhaps that discussion about bombings helped.

April 14 — Heather Green

Awoke feeling that I'm starting another shift. Whoopee. I have no idea what's coming, except that for over a week, my dreams have been bringing up vague frustrations.

At Perelandra. Clarence brought home a computer. He's figuring out how to set it up.

At the Cottage. Returned late and exhausted.

April 15 — Gold

Awoke still feeling tired and with my focus a little fuzzy.

At Perelandra. Worked in the garden all day. By 4:30 I felt chilled to the bone, and I began to feel head pressure. I showered, tested essences and left for the Cottage.

At the Cottage. I was glad to get home and get into bed. By 10 o'clock, I was sick in the Perelandra body—diarrhea, chills and body pain. At the Cottage, I had an immediate drop in body temperature. It looks like I've been hit with a stiff case of the flu, and it's a little scary because it's hit in both bodies and I've experienced vomitting in both bodies. I took essences throughout the night, and the men checked on me throughout as well. At several points in the night I felt like I was going to pass out. The essences point to a deep process going on, but I'm not getting a clue as to what's behind it. We all had our bedroom doors open for the night so that the men could hear if I needed anything, but actually I wasn't alone. They ended up taking turns sitting with me.

April 16 — Gold

I awoke after two hours of sleep feeling nausea, body aches and chills. The essences now show I'm not letting a higher shift come through to the physical. If I knew what was going on, perhaps I could let it shift. I went to sleep right after taking the essences and slept for a couple more hours. When I woke up again, all the flu symptoms were gone and I was out of the woods.

They had called Hyperithon, who monitored me throughout the night in an open coning, and he said I was doing fine. He confirmed that I was going through a deep shift and releasing pain from deep wounds. I have a choice to stop now, if I'd like—or I can go on.

I've decided to go on. I can't see any benefit to stopping now. The men say they're right with me in this.

April 17 — Ivory

Awoke with a strange, intense pain throughout my entire mid-torso area. It was a muscular pain, yet it had an odd, hollow feeling. Now what?

The essences show I'm still in process. By mid-morning, the pain subsided, so I decided I'd go to the Feldenkrais class—my teacher is good at alleviating pain and perhaps I'd get help. In retrospect I can see that I was grasping at any straw that I thought might help me.

At Perelandra. The class itself was not helpful, but I found out from the others about a bad flu going around that can drop into the muscles and cause terrible pain. It usually lasts a few days. While I was in the class, the pain returned full force.

I got into bed to rest at Perelandra and called David to tell him what was going on. He agreed it was good for me to relax at Perelandra. By mid-afternoon, the pain left—and that was that. I was finished with this stage.

At the Cottage. As the evening progressed, I could feel both bodies begin a rebuilding process. I think I've come through it. I ate a little—soup, salad and tea—napped for two hours and spent a quiet rest of the evening. The essences show, however, that I still have one issue to deal with—one more phase.

April 18 — Yellow

I slept quite late and at breakfast I promised I would have a relaxing day at Perelandra.

At Perelandra. I'm getting stronger—and I got bored with my relaxing day, so I went to town for lunch and a little shopping.

At the Cottage. I returned home tired, but okay. Shortly after arriving, I began to get ideas about what the essences were telling me about this last phase of the process. I bounced off any thought or idea that rose in my mind with several of the men, including David. I saw the core of strength my life at the Cottage gives to my work, and that the two are fully intertwined. I realized that to continue my work, I *needed* my life at the Cottage.

As I acknowledged how essential it has been for these two things to come together for me, I "saw" myself standing before a doorway that led to a new world with nature. I had the support I now needed in order to take this step, and I saw that it would move me dramatically closer to the heart of nature. What I saw then shifted to a scene that I "knew" was from my first lifetime on Earth some 5500 years ago. I was a lama living in a lamasery in the Himalayas. In this scene, I was walking along a path outside the lamasery with my closest friend. I recognized the heart and soul of this man immediately—it was David. He was teasing me about my reluctance to leave the lamasery and travel among the people to teach. He insisted I had something to give that would be helpful to others. Then he picked up a long, sturdy stick along the trail—suitable for a walking stick—and handed it to me, saying, "Here, this will give you the strength you need. Now leave the mountain and go teach!"

Here we were again. I stood before a new world with nature, one that would move me into nature's heart, and I felt certain this would result in something helpful and valuable that I could give to others. I now understood that it wasn't just the Cottage in general that was giving me the necessary strength and courage to go on. It was also David. He and I had a history of this kind of support. I looked at him and said, "Thank you." Instantly, the scene shifted back to the light-filled room I was about to enter. With that, I "walked" through the doorway and into the room.

I felt myself surrounded by a whole new framework. Its presence stabilized me, and I felt internally at peace for the first time in weeks. It was as if all the shifting and discomfort I had been experiencing never happened. By dinner, everyone knew what had occurred and gave me the heartiest of congratulations. Mickey insisted that we have a champagne toast. (I've found out that he keeps small bottles of champagne on hand, because you never know when something will need a toast.) It was an amazing night. Of course, I have no idea what specific changes my work will take on. I'm getting quite used to moving forward without the details. (What am I saying? I'm getting used to moving forward without a clue as to what is going on. It keeps the element of surprise running throughout my life.)

April 19 — Dusty Rose

At Perelandra. I had a private Feldenkrais lesson, and I thought we could work together to encourage the body to fully ground the shifts that occurred last night. I told my teacher that I had taken a big step around my work and that I felt this lesson could be helpful in stabilizing that step. This was something she could understand and work with. She worked with me intuitively throughout the hour's lesson. In the end I experienced, for the first time, the size and movement of my entire spinal column. All these years, I had visualized the spine as a *narrow* column. Now I felt how large the spine actually is, and I had a new sense of support as a result. I also felt a stronger connection between the pelvis and the head. It was a most comforting lesson, and one that gave me a new confidence. The lesson was a real breakthrough.

At the Cottage. I napped for a couple of hours. My energy level is still not at full capacity.

April 20 — Brown

I spent the afternoon in the garden doing some work that wasn't very strenuous. I had a peaceful time and was able to hold my concentration easily. I feel I have come through this latest process.

April 21 — Ivory

JAMFD

April 22 — Gold

Easter.

At the Cottage. We had an amazing breakfast, reminiscing about the things that have gone on since spring a year ago. For me, it feels like it has been a year of emotional clearing with one major pattern after another coming up for review and release. Last spring I shifted my relationship with Clarence. Then in the summer I went through all the two-week essence processes. This led to big shifts in the fall, bringing me right up to the present and my latest step with nature. Each thing was important and deep, and each required releasing and reordering, followed by corresponding physical changes. By the time breakfast was over, I was feeling quite a sense of peace, contentment and self-accomplishment. The men encourage me in these moments, saying it's good to look at my accomplishments in the context of the larger picture so that I can see how far I have come and how much I've done. I have a tendency to just keep moving forward without stepping back and reflecting.

At Perelandra. Heavy rains washed out my plans for spending the day in the garden. Basically, I banged around waiting to return home. Clarence is engrossed with the computer. I think he's found his true love.

At the Cottage. We had a family dinner, including Seamus, Max and Nicole (Butch's close friend and the singer from Seamus's band). It was a fantastic meal.

April 23 — Heather Green

JAMFD. The rose bushes arrived.

April 24 — Yellow

At Perelandra. I spent three hours digging large rose-bush holes around the outer ring of the garden. I'm half finished with this job.

I had an appointment with the chiropractor. She gave me an update on Dr. Warren. Originally, she felt he might be there to assist her, but now she knows he's there to learn from her so that he can help those souls from the Gettysburg Battle who are still in need of release. He is especially interested in her cranial work. She feels him intensely observing what she's doing every time she does anything with a client's head. His interest shows the continued dedication and work of a soul such as James Warren. She feels he'll be going back to Gettysburg to continue his work in May when I return to do the next phase there.

Perelandra body: All issues were flu-related. I had a weakened spleen—where the flu was centered—which was strengthened with two supplements. C-2 was way out to the left, and the pelvis was out. The pelvis frequently misaligns during illness, which explains why I've had to adjust it a lot recently. I needed no essences, and my other supplements tested okay.

Cottage body: The alignment was fine, no other supplements were needed, and I tested clear on the essences. In short, I was a-okay.

Max: I had a gut feeling that he needed help, and I was right. His pelvis was so badly misaligned that his entire spinal column tested weak. I adjusted him, but he tested that he needs his pelvis blocked two times daily for two weeks, essences checked one time daily for the same period, and he can only swim and walk as exercise for six weeks while the ligaments heal and strengthen. No golf. He tested that he is still going through his shift.

At the Cottage. Max stayed for dinner. This gave me time to show him how to use the wedges for blocking his pelvis. He and Tex considered canceling their trip, but I encouraged them not to. It's only for three days, and I think this trip will be good for Max. I tested him for what essences he's going to need during the trip.

After Max went to bed, I admitted to the others that I wish he didn't have to go through this and that I wanted to protect him. This gave them a chance to call *me* a Jewish mother. I'm going to miss them both, even though it's just for three short days.

April 25 — Ivory

At Perelandra. Finished the rose-bush holes. Then I showered and met my wallpaper friend in town for lunch. Two people she knows had read *Behaving* and wanted to get together with me to talk about it. So my friend arranged this lunch for the four of us. It was a strange lunch. Nothing was said about the book except that they liked my use of the word "co-creation" and had discussed that concept with the group they meet with regularly. We talked about this a bit, but, beyond that, it was a social lunch. They left one hour later, leaving my friend and me wondering what just happened—or what didn't happen. I felt they weren't sure what to say to me in person. Crazy. What a waste of time.

Back to Perelandra. I divided the rose bushes according to which ones nature said go into each section in the garden. They are all bare-rooted and have been soaking in an essence solution since arriving. I plan to start planting tomorrow.

April 26 — Gold

The men are trying to get me to sleep later in the morning. They feel I'm still coming out of the flu and shift, and I need more rest.

At Perelandra. I had another private Feldenkrais lesson that went well, then met my wallpaper friend and her husband for lunch. He's been telling me I should feel free to discuss my life in front of him and that I should be the one to bring it up and not wait for him to raise the issue. So I decided I'd call his bluff and bring up the Cottage directly to see if he would show interest. He already knew about the Cottage as something that was part of my life, but he didn't know who David was—until today. I also told him a little about the Cottage work. He really didn't pick up on any of it. He showed no visible interest, his eyes glazed over and he asked no questions. His wife—my wallpaper friend—was *no* help. In the midst of my explaining about the Cottage work, she announced (1) that a woman sitting near us was eating a huge lunch yet was so skinny, and (2) that it is interesting how the topic of nuclear power and war can put such a damper on a discussion.

Instead of taking the blame for causing an uncomfortable lunch, I saw what happened for what it was—a crappy, stupid lunch filled with insensitivity and resistance. This is a big change for me. I held my ground, and it felt good.

I spent the afternoon planting roses, finishing one-third of the job. I closed up shop, put away the bushes yet to be planted, watered the planted ones, showered and dragged on home.

April 27 — Ivory

At Perelandra. Finished putting in the rose bushes. A major job successfully completed.

At the Cottage. Tex called this afternoon to let us know all was well with Max and they're having a good time.

April 28 — Dusty Rose

At Perelandra. Spent the whole day in the garden, moving from one project to another. I was impressed at how easily the work progressed. It was never-ending, but I only did what felt right for me to do and it left me with a sense of sliding through the day.

At the Cottage. I arrived thoroughly exhausted. Max and Tex returned home this evening with terrific tales about their three days. I suspect most of the tales were exaggerated. They both look well rested. They won't tell me where they went, only that it included a town. David tells me to just be patient—I'll find out where they went. Max has been talked into staying at the Cottage for the remainder of his two weeks so that I can test him daily for essences.

April 29 — Brown

At Perelandra. Another beautiful, constructive day: transplanting, potting up, spreading stone, raking rows. . . . The day flowed.

At the Cottage. I'm returning tired these days, but not frustrated. I'm feeling good about the work, which is going very differently this year—smoother, more exact, more detailed. I sense this year is a turning point. Also, I feel all kinds of strong support for the Perelandra garden from many levels.

David and I decided we won't get back into the Universal Light work until June. May is for the garden, and I don't need any more to deal with.

April 30 — Brown

It was raining at Perelandra, so I spent the morning at the Cottage and got the fertilizer information for two-thirds of the garden. Nature wants me to put in a lot of liquid seaweed solution and kelp. This seems crazy—at the very least, it's different from the fertilizing I've done in the past.

May 1 — Gold

At Perelandra. Tilled two-thirds of the garden—all the rows I need to plant this weekend. It was a brilliant move to till in the topsoil and mulch from between the rows. This has conditioned the soil I am planting in beautifully.

At the Cottage. I talked to David about the soil work I did today and said I felt I should have conditioned my soil better before this— that I suspected I hadn't fully allowed nature to give me all the needed information. David told me something surprising. Through Hyperithon, he's been keeping up with the Perelandra garden since 1981, and has never gotten the hint that I had fallen behind in the development of the garden. According to his information, the garden has maintained its—nature's—timing. Not only was I surprised to hear this, I was also pleased and relieved.

May 2 — Ivory

At Perelandra. I added bone meal and lime where needed, then laid out the interplanting patterns using red, white and blue poker chips. The garden looks like a wild poker game that's gotten out of hand.

May 3 — Gold

At Perelandra. It's raining like crazy, but the soil is holding up beautifully. I think I'll be able to plant as planned.

At the Cottage. As I work with Max, I can feel him strengthen.

May 4 — Dusty Pink

JAMFD. Rained out of the garden.

May 5 — Heather Green

At Perelandra. The sun was out again, so I checked the soil to see if I could plant. Even with all the rain, the soil has held up enough for planting. I worked ten hours and got two-thirds of the garden in. Since it rained yesterday, I wanted to do the planting for both days so that the garden would remain on schedule.

At the Cottage. Totally exhausted, and my body is sore. Everyone is supporting me like crazy. They care, truly care about this garden. Of course, it would be a lot more helpful if they would come to Perelandra and help.

May 6 — Ivory

At Perelandra. It was not a full-energy day for me. I concentrated on the herb band planting.

May 7

JAMFD. I had another low energy.

May 8 — Gold

I basically konked out last night—I barely remember even going to bed. Once again I am looking forward to the day when I won't have to leave the Cottage, and I'll only have one body to deal with. I'll probably think I'm on vacation. The men are urging me to "blow steam" about all of this, but I can't seem to. I may feel exhausted, but I'm also grateful—grateful for my life, the adventure of it and the challenge. I'm grateful for my future and my sense of direction and stability. I enjoy feeling like I'm functioning on all cylinders. But every once in a while I get tired—bone tired. The best steam blowing I can do right now is to admit that this is making me tired. They say they're going to work on me around steam blowing. David claims to be an expert.

At Perelandra. I received a letter from a Dutch publisher requesting the Dutch rights to translate and publish *Behaving*. This book is amazing. It's been reviewed in South Africa, and now this. And it's still moving by word of mouth. Watching it move around the world like this is magical for me.

At the Cottage. Max has left the Cottage. His essence and pelvic work for the past two weeks are completed. I miss him.

May 9 — Ivory

At Perelandra. A woman from my Feldenkrais class asked me to teach her how to use kinesiology and get in touch with nature intelligences. We drove to her garden, and I gave her a lesson. She must have been ready because she understood the concepts easily and quickly. I feel like my work at Perelandra is growing in this teaching thing, and today was just one example of it.

May 10 — Apricot

At Perelandra. I had my last Feldenkrais lesson of the year—an excellent lesson, but I'm glad the series is over. I bought a trash mystery novel to read while I was at the hairdresser and ended up getting right into it. So I took the afternoon off and finished reading the book. It's been a long time since I've gotten lost in a novel. I read a good definition of a trash novel: Once you start reading it, you can't put it down—but once you finish it, you can't remember what it was about.

May 11 — Gold

At Perelandra. Composed a response to the Dutch publisher and left a copy of it on David's desk for them to go over. I'm glad they're helping me with this foreign-publisher business. I feel like I'm in over my head.

May 12 — Yellow

At Perelandra. Another chiropractor appointment.

Perelandra body: The left pelvis was misaligned just a bit, and L-5 and the sacrum were slightly out. L-5 was the key to the sacrum misalignment. I needed one essence that, to her, indicated that I was "re-wiring" for a shift toward working more with others. Of course, what this means is yet to be seen.

Cottage body: My alignment was fine, but my protein was low. I tested that now I am to drink the ninety grams of protein at one time in the mornings. I'm also testing that I need ten hours of sleep. The drain on that body is due to the present Perelandra schedule. I needed no flower essences.

Max: His pelvis is holding well and his spine tests strong. He needs a daily essence check for two more weeks, then she thinks he'll be fully stabilized.

Tex: His L-5 was out, and he needed a thoracic vertebra adjustment. He's to check himself for essences tonight.

She gave me an update on Dr. Warren. He left her office on his own about a week ago. In her mind's eye, she saw him back at the battlefield administering to one soldier after another. After he adjusted each man's cranials, the soldier disappeared from the picture.

At the Cottage. I napped for two hours. Several of us went to Nino's for dinner. I needed this break.

May 13 — Ivory

The chiropractor has given them a new incentive for bugging me about sleeping longer. They are going to drive me nuts. Max has moved backed into the Cottage so that I can test him for essences these next two weeks. I feel much better that he's with us as he goes through his changes.

At Perelandra. The garden is completely planted, except for corn and any other late plantings. What a relief.

May 14 — Gold

Hyperithon came in for lunch today. He adds a lot of laughter to the place that we all enjoy.

May 15 — Apricot

At Perelandra. Worked with a woman who was introduced to me by my chiropractor. She has asked me to teach her several things, to supply some pieces she feels are missing in her quest to "move forward." In return, she will be typing the March and April Universal Light transcripts. She seems drawn to them.

We have frost warnings for our area tonight.

May 16 — Ivory

I actually slept the "required" ten hours. The men are acting as if this was a personal victory for them.

At Perelandra. The garden survived, but they're calling for temperatures to drop in the mid-twenties tonight. I covered the transplants with straw and asked nature to help protect the garden.

At the Cottage. For the first time, we talked about what it might be like for me when I come full time—those first few days. I told them I'm really looking forward to hearing and seeing normally. They're most interested in sharing this time with me because they want to know what my changes will be. They feel strongly that I should take it slow and easy that first week. After that, they feel I'll probably be able to operate with full steam.

May 17 — Ivory

I got another good night's sleep. I must admit I'm feeling stronger and have more stamina. Switching my protein intake to the mornings seems to be helping. I'm not sure how the Cottage body can be so affected by the Perelandra schedule or how that body's energy can flow into the Perelandra body, but it obviously does. Its link must be the soul.

At Perelandra. The garden survived the cold well. I finished raking mulch around the roses, cleaned wild sorrel out of the outer ring, collected poker chips that I had left in the rows, watered everything with liquid seaweed mix and spread cottonseed meal around the blueberry bushes. This garden is way ahead of last year's.

At the Cottage. The men are flying high about the good day they had. Apparently several key coins were flipped.

May 18 — Apricot

I can feel the garden pressures easing. I'm coming to the end of that annual two-month period where it seems everything has to be done at once.

I met with one of the people today who I have talked to about the Cottage. She fully accepts this reality, and we had an easy, good exchange. It makes such a difference when I'm talking to someone who doesn't fight me on my life. I feel as if I've gone through the pain and lessons of having a lack of or limited support. Now I've released much of my disappointment and anger about this and reached a new balance, and it seems as if I'm beginning to draw a few people who can support this reality expansion.

May 19 — Yellow

JAMFD

May 20 — Ivory

Even though I'm rebuilding my strength, I can tell I'm still going through the re-wiring process that my chiropractor detected. At Perelandra, I'm taking supplements daily to stabilize the adrenals and my pelvis is needing a daily adjustment as well.

At Perelandra. The two friends who are comfortable with the Cottage information visited today. The husband met with Peter Caddy this afternoon, and Peter has asked that he (the husband) ask me to come to some potluck dinner and talk he is giving on Tuesday evening. He would like to see me. I told the husband I would call them tomorrow about my decision. The last thing in the world I want to do is get swept up into one of Peter's new-age evenings with a bunch of his adoring fans.

At the Cottage. I told them Peter was in town and trying to get me to come into the suburbs for one of his evenings. They urged me not to put myself out right now unless I really want to see Peter.

May 21 — Apricot

At Perelandra. Peter called our mutual friends again to *urge* them to get me to come see him. He wants to talk to me. He has a couple of free hours tomorrow afternoon before the potluck dinner and talk, so we would have time to talk privately. Peter has never pressed to see me like this before, so I decided to go, and I also decided to tell him about the Cottage—exactly like the dream I had five months ago about telling him.

At the Cottage. I checked with them to make sure it was okay to tell Peter about the Cottage. David said he thought it would be a good idea.

May 22 — Ivory

I had a restless night with little sleep. I guess I was keyed up about meeting with Peter.

At Perelandra. Peter and I were joined by one of the friends who supports my Cottage life. Peter has been staying at her house while he is in town, and he invited her to the meeting. As soon as I said that I think I'm working in the "Pentagon of the White Brotherhood," Peter stopped me and went out of the room to get a friend of his. When the two men resettled, Peter explained that his friend works at the Pentagon and is also working to infuse Aquarian consciousness and thinking into the Pentagon. Recently, he has run into some seemingly insurmountable walls. The two men had talked at lunch today about these problems and were unable to come up with any solutions. Peter told him answers would come. So, in I walked, and there we all sat—a little amazed at the whole thing. I told them they'd have to talk to David about the problems because I knew nothing in this area that might be useful. I called David, and we decided to meet with the fellow right after my talk with Peter. I would be the one connecting Peter's friend with David and would be translating back and forth for them.

While I was hooked up to David, Peter wanted me to ask him if he got some report Peter wrote and sent to twenty-four scientists and world leaders back in the 1950s. Peter had been able to verify that everyone received their copy of the report, except for David. David said he *still had the report* and wanted to meet with Peter about it. Peter was visibly surprised by this turn, and it was clear he had not expected this to be David's answer. He (Peter) had a full free day on September 24, when he returns to the area and offered this as a meeting date. (Just this morning, he said, he wondered what was going to fill that day.) David then asked for a preliminary meeting to be held sooner, if possible. Peter's only other free time, between now and September 24, is three hours tomorrow afternoon, starting at 3 o'clock. David asked him to pencil us in.

I then went on to give Peter the information about the Cottage and its work. He didn't blink an eye at what I was saying. In fact, it all made sense to him—including my involvement. I told him I was glad it made sense to one of us.

In the meeting between David and Peter's friend, I learned that David already knew about this fellow and his efforts. They spoke to one another, through me, for about an hour. David gave him advice about priorities and presentation in his situation. I was terribly nervous about being in the middle in this meeting, but David, the fellow from the Pentagon and Peter felt the meeting went smoothly and was obviously helpful. Peter was pleased at how well things had slipped into place around a "seemingly insurmountable" problem. I, on the other hand, was a bit in shock about the development that had occurred. I had not been prepared to function publicly as a go-between for the Cottage.

At the Cottage. I got in late. The men were still pleased about the meeting with Peter's friend. I regaled them with descriptions of the warm-up act for Peter's talk this evening, and I also asked them what the meeting would be about tomorrow, but they would only tell me it has to do with Peter's report.

May 23 — Gold

It was another long, restless night for me. At breakfast I talked to the men about my fears and apprehensions around functioning as a middleman for the Cottage. I have a concern about accuracy. They assured me I am "on" and doing fine—and the only way through my apprehensions is to keep moving. Blah.

At Perelandra. I spent time alone, preparing for my part in the meeting. I cried for about forty-five minutes—I guess I was releasing tensions, which I suspect have something to do with my re-wiring and moving through the tunnel that the chiropractor talked about. All I know is that something is happening.

Meeting with Peter. On our end, we just had Peter and me—and a thunderstorm. On the Cottage end, we had David, Hyperithon and

Butch (who was taking notes). At David's suggestion, I split so that I could be present at both ends and hear firsthand what was being said by all. Again, Peter didn't have any problems with what was going on—namely the Split Molecular Process and two bodies. All he wanted to know was what he needed to do to assist, and he was most impressed when we said he had to do nothing and that we had it all under control. The meeting was to explore the possibility of Peter doing more work with the White Brotherhood in the area of government and military. David explained that he would like to activate the necessary Aquarian changes in the government/military areas, and he would like to do a major shift globally. David then went on to describe the plan, as he and the team have worked it out so far. It would draw on Peter's work in the 1950s, and it would involve a large number of space souls to assist with the major shift. Peter's job would be to select a site on Mt. Shasta (in northern California) from which the shift would be triggered and to get the right people to that site to function as witnesses. My job would be to work with nature to prepare the site for this mission and to function as liaison between the Cottage and those chosen to witness the shift on the Earth level. David's job would be to put together the whole shebang.

After he finished giving an overview of the mission, David asked if Peter and I would like to participate. Peter agreed immediately, both to the plan and the goal. I was a bit overwhelmed by it all—I had not been prepared for this beforehand—but I agreed anyway. So I now need to go to Mt. Shasta before the meeting on September 24 to do preliminary work with nature on the site. This means Peter must locate the exact site before then. We agreed we would all meet (so to speak) at Perelandra on the 24th. David and Peter expressed that they were each looking forward to working with one another— and we closed the meeting.

When Peter and I were alone again, we talked. He was pleased that his earlier "space brother work was not for naught." He has no problems accepting any of this—however, *I* can't believe it's happening. Then he addressed my life at the Cottage. He said he's heard of people shifting from one body to another, but he has never met anyone who was doing it consciously. This, he feels, is what I am pioneering. He had many questions about the nuts and bolts of the process.

After about an hour, we exchanged private phone numbers and parted. We joked that since we had nothing else scheduled for this summer, why not be involved in a major global mission? Peter said this kind of thing is what keeps life from getting boring.

On the drive back to Perelandra, I felt like I was in a fog. I simply couldn't believe this was happening and that I would have to go to Mt. Shasta this summer to prepare a site. I feel like I am in way over my head. Plus, I think it's nuts.

At Perelandra. Clarence asked about the meeting, so I told him what was decided and what Peter and I would be doing. He got excited and even asked questions.

At the Cottage. David was sky-high. Hyperithon had left right before I got home. They all say this thing is coming together just the way they had hoped. They've officially named the project the Mt. Shasta Mission. I told them I was already getting ideas about what I am supposed to do at the mountain in September. I need to bounce these ideas off nature and find out how to proceed so that nature and the Cottage will each have the information they need after September. I have informed the men they are all crazy.

May 24 — Gold

I slept deeply and woke late, feeling I was out of the tunnel. I needed no essences and no pelvic adjustment. At breakfast, David said I would not be brought in on any of the planning for the Mt. Shasta Mission until after the garden work was completed, and then it would only be in the need-to-know areas. He doesn't want to overload me. I said that just knowing about the project was over-loading me.

At Perelandra. Decided what I needed was a quiet, *simple* day in the garden—something gentle to balance the outrageousness of the past two days. I forgot as much as I could about Mt. Shasta and just focused on the garden. Of course, my mind kept returning to the project. I keep feeling the garden is the multilevel laboratory for working out the processes needed for the project. I sense I am to use the techniques I worked with for Gettysburg and the Eisenhower

Farm in conjunction with nature as a base for what we'll be doing with the Mt. Shasta Mission.

The folks from North Carolina called, and, in honor of my new re-wiring, I agreed to do another workshop there in October.

At the Cottage. The activity around the place has picked up tremendously and the energy is high.

May 25 — Dusty Pink

I admitted to the men that I do not feel comfortable about something. It's one thing to move forward and take a risk in my own life when it's based on my insight and information, but it's quite something else to impact other people's lives based on *my* insight and information. I don't like the position this puts me in. Just voicing my fears to them gave me a feeling of greater strength and confidence. They said these feelings are natural and will become less stressful as I do more work in this larger arena.

At Perelandra. I received a call from the woman who was present at my first meeting with Peter. She told me she was impressed by my ability to just lie down in a strange house, contact David and do the job that needed to be done. She said she felt telepathically connected to David during that time. I told her generally what was decided on in the meeting the next day and my feelings about this. As if coached by David, she said she'd be worried if I didn't have some apprehensions. To her this meant I was "working from the heart and not the ego." That went a long way to settle my nerves— well, at least it allowed me to *accept* my nerves.

May 26 — Apricot

At Perelandra. I received insight from nature to test with the Soil Deva for any fertilizers needed on the garden *between* the rows. As expected, something was needed. All the while I was applying the fertilizers, I kept getting ideas about experiments to do at Perelandra to prepare for the environmental testing at Mt. Shasta—different processes to work out and directions to explore. David has suggested I keep a list of these ideas and the results of any testing I do this summer.

At the Cottage. A much-needed quiet evening for all of us.

May 27 — Gold

At Perelandra. While I worked on the Universal Light transcripts, Clarence put bales of straw on two-thirds of the garden for me to spread later after it rains. (The woman who was going to do the typing dropped out.) I worked with the session that was done right after the first trip to Gettysburg. It explained some of the connections with the Mt. Shasta Mission. I had completely forgotten much of what had been said in that session. Now some of what David said in the meeting with Peter made a lot of sense. How easily I forget these things!

At the Cottage. They had a big golf game today. David and Tex have declared Seamus totally nuts. Max joined them just for the company and the walk. He's not allowed to swing a club for another two weeks. Actually, he's holding up beautifully. He hasn't needed essences for about the past six or seven days. David assures me Max is most committed to completing the shift that he's going through.

Before dinner, we talked about the changes the Mt. Shasta Mission will bring to our respective work areas. I have the feeling that our private time is over, and that the mission sets the tone for what we're moving into. They told me it has been a privilege to know me these past two years—that "the mettle of a person shows when they're under stress." They have quickly learned a lot about me. I told them that one important thing I've learned is that, no matter what, they are there for me. They asked if the future frightened me in any way. I said I wonder if I am truly able to do all the new things I feel sure lie ahead. David said I'll probably never lose these apprehensions, that they are a sign of someone's integrity in their work. I asked if they had any fears about the future. They have only the healthy fears that help keep them honest.

May 28

JAMFD

May 29 — Yellow

I'm looking ahead to a hellishly active week. As my days become more active, I am more willing to keep my focus in the present and not project nervously ahead. Also, I'm becoming more confident about impossible-looking schedules working out smoothly.

At Perelandra. Did a nature session for the second phase of the Gettysburg Battlefield work and also got some insight about how this is going to connect with the Mt. Shasta Mission. That was a surprise. I sent a copy of the session to the Cottage so that they know what nature is saying about all of this.

The chiropractor can't go with me to Gettysburg, so I called the woman who accompanied me to my meeting with Peter. She's delighted and suggested we go this Friday. It turns out that day is perfect.

I worked on the final typing of a Universal Light transcript. Completing this job has brought me to two decisions: (1) I dislike typing these things, and (2) I need to start using the computer. It's obvious that this job is mine to do, and I've got to get at it in a more efficient manner.

At the Cottage. They tell me that Mt. Shasta is coming together quite easily and quickly. David is pleased. He's still waiting for me to be out from under the garden pressure before including me in the details of what's going on. The men decided that Clarence should be invited to be one of the witnesses on the mountain next year.

May 30 — Gold

At Perelandra. I gave Clarence his invitation to Mt. Shasta. He says he feels "honored" to be a part of the group that will be there. He had not assumed he would attend and is happy to be invited.

We had the good rain I've been hoping for, so I can concentrate on spreading the straw out on the garden. It's a big job, but I'm getting help with two days of unseasonably cool weather. Somebody is on my side. Actually, the job went better today than I ever dreamed possible. I spread straw over two-thirds of the garden.

At the Cottage. Very tired. Sitting in the lagoon helped soothe body and soul.

May 31 — Ivory

At Perelandra. Finished spreading the straw. The garden is now officially in!

At the Cottage. They're concerned about my going to Gettysburg tomorrow to do phase two. It will include seven hours of driving because I will have to pick up my friend in the suburbs and drop her off afterwards. Also, I've pushed the last two days to get the straw on the garden. I told them I feel I must go to Gettysburg tomorrow, and I must get phase two completed, because I feel there is a timing involved here. I am certain I'll be okay. I'm not sure I convinced them, but they knew they had run into my stubborn will. (Did I say I was stubborn?)

June 1 — Gold

Gettysburg. The trip was much easier than I expected. I drove up to and into the battlefield area with a sense of familiarity, knowing exactly where to go. I went to the Eisenhower Tower first to check with nature to see if the phase one work was still holding. Only one essence was needed, which I administered from the Tower. Then I got the okay to proceed with phase two. I opened the full coning and asked David where I was to plant the three comfrey plants nature had told me to bring. He said they were to be planted in a triangle configuration near the Copse of Trees—not *in* the Copse of Trees, but near it. (When I saw the wrought-iron, spiked fence surrounding the copse, I understood why David had emphasized my not going in. By now I guess he's figured out that had he not been clear I would have climbed the fence and risked impaling myself.)

The planting went quite easily, once I found a spot that had more than a quarter-inch of soil before hitting rock. It's also where the groundskeepers won't be able to mow—thanks to some boulders. As per nature's instructions, I put out a call (silently) to all who participated in the Gettysburg Battle and are still in need of healing on the soul level to return to the battlefield any time between now and next June 1. As they pass by the comfrey—which is near stop #1 on the auto tour—nature will shift the energy of the comfrey plants into their systems for the needed healing on the higher soul levels. [Comfrey Essence is for soul-level healing.]

That's all that phase two consisted of, but as soon as I was finished, I felt a deep sense of relief. I had no idea until then how much phase two had been weighing on me.

Just then, an Eisenhower Farm tour bus went by en route to the farm. My friend suggested we take a tour—just for the fun of it. It felt strange to be walking around the Eisenhower Farm—like I was in a twilight zone. I fell in love with the huge barn.

We had dinner at my friend's house, then I headed back to Perelandra. I told Clarence about what we did and the Eisenhower Farm tour. I returned to the Cottage—to eat and to tell them about my day's adventures and the Eisenhower Farm tour. I'm trying to convince David that his barn misses being used and that I could put it to good use at Perelandra.

David told me that Hyperithon called this evening to confirm that, from the human perspective, phase two was complete and in motion, and he sends his heartiest congratulations. (Nature had already confirmed that the job was complete from their perspective while I was at Gettysburg.)

June 2 — Gold

JAMFD. Took the day off.

June 3 — Ivory

JAMFD. I'm on a roll. Took a second day off.

June 4 — Gold

At Perelandra. Pulled straw in around the plants and spent about an hour connected with Elizabeth basically talking about gardening. She has a small garden, and it's in form! She even has bugs. She's looking forward to hearing about how I deal with the insect situation as the summer goes on.

At the Cottage. We all headed out to Harry's for dinner.

June 5 — Apricot

At Perelandra. It's the day before the fortieth anniversary of D-Day. Just so I could stretch my concept of time warps to its limits, I connected with David while I watched (at Perelandra) a CBS special, "D-Day and Eisenhower." Walter Cronkite introduced a program that was originally broadcast twenty years ago on the twentieth anniversary of D-Day—a program that centered around David and Cronkite. So, I had two of me, three Davids (the man I was connected to, the man in 1964 and the man in the 1944 film footage they were showing), and two Cronkites (the man today and the man twenty years ago). Plus, the TV program covered three time spans:

(1) the present, (2) twenty years ago when the original program was taped and (3) Cronkite presenting the events that occurred forty years ago. It was like mirrors within mirrors. I recognized that the cadence of David's voice was familiar to me.

His memory of D-Day is complex. He has a deep calm on these anniversary days. It's not a struggle at all, but it is complex. He says he has a memory of the exhilaration, sense of accomplishment, a mission succeeding, the horrible waiting, sadness, death, destruction.... It is a quiet memory, not one of shouts and cheers.

June 6 — Gold

The men took David to lunch—a surprise for him.

June 7 — Ivory

JAMFD

June 8 — Brown

I received a contract from the Dutch publishers for *Behaving*. I took it home and asked both David and Tex to look at it. My gut feeling is not to get in a big issue about money.

I called my friends in Holland and talked about the book contract. I also planted the seed for them to visit Perelandra this summer.

June 9 — Yellow

At Perelandra. My in-crisis friend is no longer in crisis. She has a new home, a new job and no destructive partner. In short, she has a new life.

My Dutch friends called saying they are anxious to visit to hear more about the Cottage. They are checking out travel costs now.

At the Cottage. They tell me that the Mt. Shasta Mission plans are shaping up. They're starting to include me more in the discussions.

June 10 — Ivory

JAMFD

June 11 — Ivory

I'm in a color rut, especially ivory. I feel like something is going on—again—but I have no idea what. The men feel I'm adjusting to the new, more public role in my work.

June 12 — Gold

At Perelandra. My little friend Mindy (guinea pig) died last night. She went through a fascinating process. About two weeks ago, we discovered she was passing blood through the urinary tract. I connected with her higher self to find out what she needed. She did not want to go to the vet. She wanted a private cage for a while and needed cod liver oil twice a day for two days. She tested for different essences for seven days. She slowly improved, and it was clear that her pain was gone—and her spirits picked up. Clarence and I held her each evening, something she enjoyed. Last night, Clarence gave her some Perelandra lettuce while holding her. She ate enthusiastically. Back in her cage, she snuggled in the hay and went to sleep. She died during the night.

I felt her presence around me this morning, so I decided to check her for essences. When I connected with her, she immediately appeared in my mind's eye. I talked with her, reassuring her and trying to encourage her to trundle on—as Millie had. But she kept nibbling my nose. The essence she tested for showed she needed something for "conscious and unconscious fears and courage to follow divine guidance." I worked with nature to administer the essence to her and, after taking it, she nipped me on the nose, turned with a little hop and was on her way. I sensed her leaving my presence. I felt terrific about her process and the death transition help I gave.

The men have been hounding me to get my notes about these experiences, my research and what I'm learning on computer. They say that part of my laying the foundation that's needed prior to my coming to the Cottage full time includes getting my research computerized and out to others.

June 13 — Apricot

At Perelandra. Began learning to use the computer with Clarence as my teacher. It's a snap—and it's fun. I'm surprised.

June 14 — Gold

At Perelandra. Worked on the computer. I've named it "Butch" and my printer, "Brother Butch"—the weird monk in the cellar with the quill pen. The Cottage Butch says he's honored and delighted.

June 15 — Ivory

At Perelandra. Clarence and I visited the Gettysburg Battlefield and the Eisenhower Farm—at his request. I wondered if he had some healing to go through around that battle and if he needed a comfrey infusion. At the farm, the roses were in bloom. We sat on the lawn under a tree while a young ranger told us about Mamie's influence on Ike. It was just the three of us, and her fifteen-minute lecture went on for forty-five minutes while we three discussed the Eisenhowers. She was most surprised at the information I knew about them.

I stopped by the Eisenhower Tower to do a land check with nature for the farm. All is holding just fine.

June 16 — Yellow

My Dutch friends called. The wife is coming to Perelandra next Saturday for two weeks. Suddenly, I'm swamped with getting everything prepared for her visit.

At the Cottage. A big surprise when I got home. John has returned! We had a wonderful family evening.

June 17 through 19

JAMFD

June 20 — Yellow

At Perelandra. The colors for this year's solstice are gold and white. I made four bows for the major areas at Perelandra—the cabin, the new Elemental Annex (which is to be activated at the solstice), the garden center and the house. [The Elemental Annex is the name I've given our Nature Spirit sanctuary, which was originally located in the woods near the house and the first garden. That spring in 1984, I asked nature if it was appropriate to relocate the Annex, in light of the fact that the garden had been relocated. When nature said yes, I chose a triangular configuration of trees just outside the cabin and near the new garden to "give" to the nature spirits for their new "office area" and was told to participate in the shift and activation this summer solstice.] After the bows were in place, I did the Energy Cleansing Process for the entire property.

At the Cottage. I came home for my usual evening, knowing that I would be leaving at 12:30 A.M. for Perelandra for the solstice because I needed to be present for the Elemental Annex activation. I presented each man with a small solstice bouquet of golden yarrow from the garden.

June 21 — Gold

The summer solstice: 1:02 A.M.

From the cabin, I opened a Perelandra coning and immediately saw the link between the Cottage and Perelandra. Just before the solstice moment, I invited the nature spirits to the new Annex. At 1:02, I felt the Annex fill with energy and saw it light up. I received an invitation to come join nature in the new Annex, to join their party. When I entered the Annex, I could feel the celebration all around. Then a nature spirit—a faun—stood before me and allowed himself to become visible to my naked eye. I hardly knew what to say, except "Hello" and "I love you." I made clear eye contact with this lovely faun for the longest time. It was a special and extraordinary moment. I remained in the Annex for about an hour feeling the movement and celebration going on around and within me. When I felt things settle, I returned to the Cottage and told the men about what had occurred. I had strong, deep feelings that Perelandra was now open and functioning on a new level.

June 22 — Apricot

At Perelandra. Clarence called me from work this morning to tell me that a dog had been hit near us and badly injured. He wondered if I could connect with it and test it for essences. I told him I'd try.

I opened a nature coning and asked if I was to help this dog. As soon as I heard "yes," the little black dog was before me in my mind's eye. He had died, but he still needed help through his transition. I gently pet his head and touched his face. He was sweet and appreciative. I talked to him, introducing myself and telling him what I wanted to do with the essences. All the time I spoke, he stared right into my eyes. I tested that I could proceed with the essence test. When I asked nature how I would administer the essences to him, a bowl of water appeared between the dog and me. I put the needed drops into the bowl and let him drink from it—which he did eagerly. Then I stroked his head again and encouraged him to move on. He gently licked my nose and disappeared.

Over the radio later in the day, I heard about a mine accident in Canada in which the last survivor (a twenty-two year old man) had stayed alive for twenty-seven hours while rescue teams worked to get to him. They were in voice contact all that time. When the rescuers were just six minutes away from him, the mine collapsed again and he died. The rescuers wept. This story was clearly audible to me, even though the radio was so low I couldn't hear any of the other news stories. I took this as a hint, opened the coning again and asked if I was to help this young man, as well. I was told yes, if I wanted.

I called the young man into the coning and, like the dog, he appeared in my mind's eye. He was dusty and his face was blackened from the mine, but I saw no injuries. I introduced myself, explained the essences and offered them to him, if he wished. He indicated that he wanted me to test him. Once I found out what he needed, I asked nature to assist me in administering them to him. Afterwards, I told him he was free to move on now and asked if he knew where to go. He said yes. (I was grateful. Had he said no, I wasn't sure what I was going to do next.) He thanked me—he seemed so at peace. He released himself from my vision, and I felt his energy dissipate from the coning.

Both experiences touched me deeply—and I cried. I realized this was a service I could offer, but I had questions as to whether I could take the emotional impact of it. After these two experiences, I felt drained emotionally.

June 23 — Yellow
At Perelandra. My friend from Holland arrived. I'm exhausted, so Clarence picked her up at the airport by himself, giving me a little time to rest.

June 24
At Perelandra. I had intense conversations with my friend about the Cottage. She's not challenging in tone, but she just wants to know a lot of detail about things—a lot of which I don't know.

June 25

At Perelandra. I photocopied the Universal Light transcripts for my friend to read. We are continuing to have long talks about the Cottage. I am *truly* appreciating my cabin and having my own space. It makes it a lot easier to get back and forth to the Cottage every evening. My friend spends her mornings at the house on the deck reading and taking in the sun—when it's shining. She's brought the Dutch rain. She says she enjoys these mornings alone because it's something she never gets in Holland. Now I'm not sure if she's fully comprehending the overall picture of my Cottage experiences and life.

June 26

At Perelandra. We had a Universal Light talk today and discussed the implications of the military information contained in the Gettysburg sessions. We also talked about the horizontal/vertical theory and triangulation. It's interesting to me to hear her questions and to see how this information is being accepted by someone else.

June 27

At the Cottage. Hyperithon came to the Cottage to discuss the new post-death process with me. He explained that I would not be inundated with a never-ending line of souls seeking help. Only those who are open to using flower essences would want my assistance. This service is to occur within the first seventy-two hours after death. Any healing assistance that can occur during this time would set the tone for the transition after death. Usually, healing from the death-related situation is part of a longer process that we all experience after death. By administering essences from the Earth level in that first seventy-two hours, the initial healing is accelerated, and this is most advantageous to those who have died. Hyperithon felt that this insight about the process would help me use it without the emotional drain.

This service appeals to me because for several years now I have seen the benefit of using essences during the death process. The problem has been with getting to the person who is dying or convincing others to test the essences for someone they know who is dying. Now I know we can come at this issue from the other end. In fact, the newly dead person can now come to us.

At Perelandra. Drove my friend to Skyline Drive for a relaxing day.

June 28

At Perelandra. Drove her to Gettysburg. We checked on the comfrey, which is doing fine. She asked to see the Eisenhower Farm, so we went on the tour. She was most impressed by David's simplicity and surprised an American president should live such a "simple life." She remarked that her sister in California has a more "elegant" house.

My friend's visit is intense and draining.

June 29 and 30

[Due to my schedule as a result of our house guest, I missed writing notes these two days. Also, for some reason I did not record the colors I wore during her visit.]

July 1

The schedule of not returning to the Cottage until late because of my friend's visit does not sit well or easily with me. I feel disconnected from my family, and I told them this. So, they planned a family dinner for tonight. It was something I desperately needed and, afterwards, I felt revitalized. My friend's visit is still intense and tiring. She's now resisting the Cottage reality and setting up strange resistances toward me as well.

July 2

I awoke furious at my friend's resistance and increasingly cutting comments. I talked this over with the men at breakfast, and they advised me to ignore her. This hit me as funny, and I laughed. But they kept saying, "Just ignore her. You stand your ground and make her adjust to you." Their advice and my laughter freed me from my anger.

We had tentatively scheduled a Universal Light session for this morning, so I decided, in the spirit of ignoring my house guest, I would go on with the session. It's the first one in two weeks, and I was afraid if I waited any longer, I'd get rusty. He chose an excellent topic—timing. I felt Universal Light's energy as never before—insistent, driving. He seemed anxious about getting this information across and out to others. I felt more relaxed and quite good about my translation. The men felt this was information they could implement in their area immediately.

July 3

At Perelandra. The couple who have been supporting me about the Cottage are mutual friends with my house guest and were anxious to see her, so I drove her into the suburbs to visit them. They visited with her asking about her husband, Holland, her life, and so on. I watched these two people bend over backwards to reach out to her in discussion and gesture, and she showed complete disinterest in their efforts. It was good for me to observe others having difficulty with her.

July 4

At Perelandra. Clarence and I took our house guest to see the Luray Caverns. Another good break.

July 5

At Perelandra. The house guest and I went together to the chiropractor. After I observed the chiropractor's work with her, it was my turn to be checked out. I felt tired and deeply weary when she started, but I had no specific pain or glitches to report.

Perelandra body: She adjusted the pelvis and sacrum, and the pancreas/thyroid combination tested weak. I needed one essence.

Cottage body: I needed to take one B-complex tablet, two adrenal supplements and 200 IU of Vitamin E—all of this just to deal with the drain I'm experiencing from my house guest.

It was clear to the chiropractor that I was drained and exhausted, and the two bodies were reacting to this. She would not let me scan Max or David, as we had planned, because she felt my exhaustion would put the scanning into question and make the testing unreliable. She said I need to take a two-week vacation at Perelandra and

the Cottage—no Universal Light, no computer work and no kinesiology, healing or post-death work. I am to work in the garden at
Perelandra and take a lot of walks at the Cottage. My condition
stunned us both. I knew I was tired, but I didn't suspect this. I felt
concern from David and Max throughout the examination, and I
could tell they were already planning my vacation for me. I felt
defeated by this turn of events and even cried a little. David and
Max understood what I was feeling. My chiropractor and house
guest just teased me for crying.

At the Cottage. I returned as soon as I got back to Perelandra. The
men had already drawn up my vacation schedule, which will go into
effect as soon as my house guest leaves in two days.

July 6

At Perelandra. A more relaxing day. Our guest has dropped much of
her resistance toward me. I guess observing the chiropractor working with me yesterday helped convince her of the Cottage reality.

July 7 — Dusty Pink

At Perelandra. We drove to the airport and sent our house guest
back to Holland.

July 8 — Gold

At Perelandra. Clarence had an interesting and strong dream that he
feels is about the Cottage. Because of the house guest's visit, he has
heard quite a bit about the Cottage lately, and we think this is what
triggered the dream. In it, he looked out his bedroom window and
saw two *huge*, brown, furry horses eating leaves from the tops of the
trees. It was a natural scene except for the size of the horses, and he
felt no sense of danger from them. He ran to get his camera to take
a picture of them as proof to others what he saw but, on return, the
horses were gone. The only evidence they had been there were the
holes in the tree tops where the horses had eaten the leaves. He was
disappointed, realizing anyone could explain those horses away.

He feels that the dream points out the stretch the Cottage gives
him. He knows it's real and natural—just a lot bigger.

Now that Clarence has begun to open up more to my Cottage life,

David has offered to talk with him at any time Clarence chooses and has set up the framework for Clarence to use. Clarence said he would like that, but he's not ready to talk yet.

July 9 — Yellow

At the Cottage. Max and I fulfilled our respective therapy responsibilities by going on a walk together.

July 10 — Ivory

JAMFD, with a vacation flavor. I'm resuming my puttering lessons.

July 11 — Gold

At Perelandra. I'm rereading the World War II book that started all of this for me. What a difference two years make. This time I'm not being blasted open by the material, and I'm actually able to absorb and understand what I'm reading.

July 12 — Apricot

At Perelandra. I began to experience pain on the right side of my neck—C-1 is out and it won't massage back into alignment. I sense something is trying to shift and I'm somehow resisting the change.

At the Cottage. I told the men about the neck pain at Perelandra and, as if this would do the trick, I announced that I accept whatever change is trying to occur. I want it, I'm ready for it to come in and it's time—whatever *it* is. I hoped this would help me massage C-1 back into alignment, but so far I'm not having any luck.

July 13 — Yellow

At Perelandra. Clarence is visiting his family in Roanoke this weekend. I'm looking forward to the time alone at Perelandra

At the Cottage. Had a terrific discussion with John about the process Clarence is going through to open up to my Cottage life. I can tell he's interested because he's faced with a similar challenge to consciously open to his own life at the Cottage.

July 14 — Ivory

JAMFD

July 15 — Ivory

At Perelandra. My neck pain is getting worse. My noble declarations have not resolved it.

At the Cottage. John is leaving tomorrow, so we had a big family dinner. He's been at the Cottage for a month this time—I'm going to miss him terribly. After dinner he asked me questions about the fears I've had in accepting the Cottage and what it was like for me to make the leap to fully embrace the Cottage reality. I can tell he's poised to make this leap and that he wants it. It's going to be fascinating to see what needs to happen in John's Earth life for him to consciously accept the Cottage and to call me at Perelandra.

July 16 — Gold

The Cottage and at Perelandra. What goes around, comes around. Today *I* assisted Hyperithon in placing a disk in the head of a friend on the Earth level. It was a mutual decision on their part, and appropriate for her because of her work. To assist, I split to the Cottage once I got the friend settled in my cabin. Hyperithon was already there to meet me and, when we were ready, he gave me a small, gold transistor that was about one-quarter the size of a dime. (It's the first time I've seen what one looks like.) I received it in my left hand (at the Cottage) and placed my right thumb (at the cabin) just above the area of my friend's forehead, one inch above her third-eye area. I shifted the transistor from my left Cottage hand to my right cabin thumb and focused its energy into her forehead. At no time did I touch her forehead. I felt the transistor energy pass through my hands and smoothly shift into her forehead. When it was over, I was no longer holding the transistor at the Cottage.

He now needed to activate it. For this, he held my left Cottage hand and moved energy through me, into my cabin thumb (still one inch over her forehead) and, from there, directly into the transistor. Once again, I could feel the energy move through me, and, as it activated the disk, my friend's eyelids fluttered. The whole procedure took about fifteen seconds.

Once the job was complete, I gave her the "phone number," and she tested the transistor to make sure it worked. Everything tested out fine. She told me that as soon as the transistor went into her forehead, a pressure she's had in that area for almost a year was released. She has no doubt the transistor is in her head.

At the Cottage. Hyperithon stayed for dinner. We had coffee together on my balcony and talked over today's process. It was slightly different than the one I experienced two years ago, but he said being able to work directly with me at the Cottage facilitated the process enormously. He questioned me at length about the cost my acting as an intermediary in this had on me. In all honesty, I had to admit that it felt familiar and was quite easy, and that I was getting used to shifting energy from the Cottage to Perelandra. While we were talking, the ease and casualness of the experience I was having with Hyperithon on my balcony struck me. There we were, sitting side by side drinking coffee and discussing business. It is amazing how far I've come in the four years since receiving my own transistor.

July 17 — Apricot

JAMFD

July 18 — Yellow

At Perelandra. I had a strong urge to locate John's home town in our atlas. I wondered if, at the same time, he was checking his maps to see if there really is a Jeffersonton in Virginia.

July 19 — Brown

At Perelandra. My energy is beginning to return. I mulched the garden along the east side of the cabin and had a wonderful time doing it.

July 20 — Yellow

Over breakfast the men and I talked about how tough it is to integrate the reality of simultaneous lifetimes. The only way I could deal with it was to let it happen and not think about it. I had to just let Katie's life come through me. I also told them I now understand that the ice skating training in 1982 happened in part to fully ground and activate the Cottage body. David said he knows of some of his lifetimes but hasn't experienced them as directly as I have mine— and he's not sure he would want to.

July 21 — Dusty Rose

At Perelandra. We had the couple who supports the Cottage to dinner. They also fully support Clarence and the process he's going through because of the Cottage reality. I think their support makes him feel less isolated.

July 22 — Gold

JAMFD

July 23 — Gold

At the Cottage. During a discussion I had with Tex, I found him intellectually pressing me—that old habit of his. It's been a while since he has done this with me and, this time, I called him on it right away. He apologized and backed off immediately. I can tell he's softening around this habit—at least with me. I was pleased at how easy it was for us to deal with this together this time. I didn't have to go stomping out of the room, and he won't have to dress up in a bunch of "battle-wound" bandages.

July 24 — Ivory

At Perelandra. I talked with a woman who is interested in distributing *Behaving*. She automatically leans to the Princeton Business School fallout process—flood the market and catch the fallout. I told her the book has an energy and rhythm of its own that I have tried to respond to since day one, and this is to continue. I want to let the book create its own path, and I just want to be there to quickly and efficiently respond to that direction. I told her I call this "co-creative organic marketing." It's humans and nature working together to achieve quality energy flow, facilitation and efficiency. I can feel that the book stands on its own and that it moves on its own power. I don't have to hawk it or push it—I simply have to assist it's movement. I'm not sure she grasps what I'm saying. We'll see.

I took a walk and did some thinking. I felt these past two years— the movement forward, the accomplishment and the stability it has given me. What an extraordinary two years.

July 25 through 27 — Gold, Gold, Ivory

JAMFD times three.

July 28 — Dusty Rose

The last few days have been "normal" but with an odd air about them. I've been completely ordering the garden and cleaning the cabin. Basically, I've been responding to a strong flow moving through me—hence, the crazy cleaning days. I have little idea what they mean, but I have a gut feeling something is in the air.

July 29 — Ivory

At Perelandra. The head pressure that I've been having periodically the last couple of days got much worse today. I realized I must do something about it on my own because I can't get an appointment with my chiropractor until next Thursday. That's too long to wait. I'll lose my entire week to pain and only be able to half function.

I felt the pull to work gently and quietly in the garden today. While there, one of our neighbor's cows ambled through Perelandra en route to eat the garden. Our dogs Jesse and Elsa cut the cow off on the path and were raising quite a raucous over the intrusion. As I was running up to aid in the chaos, I saw Jesse nip at one of the cow's legs and get kicked in the head. The kick stunned her, but she was still conscious. She was cut around the eye, but luckily the eye itself looked okay. I carried her to the house and gave her a strong dosage of Rescue Remedy, then called the vet. He's concerned about concussion and brain swelling. She's now at the vet overnight for observation. Elsa and I got the cow out of Perelandra. We both feel Jesse's absence.

Toward late afternoon, my head pain was still present. I didn't think I was going to have the patience to live with this any longer, so I opened a coning and asked for help. I had decided I would do whatever I was told. Hyperithon instructed me to lay down on my bed in the cabin loft at Perelandra, with my adjustment wedges and essences by my side. Then I was to split to the Cottage and lay down in the lagoon room with David by my side. He would assist and stabilize me. When I had all this arranged and was ready, I was to tell Hyperithon.

As soon as I gave him the go-ahead, Hyperithon explained that he was connecting me to the White Brotherhood "medics," and that all I had to do was lie still and let them work with me. They would be working with both bodies simultaneously.

The medics immediately began by gently holding my head for awhile. It was a comforting experience, and I could feel myself relaxing. The next thing they did was give me an image of getting Jesse back from the vet and her being completely well. That relaxed me even more. I realized that wherever my focus was directed was where they were working. I felt things happening in my head, then diaphragm, under my sternum, the pelvis, the diaphragm again, head—the right femur rotated in, and the pelvis shifted down toward the floor for a second time. I felt emotion rising when they worked on the diaphragm. When they rotated the right femur, emotions rose again and I cried a bit. They rotated the left femur gently inward, holding the rotation in place as I cried deeply. I had a sense that they wanted me to give them "permission" to continue, so I did. That's when they worked on my head one more time.

When body parts stopped "moving around," we talked—for the first time. They said that this is the medical procedure I could use from this point on and that it could be done with or without the presence of my chiropractor. For this procedure, I must be split at the Cottage so that both bodies are activated in form and can be worked on simultaneously. David is to be present at the Cottage for stabilizing and balance. I am to open a full coning, include both bodies and David, and the chiropractor, if she's present. From that coning, I am to open to the Brotherhood doctors, tell them what's bothering me and pay attention to what they're doing. If the chiropractor is present, she is to simply pay attention and do whatever is requested of her by the medics. By observing their work, she will learn new directions in her own work. I can open this process from any location on the Earth level, which means I can travel and not be concerned about my bodies possibly "going off" and being stranded. Right away, I realized that the implications of this procedure were enormous for me. They recommended that I work with them frequently and urged me not to hesitate contacting them if I feel pain. They told me how to close the coning and that, after this session, I was to go for a short walk (about one-quarter mile) at Perelandra and the Cottage simultaneously.

David accompanied me on my walk at the Cottage. As we walked along, I could feel distinct differences. I no longer had any pain in my neck, there was no pressure in my head, my hip sockets were operating differently, and there was a deeper lumbar arch that made me feel more balanced and stable. I also felt the walking was "greasing" me structurally and pumping the CSF more strongly.

I spent a quiet evening at the Cottage just letting this experience and the changes seep in. The quality and feeling of the shifts are different—deeper—from when the chiropractor works with me or I work on myself. I can tell this is a *big* step. I'm amazed and impressed. The men are pleased that my medical assistance will now be from within the White Brotherhood.

July 30 — Ivory

At Perelandra. Spent a comparatively quiet day in the garden. In late afternoon, I picked up Jesse at the vet. She's fine, but she needs to be kept quiet for another week because she's still vulnerable to brain swelling. She was thrilled to see me and to be home, and doubly thrilled to see Elsa.

July 31 — Yellow

At Perelandra. An acquaintance who knows something about astrology gave me some interesting insight about my chart. My Mars is in retrograde. She says this means it's easy for me not to know how much physical energy I'm putting out at any given time and it's easy to exhaust myself. I should pay attention to the amount of rest I'm getting.

At the Cottage. At the risk of unleashing the Jewish mothers, I discussed this insight with the men. They already knew this because Tex had done my chart not long after I joined the Cottage. This is one reason why they badger me (they used the word "coax") about my need for more rest. I said I would try to cooperate a little more from now on.

August 1 — Ivory

At Perelandra. I've been getting lots of orders for the book lately, so I spent the afternoon getting everything packed up and mailed out. My favorite thing is licking stamps.

Worked the new medical process with the chiropractor so that I could show her what I'm now doing and get her impression of the work. I split from her office to the Cottage and was joined this time by David, plus Max and Hyperithon, who wanted to observe the process as well. After I opened the coning, I was told to have David seated at my head at the Cottage and the chiropractor at my head at the other end. Then the chiropractor tested both bodies to see what condition they were in before we started. The Perelandra body was fine. The Cottage pelvis was out. She did not have Max give me the adjustment.

When we were all ready, I told the "Company docs" to start. My entire right side felt like it was being gently tilted, then lowered. This was *very* relaxing—especially the lowering part. They did this three times. Then they did the same thing twice to the left side. My focus shifted to my head, and I felt electric-like energy moving from one lobe of my brain to the other—mostly right to left. It felt like some kind of balancing procedure. The chiropractor cupped her hands on each side of my head, holding them about two inches away, and she felt the energy passing from one side to the other. They worked on the diaphragm area again, this time to the left of the sternum. My focus shifted back to the head after this. While I concentrated on that area, the chiropractor saw two "supports" forming from the left leg to the right shoulder and the right leg to the left shoulder. It created an X, with the supports crossing at the diaphragm. My left side felt like the left foot was plugged into an electric socket. I felt the left side of my neck relax, then the right side. The whole left side of my body dropped toward the floor, then the right side. The sensation of the X felt stabilizing to me. The light that I saw when my eyes were closed changed from dark lavender to white. The chiropractor said that usually signifies a clearing. She was instructed to test me for essences, and I tested for three to be taken at the Cottage level only. The Perelandra body was clear. She was asked if she understood the relationship between the X stabilization, the point at the diaphragm where the supports cross and the head balancing. She said she could *feel* it, but she wasn't understanding it intellectually. They assured her that she'd understand after observing further sessions as they work on the X.

Before closing down the coning, she checked both bodies again. Neither one of them needed adjustments, supplements or essences. I closed everything down, and she and I looked at one another. We knew we were on to something here. For me, this couldn't come at a more perfect time. It is freeing and gives me tremendous flexibility. If I need help, I can get it immediately, no matter where I am.

At the Cottage. I had coffee with Hyperithon and David to go over the medical session with them. Hyperithon told me these medical sessions are a first for the Brotherhood, as well as for me. They've not been able to transcend and stabilize realities well enough to work *directly* with individuals, and adding the coning and nature to the mix did the trick. They've also not worked with this kind of situation with two physical bodies operated by one conscious soul. My medical team has kept up with my progress with the chiropractor through Hyperithon because of his transistor. He has been able to monitor all our sessions. They all felt it was important that I go through the series of shifts and changes that have occurred over the past couple of years before opening to this new level of work. We've got ourselves quite a breakthrough.

August 3 — Dusty Pink

Finally, it has struck me that I have truly accomplished something in this adventure I call my life. I have faced it and I have done it. I've been completely focused on my journey, one step at a time, and now I've suddenly looked around and taken in the whole. I feel a deep sense of accomplishment.

At the Cottage. When I shared these thoughts with the men, they practically cheered, saying, "It's about time you realized this." We had a celebration dinner at Nino's.

August 4 — Gold

JAMFD

August 5 — Yellow

I awoke with a series of thoughts and scenes going through my head. Each scene was clear and effortless, and I was able to relax my mind and stay in the moment without frantically flipping my thoughts around, as I so often do. I felt like I was experiencing "thought stability," and that it was moving me into a whole new internal communication. This was a completely different experience for me, and I wondered if it was the result of the work of the Brotherhood medics.

August 6 — Ivory

At Perelandra. I worked in the office, and as the day progressed, I developed head pain that kept intensifying. I spent time before going home trying to ease it out.

At the Cottage. The pain worsened as soon as I arrived. I wasn't sure if I should ask for a medical session since we already have one scheduled for Wednesday. I called Hyperithon and asked his opinion on the matter. He told me to open a session immediately.

The team worked on me for an hour—the head, neck, solar plexus area and pelvis. Then they did something with the energy supports that form the X. The support from the left leg/right shoulder felt stronger than the other one. They had me visualize the right leg/left shoulder support connection. As we worked, I felt my back stiffen and arch. This reaction surprised me, and I tried to relax and ease it out. I said nothing to the team, assuming my back would automatically soften. Around three times during the session, I thought I was passing out—like slipping gently under anaesthesia. I didn't fight the sensations, and I didn't pass out. The team said little to me when they finished, except to once again urge me not to hesitate to call them whenever I need help or an adjustment. They said they depend on me for this timing as we work together. They also suggested I check essences while we were still connected.

After I closed the coning, I was fine. I went for another short walk, and I had no pain.

August 7 — Dusty Rose

At Perelandra. Today I developed back pain that kept worsening as the day progressed. I tried to relax it out, but once I got home the pain intensified again. I wasn't sure if I should test the essences, then call the medical team or call them first. I called Hyperithon for advice, and he hooked me into the team right away. They told me to test essences and said that my pain was emotion-based and not structural. I was to relax and pay attention to the definitions of the essences I test for.

I tested essences and quickly received insight that the emotional issue was directly affecting the point where the X supports cross at the diaphragm. At the same time, I also realized that I was having difficulty accepting what I have accomplished these past two years because I don't know what to do with it once I acknowledge it. When I brought up my dilemma to the men, they told me it was critical that I accept my accomplishments and that I am to tuck them away in my heart. This is what I am to do with it. It stays there forever and serves to remind me of what I can do. As they talked about these things, I remembered something about manifestation. The last step—the one that requires an enormous amount of energy and focus—is when I draw in my focus and *accept* the physical existence of the thing I am manifesting. Without this, the thing can't fully ground. I must also do this with my own accomplishments these past two years. By not doing it, I am blocking the full grounding of the X they are trying to activate in me. The men said, quite seriously, that it's too bad I'm not in some kind of army so that I could get a medal for what I've done—some tangible recognition of what I've accomplished. I told them that I felt the problem for me was that I have no framework to compare what I have accomplished to. They suggested that I let it go for now. They felt confident the answer would come.

At Perelandra. I returned to finish some office work. While there, I read an article in *The Post* about Joan Benoit, the first U.S. Olympic gold medalist in the women's marathon. In it was this quote: "My brother said something very special to me yesterday. My family was in the stadium for the [awards] ceremony and as they were walking out, someone in a wheelchair looked at him and said, 'Are you Joan's brother?'"

"He said, 'Yes I am.' And the fellow said, 'Well, tell her that Joe said she gave me inspiration to try to walk again.' That choked me up because I'm very fortunate to be the person. I have the ability to do what I'm doing. If I can let somebody hope and try to achieve something, then I think that's great. I just do what I have to do."

Joan Benoit is shy. She just loves to run, and she's not at all happy with the publicity that has gone along with her accomplishments. When I read her statement, I began to understand that being acknowledged by others as well as by yourself made sense and had purpose. I saw her struggle and mine as similar. We even say the same thing: "I just do what I have to do." This is what makes sense to us. But there is something to accepting the privilege to inspire others by our own achievements.

At the Cottage. By the time I got back home, my pain had dramatically lessened.

August 8 — Ivory

I had a medical session scheduled for today and the chiropractor was supposed to join us at the Perelandra cabin, but she never showed up. We decided to go ahead without her.

The back pain returned, and by the time I got to the Cottage for the session, it was bad. Once again, Hyperithon was with us to observe, and David was at my head. The team told me that pain is often part of process and to relax as much as possible. For both bodies, I put pillows under my head and knees to ease out the pain some. Again they worked for an hour. This time the work was *very* subtle and hard to follow. At times the back pain was bad. I felt like I was being worked on with laser beams and that there was a precision about what they were doing. In mid-process, I felt a fear or terror rising in me, almost like a pain. My back, at this point, was in extreme discomfort. Several times throughout the process, they asked me if I'd like to stop for now or continue. I told them I saw no reason to stop. (I wasn't being courageous or stoic; I was being a coward. I didn't want to deal with this pain any longer than necessary.) About a third of the way through the process, they told me to tell David to put his hands on either side of my head and hold them there for the rest of the process. Immediately, I felt my head "even out." It was an amazing effect.

I had an emotional release that made me arch my back again, and the team told me to use the wedges to support the arched position for both bodies.

At one point—after the emotional release—the team held my left foot, and I felt the X support shoot to the right shoulder, then continue up through the neck and head. They held the right foot and the same thing happened, continuing through the head. Each side of my vision broadened and cleared.

They spent considerable time adjusting my jaw into a new, relaxed position that in turn opened my neck. It was a hard adjustment for me to "allow" because I've been setting my jaw since December 1982. I needed to release this so that my neck would open and allow the X to move through to the head. The tight neck had been separating my head from the rest of the body.

This was a tough session—painful and exhausting. At one point, I commented that they were graduates of the Marquis de Sade School of Medicine. This made us all laugh, and it gave me a new depth of relationship with the team. Later they suggested that they might have to nail my jaw into its new position, thus confirming my pronouncement about their medical schooling.

After the process, the back pain was completely gone. They told me to spend time relaxing for a few days and not think about the process. I am to test for essences twice daily until our next session, and I am to walk a mile each day. They assured me that their work was going well, and I was not to hesitate to call a session if I intuitively felt I needed one or if there was any discomfort. They said the walks helped seat and ground the changes that were occurring in the sessions.

Hyperithon, David and I went for a walk before dinner. I felt content and peaceful throughout the evening.

August 9 — Yellow

I awakened hearing many voices, similar to my experience in 1974. The sound was somewhere between inner hearing and outer hearing. I told the men at breakfast, and they said we should not jump to conclusions but wait to see what this leads to.

August 10 — Gold

A strange day at Perelandra. En route to visit my two supportive friends, I came uncomfortably close to getting flattened by a tractor-trailer. The driver was going too fast: about 70 mph, carrying an oversized load—a mobile home. The fellow in the left lane two cars ahead apparently saw this guy approach fast from behind, so he panicked and slammed on his brakes. I swerved to the right to keep from getting hit. The tractor-trailer idiot jammed on his brakes to keep from running over everyone and flipped across three lanes right behind me and into the guardrail. I stopped, along with the other two drivers, to get the tractor-trailer driver out. He only had an abrasion on his forehead but his truck was totalled, and I don't think anyone is going to want to live in that house.

The afternoon with my friends and their guests was alternately fun, frustrating and useless, depending on who was interacting and what was being discussed.

I returned to the Cottage late but glad to get back to sanity.

August 11 — Ivory

This time when I awoke, I heard just one voice, but I couldn't tell what was being said or what was going on. Perhaps this is due to the re-wiring the team is doing.

At Perelandra. I worked five hours in the garden with nature on the soil-balancing process I'll be using for the Mt. Shasta Mission.

At the Cottage. Exhausted. I handed over my notes on today's work to David. He plans to show them to Hyperithon tomorrow. They feel this work is one of the keys to the success of the project.

August 12 — Ivory

The chiropractor joined me in the cabin for a medical session. She checked me first: my pelvis was way out at Perelandra. The session lasted a half-hour, and the medical team worked in the same areas as before but with more subtlety. When it was over, both my chiropractor and I realized that they had *activated* the X, and that all the work up until now has been to get the X seated in both bodies. I could feel a new level of solidity—"light solidity" and flexibility. She and I asked questions about what this will mean for me. The X is stabilizing both bodies on their electrical, molecular and cellular levels, and it will stabilize my movement between the Perelandra level and the Cottage level. It will also facilitate what I have to do at Mt. Shasta. I will note changes in my thought processes and experience greater clarity in this area. For a while, my bodies may react to the activated X, and I am to test essences daily and contact them any time I sense a reaction. I'll be going through a series of fine-tunings now, and my bodies will indicate to the team the proper timing. No essences were needed now, but I was to check again later in the day. The chiropractor gave me a final check, and my pelvis was aligned. In fact, all was fine.

After the session, the chiropractor said she felt the activated X has changed my pH balance and that I should have the team check that out.

August 13 — Dusty Pink

I had to have another medical session this morning. My entire electrical system felt like it was short-circuiting—similar to a shattering. We set it up, and the team went to work right away. Halfway through, my breathing suddenly shifted and I felt like I was trying to push something out of my right thoracic area. I felt a kind of pain— not physical, but emotional. My breathing made me feel like I was trying to give birth from my chest. Finally, I felt a release and a clearing—afterward, I was exhausted. This time David held my head throughout the entire session. They worked on my neck, then reset and opened my jaw again. They confirmed that my pH balance had changed and that I would have to limit my coffee intake in both bodies to three cups daily, down from five. When we closed down the session, I was once again fine.

At the Cottage. When I returned, I connected with my team again just to make sure everything was okay. They scanned me, did a couple of minor things for fine-tuning and declared me fine.

August 14 — Yellow

This morning, I felt much better and sensed that I was coming "out of my current tunnel." Plus, I'm getting my strength back.

At Perelandra. I took a break from Perelandra and went shopping by myself.

At the Cottage. My energy level dipped again, which lowered my spirits a bit. I had a subtle, fine-tuning medical session that lasted for only a half-hour. Sometimes it's difficult to know or feel what they're doing. I'm assuming they're doing something because I always feel better when I come out of the session.

August 15 — Gold

JAMFD

August 16 — Ivory

At Perelandra. I talked to my usually supportive friend on the phone today for one and a half hours in an effort to make some sense out of what she was saying and to calm her down. She's gone mad—temporarily, I assume—and is not being especially supportive. In fact, she's attacking me. Nothing she's saying is making sense, but she says she got guidance to say it to me.

I bounced her attacks off Clarence to see if she was saying something I should hear but am missing. He had the same puzzled reaction I did, and said, "Nothing she's saying rings true to me." His support touched me. It's been a long time since he has defended me.

Peter Caddy called, and he's located the Mt. Shasta site. He also checked it out and verified it with two "sensitives"—friends of his who channel information. I don't think this is going to matter since I know nature will be giving the final okay. He says his contacts for witnesses have come fast and easily, and that everyone is excited. I told him that I now knew from David that St. Germaine is involved in this mission. He responded, "I'll say he is!"

At the Cottage. I bounced my friend's attacks off the men, just in case both Clarence and I were missing something. They're trying to get me to see how I am to let this kind of thing run off me.

August 17 — Dusty Rose

JAMFD

August 18 — Ivory

Awoke restless, so I tested for essences. I needed one, having to do with power and standing my ground. I immediately got an insight about it not being appropriate that I take responsibility for anyone else's emotional reactions and insecurities. I am to offer a stability from within myself that they can hone in on, if they wish.

At Perelandra. Bounced this insight off Clarence, and once again he listened and participated in the discussion.

At the Cottage. I had a medical session that only lasted a half-hour, yet it was quite dramatic. I fell away from consciousness into a kind of blackout. I wasn't asleep, nor was I conscious. After remaining in this state for a while, I suddenly felt a jolt throughout my entire body, like an energy release. Then my body felt free. I must have really gotten what the essence was all about this morning.

August 19 — Yellow

At Perelandra. Called Peter Caddy and worked out the dates for my visit in September—the 10th through the 16th. Then spent several hours working on the computer.

August 20 and 21 — Ivory, Dusty Rose

JAMFD times two.

August 22 — Ivory

Medical session. I asked the team to check out three areas where I was feeling some discomfort. For a while, the work was quite subtle, then I felt changes occur. The pelvis changed alignment, the right leg (at Perelandra) adjusted, and I had a painful energy release in the PB calf and ankle on the right leg. At one point I automatically began deep breathing. Several times my jaw easily relaxed and dropped, opening my throat and making my breathing easier. The team told me that testing for essences after each session was "most helpful to the process." They also suggested that we have medical sessions every two days for awhile. They felt this would help me maintain a good balance between the two bodies.

August 23 — Yellow

Since August 21, the essences I have needed at Perelandra are the same as the ones I have tested positive for at the Cottage. This is a significant change in pattern, and it must be a result of the new medical sessions. I can tell that the team is fine-tuning both bodies to be more in sync with one another.

August 24 — Apricot

I started my period today. The men say the glow is "brighter" than normal and that it seemed to develop more strongly two days prior to my period beginning this time. I told them I would pay for them to have sunglasses if it got too bright for them. I didn't want to be responsible for eye damage.

Medical session. While at Perelandra, my right shoulder and neck constricted and became painful, so this is what the team worked on. About halfway through the session, I could feel the area begin to release, but it kept "springing" back into constriction. The team suggested I test essences for this area immediately, then they continued to work. As the shoulder relaxed, various emotions arose and were released. After forty-five minutes, the shoulder was more relaxed and partially released. They suggested that we leave it at this point tonight and that I continue testing essences for the area tonight and tomorrow morning.

August 25 — Gold

I awoke with no pain and a relaxed shoulder and neck. I had a short medical session before leaving the Cottage so that the team could check everything out. I needed no essences.

At Perelandra. I took it easy this afternoon, getting away from Perelandra and going for a drive in the Blue Ridge Mountains.

Medical session. The only indication that the team was even working on me was that my shoulder and neck were more relaxed when they were finished. When they do their subtle work, I'd swear they weren't even in the room, let alone working on me. We agreed to let everything settle in for a couple of days and not have another medical session until Tuesday—unless I have an adverse reaction. They also want me to continue testing essences two or three times a day. I left the session feeling great. I also left the session knowing the name of the person who is working with me: Lorpuris (pronounced: lor-pure'-is). I don't know how many others are on the team, but he is the "chief physician" and the one who does most of the work.

Evening. I joined several of the men for dinner at Harry's. They told me that Lorpuris is the head of the White Brotherhood "medical department" and that he knew what he was doing. He's been anxious to work with me, but I had to go through the preliminary stages of the work before he could enter the picture.

August 26 — Yellow

At Perelandra. I had a visit from a friend of my supportive friends. They felt it was important for him to hear some things about my work, so I agreed to see him. At first I was not responding to his questions about my work and life at the Cottage in a fully candid manner. After a while, I began to feel as if my soul and body were separating and that I might faint, so I checked essences. From that point on, I responded to this fellow's questions openly, and I felt fine.

At the Cottage. I talked to the men about what had happened at Perelandra, and they suggested I relax about answering people's questions. They feel I'll know intuitively what to say, and I should just say it, just let it fly.

August 27 — Ivory

When I awoke, I was in a great mood from a vivid dream. I was learning how to scuba dive, and I was especially concentrating on breathing through the scuba gear. I found the experience of moving gently in the water and breathing through the gear most relaxing.

Just before going down to breakfast, I had a strong insight about developing a set of flower essences called the Perelandra Rose Essences. It was a powerful, clear and exciting insight, and a beautiful way of sharing the Perelandra garden with others. When I talked about it with the men at breakfast, they all said they thought I was onto something.

At Perelandra. Most of my work now is Mt. Shasta related, and I have no desire to focus on anything else. I'm continuing to spend long hours working with nature to fine-tune the soil-balancing process.

At the Cottage and a medical session. When I returned, I had the worst case of cramps I've had in years. I asked Lorpuris if the presence of the X was somehow conflicting with my period, and he said it was not. My bodies are shifting and adjusting to the X, and this is causing the pelvis to misalign, which in turn is causing the cramps. While Lorpuris worked on me, my right neck and shoulder tensed up again. Finally he was able to release about fifty percent of the tension. It feels like he is re-wiring me. Lorpuris assured me that everything is going along beautifully and that both bodies are responding well, even eagerly, to the work. I should not look at my pain as a step backwards. Rather, it is a result of the many shifts I'm going through right now. We decided to leave my shoulder and neck alone for now and resume work tomorrow morning.

August 28 — Dusty Rose
A morning medical session. My shoulder and neck are much better, and they relaxed even more during this short session. At one point I felt pressure on the sternum, and Lorpuris had me test essences for this. He also "warned" me that a release was coming. We plan another session for Thursday, unless something changes before.

The men surprised me with a trip—a two-and-a-half hour drive to a seaside resort. They had rooms reserved for us at a grand old hotel, and they had a suitcase packed for me with *everything* I would need for the beach. We spent hours walking along the shore, swimming and more walking. I threw a shilling into the ocean to seal my wish to return. We had dinner together in the hotel dining room. It was wonderful. I ended up spending the entire day at the Cottage level, and I loved it. It was just the break I needed—and wanted.

August 29 — Gold
I walked around the Cottage and Perelandra with a big smile on my face all day.

August 30 — Gold
At breakfast, I realized I didn't know the name of the hotel by the sea. They told me it was the Occanside Hotel, and that this was where Max and Tex went for their vacation. When I reminded them that they had told me the two had gone to a city, they corrected me saying they told me the two had stayed close to a town—which is true. The hotel is a few miles away from a resort town. When Max and Tex came back, they had suggested strongly that I be taken there. That's why they were so mysterious about everything. When they talked with me about their vacation, they did not mention anything about an ocean, just what they did in the town. Another one of

those little, pesky mysteries finally clears itself.

Medical session. Lorpuris continued with the work he has been doing. He asked me how my work concentration has been, and I said that for about a week it has been easy, even effortless, for me to hold my focus. He explained that the X is balancing and stabilizing every cell in both bodies. I will see differences more and more. I asked if it was also strengthening my male/female balance, and he said it was, but that my relationship with the men was aiding me in this area.

This session was really difficult, creating lots of tears, pain and some deep breathing. But we just moved through it. I tested for essences to stabilize the work, then ended the session by closing the coning.

August 31 — Ivory

A vivid dream. I was trying to help a spacecraft through various levels and into the physical, five-senses level, but I was having difficulty. I finally shifted it through to the physical by supplying the craft four times more phosphorus than was available in the land where it was trying to land. I experienced tremendous physical stress while working with this craft. When I woke up, my sternum felt like it had been "exercised" during the dream, as if the power to get the craft into the physical came primarily from my sternum. I had felt power surge from that spot during the dream, and I awoke with the residue of that surge in both bodies. I also felt a slight constriction in the chest. Immediately after taking the essences I needed, emotions began welling up.

At breakfast, I told the men about what was happening. By then, I was able to identify the emotions that were rising—my fears around the Mt. Shasta Mission. I'm not sure if I can take it if this mission doesn't succeed as a result of my role in it. And I'm not sure I can handle watching them heading for the Cottage level while I remain on the mountain. As I spoke about these things, I realized I could identify the pressure I have been experiencing in my chest these past few days—and the scream I felt inside me these past few weeks. I have held this pressure inside, not wanting to burden David or the others. I felt I somehow could find the balance I needed that would allow me to make it through the day of the mission. There's so much at stake, and I am nervous about holding down the nature role in the project and being the liaison between the Earth and Cottage levels. It all seems too big, and I feel too young and tiny.

David said he is extremely confident this mission will succeed and reminded me that they have the benefit of a broader perspective about the mission that I don't have. He suggested—strongly—that I talk about my mission feelings with them and that I do this often. They are the ones who can understand what I'm going through because they are the only ones out of everyone I know who understand the scope of the mission and why I would be so stressed and nervous about it.

As he spoke, the pressure released from my chest. I had the feeling that this has been the cause of some of the emotional stress I've been experiencing during Lorpuris's work and that it was also the release that Lorpuris had warned me about earlier. It felt good to finally identify this and let it out.

September 1 — Apricot

At Perelandra. I started getting back pain, and when I tested essences it also tested that taking them just at Perelandra would hold me until the medical session later.

Medical session. Lorpuris confirmed that for some pain I experienced at Perelandra, essences taken for just that one body would hold me until he could work with both bodies later. But this would not be the rule, and I should be prepared to "come home" when necessary. He estimates that the X work will be stabilized well before Mt. Shasta. For my plane flight and jet-lag problem when I go to California in a week, he wants to see me the evening before the flight to prepare me for the trip and as soon after I arrive as possible. This should take care of the jet lag.

His work was subtle, with what felt like more laser precision. He says he usually doesn't work on both bodies simultaneously. Instead, he works on one and then the other in the same session in a related or corresponding area to the earlier work. It's not necessarily in the same spot in each body. The key is balancing and gearing the two bodies. By the time the session was over, my back pain was gone.

September 2 — Yellow

At breakfast, we talked about my purpose for telling others about the Cottage. It has been clarifying for me lately, and I wanted to bounce my thoughts off the others. The purpose for sharing my Cottage life is not to give others an example of what they are to do in their lives. Rather, it is to give them an idea of what's possible, what's out there—the options in life. It's like two hermits—one subscribes to *National Geographic* and the other does not. The one who reads about the different kinds of life around the world conducts his life with a different intent and a sense of the whole. The other hermit may do the same tasks every day, but he has a more narrow intent and understanding as he moves through them. It's the integration of what is possible that releases the creativity in our own lives. It's not that everyone has to *do* what I'm doing, but the integration of this information, these realities and the possibilities that broaden and deepen their own actions and life. It's important for me to have clarity about this because it will enable me to hold the balance as I talk with others about my Cottage experiences.

I'm also getting clearer about the "early unconscious days" prior to seeing the television movie when I was first preparing to go to the Cottage. My decision as to whether or not I would try it was made from the higher level, and this was wise. If I had decided to wait, I would now have no memory of the possibility I had put off, and I would have no pain or longing over something I was missing. I also have the feeling that the process of choosing a second body and keying in different body decisions occurred about early summer 1981. That's when I *first* started getting the idea to cut my hair, but I didn't get the urge to act on it until I was close to activating the second body. In 1981 I probably was just beginning my move to make the bodies more similar because of the initial decisions I was making on a higher level that included hairstyle.

September 3 — Apricot

Medical session. Lorpuris worked on my left side for about an hour. In response to my questions he said that both bodies are available to him and that he sees them both fully—meaning the physical level, emotional level, mental level and soul level. David holding my head at the Cottage helps ground the work through to the physical level in *both* bodies. Some of the shifts seat in instantaneously, but others take twenty-four hours to fully seat. This is why I may feel better the next day rather than right after the medical session. He confirmed my intuition that he is to be part of this Mt. Shasta trip coming up next week. As part of the result of my work on the mountain then, he will be able to get an idea of the physical impact of the mission on Earth-level people. Plus, he wants to keep close tabs on me as I go through the mission processes with nature.

I asked Lorpuris if he has ever had physical lifetimes on the Perelandra level. Yes, a number of times. His lives were always related to medicine and medical discovery. I didn't want to take it any further than this. I wasn't sure what I would do with the information.

September 4 — Ivory

I had more jitters about my possibly being the weak link in the Mt. Shasta Mission. I am concerned that I won't be able to release my fears and that this in itself might adversely affect the mission. The men didn't pass off what I was saying or insist I was just feeling nervous and being silly. Instead, they all said what I was feeling was natural and that they would be worried if I didn't have them.

September 5 — Ivory

During breakfast the men said they noticed I am really getting geared up and focused for my trip to California. David said, "Waiting is damn hard, isn't it." That about said it all.

At Perelandra. I'm working long hours with nature to finish the final notes I'll be taking to California and fine-tuning the processes I'll be working with. For some crazy reason, I feel confident and strong about this work with nature. I'm just "shy" about applying it to something like the Mt. Shasta Mission.

Medical session. Lorpuris gave me what felt like a straight Feldenkrais lesson, concentrating again on my left side. When I got up, I felt like I had been through a Feldenkrais lesson.

September 6 — Gold

Hyperithon arrived at the Cottage for a full day of Mt. Shasta meetings.

At Perelandra. I continued preparing the work for the trip.

At the Cottage. An easy evening. But I was disappointed that Hyperithon did not stay for dinner.

September 7 — Gold

Awoke in deep pain due to a tight left psoas and thigh. I decided just to get on with my day. I didn't feel like stopping to have a medical session right then.

At Perelandra. My wallpaper friend is back in town. She called and asked me to meet her in town for lunch. She sounded odd. Then a half-hour later she called again to say she couldn't meet me and that she can't talk yet. I'll understand later, she assures me.

The psoas pain intensified, so I broke down and had a medical session. I told Lorpuris that I'm tired of this particular pain. He said that perhaps he could do something about it. He began working subtly. Then, for what seemed like forever, the pain really intensified. I wanted to curl up in a fetal position, but Lorpuris kept urging me to remain in a straight position. Without consciously willing it, I began to pant deeply, like I was trying to push something out of me. It was the most difficult session so far. My neck felt like it weighed a hundred pounds, I felt deep discomfort all over, and I was panting. Then suddenly I was quiet. My breathing was effortless and almost imperceptible. I felt my body in a new state of peace, and I realized that my psoas and thigh were no longer in pain. In fact, the psoas felt warm and soft. I told Lorpuris that I could still feel weight in my neck, and he said he'd take care of it in a minute. I did a few more deep breaths and then I felt the peace again. When David held my head, the neck weight disappeared. Shortly, Lorpuris said I could test essences and close the coning. He urged me to call a medical session any time I feel discomfort. I was surprised at how quickly he wrapped up this difficult session.

At Perelandra. Right after I returned fully to Perelandra, the phone rang. It was my wallpaper friend again asking if she could meet me in a half-hour in town. She still sounded awful, so I said I would meet her.

My friend's husband has announced that he wants to end their marriage and has pulled the rug completely out from under her. She's devastated. As I listened for two hours, I noticed that I stayed strong, stable and calm.

Medical session. I had only a slight tightness in the left thigh, but the psoas was fine. I decided to see Lorpuris so that we lose nothing from this morning. In fact, he gave me part two—all subtle work. He says he couldn't be more delighted with how well this morning's work has held, especially in light of the intense lunch with my friend. When we finished, I had a revitalized sense of calm and peace.

September 8 — Apricot

Awoke *strong*.

At Perelandra. Talked to my wallpaper friend for about five hours, and I was still able to remain calm throughout.

Medical session. We agree that I am ready for the Mt. Shasta trip. I was concerned that I have not been able to exercise for the past several weeks because of all the adjustments and that I might not be in the best shape for the mountain work. Lorpuris assured me that I won't be out of shape for Mt. Shasta. On the contrary, he says I'll be in excellent condition. I'll have to take his word for it and see once I get out there. Lorpuris has been most complimentary to me about our work together. We're getting quite a partnership going. I realize I have a strong trust in him and that I also have warm feelings toward him.

September 9 — Ivory

At the Cottage. I translated a Universal Light session for the Mt. Shasta trip. He gave me insight from his perspective that I feel will be most useful as I work with nature on the mountain.

Medical session. This one was in preparation for the trip. It was subtle, and Lorpuris said he was adding the finishing touches to the work we've been doing. He told me to use my trip this week to notice the changes in how I function. I'm to just notice them and not think about them. They'll make me smile. We agree that I'll connect with him during all my Mt. Shasta work so that he can observe and collect his own data.

At the Cottage. Max joined us for a send-me-off dinner. I went to bed early and fell asleep easily. This is a change because usually I'm restless before a trip. I've never before felt such support—David, Lorpuris, Hyperithon, Max, all the others at the Cottage. Everyone seems to be focused on this trip.

September 10 — Gold

My trip to California was uneventful. Peter Caddy and his new wife picked me up in Redding and drove me to their place in Mt. Shasta. It's beautiful country. I had a late dinner with the small community of people who live and work with the Caddys. After dinner, they asked me to join them while they dedicated their new medicine wheel. For the dedication I gave a small natural quartz crystal that I happened to bring along from Perelandra. Afterwards, Peter and two other community members asked me questions about the Cottage, which was when I learned that Peter had filled some of them in on the bare details of the Cottage and its work. He had not talked about the Mt. Shasta Mission, however—at least no one else mentioned it.

At the Cottage. By 11:30, I was showered, in bed in the guest room at the Caddy house (which was in the basement) and back at the Cottage. We hooked up a medical session for recalibrating the bodies to the Mt. Shasta time and whatever else was needed to eliminate jet lag. The session didn't take long.

Right after I closed down the coning, something strange happened. I automatically curled up in a tight fetal position at Shasta and began to shiver uncontrollably. I also was hit with a deep feeling of insecurity, and it was difficult to focus. David insisted that I re-open the medical session. Lorpuris checked the two bodies and said everything was okay from his end. So I went to bed and assumed all would be fine, but I couldn't get to sleep. As soon as I started to drift off, it was like I hit some internal trampoline and would bounce right back up to a state of alertness. It was irritating. I think I managed a total of two hours sleep.

I had breakfast with the men and left the Cottage early so that I could get comfortably situated at Shasta before joining everyone there for breakfast. We were still puzzled and surprised at what happened last night and at my inability to get to sleep.

Mt. Shasta. As soon as Peter saw me, he asked how I had slept. I told him a little about what happened, and he informed me that, a hundred years ago or so, there was a massacre of Native Americans in the area and the guest bedroom was located right over the mass grave. The Caddys have had trouble with that room before and they've had three medicine men working on getting the souls out and moved on, but new souls keep coming into the grave. They can't figure out what's going on. Now last night made sense to me—especially the cold chills and strange emotions. I must deal with this situation tonight so that I can get some sleep.

I checked out the mountain site with Peter, his wife and a psychic friend of theirs who wanted to go along. Both Peter and the psychic friend showed me two sites they felt were suitable. I checked with nature and both tested negative. After much walking and using kinesiology and intuition, Peter's wife and I found the site that nature wants. I opened a coning with the Cottage and was told by David that this nature-approved site was the one they wanted to use. I spent about an hour doing all the testing with nature that was needed and planned for, plus a few unplanned tests nature asked me to do with them. By the time I finished, both Peter's wife and I realized that nature would be using the minerals at the site to stabilize the mission activity.

I closed down my testing just as Peter came up the mountain to find us. His friend had located another site, and she was angry that I had not listened to her guidance. She was convinced this new site was the one. I asked David what I should do, and he suggested the diplomatic approach. I was to go to the friend's site, open to nature, do a few of the tests and let her see the test results so that she would know that (1) we tried her site, and (2) it didn't hold up in the testing. I wasn't too thrilled about doing more testing, but the diplomatic approach made sense.

While I opened the full coning and worked with nature at the second site, the psychic became more and more agitated. She left us and began furiously pacing off a huge star in the middle of her site. I was having difficulty holding my focus, and Hyperithon, sounding alarmed, asked what was going on. I described what the psychic was doing and what I was experiencing, and told him I felt like I was being hit by massive waves of disruptive energy. That was exactly what he was picking up, too. Hyperithon told me to ask Peter's wife to stand between me and the pacing psychic so that I could complete the closing down of the coning. When Peter's wife stood between us, she said she could feel the disruptive energy hitting her back.

I was furious at this woman's lack of consideration and rudeness. I was also stunned that an older woman who had been "in the psychic trenches" for many years should act so irresponsibly. I could hardly speak to the woman. Diplomacy was the last thing on my mind.

When I got back to the Caddy house, I "called" the Cottage and assured David and Hyperithon that I was fine—tired, but fine. Also, I felt good about the testing at the first site. They confirmed that this was the site they will use.

Evening. I still had to deal with the mass grave situation so that I could get some sleep. I opened a full coning and asked to be connected to the souls. I ended up having a lovely experience with twelve gentle, grateful souls who needed flower essence testing so that they could balance, detach and move on. One by one I worked with them. Some of them touched my cheek and had tears in their eyes. Some said "thank you." It was a beautiful experience. After finishing the work with the souls, nature told me to soil balance and stabilize the grave-site area. This would shift the soil into balance and "close the door" on the grave so that no other souls would be drawn into the site. I finally completed the work after two hours, then I took a shower, returned to the Cottage, had soup with the men while we talked over the day and went to bed. I slept peacefully.

September 12 — Apricot

Mt. Shasta. Peter read my notes from the work I did last night on the mass grave to the community members. This led to a discussion, and I told them I was sorry they missed the experience.

Peter has asked me to get soil readouts from nature on each of the community gardens, so I started this work today. This got me out of the house—something I wasn't complaining about at all. I noticed right away that I wasn't sore from all the trekking around the mountain that I did yesterday. Also, I'm not feeling any jet lag.

As I did the nature work, the community members began coming out, one by one, to talk to me. One woman raised a caution flag for me. She's a counselor who doesn't mind violating the confidentiality of her clients. My instinct is to stay away from her.

Another woman seemed sensitive, intelligent and calm. She has a Ph.D. in "psycho-counseling." But she has decided that this community is not where she needs to be and plans to leave soon.

September 13 — Ivory

Mt. Shasta. I'm amazed at my stamina. I spent all day doing soil work and listening to community members. I feel like I should be hanging out a shingle. Their major complaint is about Peter's strong-willed domination of the community. I'm doing a lot of essence work with these people, and because of this I have become privy to their emotions and pains. It allows me to know them deeply and quickly, and I'm touched by the special access I have to them through the essences. I feel a responsibility about all of this and I find it humbling.

The one thing I requested from the Caddys in August when I accepted their invitation to stay with them was a private room so that I could switch back and forth to the Cottage without interference. This they assured me I would have. They told me today that I would need to vacate my room because a board member of the community was arriving this afternoon, and asked that I sleep on the couch in the community living room. I didn't think things could become more absurd than this. Luckily, the members I've been helping conspired to get me a private room at the small resort just next door—free of charge, too. I ended up in a glorious private room surrounded by *quiet*—something I haven't had since arriving. Going back and forth to the Cottage from there was like a vacation, and it was much easier for me to hold my focus at the Cottage.

September 14 — Yellow

Medical session. I took advantage of the quiet and privacy by staying later at the Cottage and having a medical session. Everything is holding up fine. The pelvis in the PB was slightly misaligned, but that was it. We're all happy with how well I'm maintaining balance under the various stresses. A medical session with smiles all around.

Mt. Shasta. Returned around noon to continue the garden soil readouts. Peter asked me to speak to the board members about the work I've been doing with the garden soil and the release of the souls. I spoke to them for about forty-five minutes, and they seemed receptive. I urged them to stabilize the community and its work by working with nature to stabilize the grounds. This potential aid awaits them. I also urged them to understand emotions and energy, and to cleanse their community on a regular basis. I think they heard me.

September 15 — Ivory

Mt. Shasta. I spent the afternoon with the fellow who will be taking over the responsibility of the community gardens and grounds. Our ideas, feelings and approach to this land are similar. He's quite open to nature.

A new process. I opened White Brotherhood medical sessions with three members of the community who I felt needed this kind of help. I checked everything out with Lorpuris beforehand, and we set up a procedure. I opened the coning and scanned the person with both hands so that they could be "handed over" to the appropriate medical team. I encouraged each person to talk to their team about the key issues and express what they felt during the session. I functioned in David's role by placing my hands on their head, and I tested them for essences throughout and at the end of the session. Each person's session was different and most helpful. It was remarkable to see their changes and gratifying to hear them talk so positively about the experience. Developing the medical session process so that others can use it is definitely worth pursuing.

At the Cottage. I arrived quite late. Mickey fussed at me and made me have some soup before going to bed. I had a medical session to prepare for the trip back to Perelandra, then I went to bed and slept well.

September 16 — Gold

Returned to Perelandra. Hooray.

September 17 — Dusty Rose

While getting "debriefed" about the trip by the men at the Cottage, it suddenly hit me that now is the time to expand Perelandra to include a third person. If Perelandra is to continue expanding in work and service, I'll need help. While talking to them about this, I saw an image of the community member at Mt. Shasta who knew she would be leaving soon. The men urged me to write to her right away.

September 18 — Yellow

Medical session. I didn't do the second half of the return-trip medical sessions until today because I was just too tired when I got back to Perelandra Sunday and yesterday. Lorpuris suggested that I make every attempt to have a session *just* before and *just* after a trip, even if it means I fall asleep during the sessions. He feels he can save me a lot of wear and tear when I travel by doing this. We are all pleased with how well I held up throughout the entire California trip. Actually, I'm amazed.

At Perelandra. I bounced off Clarence the idea of expanding Perelandra to include a third person. He was surprised at how much work goes on around Perelandra and open to the idea of my getting help—once he got over the initial shock of the idea. I'll be writing the woman in California soon.

September 19 — Dusty Rose

JAMFD

September 20 — Ivory

Medical session. My right ear started throbbing. Lorpuris worked on it for about forty-five minutes, saying it was Mt. Shasta "fall-out." When he was finished, the ear pressure was reduced by about eighty percent, and I had no pain. All I could feel was a little pressure. But he said I would have to put up with periodic "pain spasms" in that ear for another two or three days.

September 21 — Apricot

The ear spasms were terrible, and getting a head cold at Perelandra didn't help the situation.

Medical session. Lorpuris said it is better to address the ear problem gradually rather than just "popping the pressure." He told me I would see a noticeable difference with my ear tomorrow and suggested that I not sleep on it tonight. He also said I don't have a head cold and that what I *did* have would clear up overnight. The essences I tested for made me suspect that I'm dealing with resistance and fear around expanding to include a third person at Perelandra.

September 22 — Ivory

Fall equinox: 4:33 P.M.

My ear was wonderful! No pain all day. Boy, did this ever put a smile on my face. I really felt how immediate and *physical* this White Brotherhood medical work can be. This was such clear evidence of the effectiveness of working between levels and that the higher levels are not beyond our basic day-to-day life on Earth—or the day-to-day life on the Cottage level.

At Perelandra. I worked hard in the garden to give it as much of an autumnal shine as possible before the equinox. I pulled out old plants, deadheaded flowers, covered the bare rows with straw and marked the rows with stakes.

At the Cottage. I shifted a bouquet of flowers from the Perelandra garden for the equinox. Mickey placed them on the living room coffee table, along with a lighted candle. Max surprised me by joining us. I opened a coning, including Perelandra and the garden, then I silently called in next year's cycle for Perelandra, and followed it with the call for my personal cycle. As soon as the moment hit, I saw the center of the garden become energized and a shaft of light rise from it. It moved up, connected with the Cottage, moved through the Cottage and into the universe. As the light reached into the universe, it "blossomed" into a beautiful, soft, white lotus. The lotus opened broadly and fully, giving me quite a picture as it was set against the full dark depth of the universe. The energy of the equinox, having moved through the center of the garden and the Cottage, was made available to all through the lotus. It was a dramatic experience.

I shared what I had seen with everyone, and we talked about it a bit. Then we had a family dinner celebrating the new cycles.

September 23 — Ivory

At Perelandra. Spent all day in the garden to finish giving it its autumnal shine. It looks beautiful.

September 24 — Yellow

This was the day of the Mt. Shasta meeting at Perelandra with Peter Caddy. I left the Cottage with everyone telling me to just relax.

At Perelandra. The first thing Peter did after he arrived was give me an update on the fellow who worked at the Pentagon. Everything David had stressed to him in the spring worked out perfectly. He followed David's advice and stood his ground at the Pentagon. Instead of getting fired, he said what David had suggested and ended up getting transferred to a more advantageous position. This was terrific confirmation of that spring meeting and just what I needed to boost my confidence for today.

The meeting. At Perelandra, we had Peter, the chiropractor and me. As a result of my testing at the site a couple of weeks ago, Lorpuris and Hyperithon suggested that my chiropractor be included in the "Perelandra team." Based on the results of having monitored me and Peter's wife during my work on the mountain, they feel strongly that the witnesses who will be coming from the Perelandra level will need adjustments and balancing if they are to get through the mission with their sensory systems functioning well. At the Cottage were David, Butch, Tex and Hyperithon. Lorpuris and Universal Light were connected to us in the meeting through the coning. My chiropractor's daughter, who was amusing herself at the cabin with us, was placed in a protective bubble so that she would not be adversely affected by the intense coning energy.

David conducted the meeting. He restated the purpose and goals of the Mt. Shasta Mission and made sure Peter, the chiropractor and

I knew what was going to happen on the mountain.* He announced that the projected mission "go" dates were between July 14 and 17, 1985, with the primary target date being July 15.

After several questions about some of the technical aspects of the mission, we turned our attention to the medical considerations that have arisen. I had briefed my chiropractor about the mission as I understood it a week ago, and David asked if, after hearing every-thing today, she was committed to the mission. She said she'd give a definite answer by the end of four weeks, but she felt it would be yes.

David said that it was critical that everyone at the Mt. Shasta site be physically stabilized so that their sensory systems functioned well throughout the mission. To this end, David had Lorpuris and Hyper-ithon put together a simple body process that could be used to prepare everyone coming to the site prior to the mission. The process was to be shifted from Hyperithon through me to each in-vitee. Then the chiropractor could get a full readout of how each person's body will react on the mountain during the mission, and we can work to shore up any weak spots prior to that time. We did the process two times with Peter and found out that the more we do it the more the body *learns* and is able to adjust to the special cir-cumstances of the mission without misaligning, draining or short-circuiting. In short, Peter's body responded much better to the process the second time than it did the first time. This was exciting news. The net result is that everyone who plans to be present for the mission needs to be at Mt. Shasta one week prior to the mission dates so that we can move them through the process at least two (but preferably three) times. We also decided that the chiropractor and I will try to work with invitees on the east coast this winter and spring so that we can make the work load at Mt. Shasta a little more manageable.

Peter has been getting the "witness list" from St. Germaine and feels there will be about twenty to twenty-five witnesses present on

* The Mt. Shasta Mission will be fully described in a forthcoming book. I am giving the information you need now for *Dancing*. I'm sorry if you feel frustrated by the ab-breviated information throughout this book regarding the mission, but that is a book in itself.

the mountain. David warned him about not including any press people because this was not to be a "glitzy publicity show."

David asked if we understood the mission and what we are each to do. Peter re-stated his understanding of what's to happen on Mt. Shasta, and after making a few minor corrections David okayed Peter's statement of the mission. When we ran out of questions, we ended the meeting, and I closed down the coning.

Peter immediately called the first six people on his list and got everyone on the first try—which he pronounced a miracle. He explained the mission to each of them, and they all agreed to participate. No one seemed to "blink" about Eisenhower being in charge of the project. The chiropractor and I will be meeting with the first two invitees next Wednesday so that we can do the body process with them.

September 25 — Dusty Pink
At Perelandra. I wrote to the woman in California regarding expanding Perelandra to include a third person. Writing it gave me a chance to clarify my thinking and emotions. This move feels solid.

Medical session. Lorpuris said that my bodies are holding the memory of the medical work well. He suggested that we have sessions after any difficult Perelandra or Cottage work so that he can help me release any tension I might be holding. I am to go on R&R through Friday: no translation work, no office work or notes. At one point, I asked him why his work is so much more powerful than anything I've experienced on the Perelandra level. He said the disciplines I am familiar with work with one level only, and this then gradually feeds into the other levels. The team works with all levels simultaneously [physical, emotional, mental and soul], and their work is more efficient and effective because of this.

September 26 — Apricot
At Perelandra. I almost had a quiet R&R day. First I had a two-hour lunch with Peter Caddy, talking about how he can protect himself from psychics (especially women) with power hangups. Then I had a good one-and-a-half-hour talk with Clarence about his life. The day ended with a phone call from a woman who just needed en-

couragement about her difficult and complicated life.

At the Cottage. Returned amazed at my "counseling" day. Good grief. I also returned with a strangely fluttering stomach. David insisted we do a medical session right away.

Medical session. Lorpuris said that the fluttering stomach indicated that I am ready for the next step. This will begin on Saturday at our scheduled session. He suggests that I not see my wallpaper-friend-in-crisis until after Saturday, if possible.

September 27 — Ivory

My wallpaper friend called and asked me to *please* accompany her into Washington for an appointment. She was concerned about the drive and the appointment. I told her I'd have to call her back. Besides being told to hold off seeing her until after the next medical session, I was also planning to go out to dinner with several of the Cottage men this evening, and I knew I would be late in returning if I accompanied my friend to Washington. I called David, who called Lorpuris and then called me back. The boards have been cleared for me to be with my friend. I am to test essences after seeing her, and the men and I will have our dinner out tomorrow night.

After her appointment, my friend took me out to dinner, and after dessert she told me the rest of the story regarding her husband's announcement to end their marriage. The issue was hardly that he had fallen for another woman. He had become involved with a married woman, and when she announced to her husband that she wanted to leave him (about two weeks ago), he killed himself. The words hit my solar plexus like bowling balls. Now I know why my friend has been *so* devastated by all of this.

At the Cottage. I held myself together for her, but as soon as I got back to the Cottage, I talked to the men about what she had said. I told them I felt like my friend's situation involved a deep violation of trust, and I was having trouble getting it into some balanced perspective in my life. I was just glad to be home.

September 28 — Ivory

I awoke feeling someone had crapped in my universe. Surely there was something I could do to balance or counteract the piece of garbage my friend's husband and girlfriend had helped create. While I was talking about this with the others at breakfast, it hit me that it was *emotional* garbage and that maybe I could somehow use essences to counterbalance it. The men didn't know, but they said it was worth a shot.

I opened a coning and included Universal Light. I asked if it was appropriate for me to be working in a coning with them for this kind of issue and was told that it was. Immediately, I saw the faces of the four adults involved in this mess. I asked if I should proceed with an effort to balance what has happened or if it was inappropriate to address this specific issue. I wanted to make sure I wasn't intruding or interfering in something that was not my concern. If they said it was not appropriate, I was prepared to just close down the coning. I got the okay to continue. While looking at the faces of the four people, I was told to test essences for the emotions around the relationship issues that were released to the universe by them. Four essences tested positive. I was then told to give one drop of each essence to each person. One by one, they came forward to me (voluntarily), and I administered the drops. Finally, I was told to release a drop of each essence to the Perelandra nature spirits. When I did this, I saw nature spirits moving the essences to the center of the garden and into the light "tunnel" that had formed during the equinox. The essences released in a million drops of mist into the universe through the lotus. As I watched, I felt my own balance stabilize. Hopefully, this will help balance the situation as far as the universe is concerned and will assist the four in moving through the mess as well. I guess this is why they needed to receive the drops individually.

Evening. We decided not to go out to dinner and had nice quiet family time in the living room, enjoying the first fire of the year.

Medical session. This was a long and difficult session. I experienced a heightened sensation of *painful* vibrations throughout both bodies. Periodically my bodies would jump, as if given an electric shock. I kept asking if I was blocking Lorpuris's work in some way—this session seemed so difficult. He said I was not, and encouraged me to "hang in there" while he worked. I ended up holding David's hand tightly just to keep from curling up in a fetal position. Around mid-session, I tested for essences. Lorpuris said he wished I had had the extra two days of R&R to prepare for this, but the timing is now—so we proceeded. Afterwards, he told me to get some good rest and to see him tomorrow morning. Also, I am not to worry if I feel any "after-shocks" of vibration.

September 29 — Yellow

I slept long, not waking up until 10:30. After breakfast, I had the follow-up medical session. The work was subtle and the session lasted forty-five minutes. Lorpuris explained that my two sensory systems and my two electrical systems were shifting and expanding their function.

While he worked, I asked him if he was aware of my friend's mess. He said yes, in so far as it affects me. I asked how the husband who killed himself was. Lorpuris said that he was fine, for someone who had "forced his timing." These people, he explained, have special problems that they must deal with. They remain strongly connected to the situation they tried to leave as they continue their process of working toward resolution. This is why it's so hard for everyone concerned to release from both the problems and the person who forced the timing. The fact is, that person is still involved.

At the end of the session, Lorpuris told me to relax as much as I can. This is a major shift I am taking, and he'd like to see me tomorrow. I'm to test essences twice daily.

September 30 — Dusty Rose

At Perelandra. I arrived with soreness in the right side of my neck and back. It felt like muscle soreness so I tried to walk it out a bit, but I was unsuccessful.

Medical session. Lorpuris assures me that I'm structurally aligned and my cranials are okay. He says these most recent pains are my bodies adjusting to the present shift. He's continuing to work on the process and tells me to "keep hanging in there." We scheduled another session tomorrow. When I left this one, my body aches and pains were greatly lessened. The man knows his business. I'm starting to call him "Magic Fingers."

October 1 — Gold

Medical session. I'm experiencing energy dips at Perelandra, as if someone is pulling the plug on me. Lorpuris again said that the body pain that I'm feeling is caused by the shifts settling in and not because of conventional muscle soreness or structural misalignment. This is why the pain was not responding to gentle exercise. He explained that he had to stabilize the X work before the expansion of the sensory system could occur and that both bodies and my soul are "eager" for the changes. I am coming out of the woods now and will feel my strength begin to return. He said that by the end of the week I will see marked differences in my stamina. The neck pain was due to the changes, and he suggested that I not bother trying to understand this pain. It will move out on its own. As he talked about the pain I was having in my back, I could actually feel him touching my interior body as if he was pointing to a chart on the wall during a lecture.

October 2 — Yellow

The men are focused on helping me through the present changes. They tell me this is not something they have experienced themselves because the changes have to do with my special situation, "area of expertise" and disciplines. They're impressed with what I'm going through and fully supportive.

At Perelandra. I talked to S, the woman I sent the letter to in California, about coming to Perelandra. She said she felt honored to be asked to join me and planned to send me a letter this Sunday with her thoughts about the offer, but she probably won't be able to come before May. After talking to her, I felt strongly that she could help me expand Perelandra's work.

Got a call from the supportive friend who has been on the attack lately. She intimated that her last two difficult phone calls to me were due to her not feeling well. I let that ride. Although she is offering an apology of sorts, I'm assuming she's also telling me that when she doesn't feel well, she likes to harangue others—and because she's not feeling well, we others should overlook it. I don't buy it.

In the medical session, David expressed concern about my doing the Shasta medical process on the first two invitees tomorrow. In light of the changes I'm going through, will this be too much of a drain on me? Lorpuris assured David that he (Lorpuris) will monitor me and the invitees and will tell me to pull out of the session if I am unable to hold the work.

October 3 — Dusty Rose

At Perelandra. The chiropractor and I met with the two invitees. They are an older couple, and he says he's had two contacts with David—the first one two years ago and the second one just six months back. I explained David's connection with the Mt. Shasta Mission and the goals and objectives of the mission itself. I opened a coning that included David and Hyperithon from the Cottage and Lorpuris from wherever he is "stationed."

Hyperithon and I had already decided we would try to do the critical shift in the body process without my having to split and be present at the Cottage as well as at Perelandra. He felt we could utilize the transistor (the gold disk) for the shift.

The process. We are simulating a spacecraft landing in the person's energy field to find out what individual weaknesses the trauma of the landing will trigger in the body. First, the chiropractor strengthens and aligns the person's body. Then Hyperithon activates the craft energy, passes it to me via the transistor, and I pass it into the person's energy field through my hand, which is holding their hand. This takes about thirty seconds. Then the chiropractor checks the person's body again. What has misaligned or weakened indicates to us what to expect from them on the mountain. Neither Peter two weeks ago nor these two invitees today sensed a shift in their energy field when the craft was moved in, but all three registered *dramatic* changes in the body nonetheless. When we moved the craft into Peter's field the second time, the body didn't react nearly as strongly. In just one hour, it had already learned something about how to identify and sort the input from a spacecraft reality. One of today's invitees actually strengthened when the craft reality was shifted into his field. He had already told me he has a long history of space brother contacts—I guess he wasn't kidding, because the craft sure didn't traumatize his body today. Instead, his body strengthened.

The success of today's process means that I can work with all the invitees without the added pressure of having to split to the Cottage. *At the Cottage.* Hyperithon stayed for dinner, and we coaxed him into spending the night.

October 4 — Ivory

Hyperithon stayed long enough to monitor the morning medical session so that he would know the impact yesterday's work at Perelandra had on me. If there was a lingering problem, we'd have to modify the process. Only my PB pelvis was slightly misaligned.

At Perelandra. I had a long lunch with my wallpaper friend.

While on a walk, I began experiencing strong stomach pains and energy dips. When I got back to the cabin, I got the hit to slowly drink thirty-two ounces of water. When I finished drinking, all the symptoms had disappeared. I received insight that Lorpuris's work has increased my electricity and that I need more water now. I tested that I need to drink an additional thirty-five ounces daily for sixteen days, then check for my new water requirements after that.

October 5 — Yellow

I offered two dreams for the breakfast dream debriefing this morning. One took place in a Japanese bath house and the other included spontaneous combustion in a barn and with two flatbed trucks. They were strong dreams but none of us could figure out what they meant. I suggested that this means I win the dream debriefing and should get a prize. They said they'd get back to me on that.

Evening. We had a family cookout, then coffee in the living room in front of the fire. The weather seems to be turning cold quickly at the Cottage this year.

October 6 — Ivory

At Perelandra. I got a call from B, a member of Peter's community in California. She has decided to leave the community when the Caddy's return from a trip, and she expressed interest in coming to Perelandra to help me. (S had talked to her about my letter.) I saw the possibility of B doing the day-to-day support work (cleaning and cooking, etc.) and S helping me organize the research notes and editing. I told her I would think about it. B then asked if her boyfriend, H, could come along to do the outside work, plus he was good with construction. I told her I'd think about that also.

I had a difficult conversation with Clarence about all of this. We both talked about our fears around having others come live at Perelandra, but I said I felt I had no choice. The work was now more than I could manage. After a lot of soul-searching, Clarence committed himself to the changes at Perelandra, and immediately afterwards his whole demeanor changed. He was light, bright, excited and willing to try the new. We realized we would have to change our definition of home to include others. We talked about how we saw our positions at Perelandra and reminded ourselves that we were the ones who have done the work and made the moves for the past eleven years to have Perelandra unfold as it has. We both felt our power and positions, and I felt a strong sense of partnership between us.

I think this was an important afternoon in the growth at Perelandra and in the partnership between Clarence and me. When I left to go back to the cabin, we both had a sense of having come through something big. At the garden, I felt drawn to the center. From that location, I stated that I hoped with all my heart that this major change we're moving toward is exactly what is to be.

At the Cottage. The men have been encouraging me for sometime now to get the help I need at Perelandra, and they are completely supportive of the decisions Clarence and I made today.

October 7 — Gold

Medical session. Rather than wait the sixteen days that I had previously tested, I need to increase my daily water intake to sixty ounces now.

October 8 — Yellow

At Perelandra. Helped my wallpaper friend all afternoon.

October 9 — Gold

I had a restless night, floating between Perelandra and the Cottage in dreams.

Medical session. Lorpuris says I'm moving out of the adjustment period and that I will clearly see my energy begin to return. I felt he worked today to gently remind my body to relax with the changes. He says I'll start smiling about the changes soon. I sure hope so. I'm tired of the pain and exhaustion. I'm *very* tired of the pain and exhaustion.

October 10 — Dusty Rose

Dream: I was ice skating to a perfectly choreographed program set to a piano concerto. I *heard* the music and *felt* the movement of the skating. I literally felt an extraordinary power inside myself. I wore a white skating dress, skates with clean white boots and a diamond pendant. It was an exceptionally powerful dream.

At Perelandra. B called to say she and her boyfriend would very much like to come to Perelandra and asked if we had come to a decision about this yet. We talked money, and I found that their needs fit into what we could pay. Also, we agreed to pay for their plane tickets from California to Perelandra. I cleared this with Clarence, called B back and gave her the good news. She and H plan to come sometime in early November.

October 11 — Yellow

I committed myself to taking a three-day trip with my wallpaper friend while she attended to some out-of-state family business. I felt it was important to support her as she takes this big step, but I'm not happy about losing the days at Perelandra. However, this seems important. We have separate rooms at an inn with an adjoining bathroom. This gives me the privacy I need to shift back and forth to the Cottage.

October 12 — Ivory

I spent a long morning at the Cottage while my friend took care of business at the other end.

At the Cottage. I'm amazed at how even-keeled I'm staying despite the emotions involved in this trip for my friend. It's definitely helpful to be able to return to the Cottage in the evenings. The men are a solid base for me.

October 13 — Apricot

I was glad to get back to Perelandra and Clarence, and equally glad to get to the Cottage for a good night's sleep. It was a long, emotionally exhausting trip.

Medical session. Lorpuris worked gently while I drifted in and out of sleep. He's pleased that all the shifts and adjustments have held throughout the past four days. He and I both feel I'm out of the woods with this stage of my changes.

October 14 — Gold

We had a big family dinner to "unofficially" celebrate David's birthday. He protested a bit too loudly about all the fuss, and we just ignored him.

October 15 — Ivory

Evening. Just as I returned home, I received clear insight that the Mt. Shasta site was to be protected and that the protection was to be created with nature tonight. When I told David, he suggested I do the work right away, and said he wanted to sit in. He didn't question my insight at all. I only knew to open a coning and include the Deva of Mt. Shasta and the nature spirits working at the site. After doing this, I assumed I'd get some kind of indication about what I was to do next.

The work took almost an hour, and when we finished the site had a gold energy dome over it that was operating as a protection. We also linked both David and Hyperithon to the dome, and they will remain connected until after the mission is complete in July. This way, if anything happens at the site that needs attention, nature can contact David and Hyperithon directly. While working in this process, I could clearly feel my co-creative partnership with nature. I love that feeling. It's exciting, it's deep, and it gives me a tremendous rush when I'm working with them. I also love working with them because I *always* learn. Tonight was no different.

October 16 — Apricot

The men urged me not to be so nervous about making my work more public. They assured me that as I move forward they will be with me to help make sure the doors that open for me are "sitting straight on their hinges." They feel that the Mt. Shasta work will result in a greater demand for information about what's going on at Perelandra. I think I need these next nine months to adjust and prepare for what might happen because of Mt. Shasta.

October 17 — Yellow

After breakfast I got a clear hit to open a session with Universal Light. As a result of this session, we will have a series of sessions/ meetings with him regarding Mt. Shasta. We've scheduled three meetings next week with one day's rest in between. Possibly a fourth meeting will be necessary, but we won't know until next week. I'll be translating Universal Light to the others at the Cottage during the meetings.

During today's session, the translation process was much smoother for me than it had been prior to my work with Lorpuris. I can feel the sensory systems expanded and more in sync now. I also feel it was correct not to have Universal Light sessions during these two and a half months of medical work. I think the sessions would have added too much pressure on me during the intense early stages of the medical work.

At Perelandra. I consulted Pan regarding a new problem that has come up regarding switching the Cottage notes to the Cottage now that I'm using a bound notebook and not a loose-leaf one. Pan suggested I shift my entire notebook today as is and allow a nature spirit (assigned by Pan to work with these notes) to shift the written words to the notebook at the Cottage while I'm writing them each day in the notebook at Perelandra. The nature spirit will use the regular Perelandra coning to facilitate the shift. As soon as I agreed, a nature spirit "stood" before me. I handed him the notebook, which he split to David who was waiting to receive it at the Cottage. David confirmed the shift, and the nature spirit handed me back the Perelandra-level notebook. I wrote several "test" words on a page at Perelandra and, sure enough, David confirmed the words showed up on the corresponding page at the Cottage. The concept of this process was new to me—and amazing. What an extraordinary adventure I'm having with my co-workers.

October 18 — Gold

JAMFD

October 19 — Yellow

Clarence and I drove to North Carolina for another nature workshop.

October 20 — Ivory

It was a tough workshop. Some people wanted to participate by dis-cussing relevant issues together while others wanted me to hand it all to them on a silver platter—and the two sides were clearly ir-ritated at one another. Several people (the ones who wanted the silver-platter treatment) *told* me at lunch to "take control and get this workshop in hand." So I did, and the afternoon clearly pleased the platter group but irritated the discussers.

October 21 — Apricot

I tested essences for a woman from the workshop who works for Exxon. She said something interesting: Within the next four years, the top management spots at Exxon will change—everyone is retir-ing. I saw how this kind of opportunity for huge corporations like Exxon could facilitate their shift from Piscean to Aquarian dy-namics. And the mere presence of people like this woman (and Clarence at Xerox) could ground new intent and integrity within the structures and serve to assist this change.

I was pleased to get back to Perelandra.

October 22 — Ivory

When I returned to the Cottage this evening, I felt a terrific sense of power and strength flowing from inside me. What an extraordinary sensation.

October 23 — Heather Green

At Perelandra. Spent the afternoon with my wallpaper friend. We ended up having an early dinner together at a nearby restaurant, which required that I call the Cottage at the last minute and cancel plans that I had made with them.

At the Cottage. I talked to the men about not feeling comfortable about them always being the ones to make last-minute adjustments to changes in my schedule. They've never shown any anger or exasperation about this, but I still feel bad. Tonight, they assured me of their support and understanding, saying that they realize I'm trying to balance both levels. They say they want to be *with* me in this. I deeply appreciate this support from them. I know it's one of the things that makes this extraordinary balancing act possible—and I told them so.

Medical session. The whole session was geared toward preparing me for tomorrow's Universal Light meeting.

October 24 — Gold

I awoke nervous about the meeting. I don't like being responsible for the translation for these men—especially regarding Mt. Shasta. I kept wondering if I had bitten off more than I could chew.

Meeting. I met Lorpuris in the flesh! He's about my height (5'9"), blonde and has incredibly intense, deep-blue eyes. He's also quite soft-spoken and has an air of gentle dignity. When we were introduced, it felt like I was seeing an old, dear friend. We hugged.

The coning for this meeting was the most powerful one I have ever experienced. I opened it and carefully "built" it with nature, everyone in the room and Universal Light. The actual translation from Universal Light went smoothly—in fact, easier than any other translation I've done with him. After the meeting, Lorpuris suggested I check essences, but I only needed one. We had a coffee break at the Cottage while David and I stuffed protein, then I left for Perelandra.

At Perelandra. I felt exhausted and a bit lost, and I thought about my morning meeting with such extraordinary men.

October 25 — Gold

The second anniversary of my commitment to the Cottage. I worked with nature to place fourteen single white roses all around the Cottage for the men to find throughout the day. I just wanted them to know that I thank them and that they mean a great deal to me— especially on this day. My "influential friends" and I had fun placing the roses.

At dinner. I found that the roses were a hit, bringing a lot of smiles throughout the day as they were discovered. The men presented me with a gift that they claimed had my name written all over it. Naturally, I expected something with my name on it. Instead, I unwrapped a beautiful crystal fawn.

October 26 — Ivory

We had a late breakfast with Hyperithon, Lorpuris and Seamus joining us. Seamus stayed last night, and the other two are here for the big family dinner tonight and the second Universal Light meeting tomorrow.

At dinner. The celebratory family dinner that we had the night after my commitment to the Cottage is now officially declared a tradition. Even John returned for it. Mickey created a centerpiece with the fourteen white roses they found yesterday—it was quite striking.

October 27 — Ivory

Meeting with Universal Light. We had the same group for this second meeting as we had at the first, with the addition of John and Butch. Again, it was a strong coning and an easy translation. I'm starting to enjoy this—and I'm starting to gain confidence, as well.

My energy level even managed to stabilize at Perelandra this afternoon. I'm getting good at this.

October 28 — Apricot

JAMFD

October 29 — Ivory

At Perelandra. Got a great letter from a woman who has read *Behaving*. It gave me quite a boost.

Medical session. I have a whole different feeling about working with Lorpuris now that I've met him. I asked him for more detail about how he works with me. He explained that he works with "the soul body," the different electrical levels and both bodies on all their levels: physical, emotional, mental and soul. A major part of his focus centers around synchronizing the two bodies on all these levels. He suggested I not let a needed adjustment go over thirty-six hours before I call for a medical session. In fact, he would prefer to work with me on the same day the adjustment is needed. He also suggested that I plan to test essences one time daily, plus any time a need might arise.

Evening. I talked to David about how Mt. Shasta is going to confront and, hopefully, verify my life as I live it now, and that I am afraid I will go to the mountain and nothing will occur, thus proving this Cottage life has all been made up in my head. Again, he didn't tell me I was being silly. Instead, he said my fears were natural and healthy, and he urged me to keep talking about them and not hold them inside.

October 30 — Gold

We had a dinner discussion about power. The men said that power is the result of the coming together of one's talents, disciplines and training. They emphasized that power is the *result* of this and not the cause or reason. The balance for power is trust and integrity, and these two elements are what make power stable and creative.

After the power discussion, I had a feeling I needed a medical session. It was a tough one with a lot of electrical sensations. Lorpuris said the "power" release in me came sooner than expected, and it has moved my recent shifts and stabilization process further along. At the end of the session, I was exhausted. Lorpuris reminded me that a person's pelvis is unstable when the body is having difficulty identifying and integrating. Consequently, I may need more frequent sessions right now.

October 31 — Apricot

I awoke early, feeling restless and feeling a lot of electrical sensations. I was also tired—and I was tired of all the body shifts and changes.

At Perelandra. Spent the afternoon with my wallpaper friend.

November 1 — Heather Green

I'm waiting to find out if B and H will really be coming to Perelandra. The Caddys would like them to stay on in California. David says that waiting was invented by a sadist. I agree.

November 2 — Ivory

In the morning, we had a Mt. Shasta meeting with David, Tex, John, Butch and myself. I didn't have to do any translation work, so it was an easy one for me. The meeting lasted two hours and included a discussion about some of the nature work I'm developing for the mission.

At Perelandra. I banged around a bit. They're calling for a heavy frost tonight, and this will surely hit the garden. I feel a little pang about letting the garden go.

Medical session. I felt like my pelvis was misaligned, but it tested fine and Lorpuris assured me that it was aligned. He suggested that when this happens again I should test the pelvis on the soul level. He explained that there is a corresponding energy body system within that level that I can probably feel now whenever it needs essences for alignment. I told him I would do this, trusting that he knows what the blazes he's talking about.

November 3 — Apricot

At Perelandra. Spent ten hours talking to a counseling therapist who has read *Behaving* and felt she needed to talk with me about how the nature concepts apply to her work. I felt I was to give her support and verification as she explored possibilities. I think the ten hours was worth it, but it was *exhausting*.

At the Cottage. Returned late. Mickey set me up with soup, and then I poured myself into bed.

November 4 — Gold

I showed up for breakfast early, which did not make the men happy. They're pressing me to get more sleep.

At Perelandra. B called to say they were coming to Perelandra as planned.

My wallpaper friend called and asked me to join her for dinner. It was a long meal, and I listened a lot.

When I returned to Perelandra, Clarence talked to me about his life and feelings. I realized later that we needed this talk in order to prepare for the arrival of B and H.

At the Cottage. Returned exhausted again. I'm tired of all the intensity I've been dealing with lately. I'm just so bone-tired. I seem to be helping everyone around me through change and trauma. Can I continue to do this? Should I?

November 5 — Heather Green

I'm still not sleeping enough for the men. I'm anxious for B and H to arrive and to help me get Perelandra moving in its new direction.

At Perelandra. I had a semi-productive day, but I had a little difficulty eating because of a queasy stomach. I got the hit to test my pancreas—and, sure enough, it tested weak. I strengthened it with supplements.

Medical session. I told Lorpuris about my pancreas and my observation that it has tested weak over the past two years after especially long, intense discussions. He said we shouldn't assume that this is a pattern yet, but he would watch it more carefully around such occasions. When he finished the work, he said he estimated that I had one month of strengthening to move through now that the major shifts are completed. I'm to stick close to him and the essences.

November 6 — Gold

At Perelandra. Met my wallpaper friend in town for a three-hour lunch.

November 7 — Yellow

JAMFD

November 8 — Heather Green

At Perelandra. B and H finally arrived this evening. I stayed up late with them listening to their tales about the last couple of months in California.

At the Cottage. David insisted I have some soup when I "rolled in" late tonight. We talked about the Big Step going on at Perelandra. It still feels right, but both Clarence and I are nervous and anxious. I'm nervous about instituting and directing the changes that lie ahead for Perelandra. I'm not sure I would have the guts to make this Big Step if I didn't have the men at the Cottage to turn to for advice and support.

November 9 — Ivory

I awoke early, anxious about what I am going to say to B and H about what is going on at Perelandra. They came knowing only what they have read in *Behaving*. I've gone over in my head these past few weeks what they need to know. I'm not sure why it's so important, but it must be.

At Perelandra. "Orientation" lasted five hours. I told them about the nature work, where it seems to be headed, my connection with the Cottage and the Cottage work. They seemed to take it all in, and nothing seemed shocking to them—it was just new to them. When I was finished, I wasn't sure how much of the five hours they absorbed—time will tell.

At the Cottage. I returned exhausted—and I'm still not sure why I put so much effort into this orientation business.

November 10 — Yellow

I continue to wake up early. I've managed to hold the men's concern in check by assuring them that it is inevitable that one night soon I'll just konk out and sleep long hours.

At Perelandra. As soon as I arrived, I felt my pelvis was misaligned, but it tested fine. So I tested the "soul pelvis," as Lorpuris suggested, and it tested positive for essences. I worked with nature to shift the needed essences to that pelvis, and I was fine. I do not understand any of this.

Later, I developed a terrible sinus headache, and by late afternoon I could barely move. Clarence and I had planned to take B and H out for a little celebration dinner, and it was something they were looking forward to all day. I didn't feel I could back out because of sinuses. However, the headache intensified at the restaurant. I ate little and barely managed to get through the meal.

At the Cottage. This is clearly the worst sinus headache I've ever experienced. I opened a medical session and told Lorpuris that I was ready to go through whatever I needed to get out of this pain. But I reminded him I was a chicken about pain and "begged" him not to hurt me. He laughed and began to work quietly. Shortly, I went into a deep sleep that I didn't wake up from until 10:30 the next morning. Luckily, David had insisted I lie down on my bed for this ses-

sion, so all he had to do was cover me with the blanket after Lorpuris was finished.

November 11 — Apricot

When I awoke, the sinus headache was *completely* gone. I felt vulnerable, but I had no pain. Magic Fingers strikes again.

November 12 — Gold

David postponed our second Mt. Shasta/Universal Light meeting so
that I could have a few more days to build my energy level. I felt
terrible that I'm holding up the meeting, but he assured me that it
was not an emergency and that they could wait a couple of days.
The others fully supported his decision to postpone, which left me
no alternative but to accept his decision.

B is "attacking" the house—beginning a major cleaning from top
to bottom. H spent the afternoon in the outside shed sorting all of
Clarence's nails and screws. B seems to be an excellent worker, but
H is a bit drifty.

Medical session. Lorpuris reminded me (again) to be patient with
myself, especially while going through the changes at Perelandra
that have been triggered because of the Big Step.

November 13 — Ivory

At Perelandra. B is still working on the house and H is still floating.
I blew up at H during dinner when he announced he didn't want to
spend a lot of his time "finishing projects that have already been
started and have sat around unfinished." Earlier in the day he told
me he works best with a list of things to do so he can work on
several things at once, doing what he feels "moved" to do in the
moment. With his dinner announcement on top of this, all I could
see was H drifting around not doing much of anything. I blew even
higher when B and H "kidded" me for not helping them move the
living room furniture around today and suggested that all I seem to
be good at is managing. It struck me that they had no concept of
what I do at Perelandra and what I'm trying to balance. All they see
is someone who doesn't want to cook meals or move furniture. The
frustration got to me, and I just walked out. As I walked to the

cabin, I felt such a deep pain of loneliness. I stopped by the Elemental Annex, crying, and asked for help. I stayed there with my influential friends, collecting myself.

When I returned to the house, B and H told me that they understand that there's work to be done and that they would like to help me in the garden tomorrow. I told them I have to rest tomorrow in preparation for a big interlevel meeting at the Cottage the next day that has already been postponed once. This didn't even register with them. H said, "We're talking about working in the garden *tomorrow*. That's Wednesday, not Thursday." I decided I'd direct them in some garden work tomorrow just to get them settled down and show that I'm accepting their sudden concern.

At the Cottage. I talked to the men about the day's fireworks and explained that I feel I have somehow failed in my interaction with B and H. To my surprise, the men think my blow-up was perfect and just what was called for. They feel I've now gotten B's and H's attention. They urged me to fully assume my role as leader and accept that I am in this position. This, they say, will clear up any confusion. I suddenly got the idea to list everything I must do between now and January 1 to give these two people a clear understanding as to why I don't cook or move furniture. The men thought this was a good idea, and we all ended up working on it together. Just so B and H wouldn't think I was going to suddenly head for Tahiti after January 1, we made a short list of what I needed to do in the early part of next year.

Responsibilities between 11/13/84 and 1/1/85

At the Cottage
Interlevel meetings for the Mt. Shasta Mission
Biweekly Universal Light sessions
Weekly Energy Cleansing Process for Cottage
A medical session for Max before Dec. 1
Two medical sessions for John between now and Christmas
Four medical sessions with Lorpuris each week
Work with nature on two major questions regarding Mt. Shasta Mission
Test for critical essences for the Cottage members and Max
Cottage meetings/discussions that interface with my nature work

At Perelandra

Manage and organize Perelandra activity

Close down garden and get related devic information

Winterize roses and get related devic information

Plant bulbs: annual ring and around cabin

Cabin: cleaning

Office work:

> Computer organization and files
>
> Transcribe five Universal Light sessions, four interlevel meetings, research notes
>
> Mail out *Behaving* orders
>
> Answer correspondence

Flower essence work and research at Perelandra

Cottage notes

Edit Universal Light sessions

Death-transition essence work

Mt. Shasta Mission preparation

Medical work with chiropractor for invitees

Nature research

Trip to NYC for trustees meeting

Holidays

Support my wallpaper friend

Partnership life and responsibilities with Clarence

1/1/85 to 4/1/85

Rose Essence definitions

Set up research and get Rose Essence information

Universal Light sessions—biweekly

Mt. Shasta Mission: research and meetings

Preparation for the 1985 garden:

> Calendar
>
> Lay out
>
> Fertilizers
>
> Starting plants for transplanting

Begin indexing Cottage notes for 1982 and 1983

Continue garden research with nature

November 14 — Apricot

The men spent a fair amount of time at breakfast, giving me more pep talks on assuming my role as leader. I left for Perelandra knowing I am to "take the reins."

At Perelandra. I think my four-page visual aid worked. B and H now say they have some idea of what I'm doing and what they are supporting. I feel they are "oriented"—finally. They committed themselves to what's going on and say they now have a sense of what they are doing. They realize they can't do my work and that they need to cook, move furniture and do any other support jobs so that I have time to do my work.

I spent time working in the garden by myself. It was healing.

November 15 — Yellow

We finally had the last Universal Light meeting of this present series. David, Lorpuris, Hyperithon, John, Butch and I were all present. The meeting lasted two hours and translated well. I'm getting more used to Universal Light's energy.

Before the meeting, I had a few moments alone with Lorpuris. We talked a bit about how I am progressing, and he says he couldn't be more pleased. I told him I feel I'm getting stronger each day. He "warned" me not to be impatient when I lose energy. There's a lot of pressure on me because of the two-body situation.

November 16 — Gold

JAMFD

November 17 — Gold

I'm still not sleeping long hours, but the men have decided to stop hounding me so I won't get insomnia because of their concerns.

Much of my focus these days is Perelandra. I sometimes wonder if anyone there is putting the conscious effort into this expansion that I am putting into it. David is excellent at keeping me from exaggerating the importance or impact of any one step I take at Perelandra. (It is clear he's been through this leadership thing!) If I snap at H (he's still spacey), David tells me not to worry about it. I'm to stand my position and let H adjust to me. At times I might be upset at some less-than-graceful thing I've done, and David just laughs, saying this is "one of the perks of leadership"—it keeps us humble. Then he shows me how a particular action was actually fine, and I was worrying about nothing. Learning leadership dynamics from Dwight David Eisenhower is quite an amazing experience, I must admit.

At Perelandra. Clarence and H spread mulch in the outer ring while I trained B on the computer.

I've had to make it clear that I am not available at Perelandra before 11 A.M. because I am at the Cottage until then. They're having a little trouble grasping this concept, but I figure my saying it two or three more times will help them get it.

November 18 — Ivory

At Perelandra. Sunday. I cleaned the cabin in blissful solitude and listened to the Redskins game on the radio while Clarence worked outside on the cabin porch building my kindling bin. I felt H should have helped Clarence, but Clarence said H had a "macho thing" about watching football. He seems to feel he must assert his right to do this, and Clarence didn't want to get involved in H's trip. Plus, Clarence was enjoying his time outside alone.

Clarence says he's seeing some of the patterns in H that he himself is coming out of and that it's an excellent experience for him to see these patterns outside himself.

November 19 — Yellow

At Perelandra. Met with the therapist I had talked to a few weeks back. She says our talk "shifted" her to a new level personally and professionally and that her old patterns and mental constructs are "decrystallizing." I must admit there's interesting movement in her life and that she seems to be at a point where she must commit herself to going to the next level.

Received a request for a copy of *Behaving* from someone in West Germany. She said she read a review of the book.

November 20 — Dusty Rose

Took B shopping, feeling she needed to get out.

I ended the day with another confrontation with H over an amazingly trivial thing. He decided on his own to do me a favor, but he ended up screwing up the job badly because he really didn't want to do it. It all resulted in making more work for me. When I asked him about it, he became defensive and childlike, and he acted out some of Clarence's old games. During the confrontation, Clarence showed good strength and clarity—I could see his growth. H would not bend, nor would he admit any mistake or accept input. The evening ended in a stalemate, but I left this time feeling strong and stable— and that I had held my ground.

November 21 — Ivory

At breakfast. I asked Mickey what vegetables he wanted out of the Perelandra garden for tomorrow's family meal. He requested beets and leeks. That was easy enough.

Spent the afternoon with my wallpaper friend.

November 22 — Gold

Thanksgiving.

We don't celebrate Thanksgiving as such on the Cottage-level in England, but we use the Perelandra holiday as an excuse to have a big family meal together. Mickey loves putting these things together. We scheduled the dinner a little later so that I could be present for the Thanksgiving meal at Perelandra. It was a do-able juggling act, but I'm still not used to facing two huge meals in one day. Even though I can eat them, it's a psychological challenge.

November 23 — Apricot

At breakfast I talked to the men about how Mt. Shasta puts everything in my life and work on the line. Whether we succeed or not, I will have quite an integration job on my hands after July 15. The failure of the mission will be one thing, but its success is also something I will have to deal with. I suspect it will catapult me to a new level of faith, trust and dedication in my life and work, and I feel everything will have to be reviewed. They assured me I will not go through this alone and that they will be with me all the way. I could feel their support. I realize I won't be a sacrificial lamb.

Evening. We got into a discussion about traveling, and they teased me royally about my being able to travel to Europe in 1982 for two weeks with just twenty-two pounds of luggage. I told them I take great pride in being able to travel light. I further dumbfounded these worldly fellows by telling them that after my six-week trip to Europe in 1969, I managed to have only $25 to declare at customs. The men think I'm an alien.

November 24 — Heather Green

At breakfast I told them that the Mt. Shasta Mission has me feeling I have a *huge* pair of western boots on—maybe twenty times too large for me—and that between now and July 15 I'll go through changes and shifts that will allow me to grow into those boots. In fact, I have a sense of going through some shifts now. I feel a new stability and strength.

November 25 — Dusty Rose

At the Cottage. Worked with John on a good process for transferring information from the Cottage level to himself on the Earth level. David feels this will ensure that John will have better access to the information from his Earth-level perspective.

November 26 — Gold

John left the Cottage early this morning, and the other men had lunch with Hyperithon at Harry's. He's "in town" for some Mt. Shasta discussions.

November 27 — Yellow

JAMFD

November 28 — Ivory

I had an odd and restless night. I needed to open a window at Perelandra and found that I could barely move. It's unusual that I have to move at the cabin during the night anyway, but when I've had to, I've always been able to stabilize my focus enough to enable my body to move there. Last night my PB felt like it weighed four times its normal weight. I couldn't lift my hand or arm to crank open the window, so I slid my hand along the sill to the crank. I tried to get out of bed, but my body still felt heavy and my muscles felt disconnected. I think I was experiencing my Perelandra body while my soul was primarily "housed" in the Cottage body. It wasn't a scary feeling, but it was sure a curious one.

At Perelandra. I felt vulnerable, and I wanted to be alone.

November 29 — Apricot

When I awoke, I had clear insight about the way I am to proceed with B regarding her growth and our developing teacher/student relationship. I will get the insight about what to say to her based on her own comments. This way she can dictate her own pace. All I need to do is get the insights and communicate them to her when she indicates she's ready. It's an interesting process.

At Perelandra. B and H borrowed our truck and headed for the suburbs for a break. This is the first time I've been alone at Perelandra since they arrived. I loved the solitude.

At the Cottage. Returned feeling restless and uncomfortable. While in the medical session, I got insight that my new position at Perelandra was shifting me to a different level and requiring me to release blocks that might be interfering with my functioning at the new level. Addressing the teacher/student relationship with B catalyzed this.

November 30 — Ivory

At Perelandra. I spent a half-hour visualizing physical movement and exercise. *Very* interesting. Afterwards, I was physically fatigued. I felt I had been able to experience a much more focused, perhaps more complete, form of movement. On return to the Cottage, I noticed a difference in my physical presence and reality there. I could feel the men's presence and hear their voices more fully. It raises the question: Is this kind of visualization the tool for further expanding my sensory systems, especially at the Cottage?

December 1

At Perelandra. Worked in the garden by myself this morning and felt a deep sense of peace from being there. Then I "broadcast" the Army–Navy game to David. This year Army has a good team with a 9–2 record. Army won 28 to 10. Now we're talking.

December 2

At Perelandra. It's Clarence's birthday. I passed along birthday greetings from the men at the Cottage, which pleased Clarence. When I got to Perelandra, he informed me that B was talking to H about ending their relationship and that it was apparently tough for her. He said she looked like she had been hit by three trucks when he (Clarence) saw her this morning. H, on the other hand, looked like nothing was happening. They had been at it since last night. She was ignoring her work commitments that she had made to us for the day. In fact, both of them have assumed it is okay to ignore us altogether so that they can continue to work through their personal process. They seem to be lost in navel-gazing, demonstrating no sense of responsibility to or caring about anything but themselves.

All four of us were supposed to go to a restaurant for dinner to celebrate Clarence's birthday, but he and I decided we did not wish to go out with these two people, so we told them we were going out alone. The net result is that we had a lovely dinner and a great time.

December 3 — Heather Green

At Perelandra. Had a long lunch with my wallpaper friend.

Behaving was reviewed in a magazine in Great Britain, and I just received a copy of the review today. It was most favorable.

At the Cottage. I showed the review to the men, and they all agreed I couldn't ask for a better one.

I have a growing anger toward B and H. They're still quite focused on themselves and seem to feel Clarence and I should accommodate this. They work about three hours a day instead of the six hours that was part of their work agreement, and B complains a lot about how much hair the dogs leave around the house. The men keep telling me to stand my ground and don't try to whitewash anything. I keep getting tangled up in a good-person-vs-good-leadership conflict, feeling that they are mutually exclusive. David spent this evening "unraveling me" and showing me that a leader who is fair but stands her ground is a good person. The two qualities are inclusive and commingle. He now feels B and H are goldbrickers and that I should get them out of Perelandra as soon as possible. This is a tough stand. I keep thinking they need more time to adjust.

December 4 — Ivory

After breakfast I set up a medical session for Max that went extremely well. Lorpuris bantered with me throughout the session. I think he could feel my concern for my dad and was putting my mind at ease. He said that Max was in excellent shape. Lorpuris made a fine-tuning adjustment on his sacrum, said that Max was coming through the last phase of a karmic pattern and was now ready to fully release the old physical pattern. This is the final stage of a process for Max that was catalyzed by his fall on the ice in February 1983.

It is actually gratifying for me to be able to help my father go through this. Lorpuris told Max that he is to relax for a week—no golf, walk one to two miles daily and work only half days. This will allow the work to fully settle. He felt there would be no complications and suggested that Max stay close to me for essence testing. Max was pleased to feel things happening and adjustments taking place during the session. Because of his extensive knowledge of the human body and how it works, he was able to give Lorpuris terrific input about his present condition and feedback during the session work. I'm to test Max daily for one week for essences to stabilize the work, so David talked him into spending the week at the Cottage to make the testing more convenient for the two of us.

At Perelandra. I had a nature session about winterizing the roses, then began editing Universal Light with B.

Evening. I had a medical session that was gentle and subtle.

December 5 — Gold

I awoke feeling Max's presence in the house, and I smiled.

At Perelandra. I winterized the bird area, planted the last of the bulbs and prepared for a winter storm that the weathermen keep harping about.

At the Cottage. Napped for three and a half hours, then spent a quiet evening in the living room by the fire.

December 6 — Apricot

At Perelandra. It was a mild winter storm. I arrived at Perelandra to find B and H having breakfast at 12:30 P.M. I saw red—but kept it pretty much to myself because they claimed they would still get in their six hours of work this afternoon. I spent several hours training B on the computer.

For the first time, I see the depth of my dedication to Perelandra. Up to this point, I didn't realize how dedicated I was because I didn't have anyone to judge this by. It sounds so crazy, but it's true. I also see how disciplined I am, and that I can hold an intense focus for hours at a time—and now I see some others can't. And I also know I can't assume the same discipline and dedication from others. B and H do not have good work skills. They don't even have self-discipline.

At the Cottage. The men advised me not to treat B as a peer associate. I'm to make her earn that position.

                                              December 7 — Ivory
I awoke *angry* at B's lack of discipline and drive. I feel she is capable of much more. The men encouraged me to address this with her and to do it today.

At Perelandra. I ended up in a two-and-a-half-hour verbal battle with B. I challenged her workday at Perelandra and her poor work skills. It resulted in some kind of emotional breakthrough for her. She said she saw that how she thought I had been feeling about her was actually what she felt about herself—her insecurity, lack of self-respect and self-esteem. Her anger at me was really her anger at herself, and now she's able to see that there's much there for her to respect and appreciate. I hope this does the trick and she starts helping me rather than draining me.

At the Cottage. I returned exhausted and had a medical session right away. The fight with B had shifted to the Cottage body. Lorpuris worked with me in subtle ways again, but when he was finished I felt at peace.

                                              December 8 — Yellow
At Perelandra. Clarence is having a lot of difficulty with H. It's now clear we're dealing with an adolescent, and Clarence needs to clarify his expectations with H. He talked with H for three and a half hours, but he's not sure how much H heard. I worked with B again on the

computer, and the time went much easier for the two of us. Perhaps there was a breakthrough.

At the Cottage. I took a nap before dinner and spent the evening with Max and Tex by the fire. I find these peaceful evenings are most helpful.

December 9 — Heather Green

At Perelandra. I feel Clarence and I are in concert about Perelandra's direction and the type of person who can work and live there. We're having long and fruitful talks around this issue. I'm feeling Clarence take on strength and begin to operate as an active partner again. We spent the afternoon together, and it was the first time in quite a few years I've relaxed and enjoyed myself with him this way.

At the Cottage. I talked about the situation around H and Clarence with the men to get their input. They feel it would be better if *both* Clarence and I confront H together. H feels he can ignore Clarence because I'm the actual leader, not Clarence. My presence will indicate to H that he should listen to what is being said.

December 10 — Yellow

I'm getting much better about this birthday business. I didn't wake up anticipating pain. Once again, Mickey sneaked in a vase of roses so that I'd see them first thing.

At Perelandra. I received a big bookstore order for *Behaving.* (That was a fine birthday surprise.) Went to a mall for Christmas shopping and met Clarence there for birthday dessert.

At the Cottage. Returned with a sharp pain in my side that quickly worsened. A medical session got rid of the pain.

December 11 — Heather Green

Lorpuris sent word to the Cottage that I was to test essences this morning and that I was to test them several times throughout the day. I am getting "broadsided" by negative energy from H, and the pain I felt was an energy pain related to this, not muscle-related. The men urged me to get things settled with H today.

At Perelandra. Talked to H for four hours. When I started, the pain in my side had returned. I remained clear, straight and calm throughout, which kept H from closing down. He admitted he has personal problems that I seem to be triggering. (I'm thrilled.) The pain in my side left during my talk with H.

At the Cottage. I had another medical session, and Lorpuris said I was processing everything well and would be fine for my trip to NYC tomorrow.

December 12 — Apricot

I flew to NYC for a day-long trustees' meeting with a bunch of accountants and attorneys. I spent the night in a hotel and went to the Cottage from there. It was not an issue.

December 13 — Ivory

I flew back to Washington on a plane full of press people. They were following a man who had been a hostage in Kuwait and was now returning to the States. He was in the first-class area of our plane. Watching the press in action gave me some idea of the irritation David had to go through with the press when he was on the Earth level.

At the Cottage. I returned late and ready for bed—but I had to eat first. These double dinners could get to me.

December 14 — Burgundy

I have a deep desire to be at the Cottage full time. My Perelandra responsibilities are draining.

At Perelandra. B has announced that she is committed to going to the next level in her life and is open to me helping her. I spent time encouraging her. Then I headed to a long lunch with my wallpaper friend.

At the Cottage. I fell apart emotionally. I'm tired of balancing Perelandra, and I want to be at the Cottage full time. I *yearn* for a vacation. In the midst of my collapse, I started experiencing what felt like "thought spasms." David pressed me into a medical session immediately. My pelvis was misaligned, and this was causing occipital pressure in the head. After the session, my emotions were stabilized, Perelandra didn't feel overwhelming, and I was no longer experiencing spasms. I'm to stick close to the essences and *rest*. "Rest" has been defined by the men as time of less intense focus.

December 15 — Gold

The men responded to last night's collapse by surrounding me with love. I can feel them closing in and protecting me. They're not pressing me about anything, they're just present.

At Perelandra. I put the garden to bed.

December 16 — Dusty Rose

I slept late and had a leisurely morning at the Cottage.

At Perelandra. Had breakfast with Clarence in the cabin, then spent the day by myself working on the Cottage notes. I *thoroughly* enjoyed my day.

December 17 — Ivory

At the Cottage. The men spent the day with Hyperithon going over some Mt. Shasta planning. They talked him into spending the night. They tell me that both Hyperithon and Lorpuris will be joining us Christmas day.

Medical session. I asked Lorpuris if, after January 1, we can have information sessions together so that I can get answers to some questions I've had about health and body balance. He said he'd be delighted and looked forward to it. Then I asked if he did dental work. He said yes, all I had to do was say the word and we can start that work. I asked if the pain from his work would be bad, and he laughed, saying it would be a *very* different experience from what I'm used to. I reminded him that I'm a chicken about pain, especially when it comes to dental work.

December 18 — Apricot

Had breakfast with Hyperithon. He does enjoy his time "in form" on the Cottage level! His joy and openness about life fills the room, and he's quite the raconteur.

At the Cottage. Returned exhausted and completely lost my focus in mid-sentence—all of which led to a medical session. During the session, I experienced painful emotion around wanting to be at the

Cottage full time. I told David and Lorpuris that I wasn't sure I was strong enough to continue doing the Cottage/Perelandra thing. I cried deeply. I could feel both men supporting me emotionally. They assured me that my feelings were natural, and David stated emphatically that I must blow steam more. Their support helped me pull myself together, and I ended up feeling a little silly about thinking I couldn't continue. Lorpuris finished his work, and I was okay again—just feeling a little vulnerable.

December 19 — Ivory

I awoke feeling my strength was rebuilding.

At Perelandra. While I worked on the Life Table, I kept getting the intuition to put it together more carefully than ever this year, to pay attention to my intuition about what is included and where it is to be placed on the table. I worked quietly for several hours, and I ended up with probably my best Life Table yet.

At the Cottage. Hyperithon called to ask how I was and to give me his love and support. He had monitored yesterday's medical session, as he does all of them, and he was aware of my emotional pain and questions. I felt surrounded by love.

December 20 — Yellow

At Perelandra. I added some final touches to the Life Table and prepared the garden for the winter solstice. I cleaned the center's crystal and placed greens cut from the Elemental Annex cedar tree under it (as per instructions from nature). All while I worked I could feel a strong nature presence surrounding me.

I split the Life Table to the Cottage in the usual fashion.

B and H are acting up again. B is out of control and on an emotional downspiral. They waste my time.

At the Cottage. We had a Life Table toast: To life!

December 21 — Gold

Winter solstice: 11:23 A.M.

From the Cottage, I did an Energy Cleansing Process for both Perelandra and the Cottage in preparation for the solstice. Then I got word that I was to draw one card from the Tarot this year and I was to do it before the solstice moment.

The Speaker: The Speaker speaks.

From his mouth lightning bolts and birds shoot forth. The earth trembles. Volcanos erupt. The land shakes. There are water-spouts. Flowers spring up before his feet.

Terrible are his eyes.

Mighty are his words.

The entire universe hangs upon them.

He presents the greatest possible contrast to his predecessor, the High Priest or Hierophant. The Hierophant was silent. Before him knelt two robed figures. In one hand he held the miter of spiritual authority. The other, extended in the gesture of blessing, was usually marked with a mystic cross. As intermediary, he stood between man and God. The guardian of a mystery, his lips were sealed. He was a fitting counterpart to the veiled, mysterious, inaccessible High Priestess.

Not so with the Speaker.

The Speaker is the speaking of One. It is of the rose bared in the desert. "Where the sands were, now is bared a rose..." The speaking of the Speaker is like an eruption and it is clear that his words are no mere speech. The significance of the Book is It is Done. With love, it is done when the Speaker is with you. The key to the Speaker is his shimmering heart—in other words, love. But this is the transfigured heart. It is the heart of the One who drank the cup of fire. It is no longer tinged with the suffering that weighted down the Thinker, nor is it connected with redemption, the Hanging Man.

It is the heart of One, or the heart of hearts.

What then is the Word the Speaker speaks?

It is not the word nor is it a word. The point is that the Speaker must speak. And speaking is being, knowing and doing. His words are words that must be spoken. Once in the Kingdom, acting from within, the flow is direct and instantaneous.

Speaking is not passive. Words are an act and a necessity. Words spoken from within and from the heart are part of the One Motion. They are the Creative Word.

"Where the shifted sands were, now is bared a rose."

The Speaker, with his shimmering heart, is one of the major signatures of the present Book of T. And it is interesting that he is as completely open and outgoing as the Mother-Creator is ingoing, concentrated on her creation. Together they form the great yin-yang current of these Books. As a pair, in the former progression, they both contained, but veiled, the Mystery. Here, neither is veiled; all is revealed. But she creates inwardly; he speaks and outs [demonstrates] the creation.

The golden key in the left hand of the Speaker is the key of the heart. The black ring in his right hand is a magnetic iron ring, related to the crown on the head of the Feeler—the black iron circlet which supported the symbol of love—and it is also related to Unity, to the circle of manifestation symbolized by the O, and to the globe, the Prime Mystery, on which the Changer balances. The fact that it is black means that it includes the entire material realm. This states that entry into the Kingdom does not imply a severance between what is called material and spiritual, but that they are joined in one never-ending circle of manifestation, or in the circuit of positive-negative energy.

This is another restatement of the great Yin-Yang.

The Kingdom of heaven is on earth.

The reality spoken of in these twenty-two Books of Tarot is not nirvana, nor a leaving of this world for another one.

Why then does the Speaker wear boots, keeping his feet from immediate contact with the earth? This means that although he stands upon the earth and manifests on earth, his level of being is a higher one. He is more than an initiate. He is the dynamo of awakened beingness. He is the great transformer and conductor of the current of energy into the world. And he is in motion.

To do and be also means to speak, for the Word is an act of creation. God created the world by the Word.

And with his speaking, the Speaker is reversing the flow of energy which has been dammed up; for what has been received has been held, static, waiting for the positive-negative charges to join in one current. It is no longer a time for separations. It is a time for outing [demonstrating] what has been given and that which arises. What the Donor gave through absolute Truth and the law of balance is being released by the Speaker in energy and force.

I prepared for the solstice moment by activating the Perelandra coning, then the garden. This time I saw energy from the entire garden area draw into the garden center's crystal. A green stem moved up from the center, through Perelandra and through the Cottage. Once it got to the universe, it blossomed into a beautiful white rose. I watched the rose as the solstice moment hit. It was a dramatic and beautiful sight.

At Perelandra. B's attitude is rapidly going downhill. She's extremely hostile toward me. We had scheduled for me to give her a medical session sometime today but, once I saw the mood she was in, I knew I'd need a break before I could get through a session with her. I met my wallpaper friend in town for lunch and talked to her about B and H. My friend told me it took a half-hour of talking before color returned to my face.

En route back to Perelandra, I thought about the best direction for dealing with B. I got insight to put together an outline of expectations and intent at Perelandra and that I was to hold my focus on Perelandra, not B and H. Either they fit into our expectations and intent or they don't. I was not to try to convince them of anything.

When I arrived back, B threw a temper tantrum. Although we had not set a specific time for the medical session (other than it was to occur today), I had not been present to give it when she wanted it, and she was mad. She complained about a "splitting headache" and indicated that I was the cause. I offered to do the medical session for her headache, but she didn't want me touching her. Instead, she wanted Clarence to give her the session. He just looked at me, and I assured him I would talk him through the process. After the session when Clarence and I left the room, she didn't thank either one of us for our help.

At the Cottage. The men helped me with the outline of expectations and intent, then we went out to dinner to celebrate the solstice. An amazing yet weird day.

December 22 — Ivory

At Perelandra. B's headache was completely gone, and she still hasn't said anything to us about helping her through yesterday's crisis. These two people are really getting to me.

Clarence and I discussed the Perelandra outline, and he had some good ideas that we added. He's supportive of the idea and offered to type a good copy.

Medical session. I'm being broadsided again, and the negative energy is hitting a vulnerable area—the left psoas. Lorpuris said he doesn't feel I should let the B and H issue go over two weeks. It's too much of a drain on me, and it must be resolved. He said we did a good job just getting B connected yesterday, let alone through the medical session itself. I asked for help in understanding her, and he said she can make the shift facing her within the two-week time limit, *and* she can do it without involving me. In fact, he suggested I draw back from her. The end of her erratic behavior depends on how completely she goes through the shift, and it's impossible to tell right now if she will choose to go through it. He also urged me to take a two-week "vacation" beginning January 2. When I asked if I could stay at the Cottage two days in a row, he said no. He reminded me that the soul presence in my Perelandra body strengthens it, and I can't afford two days away from that body. He also urged me to stay close to him and not hesitate to call him throughout this tense time.

December 23 — Apricot

I awoke with my spinal column vibrating. At first it vibrated in sections, then the entire length—like sonar waves in the spinal fluid. I laid there and just felt the strong sensations. I realized that the spinal columns in both bodies were vibrating. After about a half-hour, it stopped.

After breakfast I had a medical session. Lorpuris assured me I've gone through another excellent shift and another part of my expansion. He worked on me for about forty minutes to help seat and ground the shift.

At Perelandra. Clarence and I presented "The Perelandra Expectations" to B and H. Both were quite hostile, and B became so angry that I suggested she consider leaving Perelandra. She said she would think about it. I gave them both two weeks to decide if they will accept our intent and expectations for Perelandra. If not, we would pay their transportation back to California.

December 24 — Dusty Rose

At Perelandra. Clarence and I had Christmas Eve dinner at a restaurant with friends, and left H and B at Perelandra to figure out life.

At the Cottage. John has returned. We had a late dinner and a terrific evening by the fire admiring the big tree the men decorated this afternoon. Once again Max joined in, even though he still says these men are much too picky about how the tree gets decorated. They told me he showed up this afternoon with a huge box of donuts for everyone. I think he was trying to loosen them up with a sugar overdose—which apparently didn't work.

December 25 — Gold

I awoke at 5 A.M. hearing Gregorian Chant in my mind's ear. (There were no monks in my room to account for the music. I checked.) Then I got insight on how better to explain Perelandra to B and H: All decisions and directions at Perelandra are initiated by nature, not Clarence or me. We will not allow anyone to impose their will on this process. If they can't place their will and/or ego to one side and put Perelandra's timing first (when dealing with Perelandra-related issues), they are in the wrong place and they need to leave.

At Perelandra. Clarence was cooking Christmas dinner for us all when he got a phone call from his family. His father was found dead in his apartment this morning. They think he probably died yesterday of a cerebral hemorrhage, and they feel it was quick and probably painless. Of course the news hit Clarence hard. He and I talked the next two hours while he got through the shock and regained his balance. We decided it was best that I stay at Perelandra because of the problems with B and H. Also, I can function as Clarence's outside anchor if he needs one while he's with his family. He left for Roanoke around 3 P.M.

Christmas dinner was a little grim. B and H were still hostile toward me, and B was angry she had to finish making the dinner once Clarence left. She acted like she expected him to finish that task before leaving for Roanoke, but this was too bizarre for me to believe.

After dinner I presented my new ideas about Perelandra. I pointed out that they are now where I was eight years ago just prior to my making the move into the nature work. At these two points we're equal. After that, I have eight years education, research and experience that they haven't even begun yet. We are not peers, therefore they can't participate fully in the final decision-making at Perelandra. (This is something they have felt they should be involved in and part of what is making them angry.) I also said that I felt people joining Perelandra must have a certain level of emotional maturity that will allow them to *comfortably* put aside their own wants and desires while they focus on the work. B and H must decide if they have personally developed to such a level, and if they haven't, they must leave so that they can continue their development. Perelandra does not provide this because it is not what Perelandra's service is about. We all have until January 8 to decide their future at Perelandra.

At the Cottage. I don't know if there was ever an evening when I was more glad to get home. When I got back, Hyperithon and Lorpuris were there.

December 26 — Dusty Rose

At Perelandra. Clarence called. He's doing fine in Roanoke—in fact, everyone in the family is doing well with the death and their sadness.

The pressure has dissipated somewhat with B and H.

December 27 — Yellow

At Perelandra. Began cleaning and rearranging my office while B worked on the computer. H is still showing signs of hostility.

At the Cottage. Had a medical session. My pelvis was misaligned. Lorpuris worked on me for about an hour. He said my spine shift is settling in well and he's pleased with my progress. He pointed out that I'm going through these shifts more easily now, and I agreed.

I went with several of the men to The Pub for the first time in months. I've treasured my quiet evenings at home during this intense time. Seamus's last set was special. The band played a quiet, mellow set, and the audience moved right into the mood. I couldn't help but compare this with the intense, hard-driving concert he gave at the Concert Hall last December 30 for the hospital benefit. Looking back, I feel this set the tone for the past year, at least for me and everyone around me on the Perelandra level. I wondered if tonight would set the tone for the year to come, if it was this year's New Year concert. God, I hope so. When the band finished, everyone felt something special had happened tonight.

December 28 — Gold

Max spent the night with us. I'm getting the distinct feeling that this week between December 24 and January 1 is developing into a family week. Everyone is taking an R&R—and we all seem to be spending it together as much as possible.

At Perelandra. I finished rearranging my office and prepared to start sorting my computer files.

Spent time with my wallpaper friend.

December 29 — Heather Green

I awoke feeling touched and even overwhelmed at the work I'm involved in—Mt. Shasta, nature, connecting the nature work with the Cottage work, serving as the Cottage grounder. The magic of it all hit me full force. I could hardly get myself to leave the Cottage today.

At Perelandra. I can tell B is honestly attempting to come up with an answer about her future at Perelandra. H, on the other hand, seems to be ignoring the situation.

Clarence returned. He's doing well and seems to be coming through his father's death well. We both feel it was a good decision for me not to go with him so that he could move through the experience alone. He says he got a lot out of it.

Medical session. Lorpuris told me to just observe the physical changes that are occurring now. The body knows what to do, and I don't have to ask questions in order to understand. I only need to observe and learn.

December 30 — Dusty Rose

Now I'm beginning to catch up on sleep.

At Perelandra. I have a strong feeling H must leave. He still

hasn't figured out that Clarence and I aren't going to abuse him, and
he's constantly defensive and tight-minded. He's making it uncomfortable for us.

December 31 — Gold

I have officially agreed to take an R&R for the next two weeks. I
need this.

I got into a discussion with David about nature and D-Day. He
pointed out that his partnership with nature forty years ago was conscious, in so far as he had to consciously deal with weather and
conditions, and unconscious on all other levels. With the Mt. Shasta
Mission, the partnership with nature is fully conscious and equally
important to the success of this mission as nature was to the success
of D-Day.

I love pressure. We move ahead.

JOURNAL UPDATE

B left Perelandra right after New Year's, and we asked H to leave a couple of months later. The problems that they presented us with began a series of lessons that lasted for a number of years. I had to establish a clear definition of appropriate expectations for the Perelandra staff. This hasn't been easy because I continued to struggle with what makes a fair leader who stands her ground. I also had to understand that no one else was going to figure out on his own what was expected at Perelandra. The job fell squarely in my lap. It seemed like every time I got the point, another person would come to Perelandra who would present a new twist on the lessons. Then I'd work with the Cottage men and nature to fine-tune some more and I'd restate a clearer definition of appropriate expectations. It hasn't been simple because we don't fit into the usual guidelines of a small business. I've had to create the best structure and define what constitutes an appropriate staff that addresses the unique qualities of Perelandra. One thing that became clear early on was that it is inappropriate for us to have a live-in staff. Since 1985, we have not invited anyone else to live here. Instead, while Clarence and I maintain our home at Perelandra, our staff lives in the surrounding area and commutes to work. We now have a staff that works diligently to maintain a finely run small business while at the same time working to understand and serve Perelandra's big picture. I doubt if the co-creative leadership class is over for me, but I'm not complaining (too much) because, as painful as it has been at times, it is a fascinating study of dynamics.

S arrived in May as planned, and we worked together for five months to get various written materials copyedited and ready for the public. As a result of our efforts, I put together the first Perelandra order form in the fall of 1985 and sent it out to everyone on our modest, but growing, mailing list. Over the past ten years, *Behaving* has sold 50,000 copies, and our mailing list has become substantial—and we still haven't used advertisements.

I continue to live in the cabin near the garden and still maintain my focus on a wide range of research and development with nature. My biggest change in this area is that I now have a garden assistant who does much of the physical work in the garden, thus freeing me to concentrate on the nature research for both our Earth level and the Cottage.

The Mt. Shasta Mission occurred in July 1985, but that really is another book. (My copyeditor says I was born to tease. She might be right.)

John still is not consciously aware of his participation in the Cottage from his Earth perspective. He continues to come to the Cottage two times each year and stays for several weeks each time. He and I have a £10 bet riding on this consciousness business. You see, if he opens consciously to this level of his life while still living on Earth, he will trigger the process of integrating the Cottage reality into his present Earth awareness. This means that when he dies, he will be ready and able to move directly into the Cottage full time. If he doesn't integrate the two realities before death, he will need to do it after death and will not be able to move into the Cottage until after this is completed. We don't know how long that will take. The bet is riding on who gets to the Cottage full time first—John, the much older but presently unintegrated man or me, the much younger but presently integrated whipper-snapper.

Mickey and Elizabeth remain the best of friends, and she says she treasures his support in her life. He still expresses his love for us through cooking, and we continue to be spared from having to drink David's "sludge" because Mickey makes sure there is always a pot of the "good" coffee available.

Butch and Nicole are also still good friends, and he continues to go to The Pub nearly every evening on his motorcycle to enjoy the music and to hobnob with the other regulars. He has not taken on any more music performances since that concert in December 1983. I guess he wasn't kidding when he announced back then that the strain of performing was too much.

Tex and David continue their ongoing, on-the-fly chess games. I have no idea who has won more games now. It changes all the time. Their "heated" discussions also continue on a fairly regular basis. The rest of us still ignore them.

Oh yes, they play golf every Sunday afternoon. The regular foursome includes David, Tex, Seamus and Max. They are joined by Hyperithon and John when they are around.

Petunia always goes out with them in her official capacity as scorekeeper. No one has teed her off yet, which is a miracle since she is always getting in the way. Of course, she continues to hold the upper hand because she remains "scented." They *have* to pay attention to her. The odd thing about Petunia is that she is not aging. She is a healthy, mature skunk that shows no signs of moving into old age. The usual life span for a skunk is seven years, and she's now twelve.

I have my own office at the Cottage that was just built this summer. Now that I have some place to put it all, I'm in the process of shifting information that I'll want later.

My daily schedule presently includes twelve hours at the Cottage and twelve hours at Perelandra.

The pattern of the colors that I wear each day have changed again. For a long time, I wore the same color ribbon on both bodies each day. Then about a year ago, the colors gradually reduced to just one—ivory. Even though I'm not sure what it means, I still feel it's a personal triumph.

Max remains very much a part of my life and heart, and he visits the Cottage frequently. He has expanded his ice rink operation and has bought a second one that's about a three-hour drive from us. David invested in this one with him. We're trying to get David on the ice, but he just stares at us as if this were the most foolish idea a human has ever had.

Seamus's band is still the main attraction at The Pub and continues to pull in people from all over. He's as outrageous as ever and still intensely focused on his music. For all intents and purposes, the piano at the Cottage now belongs to Seamus.

My friendship with "my wallpaper friend" is very much alive, and after all these years she seems to be quite at ease about my Cottage life. I had not reread the Cottage notes until I went through them for this book. In looking back, I appreciate the struggles my friend had with my Cottage life and feel that she demonstrated the full range of emotions a person can have in trying to support someone who is going through expansion. She wanted to help me, support me, protect me, warn me if she felt I was getting into trouble—while at the same time, she wanted to support me by not getting in my way, thus allowing me to move in my own direction. I might add that my life and direction is not something she would ever personally choose for herself. I think this in itself is important to note when thinking about what is needed for support during expansion. It is a difficult role that requires trust and faith from the support person. She proved that a support person does not need to be in sync with the expansion the other person is experiencing. When I talked to her recently about the ups and downs that she went through that are evident in the journal, she said, "You know, all things considered, we did good." I had to agree.

Clarence also demonstrated something important about support. So often when we think about jumping into the unknown, the first thing we do is look to our partners for support. And if we don't get it, we declare them insensitive, end the partnership and go in search of someone with the "appropriate" level of sensitivity. It is quite clear that Clarence was not my support person throughout this expansion and the post-expansion period. But what may not be clear is that it was inappropriate for him to be my support. He had to address his own issues while I was addressing mine. My expansion could not impinge on his timing or his direction. When a soul-triggered expansion occurs, the context of your life is part of the consideration and it does not require that those around you place their lives on the back burner for the sake of your expansion.

This brings me to the issue of just who you do talk to about your expansion. Based on my experience, I recommend that you choose these people carefully, especially in the beginning when everything is new and you are a little vulnerable. Try to remember that, as exciting as this time may be for you, not everyone wants to hear about it or is able to hear it. Once we tell someone something, we require that they process the information in some way. This is part of communication. It would be thoughtless on our part if we tried to force someone to listen to something like a ring-pass-not experience when they don't want or need this kind of information. We must consider what this person is going to do with the information. If they show signs of disinterest or their eyes glaze over, don't keep talking. Take the hint and accept that this is not the person to hear about your expansion.

In 1986 I began giving a workshop series at Perelandra, and in 1987 a workshop about my Cottage life and work called "The Mundane-Fantastic Workshop" was added to the series. People had a tendency to leave this workshop with their eyeballs spinning, so if you've had a reaction or two as you have read this book, don't feel you are alone. Now that I've written this book, I won't be giving the Mundane-Fantastic Workshop again. But don't feel you've missed anything because there is a lot more information in this book than I could ever have packed into that workshop.

By the way, a lot of nature research and development occurred during 1984 that you may wish to follow up on as a result of reading the journal. The Soil Balancing and Stabilizing Process plus how to work with nature is described in the books *Perelandra Garden Workbook* and *Perelandra Garden Workbook II*. What conings are and how to set up and use them are included in the two *Workbooks* and the book *MAP* (second edition). The Universal Light transcripts are offered in the Universal Light Series. The Post-Death Process is available for anyone who uses flower essences and wishes to offer this service to family and friends. It is the Perelandra Paper #9. The Two-Week Essence Process and the other testing processes I have developed for using flower essences well are described in the book *Flower Essences*.

Everything we offer is listed in our catalog, which we will be happy to mail to you. Our address and phone number are in the back of this book. There is no charge for the catalog.

Chapter 5

So, How Do I Get
to Carnegie Hall?

There were several areas of challenge that I experienced as a result of the Cottage expansion that I feel are universal to all expansions.

1. There is the deep desire to hang onto sanity. By definition, an expansion throws us outside the framework of our existing sanity. I have learned that it is natural and healthy to question our sanity, especially in the early stages after an expansion. But at some point we must let go of the old sanity structure so that we can shift to the new structure. This can be painful, as I described when I let go on December 20, 1982. The pain of letting go of our sanity is a difficult thing to describe to someone until that person is faced with it himself—and then I don't have to describe the pain at all. But when faced with this moment, try to remember to just let go. A new structure of sanity awaits you.

2. Related to the sanity issue are the constant questions I had about whether the Cottage expansion was real or was I fantasizing it. The human mind is capable of many miraculous things, and I wasn't sure if it included something like this. If it was real, I wanted to go on. If it was fantasy, I wanted to face this and get back on track with my life. Because the men were encouraging me by saying my questions were "normal," I felt comfortable questioning the Cottage reality for years. Every time I thought of a possible soft spot or loophole that might prove it all to be fantasy, I brought it up. In fact, if I can think of something to question today, I still bring it up. As a result of the probing, I now know for sure that I haven't been able to come up with a weakness.

Oddly, my strongest evidence that this Cottage life is real has had nothing to do with my questions. (A) I've been living this two-body life now for over twelve years, and I am far stronger in every way than I was in 1982 when it all began. If it wasn't real, I think I would be showing signs of deterioration by now. (B) I still have my sense of humor. I think that had this been a fantasy or delusion, I would have lost my sense of humor by now. (C) After twelve years of daily entries, I have never suffered from writer's block in the journal. I've always known what to record. If I was making it up, I think I would have hit a block at some point. (D) I don't think I'm capable of coming up with so many new concepts and information as I have had to face on a near-daily basis because of the Cottage. I have a fine mind, but I just don't think I'm capable of inventing all of this.

3. The challenge of integrating one life with two bodies living consciously on two separate realities was tremendous. I had to let everything fuse gradually and in good timing. For this, I needed patience—and this is very important to have during expansion integration. Having two bodies requires different thinking. There are two sets of teeth to brush, two showers to take and two sets of meals to eat. There's my personal life at the Cottage level and my personal life at Perelandra. If I go out to dinner with someone at one end, I have to juggle the schedule accordingly at the other end. In short, this expansion (as with any expansion) requires that a new life be created that will accommodate the new reality. And this involves some pretty mundane things.

4. I had to deal with new concepts nearly every day. Besides having the SMP issues and the Cottage's different perspective on life, I had to learn simple things like an English road system, different currency, different shops and customs. This takes a lot of effort and energy, and again patience and timing are our two best allies when facing this kind of massive integration.

5. During the first two or three years at the Cottage, I was scared *constantly*. Would I screw up the SMP and end up "blowing myself up in space?" Would I ever get lost? Could the Cottage men find me, if I did? Was I nuts? How will the Cottage affect my Perelandra work? If people found out about my Cottage life, would they be "scandalized" by this information and would my reputation as a nature researcher be destroyed because of it?

Underlying my fear, I had a deep knowing that what I was doing was right. I was also curious: How was this thing going to play out? And I have a deep belief that when I leap into the unknown, I am leaping into a universe of love and balance and I am okay. All of this overpowered my fears, and I was able to keep moving.

6. As you now know, the physical support for an expansion can be quite challenging. I could say I was lucky to have the chiropractor with the skills to address the physical issues that came up but, to be honest, I don't think my soul would have triggered this expansion without my having someone like her to turn to. She could successfully address the important physical expansion issues that arose for me because she had two areas of training that not every chiropractor includes: CSF pulse balancing and cranial adjustments. In fact, only about five percent of the chiropractors in the United States have cranial-adjustment training. When you are choosing a chiropractor, I recommend that you make sure this person has at least CSF pulse-balancing training. It would be even better if they had cranial-adjustment training as well.

I also do not feel my soul would have triggered the expansion had I not known how to use flower essences. Expansion and its aftermath are tough on a person's electrical system and central nervous system. This particular expansion was especially tough. Flower essences balance and stabilize both of these systems, and I feel they are an essential tool to have integrated in one's life for both daily health imbalances and the kinds of issues that arise as a result of expansion.

One key to flower essences is discerning which sets are appropriate for you to use. The essences that are most helpful for one person may not be the same for someone else. Although the two sets I used from 1982 to 1984 were invaluable to my process at that time, they were the only ones I knew about then and now I no longer use them. It makes sense that the essences best suited for me are the ones I have developed from the Perelandra garden. If you are interested in exploring flower essences, I recommend that you get the essences that are right for you and that you learn to test them using the kinesiology method. For learning how to use flower essences in general and how to test for the ones for you, I recommend the

book *Flower Essences*. It includes information about the Perelandra
Essences, plus several addresses of other flower essence producers
that you can write to for information. If you would like information
about the book and the Perelandra Essences, just contact us for a
catalog.

I still use the White Brotherhood Medical Unit for all my health-
related issues. This includes mental, emotional and soul-related
issues, as well as physical. We refined the medical process that was
begun in 1984 and made it possible for anyone who wishes to work
with the White Brotherhood Medical Unit to do so. The program is
called "MAP," and it is described in the book titled *MAP: The Co-
Creative White Brotherhood Medical Assistance Program*. It is not
meant just for times of expansion. It is designed to be used as part
of a person's regular health program.

After reading about my early experiences with MAP, you may be
reluctant to try the program. After all, I experienced quite a bit of
pain and discomfort in those early days. But you must remember
that the two-body system is most unusual and has some tough requirements that are not part of other expansions. I have been using
MAP regularly since 1984, and it is rare that I have a session that
even approaches the difficulty of those early ones. And many thousands of people have successfully used MAP since the book was
published in 1990. If you are at all attracted to this kind of help, I
recommend that you read the book. It gives all the information
you'll need.

The following is a list of how my life and world view have
changed as a result of this expansion.

1. I have *felt* the relationship between soul and body. I have an
exceptional appreciation for the teamwork that constantly goes on
between the two (in my case, three—one soul and two bodies), and
I certainly have a unique firsthand experience of what it feels like
not to have this team operating in sync. I also understand something
about what can be done to assist the body and soul to function with
a greater degree of synchronicity.

2. I have experienced a new level of how *big* life is. Prior to
1982, I had no idea life could be so expanded, and I certainly didn't

have a clue about what this might mean. "Big" includes an expanded sense of family and friends. It's obvious that I do not solely look to people on the Perelandra level for friends and family. I not only have a vibrant personal life on the Cottage level, I also have my good friend Elizabeth (David's mother) who resides on a third level—and I'm still not sure where Hyperithon and Lorpuris reside.

3. I have an appreciation of how *small* life is. The life loops give me a sense of the intricate weaving of seemingly distant and disconnected events—how life hooks neatly into itself. And talking to Hyperithon in a translation/coning setup at Perelandra and then talking to him over coffee on my balcony at the Cottage makes me think, "Small universe!"

4. The interconnectedness and interrelationship between levels is a daily practicality for me. Much of my work at Perelandra is a result of what the Cottage experience has taught me, and much of my work at the Cottage is a result of what I am learning from nature at Perelandra. And I never know when I'll open the door at the Cottage to find someone I had contact with on the Perelandra level.

5. Our lives continue. This I absolutely know. And we don't lose what we've learned and gained between birth and death. Contrary to popular opinion, we actually do take it with us. I also have job security. I know that when I leave the Perelandra level—when I die—I will be shifting to the Cottage and continuing my work with nature.

6. I feel I have a good understanding of the benefit of death that David and the others refer to so often. My whole view of death has changed dramatically. I now see it as a wonderful rite of passage that I look forward to experiencing. I also understand that there are many things I can learn *now* and apply to my life *now* that have traditionally been set aside until after death.

7. I've certainly learned that nothing stays on the back burner forever. This has encouraged me to address things that I might have considered sidestepping. Now I know there is no such thing as successful sidestepping, so I might as well address issues as they come up because I'll only have to do it later. And I also understand that timing is a factor when dealing with issues, and since the back burner is always there, I don't have to press myself into doing some-

thing before I'm ready. The issue won't go away. In fact, the exist-ence of the back burner assures me that it will be there when it's time to address it.

8. I have learned that emotional balance is not a stationary goal or a static phenomenon that, once achieved, remains forever. Emotional issues that I had successfully dealt with prior to 1982 and that had functioned as strengths had to be reviewed, modified or fully re-leased as a result of the expansion. Suddenly, my old balance was no longer acceptable in light of my new life. I have learned that emotional issues, like life, have levels. Our job is to understand an issue in a way that is appropriate to the level we are functioning on. This is emotional balance. But when our life expands, the under-standing we have around these issues also needs to expand and be addressed.

9. I have a different appreciation of what it is to function in form. I don't feel limited at all. Instead, I feel respect and awe toward this amazing team of my soul and bodies.

When I have talked to others about the Cottage expansion adven-ture, they quickly assume I stopped everything in my life so that I could focus on it. But this is not true. Throughout my expansion and post-expansion process, I remained functional. That's because this expansion occurred in proper timing. It was soul initiated and not will or ego initiated.

Here's a list of the major things I did from 1983 through 1990.

1983
  Self-published *Behaving*—first edition
  Designed cabin and helped get it built

1984
  Began working with Universal Light
  Learned computer wordprocessing
  Developed Battle Energy Release Process
  Developed Soil Balancing and Stabilization Process
  Planted and cultivated extensive rose ring
  Did Gettysburg Battlefield work

1985

Developed Perelandra Rose Essences
Worked on Mt. Shasta Mission
Organized and prepared first Perelandra order form

1986

Self-published *Behaving*—second edition
Wrote *Perelandra Garden Workbook*
Learned desktop publishing and a new wordprocessing program
Developed Perelandra Garden Essences
Began annual workshop series at Perelandra

1987

Did layout and desktop publishing work for *Perelandra Garden Workbook*
Self-published *Perelandra Garden Workbook*—hardcover
Wrote *Flower Essences*

1988

Self-published *Perelandra Garden Workbook*—soft cover
Self-published *Flower Essences*

1989

Learned racquetball (on the Perelandra level) and became the "killer of the racquetball court"

1990

Researched, wrote and published the following papers:
Perelandra Paper #1: *Co-Creative Definitions*
Perelandra Paper #2: *The Calibration Process*
Perelandra Paper #3: *Miasms*
Perelandra Paper #4: *The Body/Soul Fusion Process*
Wrote, "desktopped" and self-published the following books:
Perelandra Garden Workbook II
MAP: The Co-Creative White Brotherhood Medical Assistance Program

I have not given you this list so that you might pat me on the back—although I must admit it is pretty impressive to me. I want you to see that, while going through the post-expansion difficulties, I remained physically and intellectually functional. Anyone who has had a house built or an addition put on their home knows the kind of attention to detail that is required—not to mention patience. I taught myself three computer programs during this period, even though I had no computer experience prior to 1983. This required a lot of mental and intellectual effort. All the papers and books that were self-published had to first be researched and developed with nature. And I maintained contact with the public by developing the mail order division of Perelandra and giving an annual workshop series.

Ahhh...but I can hear you saying, "Of course she can do this. She has no children." And to this I respond, "Of course I have no children. I'm doing this." Expansion springs out of our mundane, day-to-day life. If I had children, this expansion would probably not have been appropriate for me, and my soul would not have initiated it. The juggling required to pull off motherhood and the Cottage would have been too difficult—at least for me.

And this brings me to the relationship between the mundane and the fantastic (or ring-pass-not expansion). Our mundane life is the foundation builder. It provides the tools and the training that are required for an expansion. It is what prepares us for an expansion. Everything we will need for the expansion itself and for meeting the challenges we are faced with as a result of the expansion are learned and developed in our normal, day-to-day life. For example, I moved to the country, and this naturally led to my decision to start a vegetable garden. I wanted to garden well. This led me from conventional gardening into organic gardening, and finally to the Findhorn books and co-creative gardening with nature. Nature then gave me the foundation I needed for the Split Molecular Process, plus a basic understanding of form and reality that came in handy once I started going to the Cottage. In short, everything I needed as a foundation to achieve the expansion and work through the postexpansion process was woven into my daily life at Perelandra.

When all the pieces of the foundation are in place, the soul then initiates the expansion. It automatically occurs, and you do not have to go in search for it—it will find you. The key to the expansion does not lie in the expansion itself. It lies in the mundane. The soul will not trigger an expansion without the proper foundation. So, if we focus our attention on what we wish we could be or do instead of paying attention to the quality of our mundane daily life, the foundation doesn't get built. It is a natural phenomenon of life: All that we need for our evolution is supplied to us in our daily life.

Once the expansion occurs, we go through the identification and integration process that results from it. As we identify the new elements, we then need to integrate each one into our mundane. This grounds the expansion and makes it fully useful. It also raises the level of our mundane so that our daily life includes this new, more expanded reality. In short, the mundane and the fantastic in our life superimpose on top of one another, becoming one, united whole. My daily life now is nothing like what I experienced prior to 1982. I have integrated the Cottage reality and what I have learned from it into my Perelandra life to such a degree that I now have one, cohesive life unit that includes both the Cottage and Perelandra realities. Every day I leave the office and go home—that is, I stop working at Perelandra and I go to the Cottage via the Split Molecular Process. I may not be using gas and getting stuck in traffic, but this is my working definition of the mundane act of leaving the office and going home.

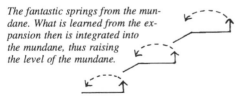

The fantastic springs from the mundane. What is learned from the expansion then is integrated into the mundane, thus raising the level of the mundane.

The integrated mundane-fantastic life

If we don't integrate the ring-pass-not expansion (or any expansion) into the mundane, it has no grounding foundation and remains virtually useless in our life. It becomes a one-time experience that only serves to "blow us away." As a result, the mundane remains one reality and the fantastic another separate reality.

An unintegrated expansion feels unsupported, and our mundane life remains separated from the fantastic experience.

All of this leads me to Frances, the South African nun who maintained contact with her best friend Helen, after her (Frances's) death. Frances had worked *diligently,* but unsuccessfully, all her life to achieve what she called "the breakthrough to the spirit." For a couple of years after death, she "talked" to Helen, describing what she was experiencing and learning about life after death. As a result, Helen wrote a book, *Testimony of Light.** During their last communications, Helen noticed a difference in Frances. She was speaking from a different perspective, as if Frances had "found her soul." The last time they spoke, Helen asked her about this change. Frances explained that everything she had sought and searched for mentally, psychically and by way of the occult in order to discover that breakthrough to the spirit for which she so longed, *she had all along.*

And there you have it. Frances is telling you that three years *after* she died, she learned that the time, effort, sweat, desire and longing she had put out in her life was for something she had all along—and she missed seeing it because of all that time, effort, sweat, desire and longing. You don't have to wait so long. David is telling you that you don't even have to die to get these things. And I'm telling you that the most extraordinary experience in your life may depend on a hair cut and a lousy television movie. Remember, the spiritual thread is in the mundane, not the fantastic. This reality that I did not know existed was there all along. My mundane ordered and disciplined each foundation piece so that when the time came and the opportunity rose, I could say "yes."

YES YES YES YES YES YES YES YES YES YES YES NO YES YES

Testimony of Light by Helen Greaves. Copyright 1969 by Helen Greaves. Published by The C. W. Daniel Company Ltd., 1 Church Path, Saffron Walden, Essex CB10 1JP, England.

Perelandra, Ltd.
P.O. Box 3603
Warrenton, VA 20188

http://www.perelandra-ltd.com

Phone Order Line:

U.S. & Canada: 1-800-960-8806 Overseas & Mexico: 1-540-937-2153
(Answered Monday–Friday from 9 a.m. to 5 p.m., eastern time.
All other times you will reach a machine.)

Fax: 1-540-937-3360

Question Hot Line: 1-540-937-3679

(Answered Tuesdays 10 a.m.–12:30 p.m., Wednesdays 5 p.m. to 7 p.m. and
Thursdays 2 p.m.–5 p.m., eastern time. All other times you will reach a machine.)

April 1999

Index